OLD NORSE FOLKLORE

A VOLUME IN THE SERIES
MYTH AND POETICS II
EDITED BY GREGORY NAGY,
LEONARD MUELLNER, AND LAURA SLATKIN

For a full list of titles in this series, visit our website at cornellpress.cornell.edu.

*A complete list of titles published in the original
Myth and Poetics series is available at the back of this book.*

OLD NORSE FOLKLORE

Tradition, Innovation, and Performance in Medieval Scandinavia

STEPHEN A. MITCHELL

Cornell University Press
Ithaca and London

Copyright © 2023 by Cornell University

All rights reserved. Except for brief quotations in a review, this book, or parts thereof, must not be reproduced in any form without permission in writing from the publisher. For information, address Cornell University Press, Sage House, 512 East State Street, Ithaca, New York 14850. Visit our website at cornellpress.cornell.edu.

First published 2023 by Cornell University Press

Library of Congress Cataloging-in-Publication Data

Names: Mitchell, Stephen A. (Stephen Arthur), 1951– author.
Title: Old Norse folklore : tradition, innovation, and performance in medieval Scandinavia / Stephen A. Mitchell.
Description: Ithaca [New York] : Cornell University Press, 2023. | Series: Myth and poetics II | Includes bibliographical references and index.
Identifiers: LCCN 2023018993 (print) | LCCN 2023018994 (ebook) | ISBN 9781501773396 (hardcover) | ISBN 9781501773402 (paperback) | ISBN 9781501773471 (epub) | ISBN 9781501773488 (pdf)
Subjects: LCSH: Folklore—Scandinavia—History—To 1500. | Mythology, Norse—History. | Old Norse literature—History and criticism. | Old Norse philology.
Classification: LCC GR205 .M577 2023 (print) | LCC GR205 (ebook) | DDC 398.20948—dc23/eng/20230522
LC record available at https://lccn.loc.gov/2023018993
LC ebook record available at https://lccn.loc.gov/2023018994

Dedicated to the memory of
Erik David Mitchell (1985–2021),
who proudly served under the regimental motto
"Our Country Not Ourselves" at COP Charkh,
Logar Province, Afghanistan, 2010–2011,
as a member of the 2nd Battalion, 30th Infantry
Regiment, 4th Brigade Combat Team,
10th Mountain Division (Light Infantry).

ſent føðþes annar slikær maðþær
(Cod. Holm. B 59, fol. 48v)

Contents

List of Illustrations	ix
Series Editors' Preface	xi
Preface	xiii
Acknowledgments	xvii
Introduction. Old Norse Folklore: An Orientation	1

PART 1: ORALITY AND PERFORMANCE   **25**

1. Orality, Oral Theory, and Memory Studies   27
2. Continuity: Folklore's Problem Child?   37
3. Performance and Norse Poetry: The Hydromel of Praise and the Effluvia of Scorn   51
4. Old Norse Riddles and Other Verbal Contests in Performance   77

PART II: MYTHS AND MEMORY   **91**

5. Skírnir's Other Journey: The Riddle of Gleipnir   93
6. The Goddess Gná   103
7. Óðinn, Charms, and Necromancy: *Hávamál* 157 in Its Nordic and European Contexts   125
8. Memory, Mediality, and the "Performative Turn": Recontextualizing Remembering in Medieval Scandinavia   149
9. Memory and Places That Matter: The Case of Samsø   169
10. The Mythologized Past: Memory in Medieval and Early Modern Gotland   189

PART III: TRADITIONS AND INNOVATIONS   **207**

11. Heroic Legend and Onomastics: *Hálfs saga, Das Hildebrandslied* and the Listerby Stones   209
12. Courts, Consorts, and the Transformation of Medieval Scandinavian Literature   231
13. On the Old Swedish *Trollmöte* or *Mik mötte en gamul kerling*   245

Works Cited   261

Index   319

Illustrations

Figure 3.1. Óðinn flying with the Poetic Mead in the shape of an eagle? Detail from Lärbro Stora Hammars III (Bunge Museum, Gotland) 65

Figure 3.2. Valkyrie with horn of mead greeting a warrior? Detail from Lärbro Stora Hammars III (Bunge Museum, Gotland) 66

Figure 3.3. Valkyrie figurine holding a horn of mead? (Historiska museet, Stockholm) 67

Figure 7.1. Scene of sacrifices? Detail from Lärbro Stora Hammars I (Bunge Museum, Gotland) 133

Figure 7.2. Wooden image of a one-eyed figure with protruding tongue in the stave church at Hegge, Norway 136

Figure 9.1. Aerial view of grave mounds, ship settings, and royal residences at Gammel Lejre 171

Figure 9.2. Grave mounds and one of the ship settings at Gammel Lejre 173

Figure 9.3. Schematic topographical diagram showing how Jelling might have appeared in the tenth century 175

Figure 9.4. Line drawings of the "Gorm stone" (DR 41) at Jelling 176

Figure 9.5. Drawing of the encounter on Samsø of the sons of Arngrímr with Hjálmarr and Örvar-Oddr 179

Figure 9.6. Map of Samsø from 1755 182

Figure 9.7. The Kanhave canal today, looking to the east 186

Figure 9.8. The Kanhave canal today, looking to the west, with a replica ship frame and reconstructed planking on the side of the canal 187

SERIES EDITORS' PREFACE

by Gregory Nagy, Leonard Muellner, and Laura Slatkin

We the three editors of Myth and Poetics II take special pride and delight in introducing this first of two volumes of collected papers by Stephen Mitchell, internationally recognized as the doyen of medieval and premodern Scandinavian studies—and as a world-class folklorist whose comparative interests range well beyond his unrivaled command of North Germanic civilizations.

The research that went into this collection of papers is universally praised for its accessibility to experts and non-experts alike. Mitchell's luminous career as a researcher is beautifully complemented by his fame, many decades in the making, as a charismatic teacher of college-level and Ph.D.-level students at Harvard: he is living proof of the adage that not only does good research drive good teaching, good teaching drives good research. Stephen Mitchell is a paragon of such an academic ideal, and this stellar book is a most eloquent proof of concept.

Preface

The opportunity to present Old Norse folklore and folkloristics through selections of my own work has been a joyous, if also daunting, experience, and I hope the choices I have made adequately demonstrate both the diversity of available materials, as well as the many useful approaches scholarship possesses for exploring the vernacular cultures of the pre-modern Nordic world. Certainly, much has been learned about medieval and early modern northern Europe over the past several centuries, yet even as our understanding improves, paradoxically, we also realize that much remains to be learned. In that vein, the studies presented here should be understood first and foremost as invitations to further work in these areas.

In selecting the chapters for this volume, I have cast the net wide and chosen studies that treat a variety of theoretical debates, genres, and issues related to Nordic cultural history, including, for example, continuity, orality, performance, and memory studies as applied to mythological, heroic, and supernatural texts and traditions. And in addition to the better-known Old Norse-Icelandic materials, I have also been careful to include topics and texts from the East Norse world, textual resources understandably outshone to the modern eye by the brilliance of Icelandic saga writing (and its widely available translations); however, the value of the East Norse evidence to a comprehensive understanding of the medieval northern world remains indispensable, as I have argued elsewhere (Mitchell 2015). Yet even as I look in these chapters to draw back the curtain and examine a number of varied historical cultural landscapes, it is also true that here and elsewhere, I return often to, and reconsider from different perspectives, a relatively small set of seminal topics and texts—the reports of an early eleventh-century *seiðr* ceremony in the Greenlandic colony; narrativizations of a wedding feast at Reykjahólar in 1119; Sturla "the Icelander" entertaining a ship's crew and the Norwegian royal couple in the 1260s; the legendary battle on Sámsey beween Örvar-Oddr and Hjálmarr against a group of berserk brothers; the roles of the mythological servants Skírnir and Gná; and so on.

As regards theoretical matters, I dismiss out-of-hand *no* approaches to accessing these remarkable cultural goods, and have over the years experimented eclectically with a variety of theoretical pathways to the worlds of the Viking Age and the Middle Ages. Some of the resulting theoretical heterogeneity in these chapters is, of course, to be accounted for by the fact that our understanding of these bygone worlds has changed over time; so too have scholarly priorities, as well as my own interests and research strategies. What I trust emerges as the consistent center of all these essays, however, is the inclination to place these materials into the context of lived lives, of performed rituals, and so on, that is—to take the example of our written narratives—never to regard these remarkable cultural goods as mere blobs on parchment consisting of gallnuts, ferrous sulphate, and other ingredients of medieval ink, but always to bear in mind a vision of, and concern for, the individuals about whom, for whom, and by whom they were written.

As regards this collection of previously published works, several of which appear here for the first time in English, I have in some instances updated the texts, mainly in pursuit of clarity, or for the purpose of improving or correcting translations (or to include newly published ones), or to rectify flaws; moreover, I have looked to unify the various style formats and to employ North American spelling conventions throughout. On the other hand, I have only occasionally added new bibliographic materials or otherwise modernized entries, preferring instead that each essay reflect the scholarly ambience of its particular cultural moment.

Naturally, articles written over several decades and drawn from a variety of journals and anthologies will employ many different bibliographic styles, as well as—depending on circumstances in an often pre-internet age—the use of many different source volumes and editions while working at various North American and Nordic libraries. It was tempting to leave these discursive reference systems entirely unchanged, but realizing, for example, how frequently certain key primary and secondary sources would need to be repeated, I was led to conclude that creating a single comprehensive bibliography would provide the most useful and clearest result. I have therefore unified the many reference systems of the original publications into a single list of works cited, divided by primary and secondary sources, and have keyed all references to a simple author-date format, whatever the original styles of the essays. Doing so has many advantages, but it also means that the number of footnotes in this text do not necessarily match on a one-to-one basis the notes of the originals.

I have also looked to employ a limited number of standard editions and translations in the essays (listed with the original texts in the bibliography), sometimes with my emendations, decisions which also entailed modest revisions of the essays. As I discovered, so many good choices of translations exist that, frankly, selecting one rendering over another was not always a simple task. Where the title of the translation is indistinguishable from the original, I use the name(s) of the translator(s) in the parenthetic references. At the same time, many texts used here have no available English translations, and in these and a few other instances, I have inserted my own. As I soon saw, however, repeated parenthetic references to "my translation" and the like became very distracting, so where no published text is mentioned, these translations should be understood to be my own. And to make the essays as accessible as possible, I have everywhere looked to provide translations or detailed paraphrases of quoted non-English materials, whether primary or secondary.

All references to medieval texts employ the titles given by the standard editions used here, irrespective of the titles of the original essays. Thus, for example, even though the poem called *Skírnir's Journey* and so on in English is variously called *Fǫr Scírnis* and *Skírnismál* in scholarship, it is here, following the editors of *Edda. Die Lieder des Codex Regius*, referred to consistently as *For Scírnis* (i.e., without the ogonek, the so-called hooked o). As to personal names, the medieval forms (such as Óðinn and Þórr) are generally used throughout with Anglophone forms inserted parenthetically on the name's first appearance in a chapter. At the same time, I have not attempted to eliminate every orthographic variation, as some cases, such as ö/ǫ (e.g., sǫgur/sögur) and c/k (e.g., Scírnir/Skírnir), have deep, and inconsistent, histories in scholarly publishing, and are here left as in the cited texts.

One final note as regards spelling: the matter of how to present in English *víkingr/víking* (the masculine and feminine forms had slightly differing associations), words used to designate pirates, adventurers, sea-rovers and other well-armed traders and raiders (and their activities), has a long and complicated history in Anglophone orthography. Writers throughout the nineteenth century employed a variety of forms—*Viking, viking, Vikinger, Wiking, Wickings,* and so on. Contemporary practice, especially as enforced by computerized spell checkers, favors the upper-case form, "Viking." That is a custom I am eager to push back against, as its use reifies the term as some sort of ethnolinguistic designation. Whatever else *víkingr/víking* meant when used in runic inscriptions, Anglo-Saxon chronicles, and other medieval sources, the terms were not primarily meant as ethnic or racial designations; thus, I prefer to use the lower-case "viking," as one would for other common nouns like pirate, pagan, or adventurer, and, to the extent practical, I use phrases like "Viking Age Scandinavians" to help distinguish the difference.

The chapters are organized around three broad categories, although I am quick to note that imposing such order is not meant to shoehorn the essays into narrow intellectual silos, especially as most of them range widely in looking for answers. Still, several central themes quickly emerged among the essays I selected. The first group—*Orality and Performance*—includes those essays largely focused on the philosophical and theoretical underpinnings for re-envisioning how we might approach the narrative and other materials with roots in the Viking and Middle Ages. The second category—*Myths and Memory*—consists of essays addressing topics concerned with what might be thought of as spiritual life in medieval Scandinavia, generally narrowed to issues connected with the residue of past pagan traditions as these are remembered and shaped under the influence of a dominant Christian culture with strong, and increasing, ties to the Continent. Here readers will find essays on various pre-Christian Nordic gods and goddesses, charms, and Nordic memory culture. The third section—*Traditions and Innovations*—includes articles highlighting important inherited traditions between and among the historically connected cultures of northern Europe, as well as examples of critical cultural developments taking place in late medieval Scandinavia.

Acknowledgments

Important as teachers are to our development as scholars, it sometimes becomes all too easy later in life to fail to mention those who first awakened intellectual curiosity in us and taught us what we know. For opening my eyes to the possibilities of an Old Norse folkloristics, I am deeply indebted to a number of inspiring and encouraging (and occasionally unintentionally terrifying) teachers, including Alan Dundes, Kaaren Grimstad, John Gumperz, Nils Hasselmo, Gösta Holm, Lauri Honko, Kristinn Jóhannesson, Anatoly Liberman, Orvar Löfgren, and especially Lars Lönnroth, whose luminous example and supportive mentorship has meant more to me over the past five decades than I can express.

Likewise, a number of academic organizations have been of incalculable importance in bringing this volume about: I especially want to thank Cornell University Press and Bethany Wasik, as well as the New Alexandria Foundation, Gregory Nagy, Leonard Muellner, and Laura Slatkin for their help in making this excellent opportunity possible. Other institutions have in various critical ways underwritten the research represented here, either by allowing me to serve as a fellow during leave years or through their generous practical support to me as a visiting foreign scholar. I am particularly grateful to the Swedish Collegium for Advanced Study, Uppsala; the Radcliffe Institute for Advanced Study at Harvard University; the University of Aarhus, Denmark (its Nordic Institute and Centre for Viking and Medieval Studies in particular); and Kungliga Gustav Adolfs Akademien, Uppsala.

Among the many libraries and archives to whom I owe a great debt of gratitude for their unfailing support, I start, of course, with my home institutions, Houghton Library, Harvard's primary repository for manuscripts and rare books, and Widener Library, the university's main research collection. Also of enormous help over the years have been the librarians, archivists, and other staff at Stofnun Árna Magnússonar, Reykjavík; Uppsala universitetsbibliotek; Kungliga Biblioteket, Stockholm; Det Kongelige Bibliotek, Copenhagen; Arkivcentrum, Uppsala; Sveriges medeltida personnamn (Institutet för språk och folkminnen), Uppsala; Visarkivet, Stockholm; Stockholms stadsarkiv; Riksantikvarieämbetet, Stockholm; Landsarkivet i Vadstena; Statsbiblioteket (now part of Det Kongelige Bibliotek), Århus; and the British Library, London. It is certainly fair to say that I would have made little progress in my various research projects without the unstinting assistance offered by those who curate and make available to the public these excellent collections.

Now in my fifth decade as a member of the Harvard faculty, I have many people to thank here "at home." I am profoundly, and especially, grateful to the students and faculty of a number of interdisciplinary instructional and degree committees on which I have been privileged to serve, including the Committee on Degrees in Folklore & Mythology (which I have chaired for several decades), the Standing Committee on Medieval Studies, and the Standing Committee on Archaeology. On these (blissfully, one is tempted to say) non-departmental entities, I have been fortunate over the years to work with many fine colleagues, some now departed, who have greatly enriched my life—a partial list from the past forty-plus years includes, in addition to, and especially, Gregory Nagy and Albert B. Lord, both of whom chaired F&M during my earliest years, Meg Alexiou, Ali Asani, Gojko Barjamovic, Lowell Brower, Philip Deloria, Daniel Donoghue, David Elmer, William Fash, Deborah Foster, Sean Gilsdorf, Ruth Goldstein, Jeffrey Hamburger, John Hamilton, Joseph Harris, Alan Heimert, Michael Herzfeld, Felicity Lufkin, Peter Machinist, David Maybury-Lewis, Michael McCormick, Catherine McKenna, Joseph Falaky Nagy, Luis Girón Negrón, Per Nykrog, Orlando Patterson, Kimberley Patton, Rulan Pian, Michael Puett, Daniel Smail, Eileen Southern, Lawrence Sullivan, Natasha Sumner, Stanley Tambiah, Maria Tatar, Evon Vogt, Nicholas Watson, Ruth Wisse, Nur Yalman, and Jan Ziolkowski.

As meaningful as has been the opportunity to serve on these academic committees, perhaps the very best professional experiences I have had while on the Harvard faculty have come while being elsewhere, a paradox that owes its existence to Harvard's generous summer study abroad programs. Through them, I have spent nearly every summer of the past two decades as the co-director of Harvard's *Viking Studies Program*. Based in the nourishing intellectual environments of two of the Nordic world's great university cities—in its early years in Uppsala, Sweden, and later in Århus, Denmark—this program, part literature and lore, part history and archaeology, has been the source of much fruitful and collaborative cross-disciplinary thinking about Viking Age Scandinavia and its legacy; moreover, in addition to affiliations with these two wonderful universities, the program has also afforded me the opportunity to spend long periods (even occasionally in thoughtful contemplation) on two of the northern world's most storied islands, Gotland and Samsø.

To those who have laid so much of the groundwork that makes these occasions possible and so enjoyable—Matilda West, Nelly DuPont, Pia Kleis, Jens Jørgen Øster-Mortensen, Christian Adamsen, the staffs at Hotell Breda Blick, Århus Diakonhøjskole, and Stavns lejrskole—I express my heartfelt thanks for their unstinting and ebullient assistance. The program also offers us the opportunity to visit a number of national and regional museums, and here again, the students and I have benefitted enormously from the goodwill and cheerful help of many institutions—in Sweden: Historiska Museet (Stockholm); Gamla Uppsala museum; Jamtli (Östersund); Glösa Rock Art Center; Kalmar läns museum; Kalmar Slott; Fornsal (Gotlands museum, Visby); and Bungemuseet (Fårösund, Gotland); in Denmark: Nationalmuseet (Copenhagen); Vikingecenter Fyrkat; Hobro Museum; Nordjyllands Historiske Museum at Lindholm Høje; Museet Ribes Vikinger; Kongernes Jelling; Museum Silkeborg; Vikingeskibsmuseet in Roskilde; Lejre Museum (ROMU); and Samsø Museum (earlier: Økomuseum, Tranebjerg).

I have saved for last mentioning the museum to whom the greatest debt *by far* is owed, namely, Moesgaard Museum. For its stunning exhibitions alone, with their power to bring alive the world of pre-historic south Scandinavia, this remarkable institution would deserve a great deal of praise, but working with the museum on the annual archaeological field school as part of the Viking Studies Program (made possible thanks to the museum's outstanding cooperation) has been nothing short of life-altering for me and for many of the students. Over the years, Torben Trier Christiansen, Daniel Dalicsek, Andres "Minos" Dobat, Lise Frost, Mads Kähler Holst, Agnete Høj Jensen, Peter Jensen, Peter Mose Jensen, Jens Jeppesen, Peter Hambro Mikkelsen, and Christina Holdgaard Schultze have brought the rewarding, educational, and sometimes backbreaking nature of archaeological fieldwork home to participants, including this codirector. They have been unfailingly gracious and patient teachers, brilliant ambassadors not only for their profession, but also for Nordic culture as a whole. I am extraordinarily fortunate to work with such remarkable people.

Similarly, all that and more feeds the gratitude I feel towards my longstanding Viking Studies Program codirectors, Neil Price and Pernille

Hermann—their wise counsel, excellent company, scholarly insights, gifted teaching, and sound friendship have regularly made a pure joy of that annual project. Indeed, the experiences of these past several decades clearly challenge the wisdom of the proverb, *Borta bra, men hemma bäst* (Away [is] good, but home [is] best)—the generosity, goodwill, happy companionship, and collegiality of these many excellent colleagues at other institutions have been useful reminders of the attractive possibilities for a life in scholarship. I would say the same thing of the many enjoyable research projects I have engaged in over the years and here I owe a special debt of gratitude to several colleagues in particular: Agnes Arnórsdóttir, Stefan Brink, Gísli Sigurðsson, Jürg Glauser, Terry Gunnell, Pernille Hermann, Louise Nyholm Kallestrup, Lena Rohrbach, and Jens Peter Schjødt.

Having undoubtedly broken every *jantelov* Aksel Sandmose ever imagined by so lavishly (however truthfully) praising these friends, I want to compound this transgression by saying a word or two about a number of other Nordicists not already mentioned, colleagues whose influence on these essays is profound. Sometimes the presence of their views is marked, sometimes it is quiet, but almost everywhere in my own work, the trace of various conversations with, lectures by, and publications from these colleagues, the quick and those no longer with us, can be found: Aðalheiður Guðmundsdóttir, Arne Bugge Amundsen, Anders Andrén, Ármann Jakobsson, Knut Aukrust, Bjørn Bandlien, Karen Bek-Pedersen, Bergdís Þrastardóttir, Karen Boe, Nils-Arvid Bringeus, Sophie Bønding, Tom Christensen, Margaret Clunies Ross, Richard Cole, Tom DuBois, Frog, Anne-Sofie Gräslund, Bo Gräslund, Kate Heslop, Shaun F.D. Hughes, Per Ingesman, Jóhanna Katrín Friðriksdóttir, Peter Jackson, Judith Jesch, Karl G. Johansson, Bengt R. Jonsson, Merrill Kaplan, Karoline Kjesrud, Barbro Klein, Jónas Kristjánsson, Sarah Künzler, William Layher, Carolyne Larrington, John Lindow, Lars Lönnroth, Maria Cristina Lombardi, Mikael Males, Agneta Ney, Guðrún Nordal, Andreas Nymark, Lis Nymark, Ane Ohrvik, Ulf Palmenfelt, Peter Pentz, Judy Quinn, Linda Qviström, Catharina Raudvere, Jonathan Roper, Lukas Rösli, Amber Cederström Rose, Daniel Sävborg, Michael Schulte, Jacqueline Simpson, Fredrik Skott, Olof Sundqvist, Tim Tangherlini, Torfi Tulinius, Natalie M. Van Deusen, Henrik Williams, Kirsten Wolf, and Torun Zachrisson. To all of you, my thanks for your good company in the remarkable worlds of folkloristics and Old Norse—and for making it all seem so worthwhile.

Saving for last those to whom the greatest debt is owed, I thank my family for their love, encouragement, patience, intelligent conversation, and happy memories. When many of the essays in this volume were written, I was, like most parents, usually scurrying between the office and the field hockey matches, football practices, baseball games, science fairs, horse shows, plays, and other activities in which my three wonderful children, Katrina, Erik, and Annika, took part. In those days, when they might understandably have looked jealously at classmates as their families set off to theme parks in Florida, we instead traveled throughout the Viking world, from Greenland to Russia and other amazing locations—I hope the memory and wonder of those trips has only grown with the passage of time. And with the most profound gratitude, I especially thank my wife, Kristine Forsgard, for her love, understanding, brilliant company, easy laughs, and unfailing support.

OLD NORSE FOLKLORE

Introduction

OLD NORSE FOLKLORE
AN ORIENTATION

We often encounter characters, themes, and motifs drawn from Old Norse folklore in the modern world, but we most frequently meet these materials by way of distinctly non-medieval paths—through, for example, the works of Richard Wagner and J. R. R. Tolkien.[1] For those who grow up in English-speaking environments, it is possible that a person's earliest experiences with "vikings" and stories about Þórr (Thor), Óðinn (Odin),[2] and the other Nordic deities will have come at an early age from chance discoveries in venerable, often-reprinted popular texts, dedicated anthologies like Annie and Eliza Keary's *The Heroes of Asgard* (1857), or even as—let's face it—slightly supplementary afterthoughts in Thomas Bulfinch's *The Age of Fable* (1855–1863).

Even more likely in today's media environment, early brushes with these wonderful cultural documents might come from Stan Lee's artistic riffs in

---

[1] These introductory remarks often mirror, sometimes with emendations, deletions and expansions, but also verbatim on occasion, my comments on Old Norse Folklore Studies in Mitchell 2000a and 2018a, as well as my plenary address at the 2022 International Saga Conference in Tallinn, Estonia; moreover, my remarks, especially in the second section of the *Introduction, Old Norse Folkloristics: Portals and Pathways*, frequently reflect my collaboration over the past several years with my co-editors, Pernille Hermann and Jürg Glauser, and some six dozen colleagues, on our pre-modern Nordic memory studies handbook (Glauser, Hermann, and Mitchell 2018), as well as the opportunities I have had to teach together with some marvelous colleagues in Harvard's Viking Studies Program over its many years in Uppsala, Sweden, and Århus, Denmark.

[2] In general, medieval forms of the names are used throughout, with the English norms placed parenthetically after the first use in the section.

Marvel's *The Mighty Thor* comics (1962–) and the related *Thor* films,[3] in television series like Michael Hirst's *Vikings* on the History Channel, and from the recent reanimation of these medieval narratives by Neil Gaiman (*Norse Mythology*, 2017). In fact, like those of many cultures in the West, Americans have been obsessed with the Viking Age and its possibilities for a very long time. Indeed, North American dreams of the Viking Age range widely, from attempts to paint George Washington as a literal descendant of Óðinn to the fascination shown by various White House occupants with "the vikings" (on which, see Mitchell 2018c).

With so many contemporary presentations of the Old Norse materials, it is easy to lose sight of the fact that posterity has bequeathed to us a substantial body of original narrative goods from medieval northern Europe, texts that richly deserve to be read in their own right. Although plentiful, these materials are at the same time not always easy to access: How are such texts best understood? What critical tools drawn from philology, folkloristics, archaeology, memory studies, ethnography, and related disciplines make us better readers (in every sense) of these cultural documents, so far removed from our world in time, space, and culture?

Or put another way, what forms of cultural competence must we acquire in order to understand these distant worlds? How, for example, does familiarity with the oral backgrounds of these texts, their performance contexts, and their relations to "tradition" (real or imagined) help explain the appeal and value of these materials to the medieval Christian descendants of "the vikings" who are our main informants? These are the central questions about the medieval Scandinavian world with which the essays that follow concern themselves, taking as they do a broad view of both the cultural monuments themselves and the theoretical keys necessary for understanding them.

But let's start at the beginning: What is "Old Norse folklore" and who were the people who made, shared, and used it? When I speak of Old Norse folklore, I am, as I have put it elsewhere, primarily focused on the expressive and customary practices of the speakers of the North Germanic dialects, communities of the pre-modern era (mainly the Viking and Middle Ages) living not only in the modern Nordic countries but also, for example, in various outposts and settlements along the Baltic perimeter (e.g., Estonia) and in the North Atlantic (e.g., Greenland, Shetland, Orkney, the Isle of Man, the Hebrides). These widely dispersed settlement areas consisted of significantly diverse sub-cultures, especially given their often extensive

---

[3] *Thor* (2011), *Thor: The Dark World* (2013), and *Thor: Ragnarok* (2017).

contacts with neighboring social groups, yet the Nordic peoples of these regions generally recognized that a broad linguistic continuity existed between and among the groups, and that they shared numerous cultural traits and traditions; moreover, they were frequently aware of and honored their historical and genealogical affinities.[4]

Put briefly, but detailed below and in the essays that follow, Old Norse folklore as it is studied today is most readily found (but by no means exclusively) through stories—myths, legends, tales, ballads, riddles, proverbs and other text-centered genres. In addition to these well-known narrative forms, expressive manifestations of Old Norse culture also included customs and behaviors, such as rituals connected to the calendar year, building and craft traditions, artistic and musical conventions, and other forms of traditional knowledge and expressions of value and heritage, everything from celebrations of "yule" (*jól*) to customary farming and herding practices.

The source materials for such omnivorous work are necessarily equally diverse. Although no folklorists examining these earlier periods would willingly exclude data of any sort from their inquiries, Old Norse folklore research typically (but by no means necessarily) centers on information gleaned from textual sources, especially the Icelandic narratives known as sagas; Latin and vernacular chronicles and other historical writings, such as Saxo's *Gesta Danorum*; religious and heroic works, such as the *Prose* and *Poetic Eddas*; letters, court records and other documents; and runic inscriptions and monuments. Also of significant value are beliefs, tales, and customs known from post-medieval times but with credible links to much earlier traditions (see the examples in Celander 1920, 1943), but so too are sources that might be all too easily pigeon-holed as "belonging" to archaeology, history, the history of religion, or legal studies. Because at its heart folkloristics is both omnivorous and highly interdisciplinary—and is always as interested in *processes* or *modes of production* as it is in *products*—no field of research falls outside the interest of the folklorist nor can data of whatever sort be arbitrarily divorced from its areas of inquiry, a perspective also shared

---

[4] Mitchell 2018a:93. See also the detailed discussion of medieval folklore in Lindahl 2000. Historically the term "Norse," deriving from words indicating "north," has connoted two ideas, both 1) things related to Scandinavia generally, especially the North Germanic dialects and the people who spoke them, as well as 2) more narrowly to Norway in particular, as is still the case in the Nordic languages (e.g., Swedish *norsk, norska*). In discussing medieval Scandinavia, "Old Norse" as an adjective is frequently applied to the entire region and its inhabitants, with the further specifications, following language histories, of East Norse (Danish and Swedish) and West Norse (Norwegian, Faroese, and Icelandic). The latter is often referred to as Old Norse-Icelandic, especially with reference to literary and cultural matters.

by other fields.⁵ Quite simply, we must go wherever good results can be had, without regard to what some may see as disciplinary trespass.

But before proceeding to how we approach these materials, let us first consider the contours of what might be called Nordic spiritual life in the Viking and Middle Ages.⁶

Viking Age and Medieval Scandinavia

There are, of course, no texts dealing with the early periods of human habitation in Scandinavia,⁷ yet later rock art and other aspects of material culture have led many scholars to agree on certain broad aspects of the magico-religious world that develops in the Nordic Bronze Age and early Iron Age, including the centrality of sun worship, which can be traced up to the sixth century CE, when substantial changes in belief systems are notable.⁸ Beginning in the first century CE, we begin to hear about the Nordic world from foreign writers, such as Tacitus (98 CE), and already in the late Roman Iron Age (first to fourth centuries CE), Scandinavians begin to leave inscriptions in stone and other impermeable materials written in the older form of runes, such as on one of the Gallehus horns (ca. 400 CE), totaling some 125 such inscriptions in this early epigraphic form.

Runic inscriptions, especially rich beginning in the ninth century with the revised runic writing system called the Younger Futhark, occasionally display elaborate poetic principles and, in addition to mainly memorial functions, sometimes treat Scandinavian legendary and mythological traditions

---

[5] For a thoughtful and productive meditation on interdisciplinarity, and our reliance on material vs. textual resources, I highly recommend Price 2020:11–15.

[6] This presentation of the Old Norse world is, of course, necessarily brief, and intended as only a compact orientation to selected themes. I have not burdened this outline with excessive bibliography—after all, virtually every sentence might lead to a separate annotated bibliography! And given the many fine English-language surveys to Old Norse-Icelandic literature and mythology now available (e.g., Clunies Ross 2010; Lindow 2021), I recommend these works for more complete introductions. In addition to surveys of this sort, especially for those seeking more granular discussions of the sagas and the worlds that gave rise to such wonderful texts, there exist a number of excellent reference volumes (e.g., McTurk 2005; Ármann Jakobsson and Sverrir Jakobsson 2017). A particularly comprehensive and valuable handbook, treating equally the archaeology, history, and cultures of Viking Age northern Europe, is Brink and Price 2008, which I strongly recommend. Nordic folklore of the Middle Ages is also extensively covered among the entries in Lindahl, McNamara, and Lindow 2000.

[7] See the relevant entries in Brink and Price 2008.

[8] See, e.g., Kaul 1998, 2004; Hedeager 2011; Gräslund and Price 2012; and Andrén 2014.

(as on the Rök inscription) and charms (as on the Kvinneby amulet). Runes continue to provide contemporary witness to Nordic cultural life throughout the Middle Ages, both in highly stylized monuments, such as the majestic Harald's stone at Jelling, and in everyday communications, such as the numerous medieval runic inscriptions, mainly on wood, found at Bryggen in Bergen, Norway. Early church activity, such as Ansgar's missionary journeys to Denmark and Sweden in the ninth century and Adam of Bremen's eleventh-century history of the Hamburg-Bremen archbishopric, provide corroborating testimony by outsiders about Nordic traditions.

Conversion to Christianity was a process initially aimed principally at the ruling class, with relatively early nationally declared adoption of the new religion in evidence in Denmark in the tenth century (cf. the so-called Harald stone at Jelling, ca. 965), in the tenth and early eleventh century in Norway (cf. the sagas of Óláfr Tryggvason and St. Óláfr), and in the peaceful declaration of the new religion in Iceland at the time of the millennium (cf. *Brennu-Njáls saga*, chap. 105), but somewhat later for Sweden, sometime in the 1060s, a date based mainly on the establishment of a bishopric in Sigtuna. In each case, missionary activity is reported to have found success first among chieftains and kings, toward whom it was directed. Although declared for the various kingdoms as a whole, questions remain—especially for Norway and Sweden, with their sometimes remote and isolated settlements—of how many decades passed before Christianity completely took hold throughout. Iceland officially declares itself Christian around the millennium, although the fondness of the Icelanders for heritage narratives connected to the pre-Christian era became legendary within the Old Norse world.[9]

The early economies of this world were mainly based on agriculture, animal husbandry and fishing, with long-distance trade to the east (i.e., Russia and the Byzantine empire) and the west (i.e., the Carolingian and Ottonian empires) in such goods as furs, slaves, walrus tusks and soapstone products, expeditions which sometimes also included raiding and piracy. Those who engaged in such piratical activities were said to be *í víkingu* (in viking) and those who practiced it were in turn "vikings." Later developments led to the

---

[9] Saxo, for example, comments on this view in the prologue to his *Gesta Danorum* and illustrates it later in the work. And famously, Theodoricus Monachus writes of his sources for his history, *et prout sagaciter perquirere potuimus ab eis, penes quos horum memoria præcipue vigere creditur, quos nos Islendinga vocamus, qui hæc in suis antiquis carminibus percelebrata recolunt* (*Historia de antiquitate regum Norwagiensium*, 3) (as I have been able to learn by assiduous inquiry from the people among whom in particular the remembrance of these matters is believed to thrive—namely those whom we call Icelanders, who preserve them as much celebrated themes in their ancient poems) (*An Account of the Ancient History of the Norwegian Kings*, 1).

formation of large-scale forces, such as the so-called "Great Army" which harried ninth-century England. The activities of such forces in England and northern France, in particular, culminated in lands in Northumbria, Normandy, and elsewhere being ceded to Scandinavian settlers, with colonies also being established in the Orkneys, Hebrides, and Ireland. Some viking adventurers traveled, and raided, into the Mediterranean; meanwhile, less bellicose relations in the east appear to lead to a series of outposts dominated by Nordic (presumably the same as the so-called Rus) merchants and traders, including Staraya (Old) Ladoga on the Volkhov River. Such sites frequently target strategic locations, such as portages around falls and cataracts, on the route to Constantinople, where especially in the tenth and eleventh centuries many Scandinavians served in the Byzantine emperor's Varangian Guard.

But, with the exception of the virtually uninhabited North Atlantic islands, in none of these cases—east or west—were the Nordic populations large enough to sustain themselves as separate communities over time, and gradually melded with the native populations. In a noteworthy example of this point, the Norman chronicler, Dudo of Saint-Quentin, writes that William I wanted his son, Richard I (d. 996), to be reared in Bayeux rather than Rouen because "Danish" was principally spoken in the former city but French in the latter, and William wanted his successor to learn and use it daily.[10]

Through a series of westward expansions—often recorded in literary sources as a pattern in which a ship is blown off course, and the reports of new lands are followed up first by individual exploration and then by settlement by an entire colony—the Norse hopscotched their way from the Scandinavian world proper to Shetland, the Faroes, Iceland, Greenland, and the New World, called by them Vínland, thus far confirmed only from the archaeological site of L'Anse aux Meadows in Newfoundland, Canada. This Norse adventure in the New World is first mentioned by Adam of Bremen and forms the core of the two so-called Vinland sagas, recorded centuries later in Iceland.

The Viking Age is generally reckoned as ending in the late eleventh century, often in association with the death in England of King Haraldr "hard-rule" of Norway in 1066. Three recognizable national kingdoms emerge in the Middle Ages: Norway, Sweden, and Denmark (which included large tracts of present-day southern Sweden and extended far down the

---

[10] Dudo, *De moribus et actis primorum Normannorum ducum*, Lib. 3. Cf. Simek 2014.

Jutland peninsula). Following the ninth-century settlement of the island, the Icelanders formed a republic centered around local and national assemblies at which the chieftains and their followers passed laws and adjudicated cases. In the second half of the 1200s, Iceland came under the dominion of Norway, and by 1397, the kingdoms of the Nordic region had been forged into the so-called Union of Kalmar under the leadership of Queen Margrete of Denmark. With Margrete no longer in power, however, things quickly fell apart, and the history of the fifteenth century may with only mild exaggeration be said to be the story of Sweden (including Finland, which had been incorporated as part of thirteenth-century missionary crusades) struggling to pull out of the Danish-dominated union.

Religion and Belief

Relatively little is known about the practice of pre-Christian religion in the northern world, although this gap in our knowledge is increasingly being filled through the hard work of archaeologists, students of religion, folklorists, and others;[11] on the other hand, we have long known a great deal about its pre-Christian mythology. That this is the case has largely to do with the fact that the Scandinavian mythological traditions were intimately connected with its poetic practice through extended metaphors known as kennings, many of which could only be understood by recourse to characters and episodes drawn from the mythology.

As a result, one of the principal sources for our understanding of this world, *Snorra edda*, or the *Prose Edda* of Snorri Sturluson (d. 1241), can be seen as an *ars poetica* intended for skalds in a Christian era in which native poetic tradition required this sort of support. This text narrates famous events in the history of the gods, and suggestively lists ways in which various words and concepts can be paraphrased in mythological terms. The pre-Christian mythological tradition is believed to be best represented in the so-called *Poetic Edda*, the main manuscript of which dates to ca. 1275. These poems—roughly half of which are mythological, the other half heroic—are generally believed to be much older than the manuscript.

The first books of the twelfth-century *Gesta Danorum* of Saxo Grammaticus also take up mythological themes, although frequently in euhemerized form, and much can be inferred from the language of the poets

---

[11] See, for example, the entries in Schjødt, Lindow, and Andrén 2020.

or skalds, as well as from their occasional presentations of mythological themes (e.g., *Ragnarsdrápa, Haustlǫng*). Some additional information about the actual practice of the pagan religion is to be found in the comments of outside observers like Adam of Bremen and in the archaeological record (for example, funeral rites). Interpretations of Scandinavian mythology have followed scholarly trends more generally—meteorological, myth-ritual, Christian-influenced, historical, and comparative (especially in line with the views of Georges Dumézil).

The stories that have come down to us overwhelmingly treat the exploits of Óðinn and Þórr against the *jǫtnar* (giants) and other representatives of the Otherworld (e.g., the World Serpent), as well as the attempts of the *jǫtnar* to possess various goddesses, especially Freyja. Typically, Óðinn's struggles involve his use of, or search for, wisdom, whereas Þórr's adventures are resolved by recourse to his might and his hammer, Mjǫllnir. Other narratives take up such tales as how Freyr gets a wife; how the gods' citadel is built; how the Vanir gods come to live among the Æsir gods; how the soteriological figure of Baldr comes to be killed; or how the enigmatic Loki leads the giants against the gods at the final battle, Ragnarǫk (fate of the gods). Yet, due to the impressive body of medieval texts on these matters that Icelandic learning and its traditions of connoisseurship in particular have preserved, as well as the undeniably impressive quality of these materials, there has perhaps been an over-reliance on these texts, with too much regard for their authority, a perspective that has lent itself to an impression that there existed greater regional and social uniformity in pre-Christian Scandinavian religious beliefs and practices than other evidence, such as place names, can support (as brilliantly demonstrated in Brink 2007).

With the Conversion, the importance to daily life of such routine aspects of Christian belief as mass, prayer, and pilgrimage can hardly be exaggerated. In the latter category, for example, significant Scandinavian pilgrimage sites included the shrines of St. Óláfr in Norway, St. Knútr in Denmark, and St. Erik and St. Birgitta in Sweden, and the significance of these sites for local economies and other aspects of the pilgrim trade, including folklore, was great. Even in post-conversion Scandinavia, religious life, although largely dictated by Christian customs, surely inherited select views (and maintained their practices) in such realms as healing and magic. Belief in witchcraft and magic is suggested throughout the sagas, and these topics are treated with much seriousness in the law codes and penitential rules of all the Nordic countries. Actual evidence of "witchcraft" is relatively scarce, however, although there are noteworthy exceptions involving the use of charm magic, such as the case of Ragnhildr tregagás in Bergen ca. 1324. In fact, the place of magic in everyday life is readily adduced from such things as charms and amulets. The late medieval, whetstone-shaped amber amulet from Dømmestrup (Denmark), for example, gives witness to this protective function with its Latin inscription, which twice reads *contra omnia mala* and once *contra ... malorum*.[12]

Tales and Texts

It is one of the paradoxes of Nordic history that Iceland, with its small population and lacking any secular court life, is often the part of medieval Scandinavia best known to us today.

Through its medieval writers, and the repository of traditions on which they often drew, Iceland gave extraordinary voice to the Nordic Middle Ages, producing hundreds of finely written *sagas*, an Icelandic word borrowed into many European languages to denote a prose narrative. Whereas by the thirteenth century the Nordic courts were actively adopting European fashions in literature, among the Icelanders (who were themselves no strangers to these new tastes, of course), the traditions associated with the Viking Age and their own heroic past continued to generate narratives of very high standards throughout the Middle Ages (although the thirteenth century has come to be viewed by modern scholars as the classic era of saga writing).

The various types of sagas are generally labelled in modern scholarship according to the callings of their principal figures: *konungasögur* (sagas of kings), *riddarasögur* (sagas of knights), *biskupasögur* (sagas of bishops), *postola sögur* (sagas of apostles), *heilagramanna sögur* (sagas of saints), or according to the sagas' relation to time: *fornaldarsögur* (sagas of antiquity) and *samtíðarsögur* (contemporary sagas, such as *Sturlunga saga*, named after one of the great clans of thirteenth-century Iceland). Among the most interesting groups of these medieval forerunners of the novel are the sagas of Icelanders (*íslendingasögur*), texts which are especially rich in such seemingly modern concepts as interiority, character development, and a remarkable feel for dialogue. The sagas present a panoramic view of medieval Nordic life, and for the student of folklore, they represent a unique opportunity to approach the cultural circumstances of medieval Scandinavia, as well as the

---

[12] On these and related matters, see Mitchell 2011.

attitudes of medieval writers toward the heroic past, whether heroic is understood in military, religious, or more personal terms.

Given the unrivaled skill with which the best of the sagas are written, it is hardly surprising that the various non-Icelandic medieval prose genres are generally overlooked. There are, however, many such texts in virtually all the vernaculars, encompassing translations of foreign originals (for example, *Sju vise mästare* [The Seven Sages]), reworkings of earlier Nordic texts (so *Sagan om Didrik af Bern* [The Saga of Dietrich of Bern]), and texts without known models (for example, *Skämtan om Abboten* [The Jest about the Abbot]). To these specifically literary forms may also be added such prolific and frequently non-narrative areas as religious prose and other forms of didactic writing, such as lapidaries, grammatical treatises and the *Konungs skuggsjá* (King's Mirror). All these materials present remarkable opportunities to mine the medieval Nordic world for folkloric materials, in which it is exceedingly rich.

Skaldic and eddic poetry, of which much survives in various contexts, are also important sources of information about the Scandinavian tradition, as previously noted.[13] Due to their great age, high aesthetic quality, and overwhelming significance with respect to Scandinavian mythology, they generally overshadow the younger forms of poetry which dominate the later periods: *rímur* (rhymes) in Iceland; *knittel*-verse in Sweden and Denmark; and the ballad throughout much of Scandinavia. The *rímur* comprise narrative poems, divided into fits, each exhibiting different complicated patterns of rhyme and alliteration. A uniquely Icelandic genre, the *rímur* are first attested in the late fourteenth century. The materials for *rímur* are largely drawn from existing prose sagas, especially those dealing with knights and ancient times, as well as from the occasional folktale and exemplum. *Knittel*, or end-rhymed epic, appears in the early fourteenth century in connection with Nordic court life, and was sometimes used to translate foreign works of literature (such as the so-called *Eufemiavisor* [Eufemia's Songs]) and to create native rhymed chronicles (for example, *Erikskrönikan* [*The Chronicle of Duke Erik*]). *Knittel* was particularly favored in Sweden, only to a slightly lesser extent in Denmark.

Ballads were sung throughout the Nordic world, although they are only rarely attested in medieval contexts (the first collections of them appeared after the Reformation). There are, however, many indications, including literary

---

[13] On which, see the texts, translations, and commentaries in the numerous volumes of *Skaldic Poetry of the Scandinavian Middle Ages*.

references and church paintings, that support the view that these "folksongs" represent a popular late medieval oral genre. The Nordic ballads are strophic, end-rhymed, narrative songs, generally associated with a lyrical refrain, and characterized by their objective style and use of so-called commonplaces. The subject matter of the ballads seems to have been limited only by the range of human imagination, and included everything from religious legends and courtly romance, at one extreme, to the supernatural and jocular, at the other. The long heroic ballads of the Faroe Islands maintained extraordinary continuity into modern times, including an association with dance.

A full accounting of resources for the study of folklore and other forms of spiritual culture in the Scandinavian Middle Ages would necessarily include, in addition to those areas mentioned above, such documents as letters, encyclopedic literature, sermons, and synodal statutes, as well as a variety of non-textual resources, including church murals, carving in wood and bone, metal work and other aspects of material culture and art, as well as folk dance and folk music. Although there exist several medieval collections of riddles and proverbs, as well as some thirty riddles in *Hervarar saga*, Scandinavia boasts nothing comparable to, for example, the Old English riddling tradition of the *Exeter Book*. Still, a reader of the sagas or of skaldic poetry will encounter a great deal of proverbial wisdom and riddle-like materials integrated into the texts.

Old Norse Folkloristics: Portals and Pathways

In his history of the Norwegian kings, the twelfth-century Benedictine, Theodoricus Monachus, comments at some length about the reputation the medieval Icelanders had for recalling ancient traditions (see above). It is a view shared by others, including the Danish historian and clergyman, Saxo Grammaticus, as well as, one suspects, the medieval Icelanders themselves (cf. Mitchell 1991b:97–98). The awareness of medieval Scandinavians to their past, its traditions and narratives, and their varying degrees of sensitivity to and concern for these materials, represents an early phase of the North's enduring cultural engagement with its own traditions, its so-called "folk memories" (*folkminnen*). During the Reformation era, serious and detailed interest in the peoples of the Nordic world, their cultures, practices, and beliefs, takes a new turn with the publication in Rome of the comprehensive ethnographic work of Olaus Magnus, *Historia de gentibus septentrionalibus* (1555).

And already in the early seventeenth century, Ole Worm in Denmark, Johannes Bureus in Sweden, and Jón Guðmundsson lærði in Iceland, for example, had interested themselves in, and were independently collecting, specimens of Nordic folklife and folklore. These efforts were made official state priorities when royal decrees—in 1622 for Denmark and Norway, in 1630 for Sweden—called for bishops to collect information on "antiquities" of all sorts in their bishoprics (Boberg 1953:144, 220, 304). Thus, as part of the struggle between the two kingdoms for political and cultural hegemony in the northern world, clergymen throughout Scandinavia ransacked their parishes for legends, memorials, runic monuments, and so on in order to add weight to the arguments of each of the competing polities to the greater claim to the North's cultural heritage. Given the resulting roots of Nordic folklore scholarship over the following centuries in nationalist, colonialist, post-colonial, and nation-building discourses, questions of memory, remembering, forgetting, and oblivion have played a considerable role in the cultural, political and intellectual debates that have for centuries figured into—often dominantly so—the study of Old Norse-Icelandic traditions (so, for example, Freeprose and Bookprose; the historical trustworthiness of the sagas; orality, oral performance, and oral composition; the disposition of the Icelandic manuscripts in the era of Icelandic independence).

To the extent, then, that folklorists are interested in the nature and uses of "tradition" (from Latin *trāditiō*, with a sense of handing over, delivery, transmission of knowledge, teaching, cf. Ben-Amos 1984; Bronner 1998, 2000; Noyes 2009), the pivotal role of cultural memory and its transmission has been at the forefront of the work of folklorists, and the field's thinking, since its earliest days. From the ambitious volumes of *Deutsche Sagen* (1816–1818) by Jacob and Wilhelm Grimm—which one scholar summarized as expressing the view that legends represent "memory in poetic garb" ("Erinnerung in poetischer Einkleidung," Fried 2012:64)—to recent studies focused on the sort of neuroimaging envisioned in, for example, the work of Harold Scheub (1998), folklorists have routinely been concerned with the interaction of cultural memory and performance in the production of narratives.

When did Old Norse folklore studies in a modern scholarly sense emerge? Nineteenth-century scholars, for example, thought it obvious that contemporary folk belief and the literature of the Nordic Middle Ages were understood to bear very significantly on each other: in Sweden's first scientific ethnology, *Wärend och Wirdarne*, with its important sub-title, *Ett försök i Svensk Ethnologi* (An Experiment in Swedish Ethnology, 1863–1868), Gunnar Olof Hyltén-Cavallius embraces a perspective on cultural memory which, even before Edward Tylor's seminal work on "survivals" (1871), views local traditions in his native Småland as reflections of earlier pagan traditions, writing, for example, that in the trolls of contemporary local folklore of the area one sees "den ursprungliga bilden af en fornnordisk Oden någon gång framskymta" (Hyltén-Cavallius 1863–1868, 1:224) (the original image of an ancient Nordic Óðinn occasionally burn through).

A century later, the Norwegian folklorist Brynjulf Alver (1962) demonstrated on more empirical grounds how folklore collected in the nineteenth and twentieth centuries sometimes reveals uncanny knowledge of, or echoes about (what we might now term, "cultural memory"), events and materials connected to the Viking and medieval periods, even the Pre-Roman Iron Age. Similar attempts have been made to assert "folk memories" connecting recently observed folklore and medieval Nordic antecedents (see, for example, Olrik 1901; Westman 1943). Recent research, frequently with a similar interest in continuities within folk traditions, have made more subtle uses of the function of memory and memory studies (Gunnell 2001b; Jesch 2008; Mitchell 2007a, 2009a), but a recognition of the fundamental conceptual relationship has remained strong throughout.

Memory Studies

The trustworthiness and accuracy of the Icelandic sagas has been at the heart of the so-called Freeprose-Bookprose debate since the term *Freiprosa* was first introduced by Andreas Heusler (1914:54).[14] The possibility of a special role for individuals with unusual abilities of recall, what Snorri Sturluson seems to mean by *gamlir fræðimenn* (old wise men) in his prologue to *Heimskringla*, and the implications of such people, the "men of memory" in their East Scandinavian legal context, has been explored in depth by Stefan Brink (2014). Gísli Sigurðsson (2004:53–92) also investigates the significance of the Icelandic institution of the so-called lawspeaker, an officially recognized "man of memory."

Accessing such rich medieval materials as these calls for a deep dive into a synthesizing study of cultural history, what most scholars working in the field mean by Old Norse folkloristics. Historically, that phrase embodies the field's twin roots in *folklore och filologi* (folklore and philology), as the

---

[14] On which see T. M. Andersson 1964:65–81; cp. Mitchell 1991b:1–6; Mitchell 2003b; Gísli Sigurðsson 2003, 2004; and Hermann 2017.

debate between these two points of view was characterized in a significant early twentieth-century academic feud.¹⁵ Famously proposed by the English antiquarian William Thoms in 1846, "Folk-Lore," as it was originally styled, is a calque on German *Volkskunde* (folk wisdom). Now widely used in international scholarship, as useful a term as "folklore" is, it can also occasionally mask telling native phrases: indicative of how the field has been popularly conceived in the North, one especially common term in the various Nordic languages for what we would today call "folkloristics," in evidence since the 1830s, specifically builds on the compound "folk memory" (i.e., *folkminnesforskning*, *þjóðminjafræði*).

This early understanding of the field of folklore study in the North is no trifling matter, especially as the role of Scandinavian folkloristics was so influential in the creation of modern international folklore scholarship. Indeed, disambiguating the specific study of Nordic folklore, including its roots in Old Norse philology, from the evolution of the field as a whole is largely impossible.¹⁶ Moreover, that the scientific study of folklore has historically been concerned with the reception, perception, use, and reconfiguration of cultural forms inherited from the past (or believed to have been inherited from the past) means, as Henning Laugerud (2010:19) notes, that "folklore studies have in one sense always been concerned with memory as a cultural phenomenon. The term folklore describes a certain kind of transmitted and collectively shared memory."

Of course, even a casual observer would think it obvious that understanding the past should be intimately connected with memory, understood broadly, yet as self-evident as that observation may seem to us today,¹⁷ it has not always been so: it was only in the aftermath of the so-called Great War that Maurice Halbwachs looked both to the past and the present and made his ground-breaking observations about the social frameworks of memory in *Les cadres sociaux de la mémoire* (1925; translated as *On Collective Memory*); similarly, memory's important role in constructing the past has been central to highly relevant contemporary questions of, for example, how to acknowledge, remember, respond to, and memorialize the Holocaust in

---

[15] Cf. von Sydow 1922a–b; Finnur Jónsson 1922; and my remarks in Mitchell 2000a.

[16] Cf. von Sydow 1922a, 1944; Boberg 1953; Strömbäck 1979a–b; Mitchell 2000a.

[17] My comments here largely build on and expand my remarks in Mitchell 2018a. Lest my emphasis here on perceived traditionality be misconstrued, I hasten to add that although this relation to the past is an important aspect of folklore, it is only one strand among many. Also vitally important is its relation to the present, a facet most readily revealed through "performance theory" and other context-oriented approaches, as discussed below.

the decades after World War II. Yet despite the significance of the development of memory studies in such relatively contemporary settings, it is notable that it is precisely studies of memory in "deep history," such as Jan Assmann's work on pharaonic Egypt (e.g., *Das kulturelle Gedächtnis: Schrift, Erinnerung und politische Identität in frühen Hochkulturen* [1992], translated as *Cultural Memory and Early Civilization: Writing, Remembrance, and Political Imagination*), that have been among the most profoundly influential works in the Humanities' recent engagement with memory studies and its refinement into such sub-categories as individual, communicative, and cultural memory (Assmann 2008).

By memory studies, most scholars primarily mean cultural memory studies, the branch of current memory theory that, broadly speaking, investigates "the interplay of present and past in socio-cultural contexts" (Erll 2008:2), that is, cultural memory as the product of representations and not of experiences (e.g., Assmann 1992; Rigney 2005). Moreover, I understand the study of cultural memory to be inherently, even stridently, cross-disciplinary, drawing on many theoretical stances that contribute to its area of inquiry (e.g., ethnohistory, speech act theory, performance studies, mediality, studies in orality and literacy, gender studies), an approach my colleagues and I employed in *The Handbook of Pre-Modern Nordic Memory Studies: Interdisciplinary Approaches* (Glauser, Hermann and Mitchell 2018). An emerging and ever-evolving synthesis between memory studies and the various disciplines that undergird and inform it offers the hope of new understandings of the Nordic Middle Ages and of memory's creative dimension (i.e., creative recall or *memoria rerum*, on which see Hermann 2009; cf. Erll and Nünning 2005). In the case of Old Norse-Icelandic literature, we should also consider the possible importance of memory that looks to maintain specific information (i.e., rote memory or *memoria verborum*; cf. Acker 1998). Also significant in such a discussion is the influence of learned culture which found in memory a kind of craft on which it too relied in the European Middle Ages.[18]

One can, of course, hear in these remarks the echoes of the once heated matters of orality versus writing, Oral Theory versus Neoanalysis, and so on, a debate which I for one regard as having been extremely useful yet

---

[18] See, for example, the items anthologized in *The Medieval Craft of Memory* and as explored by Yates (1974) and Carruthers (1990). This is an important perspective I have attempted to keep in mind in my own work treating issues of memory, tradition, and continuity (e.g., Mitchell 1984, 1985, 1991b, 2007a, 2008a, 2009a, 2012a, 2013, 2014a, 2018a, 2020a, 2020c, 2022a, 2022b, 2022c).

largely superseded by other synthesizing and more fruitful approaches (cf. Mitchell 2003b). As Pernille Hermann (2017) has noted with respect to the Old Norse-Icelandic materials, we ought now to be able to "reframe" these matters, and reconsider these key issues in the light of memory studies and the complex medial processes and changing functions of media taking place in the Norse world at that time (cf. Gísli Sigurðsson 2004; Glauser 2010; Gunnell 2016, 2018; Mitchell 2013).

The Ethnography of Communication and Performance Archaeology

Folklore's concern with just such key issues as continuity, heritage, remembering, tradition, memorialization, and innovation led to, and are largely revealed in, such ambitious theoretical stances as, e.g., the concepts of the "superorganic" (Kroeber 1917) and the "mentifact" (Bidney 1947:384; cf. Mitchell 2014a:47–48).[19] These approaches were all geared more-or-less exclusively to exploring folklore "products," whereas folkloristics has in recent decades experienced a strong movement away from this emphasis on such artifactual aspects of folklore as motifs, genres, and taxonomy, and focused instead on folklore's social and performance contexts, that is, pivoting away from the cultural documents themselves and toward the social processes by which these items are constructed and through which they acquire meaning, an orientation now usually referred to within folkloristics as performance theory. It would be difficult to overstate the significance of this performative turn for folkloristics as a whole, and for the study of the Old Norse materials in particular. The reconstruction it envisions of the cultural codes that govern communicative acts in medieval northern Europe "allows us to fill the interstices between the visible information in surviving written records and the larger picture of the past they are capable of painting; it is an approach that urges us to consider all aspects of our materials, to regard, for example, modes of production as a social process, not just the technology of ink production and other elements of the *scriptorium* (although they too are important)," as I have noted elsewhere (Mitchell 2022a:22). My own approaches to these matters have been primarily shaped by, on the one hand, what might be characterized as linguistic anthropology

---

[19] My comments here build on and extend my remarks in Mitchell 2022a.

writ large,[20] and, on the other hand, the work of Milman Parry, Albert Lord, and those inspired by their fieldwork in the Balkans, setting, as Parry wrote in 1935, "lore against literature."[21]

As befits the many purposes to which the term is yoked, performance is a broad and malleable designation covering many different, often ethnographically oriented approaches within the humanities and the interpretive social sciences. As is apparent from the well-known expression, "composition-in-performance," made famous by Lord ([1960] 2000), the concept plays a central role in the analysis of his and Parry's experiences of sung oral epic in southeastern Europe. In fact, performance is an issue to which he returns time and again in *The Singer of Tales*. And Lord's insistence on the defining significance of performance for the study of oral literature (even if he may not mean quite the same thing by performance) has been key in the reinvigoration of our understanding in a variety of historical cultures of the nature of oral literature (or as Foley later suggests, "oral-derived" texts [2011]).

That a conceptual tool like performance should be appropriate to treating traditional epic poetry and should also lend itself to discussing village factionalism in modern Africa may surprise some, but already in 1957, Victor Turner drills down with great foresight on such conflicts as ritualized performances and notes, "These eruptions, which I shall call 'social dramas', have 'processional form'" (1957:91), a view he extends significantly over the following decades (e.g., 1967, 1980). In many respects, performance (increasingly viewed as a separate discipline, Performance Studies), like memory studies, offers the possibility of an extensively cross-disciplinary academic field, encompassing not only oral theory, folkloristics, and ethnography, but also theater arts, speech act theory, and many other approaches.

For folklore, which, as one scholar mischievously noted, might be described as "a bastard field that anthropology begot upon English," performance indeed offers the possibility of overcoming the view that it is a discipline divided between those primarily concerned with the "folk" (typically viewed as being those oriented toward the social sciences) and

---

[20] E.g., ethnolinguistics (e.g., Gumperz and Hymes 1964), ethnobotany (e.g., Berlin, Breedlove, and Raven 1973), folkloristics (e.g., Bauman and Sherzer 1975; Bauman 1975), and the recognition of the importance of dynamic interactions over time within "social dramas" (e.g., Turner 1957; 1967:112–127; 1980; cf. Schechner 1977).

[21] Parry 1935. In addition to Lord's seminal study—and challenge—(1960) 2000, I have been heavily influenced by many scholars outside of Old Norse who have pursued so-called "oral theory" in other traditions (e.g., G. Nagy 1990, 2011; Foley 1991, 2002).

those focused on the "lore" (usually thought of as humanists in various language departments).[22] Like most stereotypes, that is an extreme view, but it is also a characterization not wholly without foundation. Even if folklore scholarship has never been defined by any single exclusive approach, there was one method that came close, the so-called Finnish Historical-Geographic School. This model of folklore scholarship was dominant and highly regarded throughout much of the twentieth century, giving rise to books with confident titles like Krohn's *Die folkloristische Arbeitsmethode* (1926) and Krappe's *The Science of Folk-Lore* (1930). In looking to provide folklore with its own scientific method,[23] the Finnish Historical-Geographic School developed a view that saw folklore as, in the words of its critics, "reified, persistent cultural items—texts, artifacts, mentifacts" (Bauman and Briggs 1990:79). Folkloristics conceived thus was generally uninterested in those who knew and used these materials—in other words, it represented just the sort of non-contextual view of folklore to which those who advocated a performance-oriented approach increasingly objected.[24]

In one of the early theoretical reflections on the potential value of a context-based approach to folklore, Roger Abrahams offered this succinct jeremiad on the shortcomings of the two extremes:

> Too long have the anthropologists and psychologists seen folklore as data which merely project ethnographic or psychosocial detail. Too long have folklorists emphasized the internal attributes of folklore as esthetic constructs without a consideration of how the lore reflects the group in which it exists, persists, and functions. Too long have all investigators been willing to divorce folklore from the people who perform it, or to regard it as peripheral—and therefore meaningless—or debased.
>
> Abrahams 1968:157

The corrective trend Abrahams anticipated to these issues was well expressed by Dell Hymes as the desire "to study the relation between folkloristic

---

[22] Coffin 1968, v. It is on account of this century-old friction that Rosemary Zumwalt gives her 1988 history of American folkloristics, *American Folklore Scholarship*, the sub-title, *A Dialogue of Dissent*. A similar dissent, and division, was, one suspects, mirrored elsewhere.

[23] As the author of *The Science of Folk-Lore*, Alexander Krappe, writes in the book's preface, "Folklore is, in fact has been for a considerable number of years, an historical science, having its own methods of research and admitting of the same system of checks and verifications as any other" (1930, ix).

[24] As Richard Bauman rightly remonstrated, the Finnish Historical-Geographic School treated folklore as "disembodied superorganic stuff" unconnected to "the individual, social, and cultural factors that give it shape and meaning in the conduct of social life" (Bauman 1986b:2).

materials and other aspects of social life *in situ*, as it were, where that relation actually obtains, the communicative events in which folklore is used."[25] The resulting view of "verbal art as performance," a theoretical and ethical stance (as well as the title of Richard Bauman's seminal 1975 article [expanded as Bauman 1977]), increasingly became the dominant mode of analysis in major folklore circles. It has permanently, it seems, reshaped folkloristics in very important ways, redirecting the focus of study from the "text" (or other cultural document) in isolation and toward the event or process in which such monuments are produced and used.[26]

But what about Old Norse? Where does Old Norse folkloristics fit amid all of these changes? First, it must be said that the discomfort with these changes expressed by D. K. Wilgus,[27] if perhaps not to the same degree, can also be seen within the Nordic folklore community. As Dag Strömbäck presented the issue at the end of a quarter century as editor of the prominent Nordic folklore journal, *ARV*,[28] it was a conflict between the study of folklore as he knew it, that is, as a field with intellectual roots in philology, archaeology, the history of religion, and the study of literature, against a movement that "sweeps folklore research in the direction of cultural anthropology and sociology and statistical method" (1979b:10). From our current vantage point, such fears, captured all too well in the title of one

---

[25] Hymes (1971:46), to which he shrewdly adds, "This concern is precisely parallel to the motivation of sociolinguistics research into the ethnography of speaking."

[26] At its heart, the significance of "performance theory" to folkloristics was an ideological dispute with serious methodological and theoretical consequences. Yet one cannot escape the sense that, at least in the American context, it was also a conflict in which academic politics and generational friction played their roles. When Richard Dorson refers to its advocates as "the young Turks among folklorists" (Dorson 1972:45), one senses that he does so with a degree of sympathetic approval (so Ben-Amos 2020:215); however, when D. K. Wilgus says in his 1972 American Folklore Society presidential address (published the following year) that "the behavioral approach is 'now-oriented'—and I might speculate on its relation to the so-called 'Now Generation'" (1973:244), the comment, and the address as a whole, should be understood as part of "a frontal attack on the theory, the method, and the terminology of these upstarts in folklore," as Dan Ben-Amos, one of Wilgus's main targets, puts it (Ben-Amos 2020:215).

[27] Famously, Wilgus wrote that "if a school of 'behavioral folklorists' determines that its questions are the only valid ones and that its findings cannot be applied to materials of previous researchers, then the results will not be revolutionary, but catastrophic. To be blunt, we might as well burn the archives" (Wilgus 1973:244–245).

[28] Strömbäck 1979a, 1979b. Strömbäck was the editor of *ARV* from 1952 to 1979. Published by Kungl. Gustav Adolfs Akademien för svensk folkkultur (the Royal Gustavus Adolphus Academy for Swedish Folk Culture), the journal has appeared under several slightly different sub-titles: *ARV. Tidskrift för nordisk folkminnesforskning* (1945–1978); *ARV. Scandinavian Yearbook of Folklore* (1979–1992); and *ARV. Nordic Yearbook of Folklore* (1993–).

critical assessment, "Slouching towards Ethnography: The Text/Context Controversy Reconsidered,"[29] were greatly exaggerated.

Second, the key methodological adjustment required from the perspective of those working in older fields, including Old Norse, if they were to accept the performative model, would be the transfer to their materials of the approaches developed with living folklore communities in focus—but just such an application from observed behavior to archival materials is, of course, at the heart of any number of theories, most notably the Parry-Lord project.[30]

Parry and Lord had, after all, immersed themselves in a living tradition of sung oral epic poetry in the Balkans principally as a means of better understanding the techniques available to, even likely used by, singers of Homeric and other early epics.[31] Theirs is an argument by analogy, one that at the same time advocates a broad philosophical and ethnographic reorientation—reimagining even—of textual scholarship. The significance of their work for Nordicists, it seems to me, resides in the model they provide for such (re)contextualizations of past performance practices, a model through which Lord's and Parry's work has considerably reinvigorated medieval scholarship in general.[32]

As Terry Gunnell, a leading scholar of medieval performance practices and of the effort to reimagine such practices for medieval Scandinavia, rightly comments, "If we wish to understand how Old Norse poetry was conceived and experienced by poets and audiences in the medieval period, we need to put reading and writing to one side, and to start considering these works more in terms of theatre, slam poetry and jazz improvisation, in other words, in terms of sound, vision and momentary *experience*. In short,

---

[29] Jones 1979; in fairness, it should be noted that, the tenor of the title notwithstanding, the essay's main concern is to argue for the value of the isolated folklore item, even when shorn of context.

[30] To take a famous instance within Old Norse of such an application based on modern observations, Carol Clover has on several occasions (1986b, 1993) very successfully employed the example of the Albanian system of "sworn virgins" as a means of showing how there may have existed for Old Norse a "historical prototype of the maiden warrior" (1986b:49) we see in such figures as Hervǫr in *Hervarar saga*.

[31] As I have argued elsewhere (Mitchell 2014a), although this change of perspective was to my eyes both welcome and much needed, one can also sympathize, as I readily admit I do, with Strömbäck's further comment (1979a:11) that, "my heart is captured more by the study of traditions from olden times, particularly from the Middle Ages, and by the approach which interweaves historical fact, philological interpretation and textual criticism." Of course, rather than a binary choice limited to just one of these two seemingly antipodal perspectives, as medievalists we need to meld these systems in such a way as to produce the most informative and enlightening results.

[32] Cf. my comments in Mitchell 2013 and 2018a, as well as those in Mitchell and Nagy 2000.

we need to start by considering them in terms of *performance*..."[33] Toward this end, Gunnell has himself in a series of monographs and articles demonstrated how vital our ability to envision and recognize "performance," in both its most literal and in its more extended senses, is to apprehending fully the potential of the experiences reflected in our surviving texts.[34]

Parallel to these developments among those Old Norse scholars primarily engaged in folkloristic, philological, and literary studies, archaeologists too had been responding to similar theoretical discussions and often to many of the same scholars (e.g., Turner, Schechner). Indeed, "performance archaeology" appears very much to have come into its own in recent years; however, even before the appearance of such works as *Theatre/Archaeology* (Pearson and Shanks 2001) and *Archaeology of Performance* (Inomata and Coben 2006), with their more clearly contemporary theatrical sense of performance, the essence of this performance perspective was making itself felt.

In 1989, for example, the Swedish archaeologist Anders Andrén published "Dörrar till förgångna myter. En tolkning av de gotländska bildstenarna" (later expanded as "Doors to Other Worlds: Scandinavian Death Rituals in Gotlandic Perspectives," 1993). With its innovative examination of Gotlandic picture stones and Iron Age death rituals, this forward-thinking and careful study opened new vistas for Nordic archaeology, a performance-centered approach which Andrén has continued to pursue over the years (e.g., 2012, 2014).

A number of other Nordic archaeologists (e.g., Terje Gansum, Torun Zachrisson, Jan Bill) have effectively pursued similar performance-oriented strategies, but perhaps the archaeologist who has most vigorously and most persuasively considered the implications (and possibilities) of Old Norse performance archaeology is Neil Price at Uppsala University. In a series of works (e.g., 2008, 2010, 2012, 2014, 2019, as well as Price and Mortimer 2014), Price has probed the physical and textual evidence of Viking Age funerals and considered, for example, "grave goods" (objects found in association with the burial) not just as material objects to be duly recorded and

---

[33] Gunnell 2022:1. Gunnell's point is one I have recently attempted to exploit in looking to various modern forms of aggressive verbal competitions (e.g., "the dozens") as a means of understanding similar contests in Old Norse (Mitchell 2020b). See also, e.g., Bauman 1986a; Würth 2007; as well as my other forays, Mitchell 1991b, 1997b, 2001a, 2007a, 2009a, 2011, 2013, 2018b, and 2022a. Gunnell's fulsome survey (2022), together with his entry on "Performance Studies" (2018), offer very complete reviews of the state of this approach in Old Norse.

[34] E.g., Gunnell 1995, 2001a, 2006a, 2006b, 2008, 2011, 2012, 2013, 2016, 2018, 2019, 2020; Gunnell and Ronström 2013.

catalogued,³⁵ but as elements of what Price refers to as "burial theatrics" (2014:179). That is, they are objects which demand interrogation: Where were such items placed? By whom? For what purpose? In the presence of what audience? In what sort of process? With what attendant sounds and smells? Over what period of time did the events take place? How were these events commemorated and observed? How were such practices and events reflected in, and how did they contribute to, the formulation of the narrative traditions of these communities? and so on. These are, of course, heady matters, and the various cases Price examines from Fyrkat, Birka, Trekroner-Gyldehøj, Götavi, and so on offer valuable examples of what is to be gained from such innovative approaches. As Price himself writes, "As the practical potential for recovering ritual performance increases, so will our opportunities for access to the Viking mind, in all its marvellous variety."³⁶

Emergent Perspectives

In a similar vein, important emerging approaches and perspectives, such as the study of mentalities (cf. Hutton 1981; Knuuttila 1993, 1995) and ethnohistory and ethnopoetics (Dorson 1961; DuBois 2013), have also added significantly to the toolkit of Nordic medievalists. Focusing on these perspectives, as well as on memory studies and performance studies, is, of course, not meant to exclude other, often more traditional, disciplines. Clearly, many research fields have played, and will continue to play, important roles in how we understand the worlds of the Viking Age and the traditions held by those people in later periods who knew about those worlds, even if they did so at some remove from the events themselves.

The history of religions, for example, with its focus on ritual, has also been a leading force in re-envisioning how a context- or performance-based approach can bring about new understandings of our Nordic materials.³⁷ Onomastic research too has proved to be an invaluable tool in reimagining

---

[35] "In our recording and publication it is not enough to list the contents of a grave, like an accountant's inventory. Burials are clearly organic things, developing over sequences of ritual actions," Price 2014:186.

[36] Price 2014:188. Although agreeing that "the performance paradigm has been very productive within Scandinavian pre-Christian archaeology" (2020:120), Clunies Ross offers a generally very dim view of such cross-disciplinary research, citing precisely some of the recent work in "performance archaeology."

[37] E.g., Nygaard and Murphy 2017; Nygaard 2018. For a survey, see Nygaard and Schjødt 2018.

these bygone worlds. In recent years, for example, place-names specialists (e.g., Stefan Brink), in investigating place-names with archaeologists, students of religion, and those working from the perspectives of other subjects, have contributed richly to our understanding of such Nordic institutions as the *vi* and the *þing*, assemblies with juridical and religious or cultic functions.[38]

It is primarily because of such good cross-disciplinary research results that we should prize working interdisciplinarily, of course. A further advantage to taking such a multivalent approach is that by doing so, we do not *a priori* exclude any form of data.[39] Thinking broadly about how we can access our materials, beginning by seeing them as socially constructed and socially employed phenomena, has proved critical in interpreting Old Norse folklore. For my part, I have focused primarily on memory studies and performance theory (in the latter case, especially as the idea was developed within the "ethnography of communication," or as originally styled, the "ethnography of speaking"),[40] but I do not discard out of hand any approach capable of adding to our understanding.

Thus in *Heroic Sagas and Ballads* (1991), a book-length study of the legendary sagas, or *fornaldarsǫgur*, I employ an ethnosymbolic approach to cultural memory and build on the view that these texts were understood (or agreed upon to be understood) by their audiences to be traditional—storied tales based on orally transmitted memories, or purported memories, from the past (Mitchell 1991b; cp. Mitchell 2014a). Understanding the value these works would have had in the late medieval period as "cultural forms inherited from the past (or believed to have been inherited from the past)," the study underscores the roles played by revitalization, folklorism, and "the attitudes of the Icelanders toward their past" (Mitchell 1991b:133–135, 180).

Similarly, Merrill Kaplan's study of four tales in *Flateyjarbók* (2011; cf. Kaplan 2000, 2004) carefully examines episodes in the manuscript where figures from the pre-Christian past make appearances, episodes which

---

[38] Meeting places of this sort, frequently referred to in scholarship as *tingsteder* (lit., "thing sites"), have been the subjects of significant archaeological and onomastic scrutiny. For orientations, see Brink 2003, 2017, 2018, 2020; Vikstrand 2001; and Sundqvist 2016, as well as the very substantial two-volume collection of essays in *The Journal of the North Atlantic* (special volumes 5 [2013] and 8 [2015]), introduced in Sanmark, Semple, Mehler, and Iversen 2013.

[39] My unapologetic antipathy toward constipated disciplinary fidelity is, I am certain, obvious throughout this volume, and is, I suppose, to be expected, as my training and degrees included the highly synthesizing fields of philology and anthropology (encompassing, as is typical in North America, folklore and archaeology).

[40] Cf. Hymes 1962; Bauman 1975, 1977; Bauman and Briggs 1990; and my comments in Mitchell 2022a.

constitute "a guide for thinking about the narrative goods of the pagan past, and for reusing them" (Kaplan 2011:194). And in his important examination of the relationship between oral sources and Old Icelandic literary texts, especially with respect to the so-called *Vínland sagas*, Gísli Sigurðsson (2004:253–263) utilizes the comparative study of oral traditions, embracing the expression "floating memories" as a means of capturing the process that views our extant texts as the results of multigenerational tale-telling, "in exactly the way we might expect of stories and information preserved by memory and passed on by word of mouth" (Gísli Sigurðsson 2004:301).

A variety of sometimes established, sometimes emerging theoretical models offer modern students of the Nordic Viking and Middle Ages extraordinary opportunities to gain a purchase on the endlessly fascinating world being reflected in the Norse materials. From my current perch, now more than fifty years since I was first made aware of the genius of the Nordic Middle Ages as an undergraduate at Berkeley, it seems to me that folkloristics continues to be among the most important portals we possess into the Old Norse world. Despite my own partisan position, however, I believe strongly in the value of cross-disciplinary research—yes, of course, with our feet firmly planted in specific academic areas, but also with our eyes very much open to advances in neighboring fields—so, in that sense, the disciplinary tags we use to describe our work are themselves not the key concern. It is rather how we choose to look at things.

The sort of re-orientation I envision about how we should approach our materials was perhaps best expressed by the Anglo-Swedish archaeologist Neil Price in his fine recent history of the Viking world, where, speaking of older works, he notes (2020:6), "the focus has largely tended to be on what the Vikings did rather than on why they did it. There is a sense in which this viewpoint is looking through the wrong end of the historical telescope." In taking what he subsequently refers to as "the opposite approach, working from the inside looking out," Price sets an admirable example of what is to be gained in taking the broad view.

I hope readers will feel that the chapters that follow adhere to this same high standard and offer the opportunity to consider, or perhaps, to re-consider, some of the great problems and some of the great cultural monuments with which Nordicists concern themselves. And I trust as well that the essays demonstrate the possibility of retaining what was good about traditional folklore studies, such as it was envisioned by Strömbäck, with its roots in philology, archaeology, the history of religion, and the study of literature, while at the same time highlighting the field's ability to evolve and reinvent itself positively through emergent methods and perspectives.

PART I

Orality and Performance

Chapter 1

ORALITY, ORAL THEORY, AND MEMORY STUDIES

In Old Norse scholarship, "orality," "Oral Theory," "oral text" and similar terms commonly indicate two related but historically distinguishable approaches to the medieval materials.[1] In one case, such locutions have been used very broadly to refer to a wide range of ideas discussed since at least the late eighteenth century relating to how historical, mythological and legendary materials, for example, were believed to have been narrativized and performed anterior to and/or outside of writing. In the Nordic context, this approach was both philosophical and deeply political. In the other instance, "Oral Theory" and related terms (e.g., "oral tradition") have, since the ground-breaking research on oral epic singing by Milman Parry and Albert Lord in the 1930s—expressed most famously in Lord (1960) 2000 and the substantial research it has inspired in a wide range of language traditions and periods—been used to take the lessons of that work, as well as other evolving oral-centered methodologies, and apply them to the Old Norse situation. These now largely merged lines of thinking share a number of concerns with memory studies, although the overlap is not absolute.

State of Research

Students of folklore and others with a stake in so-called oral literature might well be forgiven for asking whether or not memory studies does not simply

---

[1] Original publication: "Orality and Oral Theory." In *Handbook of Pre-Modern Nordic Memory Studies: Interdisciplinary Approaches*, ed. Jürg Glauser, Pernille Hermann, and Stephen A. Mitchell, 1:120–131. Berlin, 2018.

represent a question of "new wine in old skins": after all, some "discoveries" made within memory studies do indeed appear to be simple re-packagings of ideas that are very old within folklore studies (e.g. "memory communities" for "folk groups"). And importantly, folklore as a field has always had an eye on memory, whether the communicative memory of individuals or a folk group's collective memory. Do memory studies in fact differ from studies of orality and performance practices, and can the two be disambiguated?

It is apparent that the answers cannot be reduced to simple binaries, for the two fields share much but also differ in their orientations and the questions they seek to answer. Modern memory studies in all its diverse forms, as expressed in the works of, among others, Aleida Assmann, Jan Assmann, Paul Connerton, Astrid Erll, Andreas Huyssen, Jacques Le Goff, Pierre Nora, Ann Rigney, and Richard Terdiman, is, after all, only a few decades old—the works of e.g. A. Assmann, J. Assmann, and Hardmeier (1983) and Le Goff (1988) may be taken to represent convenient early milestones in these modern developments. Even the venerable early considerations by Maurice Halbwachs about collective memory (1925, 1950) have not yet been around for as much as a century.

By contrast, orality's engagement with memory—perhaps best visualized emically in the anthropomorphization of "the tradition" in the form of legendary performers like Homer, Ossian, Ćor Huso, or, in the case of pre-modern Nordic oral poetry, Bragi (cf. Foley 1998)—represents a form of abstraction that dates back millennia. Moreover, it is telling that the compound "folk memory studies" in the various Nordic languages (e.g. *folkminnesforskning, þjóðminjafræði*) has been used since at least the early nineteenth century as a primary means of expressing what in English was in that same period re-named Folk-Lore as a substitute for the earlier phrase, "popular antiquities"—and in all of these cases there existed consistent and concomitant connections to orality, tradition and cultural memory.

Perhaps a convenient if somewhat over-simplified means of disentangling the two approaches, especially for those interested in the pre-modern, would be to say that where students of orality, oral tradition, and so on look primarily to understand the means by which cultural monuments are produced in artistic performances or re-enactments (cf. G. Nagy 2011)—and by extension to exploit re-contextualizations of performance practices as a means of analyzing meaning within specific cultural contexts—the student of modern memory studies is primarily concerned with how the past is created collectively and, especially, with the purposes and values of how it is used in the present.

Thus, one sees, for example, in Lord's discussion of a young singer's informal apprenticeship that there exists a reliance on memory in a sophisticated sense ([1960] 2000:36; see below) according to which memory in Lord's thinking is viewed as an important generative technology, or art, writ large, useful and functional in terms that would have been readily appreciated by an experienced ethnographer like Bronislaw Malinowski. By contrast, memory studies tends to have other ambitions: to take a notable example, Terdiman writes of his major work on memory that it is a book "about how the past persists into the present," arguing further that "there is another side to memory—memory as a problem, as a site and source of cultural disquiet"— his book's goal is thus "to reconceive modernity in relation to the cultural disquiet I term the memory crisis" (Terdiman 1993, vii–viii). Emphasizing a somewhat different research interest—"the link between collective memories and identity politics"—another leading memory studies scholar explores how "memories of a shared past are collectively constructed and reconstructed in the present rather than resurrected from the past" (Rigney 2005:13–14).

Caution is naturally in order: memory studies has many branches, orientations and followers and no small sub-set of writers can be understood to encompass its multifaceted interests. Moreover, one does not want to reduce the differences between studies of orality and memory studies to a mischaracterizing binary in which one group focuses on questions of technique— *memoria verborum* (i.e. rote memory), *memoria rerum* (i.e. creative recall) and all that accompanies such debates—versus the supposed focus by the other group on contemporary society's relation to the past in which memory is conceived as (mere) modality and mediating psychotechnology. Neither image would be accurate and inherently the perspectives of those interested in orality, oral literature, folkloristics and so on, and those engaged in memory studies share considerably overlapping sets of concerns. They have learned, and will continue to learn, much from each other; moreover, scholars need not belong to only one group (see e.g. the essays in Ben-Amos and Weissberg 1999).

Orality

Consideration of what constituted oral tradition in the hyperborean Middle Ages (and how to access it) is subject to many factors, including how much of the medieval materials have survived; the use of analytic tools developed for non-Nordic texts, Homeric epics in particular; and the influence of early modern nation building in shaping how these texts have been experienced. Perspectives on such inherited cultural goods were in the eighteenth and early nineteenth centuries heavily influenced by the writings of Giambattista Vico, Friedrich August Wolf, Johan Gottfried Herder, Karl Lachmann and others, debates about so-called *Naturpoesie* (natural or "folk" poetry, conceived in opposition to *Kunstpoesie* [art or elite poetry]), and epic construction through the so-called *Liedertheorie* (song theory) (see T. M. Andersson 1962, 1964:1–21).

Moreover, since the Union of Kalmar in the late fourteenth century, Norway and its overlordship of the Norse colonies in the North Atlantic had passed to Denmark. With the Napoleonic era, the map of Scandinavia was substantially rearranged, and an era of significant agitation for Norwegian and, to a lesser extent, Icelandic political independence ensued. In that world of Romantic nationalism and inter-Nordic colonialism, few cultural goods were as significant as the eddas and sagas, those unique literary windows on the medieval North. Who "owned" them—that is, who created them, whose traditions they represent, whose unique literary achievement they were to be credited as being, and so on—played a meaningful role in justifying Norwegian claims to nationhood in the modern era. If early ideas of a fixed oral tradition were correct, nationalists could argue that the Icelandic literary enterprise of the thirteenth century was "really" a displaced exercise in Norwegian creativity, and the greater the degree to which this oral tradition could be argued to be a practice harking back to the mother country, the greater the nationalist claim to these prized literary works—and the more legitimate the Norwegian demand for complete independence (T. M. Andersson 1964:65–81; Mitchell 1991b:1–6).

In this sense, discussions of orality were not only an academic debate, but rather a substantive argument deeply embedded in a serious political dilemma. And it was a debate with a lengthy hangover: Harald Beyer's *Norsk Litteraturhistorie* (*A History of Norwegian Literature*) was published in 1952, well after the political debates themselves had been resolved, yet even here the text emphasizes that "the rise of the written saga must be seen against this background of learned antiquarianism *in the pioneer society of Iceland*," and even refers to the Icelanders—by now, some 400 years after the beginning of the *landnám*—as "*emigrated Norwegians in Iceland*" (1952:44; *emphases added*). Oral sagas and eddic poetry were in this scheme seen as reified cultural memories.

Over time, these positions developed into largely opposing schools of thought: on the one hand, those who emphasized the oral, performed roots of the extant written sagas, what has come to be called the "Freeprose" position, and, on the other, those who stress the sagas as the written products of individual authors influenced by Continental models, the so-called "Bookprose" position, terms proposed by Andreas Heusler (1914:53–55). No modern scholar believes in an absolute dichotomy between these views, and the general question of how to account for this unique medieval genre has been posed as follows, "[...] is the background to the sagas' art to be conceived of as native and essentially spoken (or verbal, or performed, or recited), or is the background based on foreign models in which the key aspects of composition have been shaped by literacy?" (Mitchell 1991b:1).

Oral Theory

The second approach, what is often called Oral Theory—nomenclature that often troubles adherents, as it tends to ignore the hard evidence of the original study—draws inspiration from many of the same early Homerists mentioned above. The Homeric problem Milman Parry sought to solve might reasonably be formulated as follows: how was it possible that the *Iliad* and *Odyssey*, two of the finest works of western literature, appear simultaneously at the very moment of writing's inception in the west? The answer Parry proposed, of course, was that rather than being written creations, these epics were in fact the products of many generations of oral narration—writing made it possible to record them, but this new medium was not itself responsible for creating them. What distinguishes Parry from other Classicists who had posed the "Homeric Question" before him was not only his view that the *Iliad* and the *Odyssey* were originally the products of an oral tradition that was older than any written literature, but rather his formulation of a method for *testing* this hypothesis, a procedure which moved the debate from focusing solely on the content of orally produced songs to the actual process through which such songs are produced in performance, and an approach that asked the humanities to adhere to the scientific method (observation; hypothesis formulation; testing; validation, or modification, of the hypothesis). This goal Parry and Lord pursued vigorously by examining the living tradition of south Slavic oral poetry and learning how it functioned. In Parry's own words, the problem and proposed solution is this:

> If we put lore against literature it follows that we should put oral poetry against written poetry, but the critics so far have rarely done this, chiefly because it happened that the same man rarely knew both kinds of poetry,

and if he did he was rather looking for that in which they were alike. That is, the men who were likely to meet with the songs of an unlettered people were not ordinarily of the sort who could judge soundly how good or bad they were, while the men with a literary background who published oral poems wanted above all to show that they were good as literature. It was only the students of the "early" poems who were brought in touch at the same time with both lore and literature.

Parry 1935:3

Parry's untimely death left to his assistant, Albert B. Lord, later the Arthur Kingsley Porter Professor of Slavic and Comparative Literature at Harvard University, the completion of this bold project. In Lord's seminal analysis of their findings, *The Singer of Tales* ([1960] 2000), he demonstrates the process by which singers learn their craft and the methods they employ in singing epics of great length, several aspects of which are of particular relevance to memory studies.

In the Yugoslavian case, those who aspire to become oral poets begin the process early, through informal training in adolescence, which Lord summarizes as "first, the period of listening and absorbing; then, the period of application; and finally, that of singing before a critical audience" ([1960] 2000:21). During this informal and lengthy period of "enskilment" (see Gísli Pálsson 1994), singers "lay the foundation," in Lord's phrase, learning the stories, heroes, places, themes, rhythms, formulas, and the other tools they use in composing their own multiforms of these songs. It is not difficult to see in this process the broad understanding of memory, as a noted scholar in the field writes, "in the sense of an embodied storehouse," "a craft and as a resource that can be trained to contain immense amounts of information" (Hermann 2020).

An important distinction Lord draws is between traditional singers of this sort and those who sing but are using memorized (often published) texts—"we cannot consider such singers as oral poets," he writes, "They are *mere* performers" ([1960] 2000:13). The traditional singer learns the craft at such a level, that over time he is able to compose, or recompose, the songs himself, not as memorized text, but as story-telling in which he uses the specialized tools of the tradition's poetic language:

> When we speak a language, our native language, we do not repeat words and phrases that we have memorized consciously, but the words and sentences emerge from habitual usage. This is true of the singer of tales working in his specialized grammar. He does not "memorize" formulas, any more than we

as children "memorize" language. He learns them by hearing them in other singers' songs, and by habitual usage they become part of his singing as well. Memorization is a conscious act of making one's own, and repeating, something that one regards as fixed and not one's own. The learning of an oral poetic language follows the same principles as the learning of language itself, not by the conscious schematization of elementary grammars but by the natural oral method.

Lord [1960] 2000:36

Lord's generative model, implicitly anticipating important aspects of what later emerged as transformational grammar and discussions of deep and surface structures, is critical to so-called Oral Theory, insofar as it is the key finding behind the concept that traditional oral poets compose in performance, and are neither repeating memorized texts nor engaging in improvisation, extemporization, or other autoschediastic utterances. "My own preferred term for that type of composition is 'composition by formula and theme.' 'Composition in performance' or possibly 'recomposition in performance' are satisfactory terms as long as one does not equate them with improvisation [...]" (Lord 1991:76–77).

Significantly for the issue of memory and memory studies, Lord also describes the phenomenon of "multiformity" (99–102), essentially the same feature of oral poetry Zumthor (1972) later popularizes as *mouvance* (although their points of view differ somewhat). Lord's formulation is especially apt, as he speaks not of the song but of songs; that is, to a singer and his audience, since the subject matter is "the same," they will identify different performances as being of "the same song," even though these performance-generated oral texts may differ markedly as regards length, focus, and other matters of treatment (something we must do as well in cataloguing texts). But, of course, they are not truly "the same," since they are never fixed or memorized, and can vary greatly. Thus, in a famous example, *Ženidba Smailagić Meha* (The Wedding of Meho, Son of Smail) was recorded on two occasions, separated by some 15 years, from the most renowned of the singers in the Parry Collection, Avdo Međedović (Lord 1956). In July of 1935, Avdo's performance ran to 12,323 lines; in May of 1950, he performed "the same song" in 8,488 lines. They are both complete, full recountings of the story, but differ precisely in how Avdo treats the performances.

In addition to these direct findings about south Slavic traditional oral poets, among the most important results of applying the Parry-Lord observations to other tradition areas, has been the reevaluation of just what we should hope to find—not merely duplications of Parry and Lord's original methods for, e.g., testing the use of formulas or the mechanics of composition in performance, but also tools for such important perspectives as recontextualizing performance practices (e.g. G. Nagy 2011; Mitchell 2013; cf. Harris and Reichl 2011). Further ramifications of the Parry-Lord project are to be seen in the fact that two prominent theoretical approaches to folklore and oral literature—ethnopoetics and performance studies, both of relevance to memory studies—were clearly anticipated in Lord's writings (see, e.g., DuBois 2013 and Gunnell 2008). As Bauman notes in his highly influential *Verbal Art as Performance* (1977), *The Singer of Tales* is one of the first works to conceive of folklore texts in terms of "emergent structures." Continuing, he writes, "one of Lord's chief contributions is to demonstrate the unique and emergent quality of the oral text, composed in performance. His analysis of the dynamics of the epic tradition sets forth what amounts to a generative model of epic performance" (Bauman 1977:38–39; cf. Mitchell and Nagy 2000). It is certainly the case that Parry and Lord's observations on south Slavic song culture had profound impact throughout the humanities, and it is presumably no coincidence that just four years after *The Singer of Tales* first appeared, Andersson concludes his impressive history of the Nordic situation with the sentence, "The inspiration of the sagas is ultimately oral" (T. M. Andersson 1964:119).

Pre-modern Nordic Material

Capturing the essence of the Nordic localization of the so-called Great Divide, Sigurður Nordal once described the Bookprose-Freeprose controversy as the Scylla and Charybdis between which saga scholarship has tended to sail ([1940] 1958:65)—should the medieval Icelandic texts be seen as products of a memorizing oral culture or as a situation where "sagawriting existed in a social vacuum, that written sagas were influenced only by other written sagas," as one scholar noted (Lönnroth 1976:207)? Or, as a later writer less generously characterized the Nordicist's dilemma, there was not much of a choice between "a desiccating formalism dedicated to a fixed text and an equally alkaline literary criticism that saw only words on a page" (Mitchell 2003b:204).

The significance of Oral Theory's contributions to the debate—fortified by complementary approaches (e.g. Zumthor 1983; Schaefer 1992) and sympathetic advocacy (e.g. Ong 1982; Goody 1987; Foley 1988, 2002)—was to offer compromises between the two century-old extremes in Old Norse scholarship, compromises that often resulted in new models and novel exploratory ingresses to the texts (e.g. Lönnroth 1976; Byock 1982; Harris 1983; Bandle 1988; Glauser 1996; Mundt 1997; Acker 1998; Gísli Sigurðsson 2002; Mellor 2008; cf. Ranković, Leidulf and Mundal 2010), resulting in emerging symbioses (see, e.g. the reviews in Harris 2016 and Hermann 2017). Oral Theory, particularly in the context of the so-called "ethnography of communications," has also led to much interest in the production of Norse oral compositions and their delivery in medieval Scandinavia, especially the frequently noted performance contexts of eddic and skaldic poetry (e.g. Lönnroth 1971; Bauman 1986a; Acker 1998; Harris 2000a-b; Mitchell 2001a; Gunnell 2013; Clunies Ross 2014).

That one can discuss a text from the Middle Ages as being oral naturally strikes many observers as paradoxical, since it cannot be literally true, and Lord himself acknowledges this point in what he refers to as "the merging of the world of orality with that of literacy" (1986:19). Still, the power of orality, or of the idea of orality, as a key ingredient in the cultural kit seems to have been strong, and when mirrored in writing has been called "fictionalized orality" (*fingierte Mündlichkeit*) (Goetsch 1985), a phenomenon also in evidence in the medieval North (cf. T. M. Andersson 1966). Recognition of both unconscious reflections of orality in the medieval texts, as well as of this more consciously applied oral style, was observed early on in scholarship, and the need for a descriptor for such materials was met by Foley, who coined the phrase "oral-derived text" to describe "manuscript or tablet works of finally uncertain provenance that nonetheless show oral traditional characteristics" (1990:5; cf. Quinn 2016). The phrase is intended, as Foley states elsewhere (2011:603), "As an alternative to the simplistic binary model of orality versus literacy, the concept of oral-derived texts suggests a broad range of diverse media interactions: from autographs through dictation to scribes and on to multiply edited manuscripts and works written in an oral traditional style."

Perspectives for Future Research

Just as emerging perspectives like New Philology have re-energized manuscript studies, orality and Oral Theory have similarly re-vitalized the study of medieval literature and made available a variety of techniques to move serious scholarship beyond merely viewing the texts as ossified words on a manuscript page (cf. Gísli Sigurðsson 2008), leading to a healthy integration of oral-centered approaches with adjacent methodologies (e.g. ethnopoetics, ethnohistory, performance studies), symbioses that promise much (see DuBois 2013; Hermann 2017). Similarly, the specific intersection of orality and memory studies is significant, and one expects that so interdisciplinary and methodologically agglutinating a field as folkloristics will enthusiastically embrace the lessons to be learned from memory studies. The interplay between Oral Theory/orality and modern international memory studies within Old Norse studies has only recently been taken up in earnest (e.g. Mitchell 2013; Hermann 2017; Hermann 2020), but promises bright prospects for future research.

Chapter 2

CONTINUITY

FOLKLORE'S PROBLEM CHILD?

Introduction

Few topics play a more central role in the way scholars have thought—and, in some cases, continue to think—about medieval folk cultures than has the issue of continuity.¹ The possibilities of making useful and empirically grounded connections over time between and among cultural documents, understood broadly, are indeed enticing, especially for those focused on northern Europe, where unbroken chains of tradition might lead us from our late medieval data back into the deep past, to the earlier worlds hinted at in the writings of Adam of Bremen, Rimbert, even Tacitus, as well as to the recoverable outlines of late Iron Age material culture revealed by modern archaeology.

Thus, with luck and hard work, it was hoped, the continuity argument might fill the interstices of our textual data, and, correspondingly, clothe the postholes and other echoes of "lived lives" of countless dig sites in cultural context and human values. By means of continuity and tradition, scholars could make the leap from, say, the thin gruel of an insouciant reference by a Latin author or the settlement design of some immiserated polar outpost

---

[1] Original publication: "Continuity: Folklore's Problem Child?" In *Folklore in Old Norse – Old Norse in Folklore*, ed. Daniel Sävborg and Karen Bek-Pedersen, 34–51. Nordistica Tartuensis, 20. Tartu, 2014.
   My comments here build on and extend my presentations at the 2011 meeting of the Old Norse Folklorists Network in Tartu, Estonia, and the Folklore Roundtable in 2012 at the 15th International Saga Conference at Aarhus University, Denmark, as well as several previously published works (especially 1991, 2000, 2007, 2009, and 2012). I am very grateful to Barbro Klein, John Lindow, and Jens Peter Schjødt for their very helpful comments on earlier drafts of this paper.

all the way forward to the spectacular "thick descriptions" provided by thirteenth- and fourteenth-century Icelandic sagas and other writing.[2]

Thus, in the first case, Paul the Deacon's eighth-century story of how Frea tricks Godan into giving victory to the Lombards over the Vandals can be better understood against (and, in turn, give a more comprehensive understanding of) the thirteenth-century prose introduction to the eddic poem *Grímnismál*.[3] And in the second instance, one can appreciate how the discovery of the so-called Þjóðhildarkirkja, the chapel at Brattahlíð in Greenland, which, according to the traditions recorded in *Eiríks saga rauða* (212 [chap. 5]), was built—not without controversies—for Eiríkr's wife, Þjóðhildr, become much more than the unearthing of the foundation stones of just another *úthús* (cf. Þórhallur Vilmundarson 1961).

This is heady stuff, and one need not be hopelessly romantic to see that such connections can have important consequences—the fascinating recent debates surrounding the figures from Lejre and Uppåkra (T. Christensen 2010c; Helmbrecht 2012) are only the latest discoveries to underscore the significance and consequences of the continuity argument. It is, however, also clearly difficult terrain to untangle from, on the one hand, the seemingly futile but intellectually driven search for authenticity, to borrow the evocative phrase used by Regina Bendix in her important study of folklore's social and academic roots (1997), and, on the other hand, the echoes of a field which, like its sister disciplines, archaeology and physical anthropology, was all-too-easily seduced by National Socialism's racially motivated hyper-nationalism.[4]

With post-war awareness, it is difficult indeed to read, for example, the works of a man like Otto Höfler on our topic, although he was certainly a scholar capable of great insights. A follower of Rudolf Much's views about the continuity of Germanic traditions and culture and himself a prolific writer on the topic, Höfler was, one has to believe, a much more enthusiastic

---

[2] On such traditions, their durability (i.e., continuity) and purpose, see Gísli Sigurðsson 2002, 2004. I note at this juncture in a general way that although some writers are content simply to wave off such parallels in the historical record as mere accidents or coincidences (without, it is important to add, suggesting alternative explanations), I find such stances unsatisfactory, to put it mildly.

[3] See J. S. Martin 2000 and the literature cited there.

[4] Bendix 1997; for an excellent overview of the relationship of these disciplines to Nazi ideology, see, e.g., B. Arnold 2006 (especially on the so-called Cinderella explanation); Lixfeld 1994; and the essays in Dow and Lixfeld 1994, and on the related area of runology, Björn Andersson 1995. For additional analyses, especially with regard to the Nordic situation, see the essays in Raudvere, Andrén, and Jennbert 2001 and Garbering 2010

supporter of the Third Reich than the relatively neutral post-war judgment of him as "merely" an intellectual fellow traveler (*geistiger Mitläufer*) makes him sound. When his observations about scientific matters, often of real substance and interest, are held up against such moments as his urging that a broad image of German origins capable of overcoming the occasional "breaks" in its development be created (or shaped, designed, and so on: *zu gestalten*), the resulting dissonance between scholarship and political activity, made all the worse by his dedication to the cause of National Socialism, easily makes one question the quality and motivations of all his judgments.[5] I raise this point, not to pull at the sutures of wounds from an evil era back before most of us were born, but exactly because this history is the moral and biographical predicate that has shaped many of our personal, and institutional, reactions to discussions of continuity since the middle of the last century,[6] and it has no doubt also played its role in the view many folklorists have developed about continuity in recent years.[7]

These are all important factors in modern receptions, perceptions and discussions of continuity, and I admit that I raise all of this in a slightly confessional mode, precisely because I *do* believe in both the empirical reality of *some* continuities and traditions within northern Europe (although I hasten to emphasize, not in any blanket fashion or with any predetermined political perspective on their value); moreover, I am also convinced that such *provable* links to past practices, belief system, codes of behavior, linguistic usages, and so on offer us useful data points and insights into the study and understanding of the past.

---

[5] E.g., Höfler 1937; 1938:26. See, e.g., the critique in Behringer 1998 and the literature cited there.

[6] Cf. the comments in Gerschenkron 1971, which highlight some of the important differences between the German and Anglophone experiences with this issue. Many years ago, my own anodyne (and, I suppose, typically American) views of the consequences of the continuity debate—a perspective I would characterize as broadly positivistic and historicist— came up against those of a departmental colleague, a gentle, older scholar of medieval drama, and, significantly, a childhood survivor of the fire-bombing of Dresden: as I came to perceive, he simply could not accept a purely academic discussion of continuity. Having grown up in, and survived, a world shaped by the perversions of such views, he regarded all discussions—and therefore, uses—of the tradition and continuity question as politically charged and deeply suspect.

[7] Of course, many times this is a matter of where one's intellectual heart is, but this knotty history may *help* explain (although not fully address) the eschewing in recent decades of the past as a research area by many folklorists, who, under various theoretical guises, deeply, too deeply some may think, embrace an emerging paradigm of intellectual presentism. Cf. the remarks by Strömbäck 1979b, as well as my own attempts to contextualize this debate in Mitchell 2000a.

Thus, I start, and end, my thinking about this issue with the view that even if such concepts as continuity and tradition have been abused by some and employed toward horrible ends, or have been determined to be intellectually unfashionable by others, the facts remain what they were: traditions exist; there are connections and continuities over time; these realities influence behaviors, as they have always done; *and* if we want to understand those bygone worlds, then we must figure out what to do about, and with, such materials as key access points to historical cultures.[8]

The Place of Continuity in Folklore Studies

In giving a tour of Harvard to a German colleague some years ago, I had just pointed out that hallmark of the American college campus, a building about which tales of a peculiar, even bizarre, bequest by the donor circulate. Enraptured by the strangeness of it all, I assume, my colleague burst out excitedly, "I love it! It's like Britain—it makes no sense, but it's *tradition!*" That remark is no doubt unintentionally uncharitable both to a very great nation and a very durable cultural concept, but it reflects the sort of view about the nature of folklore once held by luminaries in the field.

After all, to many early scholars, folklore was that cultural oddity that did not fit in or make sense in modern society, e.g. the superstition about the number thirteen or the business about the black cat and bad luck; in other words, folklore was understood to be like the famous scene Andrew Lang paints of the flint spearhead being found in a freshly plowed field, *viz.*—a cultural artifact from the past that emerges unthinkingly and awkwardly in, and into, the present.

Or in Lang's own words, "There is a form of study, Folklore, which collects and compares the similar but immaterial relics of old races, the surviving superstitions and stories, the ideas which are *in our time but not of it*" (1893:11; emphasis added), to which he adds,

> ...the student of folklore soon finds that these unprogressive classes retain many of the beliefs and ways of savages, just as the Hebridean people use spindle-whorls of stone, and bake clay pots without the aid of the wheel, like modern South Sea Islanders, or like their own prehistoric ancestors. The student of folklore is thus led to examine the usages, myths, and ideas

---

[8] Cf. Gailey 1989:144, "Dan Ben-Amos put the situation succinctly when in a conference in 1984 he noted that 'In folklore studies in America *tradition* has been a term to think with, not to think about.'"

of savages, which are still retained, in rude enough shape, by the European peasantry. Lastly, he observes that a few similar customs and ideas survive in the most conservative elements of the life of educated peoples, in ritual, ceremonial, and religious traditions and myths. Though such remains are rare in England, we may note the custom of leading the dead soldier's horse behind his master to the grave, a relic of days when the horse would have been sacrificed.

Lang 1893:11

Of course, the concept of *tradition*, with its inherent sense of agency etymologically secured (< *to hand over, deliver, entrust*, and so on), has given rise to any number of attempts at dissection, both its place in the study of folklore, and as part of grander schemes for the illumination of history and human nature.[9] By contrast, the more amorphously constructed concept of *continuity* (< *hold together*) has, it seems to me, been much less subject to analysis, but the two ideas can never be entirely divorced from each other. I want to mention just a few approaches which I have found useful in considering the kinds of materials that history and the archives have serendipitously bequeathed to us and which suggest how we might fruitfully investigate these concepts.

One important early strand of this discussion concerned the so-called "superorganic." This neologism, used first in 1862 by the British sociologist Herbert Spencer, was enthusiastically embraced by, and is now more frequently associated with the works of, Alfred Kroeber. At its heart, and appearances notwithstanding, the concept of the superorganic is largely concerned with agency; it is an attempt to give expression to the reality of "social life or culture,"[10] by contrasting the "cultural society of man" with the "cultureless pseudo-society of the ants and bees."[11] It is not difficult, of course, to see how Kroeber's formulation—[a] "body of 'superorganic products' that is carried along from individual to individual and from group to

---

[9] Cf. from the folklore perspective, e.g., Ben-Amos 1984; Bronner 2000; Gailey 1989; Glassie 1995, as well as from such adjacent fields as sociology, e.g., Shils 1981.

[10] Kroeber 1918:634, who suggests as possible synonyms, "the civilizational or superorganic or, better, superpsychic." Cf. Kroeber 1917.

[11] "That the social insects do not learn or acquire knowledge as groups; that they totally lack tradition; that substantially all their activities are inborn and determined by organic heredity, or depend on individual psychic experience acting upon hereditary faculty; in short, that they totally lack any body of 'superorganic products' that is carried along from individual to individual and from group to group independent of the nature of these individuals and groups," Kroeber 1918:643.

group independent of the nature of these individuals and groups"—would find ready acceptance in the folkloristics of the early twentieth century, as well as in allied disciplines, as a useful means of conceptualizing both tradition and continuity, especially when viewed in the context of folklore's emerging theoretical paradigm, subsequently codified as *Die folkloristische Arbeitsmethode* (Krohn 1926).[12]

The work, aims, and methods of this view of folkloristics, what we today call the Finnish Historical-Geographic Method, clearly anticipated and overlapped with the concept of the "superorganic." Already in the nineteenth century, Julius Krohn had developed a view of Finnish folk poetry that, although very interested in, for example, the biographies of its practitioners, nevertheless understood the materials as in some sense possessing an existence "above" or "beyond" the level of the individual. As Jouko Hautala writes, "Julius Krohn thought of folk poems as if they were organisms independent of their carriers: nobody had created them, but they have originated spontaneously, under the influence of psychological laws, and their development has also followed laws which work in an almost mechanical manner."[13] The hallmarks of the Finnish School—its careful documentation of materials, the organization of these materials into motif-indexes (and the usefulness of Inger Boberg's *Motif-Index of Early Icelandic Literature*, even if incomplete, is not lost on anyone in our field), the search for archetypes, and so on—are well-known and famously became the dominant approach to folklore in the early twentieth century. Subsequent critiques have naturally tended to focus on the rather intellectually arid aspects of the approach and drawn pictures, not wholly undeserved, of a remote and uncaring view of folklore and its users.[14]

On the other hand, at a time when Lang and many others viewed folklore almost exclusively as a survival from the past, and at the same time Kroeber was developing his views of the superorganic, Kaarle Krohn, as Elli-Kaija Köngäs-Maranda has noted (1963:78), "clearly objected to the survival

---

[12] To some extent, Kroeber's views draw on, and look to mediate, the opposing perspectives of Spencer, Durkheim and Boas. See also the discussion and literature in Mitchell 2007a and 2012c, where I have attempted to tease out the possible continued usefulness of Kroeber's ideas in several Nordic-themed essays.

[13] Quoted in Köngäs-Maranda 1963:77.

[14] Indeed, if one's only experience of the results of the Finnish Historical-Geographic method were, e.g., Archer Taylor's Black Ox study, one could certainly be forgiven for having strongly skeptical views about the interpretive possibilities of such an approach: many details and much hard work, one imagines, but exactly what is the intellectual pay off?

theory and stressed the point that folklore is an integral part of folk life and carried on by the force of its function." Folklore as cultural goods may still have been conceived as existing independently of ("above," "beyond," and so on) individuals but, on the other hand, it did not exist outside of society or the experiences of those who make up such communities.

In a key reconsideration of the superorganic in the late 1940s, David Bidney took up exactly this issue—and added, so far as I know, a new term to our vocabulary, the *mentifact*, described by him as a conceptual symbol "comprising language, traditions, literature, moral, aesthetic and religious ideals."[15] And very importantly, he argued,

> cultural objects *per se*, whether artifacts, socifacts or mentifacts, are but inert, static matériel or capital for cultural life, and that of themselves they exert no efficient, creative power. Only individuals or societies of men can spontaneously initiate and perpetuate cultural processes which may result in superorganic cultural achievements, and hence there can be no autonomous cultural process independent of human intelligence and voluntary effort...
>
> Bidney 1947:384

Although the soci- or sociofact appears to have had some scholarly traction, the idea of the mentifact is not one that seems to have found much favor with either humanists or social scientists. It is not difficult to see how it proceeds from the theory of the superorganic and looks to cover some of the same territory, such as explaining the persistence of beliefs, narrative and behaviors over time, and how it still—the deeply wrong-headed notion of these materials as "inert" and "static" notwithstanding—suggests a useful analytic tool in other ways. And as Bidney's comment underscores, there is

---

[15] I have no idea who originated this term and its cousin, sociofact (or socifact), but certainly the widely bruited about view (e.g., Wikipedia's entries for "Mentifact" and Huxley himself as of the date of this writing, 3 February 2013) that mentifact "is a term coined by Sir Julian Sorell Huxley" in his 1955 editorial in *The Yearbook of Anthropology* cannot be correct, given that already in 1947 Bidney used it without bothering to note its origins. Neither *The Oxford English Dictionary* nor any other dictionary I have been able to consult lists the term. On the other hand, given Huxley's fame as a popular science writer, the fact that his essay (Huxley 1955:16–17) states the following undoubtedly contributed to the notoriety of the term: "...a culture consists of the self-reproducing or reproducible products of the mental activities of a group of human individuals living in a society. These can be broadly divided into artifacts—material objects created for carrying out material functions; sociofacts—institutions and organizations for providing the framework of a social or political and for maintaining social relations between its members; and mentifacts—mental constructions which provide the psychological framework of a culture and carry out intellectual, aesthetic, spiritual, ethical or other psychological functions."

no inherent conflict between the continuity of such cultural goods across time and the necessary input of individuals who tell, use, and "own" such goods.

Although not concerned exclusively with folklore as such for the most part, a series of important discussions about the nature of memory and past awareness, of mnemohistory, has contributed importantly to this debate through the past century.[16] In fact, it would seem obvious that to a high degree the notion of memory would be paramount to the study of continuity in folklore, yet that "obvious" fact is not much in evidence, much of the work in this area having been developed by social historians working within a Durkheimian framework.[17] From Maurice Halbwachs' innovative studies of *collective memory* and the social construction of memory (1925:1950), to the notion of *ethnic memory* and its focus on pre-literate-normative societies (as in Le Goff 1988), to the discussion of *cultural memory*, the *handing over* [!] of meaning across generations, and the idea of *communicative memory* between individuals (as argued in J. Assmann 1992, 1995, 2006), memory studies provide a very productive framework for the consideration of the transmission and preservation of traditions.[18]

Among these broad categories of theories with important ramifications for considering the traditions of past societies, I will mention just one more, an approach to folklore that looks to put the telling or enactment of folklore, the "doing" of folklore, at its center, that is, a view of folklore that promotes a dynamic, communicative and re-contextualized conception of past materials.[19] The various approaches I am somewhat awkwardly gathering together in this group developed to a significant degree as dissatisfied responses to what was understood to be the overly positivistic approaches of earlier scholars, as exemplified by those associated with the Finnish School. Thus, as two of its advocates write, "A second major shift of perspective captured by the notion of performance occurred in folklore, founded on a

---

[16] On this issue, see especially DuBois 2013, as well as, more generally, the other essays in Hermann and Mitchell 2013.

[17] In fact, memory studies has deep roots within the social sciences, going back to Emile Durkheim and extending from Frederic Bartlett to Maurice Halbwachs to Fredrik Barth; it holds that remembering is always social in that those semiotic systems with which we are inculcated by our interactions throughout life shape not only what, but how, we remember.

[18] On the ramifications of memory studies for medieval Norse studies in general, see the essays in Hermann and Mitchell 2013; Herman, Mitchell and Agnes S. Arnórsdóttir 2014; and, e.g., Hermann 2009 on the significance of these findings for the study of Old Norse literature.

[19] Within Old Norse studies, important applications can be found in, e.g., Bauman 1986a, 1992; Gunnell 2001a; and DuBois 2006. For an overview, see Mitchell 2013.

reorientation from a traditionalist view of folklore as *reified, persistent cultural items—texts, artifacts, mentifacts*—to a conception of folklore as a mode of communicative action" (Bauman and Briggs 1990:79; *emphasis added*).

As the authors' tone makes apparent, this approach was to a great extent developed in reaction, and even in opposition, to earlier theoretical orthodoxies, or as Bauman himself had earlier reasonably summarized his, and many others', frustration with this older ossified image of folklore as "... collectively shaped, traditional stuff that could wander around the map, fill up collections and archives, reflect culture, and so on" (Bauman 1986b:2). Instead, he notes, "[m]y concern has been to go beyond a conception of oral literature as *disembodied superorganic stuff* and to view it contextually and ethnographically, in order to discover the individual, social, and cultural factors that give it shape and meaning in the conduct of social life."[20]

Continuity and Old Norse Folklore

The significance of the analytic stance Bauman advocates, which draws inspiration from performance studies, speech act theory, communication theory, studies of living oral traditions (so-called "oral theory"), and a variety of other approaches, has been profound, not least in Bauman's own work, when, for example, he applies these ideas to Old Norse cases (1986a, 1992). And one readily sees the effects such enlightened approaches as "oral theory" have had among those working in disparate and often archaic traditions, such as Gregory Nagy and the late John Miles Foley.[21] And as the example of all three of these scholars makes apparent—pointedly, Bauman as well—there is no inherent conflict between respect for the older empirical data and the application of modern theoretical stances. In other words, the occasionally heated and even hyperbolic rhetoric of an emerging theoretical position notwithstanding, there is no reason to throw the baby out with the bathwater: one can take forward-leaning theoretical views of the materials, yet at the same time recognize that some of the traditional approaches to

---

[20] Bauman 1986b:2; emphasis added. See my comments on this point in Mitchell 2012c, and for an excellent example of this question in the Nordic context, see the treatment of Grýla in Icelandic, Faroese and Shetland seasonal traditions in Gunnell 1995:160–178.

[21] The examples here are voluminous, but to mention just a few, Nagy 1990 and 1996, and Foley 1991 and 1995.

folklore studies (e.g. motifs and motif-indexes) can continue to be useful tools.[22]

In my own attempts several decades ago to struggle with these issues—highly traditional texts and evolving interpretive paradigms—in the case of the Icelandic *fornaldarsögur*, a set of texts whose signature characteristic, I argued, was their perceived continuous relationship to Nordic traditions, I looked to resolve the question of what tradition meant by pointing to three factors: that the narratives were shared within the Icelandic community (*communality*); that they were anything but ossified but rather showed a great deal of individualization and reworking (*variation*); and that they had roots going back over time in their Nordic environments (*continuity*). Moreover, I argued that these texts did not merely exist in some sort of vacuum but rather were important psychological tools in the arsenal of the colonized late medieval Icelanders and could be, and were, used in the service of both their authors' and sponsors' personal ends and to support an embryonic sense of nationalism.[23] Thus, the genealogies of leading Icelanders (e.g., Ari fróði, Haukr Erlandsson, Steinunn Óladóttir) are sometimes carefully tied to the heroic figures who people these texts (Mitchell 1991:123–125), pointing to a fourth important aspect, *function*.

In an attempt to capture the essence of this argument, I used a biological metaphor in *Heroic Sagas and Ballads* as a means of explaining continuity and tradition in the case of narratives and beliefs, an image to which I would like to return, demonstrating what I had in mind with a single, more recently developed example.[24] Walking in a field or forest, or in our own yards, we are likely to encounter the sight of mushrooms growing, often large clumps of them, sometimes "arranged," seemingly, in so-called "fairy rings." Yet those mushrooms (or other fungi) are only the most visible signs of something much larger taking place out of sight. For unseen by our eyes, yet existing

---

[22] See, e.g., the essays in the special issue (volume 34) of *The Journal of Folklore Research* on "Tools of the Trade, Reconsidering Type and Motif Indexes."

[23] Mitchell 1991b:44–46 *et passim*. I was hardly inventing these ideas, of course, but rather building on the work of others: see the literature cited there.

[24] On the historical dangers involved in using such metaphors, see Valdimar Tr. Hafstein's intelligent arguments (2000); on the other hand, I do not sense that this one falls afoul of his warnings. I should note that I owe this useful metaphor to conversations long ago with my wife, Kristine Forsgard, an ethnobotanist by training, who first drew my attention to the similarities between tradition and the way mycelium functions. The fact that I am writing up these notes as I work at The Swedish Collegium for Advanced Study in buildings originally given by Gustav III in honor of Carl Linnaeus, the "flower king," only strengthens my sense that this is a particularly apt parallel.

virtually everywhere in temperate climates, is the truly active, vegetative part of the fungus, the so-called mycelium, made up of fine filaments, the hyphae, running through the soil (or other medium). It is this part of the organism which under various conditions will form a so-called "fruiting body" and push up as a cluster of mushrooms (Mitchell 1991b:179–181).

So, although what we see on the landscape is a mushroom, that is only the most visible part of something much, much larger, something generally unnoticed, but something absolutely critical to the very existence of the organism. In a similar vein, I would argue (and have), the parallel situation *can* (but need not) obtain in our materials and, again, *can* offer us one avenue for understanding them.[25] As folklorists interested in medieval Nordic materials, we are necessarily in possession of data points only, and very, haphazardly preserved over time—information recorded by one circumstance or another but before modern times, surely not as the result of anything like a scientific process. Therefore, we must necessarily learn to work with serendipitously recorded information.

To take what I believe to be a remarkable example of this process in our historical materials, of this metaphor in action, several late fifteenth-century Swedish trials involve accusation of rituals and the worship of Óðinn in the Stockholm-Uppsala area.[26] These trials are also generally connected not only with charges of apostasy from the authorities but also with attempts on the part of the accused to acquire wealth. Are such trials "mere" coincidences, or do they fit larger patterns? And if larger patterns emerge from the empirical data, are we justified in hypothesizing how they may have suited the arsenals of survival with which medieval and early modern Swedes sought to arm themselves against poverty and starvation? I certainly believe we are, and in pursuit of such an explanation was astonished to discover that in the centuries after these late medieval trials very similar scenarios emerged from the archives: a sixteenth-century Swedish chronicler states that people who amass wealth "serve Óðinn"; an early seventeenth-century trial in Småland concerns a man who goes through a ritual pledging himself to Óðinn in order to get money; and a late seventeenth-century commentator, also in Småland, notes in marvelous detail that those who want to get rich invite Óðinn to their homes, and even cites examples of those who found temporary success from such rituals; and there are other similar modern data points. All of these

---

[25] Most directly in Mitchell 1991b, 2007a, 2009a, and 2012b, although I have understood this to be a useful strategy in other instances as well, if more obliquely (e.g., 2011).

[26] On these trials and all other aspects of this discussion, see Mitchell 2009a.

cases involve both Óðinn and wealth, and when we look back in time at the evidence, the association apparently made by early observers between this god and the Roman god of commerce and trade, Mercury, takes on added significance, as do references in the medieval record to Óðinn's association with wealth (e.g. a medieval runestick from Bergen which invokes Óðinn in an attempt to recover lost wealth [B 241 M]; *Ynglingsaga's* statement that he knew about hidden treasures).

In other words, I believe we have here a parallel to our mycological analogy: just as mycelium may run through the ground without developing into a fruiting body, and then suddenly erupt into a clump of mushrooms, so too here, I suspect, there has existed a tradition according to which Óðinn was connected with wealth and therefore appealed to by people in order to acquire riches; moreover, it was a tradition that continued over a number of centuries, at least from the medieval period until the eighteenth century, if not both earlier and later. Or so I have argued based on the evidence.

After all, what else could such data points mean? They are consistent in their references to Óðinn and wealth, not merely random references to the name or the like. Could they all possibly be "mere coincidences"? Are they simply proof of the so-called "infinite monkey theorem"? Or is there not more to the fact that the data just happen to line up correctly, by which I mean they are coherent, fit known or discoverable patterns, and are explicable based on empirical data? As opposed to a nihilistic world whose alternative explanation must rest on randomness and chaos, Occam's razor looks pretty attractive in my view.

Conclusion

I purposefully gave this essay, "Continuity: Folklore's Problem Child?", a contentious title. This decision was in part due to the fact that I wanted to address what appears to me to be a difficult moral and intellectual issue for the field, as well as the resulting trend in modern folklore studies away from considerations of temporality—that is, continuity and tradition. As I suggested above, historically this may be due to some degree to the evil ends to which the field was put by National Socialism. In that case, that continuity has indeed been a problem results, of course, from those who have misused it, not from any inherent flaw in the concept or the sorts of information it can offer us.

But the tendency to avoid such concepts as continuity (and the historical component as a whole) may have other roots as well. Thus, for example, in an influential article, Robert Georges and Alan Dundes formulate a concept of tradition that notably relies mainly on multiformity and, importantly, tends to leave aside the temporal dimension, certainly so as a necessary ingredient in any event:

> By *traditional* we mean that the expression is or was transmitted orally and that it has or had multiple existence. Multiple existence means that an expression is found at more than one period of time or in more than one place at any one given time. This multiple existence in time and/or space usually, though not necessarily, results in the occurrence of variation in the expression.
>
> Georges and Dundes 1963:117

Of course, this perspective, it could be argued, may be especially relevant to American and other immigrant-dominant situations, or perhaps, less intellectually, this was just the opening salvo in the attempt within the sharp-elbowed academic world to hive folklore as a discipline off from history and language departments.[27]

But even for those whose research interests are entirely focused on the "now," it cannot be without important evidentiary value that a cultural good can be shown to have existed over time within the community that has, practices, tells or otherwise uses an item of folklore, even though that may in itself be insufficiently explanatory, of course. An obvious example of this point to me would be the ritualized exchange of insults, so-called "dozens" ("sounding," "woofing" and so on), a phenomenon well-studied over the decades with respect to modern American youth culture (and even

---

[27] The intellectual, and administrative, independence of folklore as an academic field has been at the heart of much debate and strife, in the United States at least as much as elsewhere. For an excellent overview of the early history of the discipline in the U.S., see Zumwalt's 1988 *American Folklore Scholarship*, whose sub-title, *A Dialogue of Dissent*, underscores the often fractious nature of this history. Cp. the remarks in Dorson 1972, which are mainly of interest today as a rather under-, or even ill-, considered view of the issue. With regard to the desirability of identifying "American folklore," rather than "folklore in America," it seems obvious to me that Dundes and Georges are looking for an efficient means of removing the study of American folklore from its Old World swaddling clothes, the sort of view reflected in the remarks by William Wells Newell in his 1888 description of what the work should be of the newly founded *Journal of American Folklore*, where he famously cites various categories of folklore *in* America, that is, "the fast-vanishing remains of Folk-Lore in America, namely: *(a)* Relics of Old English Folk-Lore (ballads, tales, superstitions, dialect, etc.). *(b)* Lore of Negroes in the Southern States of the Union. *(c)* Lore of the Indian Tribes of North America (myths, tales, etc.). *(d)* Lore of French Canada, Mexico, etc." Newell 1888:3.

commercialized in the *Yo Momma* TV series), but with important roots and analogues in Africa (e.g., Ewe *halo*) and Europe (e.g., Old Norse *senna*).

In the hope of avoiding being branded theoretically retrograde, let me note that I heartily and emphatically approve of and embrace emerging approaches to our material, but with the difference that I do not want to do so at the price of losing what was best about the old alliance between *folklore och filolgi*, a view I note that I share with many others.[28] With that thought in mind, I want to close this brief theoretical perambulation by quoting a man who perhaps knew more about the nature of tradition in the Old Norse world and the possibilities of continuity than anyone else of his day, Dag Strömbäck.

Shortly before Strömbäck's death in 1978, in contrasting the folklore studies on which he had been nurtured with the emerging trends of the mid-70s, where tradition and continuity were being actively demoted as windows into the thought world of folklore, he wrote: "I willingly admit that my heart is captured more by the study of traditions from olden times, particularly from the Middle Ages, and by the approach which interweaves historical fact, philological interpretation and textual criticism" (Strömbäck 1979b:10–11). Here, I think Strömbäck had, as was so often the case, the *bons mots*. But perhaps not the last ones: for one can share, and accept the value of, Strömbäck's love for "historical fact, philological interpretation and textual criticism," *and* marry that perspective to folklore's modern search for meaning. In my opinion, both views are enhanced by a proper appreciation of folklore's "problem child," continuity.

---

[28] On this point, see Mitchell 2000a, as well as Bauman 1996.

Chapter 3

PERFORMANCE AND NORSE POETRY
THE HYDROMEL OF PRAISE AND
THE EFFLUVIA OF SCORN

How should we moderns "read" a medieval text?[1] Thanks to the work of many scholars, not least the pioneering studies of Milman Parry and Albert Lord, we are today able to understand the nature and implications of a preserved medieval work's background as an oral text much better than did the early and brilliant (but narrowly gauged) generations that included such giants within Old Norse as Jacob Grimm, Konrad von Maurer, Theodor Möbius, Rudolf Keyser and N. M. Petersen.[2] Given these advances in our understanding of orality, performance, and the ethnography of speaking, how do

---

[1] Original publication: "Performance and Norse Poetry: The Hydromel of Praise and the Effluvia of Scorn." *Oral Tradition* 16:1 (2001), 168–202.
   By "read," I mean here the full range of decocting techniques employed by modern scholarship, including but not limited to those associated with traditional philology and folkloristics, as well as such emergent approaches as those collectively known as "cultural studies." This essay was delivered as the 2001 Albert Lord/Milman Parry Memorial Lecture under the sponsorship of the Center for the Study of Oral Traditions at the University of Missouri. For their encouragement, sage comments, and helpful criticism, I warmly thank John Foley, Joseph Harris, Gregory Nagy, and John Zemke.

[2] Already as Parry was in the early stages of his research project in the Balkans, he envisioned its implications for the older works of northern Europe: "My purpose in undertaking the study of this poetry was as follows. My Homeric studies [...] have from the beginning shown me that Homeric poetry, and indeed all early Greek poetry, is oral, and so can be properly understood, criticized, and edited only when we have a complete knowledge of the processes of oral poetry; this is true for other early poetries such as Anglo-Saxon, French, or Norse, to the extent they are oral. This knowledge of the processes of an oral poetry can be had up to a certain point by the study of the character of a style, e.g., of the Homeric poems; but a full knowledge can be had only by the accumulation from a living poetry of a body of experimental texts." From Parry's "Project for a Study of Jugoslavian Popular Oral Poetry" in the Milman Parry Collection of Oral Literature, 1. Quoted in Mitchell and Nagy 2000, ix.

we decode the social, religious and literary worlds of northern Europe in the Middle Ages? How, for example, do we understand the role of poetry in Nordic society and how do we view the composition of poetry in that world? And how do we take advantage of these advances while at the same time resisting the temptation to ignore what can be gained by old-fashioned philology and the study of mythology?[3] Of course, the role of orality in the composition of Old Norse poetry and prose has been a dominant heuristic theme in the history of modern scholarship in that region. Whether investigators have been focused on such literary and cultural issues as compositional techniques, or modern nationalistic efforts to lay claim to these wonderful medieval texts from the periphery of Europe, or the historical value of the contents of such works, the degree to which the basic shape, form and character of these materials was imparted by a background either in a popular (and thus oral) or a courtly and ecclesiastical (and thus written) cultural matrix has been at the heart of a generations-long debate, an argument that significantly parallels the concerns of Homeric analysts and unitarians.[4]

In Old Norse studies, these opposing views came to be crystallized around the dichotomy *Freiprosa–Buchprosa* ("Freeprose–Bookprose"), scholarly strife that also reaches back into the nineteenth century. As with comparable debates in adjacent fields, serious intellectual goods were at stake in this heavily dichotomized clash of views between advocates of an essentially neo-romantic and passionately democratic perspective, on the one side, and a fundamentally restrictive and equally passionate elitist view, on the other.[5] In addition, the Freeprose–Bookprose debate in northern Europe was fraught with significant nationalist overtones that can be conveniently summarized as "Who owns the sagas?" Are they to be understood as part of the cultural legacy of all of Scandinavia, the product of an oral culture that had migrated to Iceland in the ninth and tenth centuries and had been recorded there in the 1200s (and thus cultural goods to which other Nordic countries, Norway in particular, might legitimately lay claim)? Or are they the product of a

---

[3] Cf. Bauman 1996, 17: "...the enduring importance of the intellectual problems that the philological synthesis was forged to address constitutes a productive basis on which we as folklorists might orient ourselves to our cognate fields and disciplines."

[4] On the Homeric debate, see Foley 1988:4–6 *et passim* and G. Nagy 1996a:93–94, 133–134 *et passim*, and the relevant entries in Foley 1985 (available online at http://www.oraltradition.org).

[5] Cf., for example, T. M. Andersson 1964; Byock 1984; and Clover 1985, 239–240; for a recent review of positions, see Harris 1998; on the outlines and implications of the Freeprose–Bookprose controversy, see Mitchell 1991b:1–6 *et passim*; for a review of works on eddic poetry, see Harris 1985 and Acker 1998, 85–100.

specifically written literary culture that develops uniquely in Iceland in the Middle Ages (and to which only the Icelanders might lay claim)? This debate needs to be understood against the backdrop of inter-Nordic colonialism and the fact that the nineteenth-century nationalist movements in both Norway and Iceland were at just this point in time agitating for independence after more than half a millennium of political and cultural dominance from afar. The Freeprose–Bookprose debate was then not "only" about literature and culture, and not "only" a matter of concern within the rarified atmosphere of the academy. It was all of that, to be sure, *plus* an emotionally charged political topic about which many had opinions and in whose outcome everyone in that region of the world had a stake.

Whereas one might reasonably expect to gain a great deal from a close examination of the oral-written debate in Old Norse studies in those earlier periods, for the most part this opportunity was seriously compromised by inflexible and unsubtle thinking by advocates of the two opposing sides of the argument. In recent decades, however, a number of those in the field have advocated a view that looks to take the best of the hardened Freeprose–Bookprose positions and forge a synthesis that has no *a priori* theoretical conclusions but looks only for practical and useful ways to understand the texts that the antiquarianism and narrative sensibility of the medieval Icelanders have bequeathed to us.[6] Perhaps one of the most important developments in this kind of thinking has been the realization that the question should no longer be styled as, to quote one noted scholar's confident conclusion in 1964, that "the inspiration of the sagas is ultimately oral."[7] This sort of understandable (if regrettable) formulation can naturally only give rise to endless debate—we will never possess the sort of litmus test that would allow us to address without doubt such an assertion. Rather, the question needs to be framed as "How do we best understand the Norse materials?"

Fortunately, just as the pronouncement concerning the ultimate "orality" of the sagas (above) appeared, a promising way out of the morass was being developed by anthropologists and folklorists: what is variously referred to as

---

[6] Cp., for example, the sometimes contrasting views in T. M. Andersson 1966, Lönnroth 1976; Lönnroth 1978; Byock 1982; Clover 1986a; Harris 1983; Mitchell 1987; Mitchell 1991b; despite the different orientations of the authors, however, they appear to share the view that a new synthesis of approaches is a desideratum.

[7] T. M. Andersson 1964, 119. It should be noted that Andersson's early embrace of the oral character of the sagas seems to have loosened considerably in the intervening years.

the "ethnography of speaking," performance studies, and so on.[8] The tenets of such an approach—that we conceive of such cultural monuments as artistic communication and attempt to situate them in history and social life using tools drawn from a wide variety of disciplines—do not from today's vantage point sound especially earth-shaking, but occasionally the results have been. In addition to its inherent intellectual benefits, a performance-based analysis of Old Norse literature brings with it a further advantage—namely, it allows scholars in the field to step back from approaches that are implicitly politically sensitive within the discipline; in other words, it represents an important means of escaping the fossilized and largely unproductive positions associated with the *Buchprosa–Freiprosa* debate. Some years ago folklorist Richard Bauman applied this "ethnography of speaking" approach specifically to Old Norse in an important discussion (Bauman 1986a; cf. Bauman 1992), but one that, unfortunately, has been largely overlooked by scholars of Old Norse. To a great extent, the following comments owe their existence to the works of Bauman, Geertz, Hymes, Foley, Nagy, and so many other practitioners of such studies—all of whom implicitly (and several explicitly) build on Parry's and Lord's ethnographic observations from the 1930s, a project looking to set "lore against literature,"[9] the lore of a living tradition against the literature of a long-gone world.[10] The collective approach that precipitates out of the works of these scholars exhibits far less rigidity than did the old oral versus written debate. Moreover, the emerging consensus shows how by understanding living traditions of oral literature, by a sophisticated application of folklore theories and practices, and by abandoning what were still in the main (although heavily disguised) legacies of nineteenth-century romanticism and class wars, we can improve our ability to apprehend the long-lost cultural moment of the medieval literary enterprise. Toward these ends, I present in the sections that follow: 1) a discussion of poetics and

---

[8] The clarion cry of this new movement had already been sounded in 1959 with Erving Goffman's *The Presentation of Self in Everyday Life*, but with respect to our materials, the beginnings are much more naturally seen, I would argue, in Hymes 1962, followed shortly thereafter by Hymes 1964, an introduction to a collection that included such influential studies as Frake 1964. Within the anthropological tradition, the works of Dell Hymes, Clifford Geertz and Victor Turner have been of particular moment, perhaps especially on those of us in allied fields. A specific, and early, application of such a contextualizing approach to the Icelandic sagas can be seen in Turner 1971.

[9] E.g., Bauman 1977; Bauman 1986b; Foley 1991, 1992, 1995; Geertz 1973; Hymes 1962, 1964; G. Nagy 1990, 1996a, 1996b. The phrase "lore against literature" I take from the 1935 typescript of Milman Parry's "The Singer of Tales" in the Milman Parry Collection of Oral Literature, 3. Quoted in Mitchell and Nagy 2000, viii.

[10] This symbiosis is deftly outlined in Foley 1995:1–29.

performance in the Old Norse world, specifically, of how a range of alimentary images is used in Old Norse conceptualizations of poetry, and then 2) a discussion of how our appreciation for this metaphor enables us to understand in new ways important aspects of performance, and the representation of such performances, in the Old Norse world.

Poetry, Potables, and Physiology

Before examining how Icelanders understood and presented the performance of poetry in the narratives of the thirteenth century (mainly), it is important to recognize the high status poetry had in the Nordic world, a region notably devoid of epic verse but otherwise much enamored of the art of poetry. Indeed, poetry was so highly prized in the Old Norse world that the chief god of their pagan pantheon, Óðinn, was reported to have spoken entirely in meter ("Mælti hann allt hendingum, svá sem nú er þat kveðit, er skáldskapr heitir") and in that context, it is said that his priests were called songsmiths (*ljóðasmiðir*) (*Ynglinga saga*, 17 [chap. 6]). The most famous and prized form of poetry in the world of northern Europe from the ninth to the thirteenth century was a style of verse that represented a metrically very demanding development from the original narrative forms of verse common to the Germanic world. This kind of poetry was associated with the skalds, the court poets, mainly Icelanders in later periods, who declaimed their works at the various Nordic courts.[11] So central to the Scandinavian world was this verse form that its acknowledged originator within Old Norse tradition appears to have been raised to godhead status within a century of his death. Bragi Boddason the Old is the oldest known skald, a historical ninth-century figure, famous as the primogenitor of the art. But Bragi is also the name of the god specifically associated with poetry. According to our principal guide to the world of Norse mythology, Snorri Sturluson's thirteenth-century *Edda*, "There is one [god] called Bragi. He is renowned for wisdom and especially for eloquence and command of language. Especially he is knowledgeable about poetry, and because of him poetry is called *brag*" (Faulkes, 25) (Bragi heitir einn. Hann er ágætr at speki ok mest at málsnild ok orðfimi. Hann kann mest af skáldskap, ok af honum er bragr kallaðr skáldskapr) (*Edda Sn* 1, 25). This apotheosis of Bragi Boddason the Old into the god Bragi is by

---

[11] For an introduction to skaldic poetry, see Holtsmark 1982b, Frank 1978 and Frank 1985; although dated, Hollander 1945 remains a useful overview.

no means certain, but represents the widely accepted understanding of the relationship.[12]

The complete aetiological myth about the origins of poetry is, significantly, a story told in Snorri's *Edda* by the god Bragi himself, where it is Óðinn who acquires poetry for men and the gods from the giants. Briefly, the story runs as follows: as a resolution of the Æsir gods' war with the Vanir gods, a man named Kvasir is created from the spittle the gods have spat into a vat (cf. the version in Snorri's *Ynglingasaga*, 12–13). Kvasir is so wise that no one can ask him a question he cannot answer, and he spends his days traveling and teaching people. The dwarves secretly kill him, drain his blood, mix it with honey, and turn it into the mead that makes all who drink it a poet or a scholar ("hverr er af drekkr verðr skáld eða frœðamaðr") (*Edda Sn* 2, 3). The dwarves, when asked about Kvasir, claim that he has suffocated on the wealth of his knowledge because no one was sufficiently educated to ask him questions. Now the giants come into possession of the mead, and Suttungr places it inside a mountain called Hnitbjǫrg watched over by his daughter Gunnlǫð. Óðinn arranges for the servants of Suttungr's brother to kill each other and he works in their place in expectation of getting hold of the mead as a reward. When he is refused a drink, Óðinn has the brother bore a hole into the mountain; the god changes himself into a snake, and crawls through the hole to the place where Gunnlǫð guards the mead. Óðinn sleeps with Gunnlǫð for three nights and she allows him to drink three draughts of the mead. He consumes all the mead, turns himself into an eagle and flies back to the home of the gods, pursued by Suttungr, also in the shape of an eagle. When Óðinn arrives in Ásgarðr, he spits the mead up ("... þá spýtti hann upp miðinum") (*Edda Sn* 2, 5) into the containers the other gods have set out. But during his escape, as Óðinn looks back and sees Suttungr chasing him, "... he sent some of the mead out backwards, and this was disregarded" (Faulkes, 64) (... hann sendi aptr suman mjǫðinn, ok var þess ekki gætt) (*Edda Sn* 2, 5). Anyone is allowed to use it, and that is what is known as the poetaster's share ("Hafði þat hverr er vildi, ok kǫllum vér þat skáldfífla *hlut") (*Edda Sn* 2, 5). Otherwise, Óðinn apportions the mead out to the Æsir and "... to those people who are skilled at composing poetry" (Faulkes, 64) (þeim mǫnnum er yrkja kunnu) (*Edda Sn* 2, 5).

This myth, especially in its full and complete form, is, of course, chock-a-block with symbols and meaningful associations; naturally, there exists a

---

[12] See Mogk 1887 and Turville-Petre, who notes that "[Bragi] was an historical poet, whom mythological speculators had promoted to the rank of godhead" (1975:186).

long list of interpretations, not least those based on the story's connections with other traditions, especially Indic and Celtic, that suggest a background in Indo-European mythology.[13] The centrality in this myth of what looks to be a reflex of Greek *ambrosia* and Vedic *soma* and *amrita*—an intoxicating drink whose consumption imparts special power to the drinker—has naturally been the focal point of much scholarly attention.[14] And part of our understanding of this myth is the "shamanistic" view according to which Óðinn changes himself into a snake, drinks the hydromel, escapes as a bird and regurgitates the mead for the use of the gods and men—much as a bird would do in feeding its young. A recent observation has added a further, fresh perspective on our aetiological myth of the acquisition of poetry, and that is the degree to which it relates to *comparanda* from several traditions where similar myths apparently look to explain text as recomposition-in-performance. Citing examples from Persian, Telegu, Irish, French and Greek, Gregory Nagy points out that in a number of traditions there exist myths in which "the evolution of a poetic tradition [...] is reinterpreted by the myth as if it resulted from a single incident" (G. Nagy 1996a, 70). In these instances, the myth treats the tradition as though it were an original book that has been scattered and is now held by various performers within the tradition, a scenario in which "... paradoxically a myth about the synthesis of oral traditions [...] is articulated in terms of written traditions" (O. Davidson 1985, here quoted from G. Nagy 1996a, 70). Clearly our Norse myth about the origins of poetry is of a somewhat different sort, yet there are important points of contact as well. In our materials we have a story in which poetry has a single origin in the anthropomorphic being Kvasir, the wisest man in the world, who is slain (dismembered?) and his blood turned into the stuff of poetic composition. This elixir is rescued from the Otherworld of giants and dwarves by Óðinn, acting on behalf of men and the gods. But this potent liquid is, despite Óðinn's best efforts, not restricted to those whom he chooses but is in the form of the "lost" portion also spread out in the

---

[13] Discussions on this issue range from the imaginative (e.g., Stephens 1972) to the skeptical (e.g., Frank 1981). For a general orientation to this myth, see Turville-Petre 1975, 35–41; perhaps the broadest frame for understanding the text has been suggested in Meletinskij 1973, summarized and developed in Meletinskij 1977. This myth is also found in *Hávamál* 104–110, and referred to in several 10th-century skaldic verses, as well as the eighth-century (?) Lärbro stone on Gotland.

[14] On the parallel of Indra obtaining *soma*, see especially Dumézil 1973; the parallels to the use of spittle are explored in Stübe 1924; on the broader associations with the use of intoxicating liquors, see especially Doht 1974. Of course, the connection between other intoxicants, such as wine, and poetry is known in many other traditions in roughly comparable periods. See, for example, Harb 1990 and Scheindlin 1984.

world and available to all. As in those other traditions, Norse composition as articulated in the form of the mead is scattered through the deeds of the principal deity.[15]

This reification of poetry—projecting inspiration, skill with words and wisdom into the physical image of mead—is widely employed in the Norse world. The poet consumes intoxicating drink and then metaphorically "regurgitates" words of poetry, just as Óðinn has consumed and regurgitated the mead. This connection between such liquids, wisdom, and poetry is strong in Norse tradition. In fact, in addition to the mead of poetry, Norse mythology also speaks of a special elixir containing all wisdom coming from the well of Mímir, a figure who can boast numerous associations with wisdom, knowledge, and foresight. It is for a drink from this well that Óðinn gives one of his eyes. Once he has quaffed the liquid in exchange for the partial loss of his physical sight, he gains insight.[16] A connection rarely made with this aspect of Óðinn's career is the degree to which it would appear to conform to other culture heroes who are viewed as being formative in the creation of the poetic tradition—Homer as a blind singer is the prime example, of course, but one notes also the existence of a figure like the Ćor Huso about whom Parry heard so much in the Balkans of the 1930s.[17] To what extent an Icelandic poet who engaged in the composition and recitation of his art was mindful of such filiations as those with Óðinn is uncertain, although both in the Norse world and elsewhere the argument has been made that poets were aware that their craft had divine inspiration, perhaps even a mimetic function during the performative moment.[18]

How thoroughly Óðinn's acquisition of the poetic mead was meaningfully integrated into Norse presentations of poets and poetry is indicated by the

---

[15] Cf. the remarks in Foley 1998 and Foley 1999:49–63, where Foley demonstrates "how the legendary singer, although represented as a once-living individual by the lesser, real-life bards who follow in his footsteps, is also a way of designating the poetic tradition" (1998:149).

[16] Cf. Andrews 1928, whose clever construction of this complex is worth noting: he suggests that Mímir is actually a skull used as a drinking vessel, and thus would be the fountain of wisdom from which Óðinn drinks.

[17] See the remarks on Isak/Hasan Ćoso, Ćor Huso, and Homer in Foley 1998 and Foley 1999, 49–63.

[18] Cf. the Homeric case as outlined in G. Nagy 1996a:96–97: "I must insist that this kind of 'acting' in the context of archaic Greek poetry is not a matter of pretending: it is rather a merger of the performer's identity with an identity patterned on an archetype—a merger repeated every time the ritual occasion recurs." On the relationship between the skald and his art see, for example, Clover 1978 and the works noted in Frank 1985:180–181. For the specific example of Egill Skalla-Grímsson in this regard, see M. Olsen 1936.

following scene from *Egils saga Skalla-Grímssonar*, a saga whose eponymous hero is often associated with Óðinn.[19] In this tale, Egill's enemies have plotted to kill him and his men by poisoning them. Egill undertakes to consume all the alcohol as the only one who will not be harmed by the poison:

> One man was given the job of serving each toast to Egil and his men, and kept egging them on to drink up quickly, but Egil told his men not to have any more, and he drank their share, that being the only way out of it. When Egil realized that he couldn't keep going any longer, he stood up, walked across the floor to Armod, put both hands on his shoulders and pressed him up against the pillar, then heaved up a vomit of massive proportions (*Siðan þeysti Egill upp ór sér spýju mikla*) that gushed all over Armod's face, into his eyes, nostrils and mouth, and flooded down his chest so that he was almost suffocated. When he recovered his breath he spewed up (*þá gaus upp spýja*) and all of his servants there began to swear at Egil. What he'd just done, they said, made him the lowest of the low, and if he'd wanted to vomit (*spýja*) he should have gone outside, not made a fool of himself inside the drinking hall.
>
> "I shouldn't be blamed by anyone for this," said Egil, "I'm only doing the same as the farmer. He's spewing (*spýr*) with all his might, just like me."
>
> Then Egil went back to his seat, sat down and asked for a drink. After that he recited this verse at the top of his voice:
>
> With my spew I swear
> Thanks for your sociability!
> We have witnesses that
> I could walk the floor:
> Many a guest's gift
> Is even more gushing;
> Now the ale has ended up
> All over Armod.
>
> Armod jumped to his feet and ran out, but Egil asked for something more to drink. The housewife told the man who had been serving all evening to carry on as long as they wanted to drink, and make sure they had enough. The man took a great ox-horn, filled it and gave it to Egil, who swilled it down in one draught. Then he said:

---

[19] Many aspects of Egill's career tie him to Óðinn, such as the gouging out of Ármóðr's eye, making him appear like "one-eyed Óðinn." See M. Olsen 1936 for a treatment of this relationship on more aesthetic grounds.

> Let's swallow each swig
> This sailor keeps serving;
> The bard is kept busy
> With barely a break:
> Not a lick shall I leave
> Of this malted liquor,
> Though the fellow keep filling
> Fresh horns till day break.
>
> Egil kept on drinking for some time, tossing down each horn he was given, but there was little fun to be had in the room as not many were still drinking. Then Egil and his companions got up, took down their weapons from the wall where they had hung them, and went over to the granary where their horses were kept. There they lay down on the, straw and slept through the night.[20]
>
> *Egil's saga*, 188–189

Crude though we understand this scene to be, many have perceived in it a reflex of ancient concerns with intoxicants, ingestion, and the production of poetry as a kind of regurgitation, a recurring theme in this saga in particular.[21] Of interest in this connection is the fact that the author of *Egils saga* here uses the verb *spýja*, cognate with the term used in the corresponding section in *Snorra edda* about the acquisition of the poetic mead, *spýta* (< **spyēu-*, **spyū-* ; see Buck 1988:264–266), rather than, for example, *hrækja* ("to spit"). Important here too is the fact that Kvasir himself is made from the spittle the gods have spat into a vat. The conservative lexical choices of the saga's author, often suggested to be Snorri Sturluson himself,[22] have been shown elsewhere to reflect deep connections to Norse traditions (e.g.,

---

[20] The translation here of *Egils saga* is from the peerless text of Hermann Pálsson and Paul Edwards, *Egil's saga*, 188–189; all inserted citations from the original are to *Egils saga*, 225–227 (chap. 71).

[21] This same image of consumed liquid and produced poetry is used commonly elsewhere in *Egils saga*, as when, heavily despondent and contemplating death after his son has died, Egill refuses all food and drink. Egill's daughter tricks him into drinking milk and he goes on to compose one of his most famous poems, *Sonatorrek* (*Egils saga*, 245–256 [chap. 78]). The concatenation of the rules of hospitality, drinking, vomiting, and poetry is pointedly used as well when Egill visits the king's steward, Atleyjar-Bárðr (*Egils saga*, 106–111 [chaps. 43–44]). Medieval texts frequently employ the image of vomiting to a different end, often the idea of the non-contrite sinner returning to his sins as a dog returns to its vomit. See Toswell 1993 for a discussion and further examples.

[22] The classic formulation of this argument is Hallberg 1962.

Mitchell 1998), and we may here have another instance of this trend. Not only are such themes woven into the subtle nature and meaning of every part of the narrative, the same reflexive awareness of poetry's archetypal background in the consumption of liquids and other sustenance is marked in Egill's poetry itself. Indeed, Egill frequently uses metaphors based on this association, paraphrases that specifically conjure the image of Óðinn's original act of bringing poetry to humanity—"arnar kjapta órð" ("seed or produce of the eagle's beak"); and "Viðurs þýfi" ("Óðinn's theft") (*Egils saga*, 276 and 185).

In fact, kennings, those elaborate metaphors in which Old Norse poetry delights, confirm and extend this association: paraphrases for the art of poetry include "Óðinn's drink," "the Æsir's drink," "Kvasir's blood," "dwarfs' drink," "the rain of dwarves," "Suttungr's mead," and "the liquid of Hnitbjǫrg." Óðinn's trip back to Ásgarðr in the shape of an eagle has also given rise to metaphors for poetry, as well as some opportunities for understanding yet further how the Norse viewed the full range of this image. Early in the twelfth century, Þórarinn stuttfeldr uses the kenning "leirr ens gamla ara" ("the mud of the old eagle") to refer to poorly executed poetry.[23] The reference comes in the context of what amounts to a competition between court poets, and in his verse, Þórarinn mocks both the bravery and poetic skill of his adversary. The kenning is built, of course, on Snorri's story, outlined above, of how Óðinn acquires the Poetic Mead, but "spills," as bowdlerized translations often gloss it, some of the mead during his escape.[24] What the text says, however, is that "he sent some of the mead out backwards" (at hann sendi aftr suman mjǫðinn). This is not a case, as it often seems from polite translations, of spillage: Óðinn quite literally excretes this portion of the mead. This defecated mead has no merit or value, is not watched over by anyone, and this exudate, rather than the regurgitated mead, is what poetaster's consume, with obvious results. "The mud of the old eagle" is euphemistic—the phrase quite clearly refers to "the dung of the old eagle" (cf. *leirr* "mud, filth, dung"; cf. *Lexicon poeticum*, 368). Þórarinn's meaning could not be more clear: his enemy's poetry is shit.

That this physiological frame of reference was, like the larger myth from which it derives, well-known and well-used can be established by exploring

---

[23] *Skj*, 1:464. In addition to this twelfth-century occurrence, there exist both thirteenth- and fourteenth-century examples. See Frank 1978:100–101.

[24] Jean I. Young's well-known translation from 1954, for example, reads, "It was such a close shave that Suttung did not catch him, however, he let some fall, but no one bothered about that."

some of our saga texts. In Sturla Þórðarson's thirteenth-century *Íslendinga saga* (part of the so-called *Sturlunga saga*), we are told of troubles in the region around Miðfjǫrðr and Víðidal. At the heart of this discord is a man named Tannr Bjarnason: "hann var orð-illr, ok orti, ok niðskar; enngi var hann manna sættir" (*Sturlunga saga*, 1:320) (a spiteful gossip, a man who spread rumor and malicious statements, and was on good terms with no man) (McGrew and Thomas 1:155). In typically laconic saga-style, we are immediately told that a certain lampooning verse appears in the region about the sons of Gísli, but its author is quite clearly to be understood as Tannr. A killing takes place, and now as part of the renewed verbal war, the men of Víðidal tell a mocking story about the men of Miðfjǫrðr, according to which the latter make up a mare: one man is the back of the mare; another, the belly; yet another, the feet; still another, the thigh; and Tannr, "the arse. For, they said, he shat on all who had anything to do with him with his slanders" (arzinn; hann savgþv þeir skita aa alla þa, er við hann attv, af ropi sino) (*Sturlunga saga*, 1:320). This little slice of life from thirteenth-century Iceland draws on and explicates the myth of Óðinn's acquisition of the poetic mead—that myth is not just an explanation for how poetry came to be, or even why poor or inadequate poetry exists, but rather points to the social origins of versecraft.

Many of the Old Norse terms connected with poetry derive from words that designate this sense of caviling or defaming. And although the synchronic moment, in this case mainly the thirteenth century and the periods immediately adjacent to it, is our principal subject, our understanding of that period is necessarily informed by the diachronic perspective. A short digression into etymology is then not out of order. Thus, *hróp* (vb., *hrópa*), for example, has here the old sense of "slander, defamation" (cf. Old English *hropan* "to shout, proclaim, howl"; modern Swedish, etc. *ropa* "call, cry, clamor"; cf. Low German *rufen*).[25] Of related interest is the probable etymology of the terms for poetry, poets, and so on, *viz.—skáld* (whence, *skáldskapr* "poetry," and so on). Despite a long-standing debate about the derivation of this term,[26] scholarship overwhelmingly accepts that it is cognate with English *scold* and, indeed, with a whole host of terms relevant to this discussion (e.g., MnEng *say, scold*; ON *saga* [all derived from **sekw-* "to say, utter"]). The

---

[25] See de Vries 1961, 260; Buck 1988:1250–1251.

[26] See the bibliographic discussion on this and related points in Holtsmark 1982b and Frank 1985:180–182, as well as the references in Vries 1961. Important elements of this discussion are to be found in M. Olsen 1911, von See 1964, and Steblin-Kamenskij 1969. Of related interest is the proposal in Werlich 1964 and 1967, refuted by Hollowell 1978.

very etymology of the act of poetry in Old Norse thus suggests a performative character. A related image emerges in *Þorleifs þáttr jarlsskálds*, where Þorleifr employs the outward appearance of delivering praise poetry in order to gain a hearing at the Norwegian court. Once he has secured the venue, he recites instead an insulting lampoon (*níð*) to the king as a reward for the king's earlier misdeeds. This same corrective quality is further underscored by medieval Nordic law, which contains provisions for what it terms a *skáldstǫng* ("libel-pole").[27] Nineteenth-century Icelandic popular tradition knew of such a concept, a custom believed to be a reflex of older practices:

> The beina-kerlinga-vísur of mod. times are no doubt a remnant of the old níðstǫng;—certain stone pyramids (varða) along mountain-roads are furnished with sheeps' legs or horses' heads, and are called beina-kerling (*bone carline*) [...] a passing traveller alights and scratches a ditty called beina-kerlinga-vísa (often of a scurrilous or even loose kind) on one of the bones, addressing it to the person who may next pass by...
>
> *níð*, n. Cleasby 1874, 455

Grettis saga Ásmundarsonar presents a scene that echoes this same idea: late in Grettir's career, he steals a horse and is chased by the owner of the horse over a long distance. During the chase, Grettir stops for rest and food, composing verses as he does so, sometimes teaching the stanza to those nearby. His pursuer mimics this behavior, stopping at the same places and also composing poetry. When the two finally end the race harmoniously, they compare notes about their versecraft, assembling the whole episode for each other, have much fun from it, and part the best of friends (*Grettis saga Ásmundarsonar*, 147–153 [chap. 47]). The vignette cited earlier from *Egils saga* raises another important opportunity for our understanding of Norse poetry *in situ*: Egill is traveling and has taken shelter with Ármóðr. His "gushing" behavior thus comes in the context of his being a guest (and, of course, at the same time, the host is trying to poison him). Hospitality—and its rules—becomes then one of the central stylized features of this marked form of performative behavior. Utterances of skaldic verse can come almost anywhere and at any time (the so-called *lausavísur*; cf. Lie 1982), if we are to believe the contexts provided in the narrative frameworks in the sagas, but marked, stylized presentations of elaborate praise compositions come predominantly within the asymmetrical context of guest-host relationships,

---

[27] Cf. *NGL* 1:430; more generally, see de Vries 1961:481; Falk and Torp 1904–1906; Hellqvist 1957; Buck 1988:1298–1300.

especially as this literary marketplace increasingly comes to be characterized as Icelanders traveling from afar to the various Nordic courts. Old Norse literature is not so well-known as is Homeric literature, for example, for an obsession with the rules of hospitality. Still, large sections of the eddic *Hávamál* treat this issue (e.g, st. 2), encouraging reciprocity between host and guest (cf. st. 42: *gialda giof við giof*) (and repay gifts with gifts), and the equitable treatment of strangers (sts. 2–7). The specific relationship between the king's hospitality and the poet's duty to respond with verse is noted directly in *Egils saga Skalla-Grímssonar*, when the eponymous hero comments in his so-called "Head Ransom" (*Hǫfuðlausn*) that he is responding to the king's hospitality, in return for which he should praise the monarch, bringing poetry (= "the mead of Óðinn") to England, "Buðumk hilmir lǫð/ þar ák hróðrar kvǫð/berk Óðins mjǫð/á Engla bjǫð."[28]

The ethnography of giving and receiving in medieval Scandinavia suggests that beyond the transparent and readily apprehended character of this relationship, much more subtle and complex filiations are acted out through various reciprocal acts of munificence (cf. Gurevitch 1968 and Mitchell 1983, with bibliography). The distinction between native purveyors of skaldic poetry, essentially an "aristocracy of the mind" within Norse society, to whom remuneration is owed in the form of hospitality, fellowship, and community contrasts sharply with the image that emerges of professional entertainers for whom little respect is shown (cp. the case of Old Swedish *lækæri* "player" in *SGL*, 1:36; cf. Mitchell 1997b). That mead and hospitality were intimately connected in Germanic tradition has been the thrust of much scholarship and appears to be a common feature of the archaeological record, including the panel on the Gotlandic Lärbro stone that appears to parallel the story of Óðinn and the acquisition of the Poetic Mead (figure3.1) and the many "valkyrie" figurines holding beakers of mead (?) recovered in northern Europe (figures 3.2–3.3) ; moreover, a number of literary texts treating the Germanic world, from *Waltharius* to saints' lives, testify to aspects of this same tradition (cf. Enright 1988; Bridges 1999). One scholar has argued that this image is reflected in *Beowulf* when the hero is welcomed by Wealþeow behaving within this "valkyrie tradition" (cf. Damico 1984). Despite the many differences of their views, all of these scholars argue that the triptych of mead, poetry, and hospitality possesses widespread and deep roots in northern Europe.

---

[28] *Hǫfuðlausn*, st. 2 (*Egils saga*, 186 [chap. 60]). End-rhyme is one of the special additional features of *Hǫfuðlausn*, leading to the following rendering in the translation, *Egil's saga*, 158: "And now I feed / With an English king: / So to English mead / I'll word-mead bring."

Figure 3.1. Óðinn flying with the Poetic Mead in the shape of an eagle? Detail from Lärbro Stora Hammars III (Bunge Museum, Gotland). Bengt A. Lundberg / Riksantikvarieämbetet. Licensed under CC BY-SA 2.5 via Wikimedia Commons. https://commons.wikimedia.org/wiki/File:Bildsten_Stora_Hammars_3_-_KMB_-_16000300017716.jpg.

Performing Poetry

Mindful of the truth of the comment that "oral tradition comes to life in performance" (G. Nagy 1996a:19), let us examine the fictional representations of such scenes in documents against the background of our discussion of hospitality, reciprocity, and this new understanding of the alimentary view of poetic creation among the Norse, and see if we cannot "unpack" the materials and arrive at a better understanding of the texts. It would seem to me to be obvious, but nevertheless worth noting, that the "cultural moment" is in every case for me contemporary with the written formulation of the surviving text—thus, a scenario set in the twelfth century but coming to us in a text composed in the thirteenth century should clearly be understood (barring convincing evidence to the contrary) as a thirteenth- and *not* a twelfth-century phenomenon. Thus, although our texts treat many different periods, we must regard these settings as of little importance in this instance and focus on the period from which the documents derive, in most instances cited here, the 1200s (see my comments in Mitchell 1991b, xii–xiii).

Figure 3.2. Valkyrie with horn of mead greeting a warrior? Detail from Lärbro Stora Hammars III (Bunge Museum, Gotland). Bengt A. Lundberg / Riksantikvarieämbetet. Licensed under CC BY-SA 2.5 via Wikimedia Commons. https://commons.wikimedia.org/wiki/File:Bildsten_Stora_Hammars_3_-_KMB_-_16000300017716.jpg.

In one of the most famous scenes of *sagnaskemmtan* "saga entertainment," *Þorgils saga ok Hafliða* (composed ca. 1237), we are told of how at a wedding at Reykhólar in 1119 several prosimetrical sagas are narrated, at least one of them including a long poem (*flokkr*) at the end. Yet for as often as this episode has been examined, the activities of the wedding guests in the period leading up to the saga narration are rarely connected with this well-known scene.[29] In this earlier episode, the saga tells of how various guests engage in dueling lampoons.[30] As the wedding feast progresses, the drinking keeps pace, and we are variously told that "there was no shortage of good drink" (skorti ok eigi drykk góðan), later that "They all now drank happily and the drink soon made them boastful" (Drukku nú glaðir, ok rekkir þá brátt drykkinn), and yet further that "Everyone now began to drink heavily

---

[29] E.g., Liestøl 1945; Dronke 1947–1948; Foote 1955–1956; Lönnroth 1976:170–172; von See 1981.

[30] These stylized insults resemble, but perhaps do not rise to the level of, the so-called *senna* or *mannajafnaðr*. On the *senna*, see especially Harris 1979. Cf. Swenson 1991, although she does not take up the case of *Þorgils saga ok Hafliða*.

Figure 3.3. Valkyrie with horn of mead? (Historiska museet, Stockholm.) Photo by Gabriel Hildebrand, 2011-11-08. Creative Commons Attribution 2.5 Sweden, SHM 128, Picture 341369, Item 108864. https://mis.historiska.se/mis/sok/bild.asp?uid=341369.

and grew somewhat intoxicated" (Þeir drukku nú ákaft, ok fær á þá alla nǫkkut).[31] One exception to this heavy carousing is a guest named Þórðr, who is described as "not much of a drinking man" (ekki mikill drykkjumaðr [19]), cursed with a bad stomach, labored breathing, dyspepsia, a receding

---

[31] The wedding scene and its entertainment play out in Þorgils saga ok Hafliða, 18–22. All subsequent references to Þorgils saga ok Hafliða are given parenthetically in the text.

hairline, and sour breath. These features become the cause of several versified lampoons by other guests—e.g, "Whence comes this stink?" / "Þórð is breathing at table" (41) (Hvaðan kennir þef þenna? / Þórðr andar nú handan [20]). Þórðr responds in kind to each of the taunts, and his retorts and those of the others underscore the association between imbibing, items expelled from the mouth, and poetry. In fact, the image of poetry—apparently bad poetry—is in these exchanges explicitly expanded to include breathing (*andi*) and belching (*repta*), in particular the association between poor poetry and mephitic stench of constant burping.

But what seems to be a jovial time for all—Þórðr is said to laugh heartily at the versified calumnies—turns bitter when a voice from the movable benches, where the low status guests are seated, utters an apparently more insulting and mocking verse. When Þórðr inquires of his hostess who the man is, and is told by her, he says that he will leave immediately if the offending poet—or poetaster—is not asked to depart. The refusal to turn him out precipitates a crisis and in the end Þórðr leaves, but not before two more insulting verses (presumably by the same man) have been thrown at him, and the episode concludes by noting that "it is not told that anyone spoke of giving him gifts" (43) (En eigi er getit, at neitt yrði af gjǫfum við hann [22]). This phrase must be understood as a clear indication that the host-guest relationship has broken down entirely by the time Þórðr moves to other quarters. Immediately after this scene, the saga says that "There was increased merriment and joy now, good entertainment and many sorts of amusements—dancing, wrestling, and storytelling" (43) (Þar var nú glaumr ok gleði mikil, skemtan góð ok margskonar leikar, bæði dansleikar, glímur ok sagnaskemmtun [22]).

After this section follow the vastly better known comments about the famous *fornaldarsaga* narrations with their verses: Hrólfr tells a saga about a viking, a barrow robber, and a berserker, "with many strophes too" (44) (... ok margar vísur með [22]), while the priest Ingimundr narrates a story about the skald Ormr of Barra, "with many verses and, towards the end of the saga, many good *flokkrs* [poems] which Ingimund himself had composed" (44) (ok vísur margar ok flokk góðan við enda sǫgunnar, er Ingimundr hafði ortan [22]).[32] The sub-text of this portion of *Þorgils saga ok Hafliða* treats matters of status, host-guest responsibilities, and other aspects of the reciprocal relationship of this important dyad. If we consider these scenes in tandem, as

---

[32] Cf. Harris 1997:134–135, on the prosimetrical character of the saga described here and the question of how tradition may dictate "a recurrent formal arrangement in which longer poems cluster at the end of a saga."

Chapter 3. Performance and Norse Poetry   69

they are presented in the saga, it would appear that one of the more honored and high-status guests has been insulted in verse by one of the low-status guests, but as this man is part of another high status guest's followers—and indeed, even acts as his proxy in some ways—the hostess refuses to honor Þórðr's request and he leaves in a huff. The scene as a whole forms a metanarrative in which the lampoons function as a proxy discussion about the host-guest relationship.

Although skaldic poetry was known throughout the Nordic world and is common enough in entirely domestic contexts in Icelandic sagas (e.g., *Grettis saga Ásmundarssonar*), the *locus classicus* for the *dróttkvætt* stanza is the *court*, as its very name implies (< *drótt* "comitatus"), and it is here we see the most elaborate presentations of it at work.[33] It would seem that each of the Nordic courts plays a role as the recipient (or would-be recipient) of this kind of poetry,[34] but none more so than the Norwegian court, to which Icelandic skalds travelled in hopes of delivering their elaborate poems and in still higher hopes of receiving remuneration, perhaps of even becoming a king's man (cf. *Kounungsskuggsjá*).

Instructive in this regard, in part because it seems so atypical, is *Sneglu-Halla þáttr*, one of several dozen short narratives interwoven into the lives of the Norwegian kings.[35] *Sneglu-Halla þáttr* differs from most of these short narratives, or *þættir*, by virtue of its relative lack of cohesive structure, apart from what seems to be the author's need to supply a narrative to accompany Halli's poetry. This story gets off to an unusual start, it would seem: as Halli's ship arrives in Norway, they are greeted by some passers-by, one of whom, "a man in a red tunic," turns out to be the king (Haraldr Sigurðarson, sometimes called *harðráði* "hard-rule," d. 1066). After he greets Halli and discovers that they have spent the night at a certain location, the king insultingly inquires, "Didn't old Agði screw you?" (Andersson and Gade, 240) (Sarþ hann yðr eigi þá Agði) (*Sneglu-Halla þáttr* M, 270]). Halli responds in the negative and when the king asks why this is so, Halli says in turn to the king, "he was waiting for a better man and was expecting you this evening" (Andersson and Gade, 244) (beið hann at betri manna, vænti þín þangat í kveld) (*Sneglu-Halla þáttr* M, 271). In fact, as jarring as this comment and its response may strike us today, it is a fitting opening for a tale filled with competitive, male

---

[33] Cf. Frank 1978, 21–33 for a general orientation to the *dróttkvætt* verse.

[34] See, for example, Mitchell 1997b on this point.

[35] *Sneglu-Halla þáttr* exists in two versions, one in *Morkinskinna* and another in *Flateyjarbók*, marked here as M and F respectively, with page numbers provided parenthetically in the text.

witticisms. When later Halli is presented at the court, the king says that he must find his own lodgings, "...but I will not be stingy with food for you" (Andersson and Gade, 244) (en eigi spari ek mat við þik) (*Sneglu-Halla þáttr* M, 271). Halli takes up residence and the king sets a series of poetic challenges for him and his opponent, the court skald, Þjóðólfr, especially verses composed "on the spot," based on events that have unfolded in front of them, such as a fight between a smith and a tanner. When Halli engages in a prank that impugns the quality—and especially the quantity—of the food from the king's table, the king responds to his hijinks that very night.[36] He has an entire roast pig sent to Halli's table with the following instructions: "Take this to Halli and tell him to compose a stanza before you get to his place. Deliver that message when you get halfway across the floor, and if he does not get the stanza finished, it will cost him his life" (Andersson and Gade, 246) (Fœr þetta Halla,' segir hann, 'ok seg honom at hann hafi ort vísu áðr en þú kemr fyrir hann, ok mæl þat þá er þú kemr á mitt gólfit, ok ef eigi er þá ort sér hann bana sinn) (*Sneglu-Halla þáttr* M, 275). Surprisingly, Halli manages this difficult assignment and thereby saves his life.

Attitudes toward this *þáttr* have generally been negative because of its apparently elusive, unsatisfying structure, but we are now better prepared to understand its intent: the abbreviated *senna*—the ritual exchange of insults—that begins the episode carries the burden of the narrative's meaning, and frames the *þáttr*'s fascination with hospitality, imbibing and eating, and competition, especially in the form of poetry. Indeed, virtually every element of this tale reflects concern with the reciprocal obligations of the guest and his host as they are actualized by consumption and poetic production. In the late fourteenth-century variant of this *þáttr* found in *Flateyjarbók*, for example, it was said to have been the king's custom to eat just a single meal each day, and when he had his fill, he would call for the tables to be cleared immediately, even if many were still hungry:

> King Harald's custom was to eat one meal a day. The food was served first to him, as would be expected, and he was always very well satisfied by the time the food was served to the others. But when he was satisfied, he rapped on the table with the handle of his knife, and then the tables were to be cleared at once. Many were still hungry (*voru margir þaa huergi næri mettir*) (*Sneglu-Halla þáttr* F, 417). It happened on one occasion that the

---

[36] On Sneglu-Halli's transgressive behavior and the broader structural elements among such *þættir* of what Harris, in an adaptation of Vladimir Propp's schema, terms Alienation/Reconciliation, see Harris 1972:7–8, 11. On this narrative and the broader theme of verbal wit, see Harris 1976b:7–16.

king was walking in the street attended by his followers, and many of them were not nearly satisfied (*voru margir þaa huergi nærri mettir* (*Sneglu-Halla þáttr* F, 417). And then they heard a noisy quarrel at an inn. It was a tanner and a blacksmith, and they were almost attacking one another. The king stopped and watched for a while. Then he said, "Let's go. I don't want to get involved in this, but, Thjodolf, compose a verse about them" (*en þu þiodolfr yrk vm þa visu* (*Sneglu-Halla þáttr* F, 417).

The Tale of Sarcastic Halli, 696

The treatment of this subject—the stinginess of the king at his table, and Halli's poetic and mocking responses—is, in fact, the principle sub-text of the *þáttr*, as Halli time and again notes the hunger King Haraldr's guests must endure and his own reactions to the condition. That the person responsible for the *Flateyjarbók* version of the tale apparently understands that the audience needs to have this meaning in mind and underscores the point by adding in the explanatory remarks about the king's dining habits is undoubtedly attributable to the demise in the receptiveness of the Nordic courts to skalds and skaldic verses in the century and a half that separate the *Morkinskinna* and *Flateyjarbók* versions of *Sneglu-Halla þáttr*. In other words, by the end of the fourteenth century, the once-flourishing interconnected relationship between the various dyads of poet : praised, honorer : honored, supplicant : superior, sender : receiver, Icelander : non-Icelander, guest : host has passed into oblivion, and for the audience to apprehend fully the nature of the text, it needs the clarification the later editor has supplied (cf. Mitchell 1997b).

Yet of all scenes concerning the oral presentation of poetry and prose in the Old Norse world, the one that holds the most meaning for us—exactly because it provides us with a remarkable "snapshot" of distinctly different models of literary activity in the thirteenth century rather than a single uniform model, as is sometimes assumed—is the story of Sturla Þórðarson in *Sturlu þáttr* and its famous scene of saga narration and declaimed praise poetry.[37] The text reports events that took place in 1263, when the Icelander Sturla Þórðarson came to King Magnús Hákonarson of Norway, to whom he has been defamed, looking to repair the damage of the misrepresentations.

---

[37] Cf. my earlier comments on this scene, Mitchell 1991b:98–102, and Mitchell 1997b, discussions on which the current reading builds. Although I do not make direct reference to the "ethnography of speaking" in these earlier works on *Sturlu Þáttr*, I take this opportunity to note the important influence this area of anthropology (and especially an encounter with Frake 1964, and the approach implicit in it, early in my studies in anthropology) had—and continues to have—on my conceptualization of cultural questions.

Reminiscent of the king's behavior in *Sneglu-Halla Þáttr*, the king here refuses to listen to him, but does allow him to accompany the royal party on board ship, supplying him with food:

> And when men lay down to sleep, the king's forecastle-man asked who should entertain them. Most remained silent at this. Then he asked: "Sturla the Icelander, will you entertain us [*skemta*]?"
>
> "You decide," says Sturla. Then he told (*sagði*) *Huldar saga, better and more cleverly (*betr ok fróðligarr*) than any of them who were there had heard (*heyrt*) before.
>
> Many thronged forward on the deck and wanted to hear (*heyra*) it clearly, so that there was a great throng there.
>
> The queen asked, "What is the crowd of men on the foredeck?"
>
> A man says, "The men there want to hear (*heyra*) the saga that the Icelander is telling (*segir*)."
>
> She said, "What saga is that?"
>
> He replied, "It is about a great troll-woman, and it is a good story and is being well told (*vel frá sagt*)."
>
> The king told her to pay no heed to this but to sleep. She said, 'I think this Icelander must be a good fellow and much less to blame than he is said to be.'
>
> The king remained silent. People went to sleep for the night. The following morning there was no wind, so that the king['s ship] was in the same place. When the men were sitting at table during the day, the king sent to Sturla some dishes from his table. Sturla's companions were pleased at this, and [said], "Things look better with you here than we thought, if this sort of thing goes on."
>
> When the men had eaten, the queen sent a message to Sturla asking him to come to her and bring with him the saga about the troll-woman (*bað hann koma til sín ok hafa með sér trǫllkonu-sǫguna*), Sturla went aft to the quarterdeck then and greeted the king and queen. The king received his greeting curtly but the queen received it graciously and easily. The queen then asked him to tell that same story (*segja þá sǫmu sǫgu*) that he had told

in the evening. He did so, and told the saga for much of the day (*sagði mikinn hluta dags sǫgu*). When he had told [it] (*hafði sagt*), the queen and many others thanked him and understood that he was a knowledgeable and wise man (*fróðr maðr ok vitr*).[38]

As a result of his well-told troll saga, Sturla is given the opportunity the next day to declaim a panegyric he has composed in honor of the king, and he later delivers a further praise poem in honor of the king's father. Sturla's performances and poems ingratiate him to the king, and eventually the king awards Sturla what must have been one of the great literary commissions of the age, the responsibility for composing his father's saga, *Hákonarsaga Hákonarsonar*. Attempts to assess carefully whether the narration of *Huldar saga* is to be understood as one about saga reading (the phrase "bring the saga with him" being understood as implying a manuscript) or saga telling (the phrase "better and more cleverly" being understood as implying an unfixed text) abound.[39] Despite the discord and consternation the episode has engendered among such excellent readers of saga literature, a reasonable solution to its apparently contradictory information is available.

The author's handling of the scene betrays his concern with a whole series of distinctions between the Norwegian court and his Icelandic hero: in one case, he is portraying a Danish-born queen who now lives at the Norwegian court, an institution that had been the center of an active translation industry for at least 35 years and possessed a noteworthy library. When she calls for Sturla to entertain them onboard the becalmed ship, the cultural frame established by her background (that is, the royal courts of Denmark and Norway) anticipates an entertainer who will come forward with a manuscript from which he will read. In fact, Sturla has no such manuscript. He arrives with no other possessions than his native talent and from it re-builds his career, and, indeed, Sturla's lack of worldly goods is underscored by the fact that he has with him no provisions, but must live instead off the good will of the royal couple. The ability of "Sturla *the Icelander*" to use poetry and saga narration as the means to become a Norwegian court favorite reflects a widespread idea in Scandinavia concerning Icelandic antiquarianism and narrative skill, a view one finds already in twelfth-century Norwegian and Danish historiographers, and one the saga's author is only too happy to perpetuate

---

[38] *Sturlunga saga*, 2:325–326. The compilation as a whole probably dates to ca. 1300.

[39] E,g., Stefán Einarsson 1957:158; Hermann Pálsson 1962:52; Hofmann 1971:135–175; Lönnroth 1976:172; Clover 1982:194. Cf. Mitchell 1991b, 1997b.

and exploit.⁴⁰ Thus, the forecastleman's question, "Sturla inn íslenzka, viltu skemta?" ("Sturla the Icelander, will you entertain us?") which introduces Sturla's obviously oral narration of *Huldar saga, contrasts pointedly—and is intended to contrast—with the queen's request that Sturla be sure "to bring the saga" with him when he comes before the royal couple. Here the author has neatly juxtaposed the traditional and modern, the non-elite and elite forms of literature (that is, "unaided narration" and "manuscript-based narration"), appropriate respectively to the ship's forecastle and its quarter-deck, and the text carefully emphasizes the national, social, and aesthetic differences between the two forms as they are practiced and anticipated. In this episode, in fact, we witness the wide range of literary possibilities at mid-century: oral saga narration (Sturla's two recitations of *Huldar saga); declaimed skaldic poetry (the panegyrics to Magnús and Hákon); and the written and read saga (Hákonarsaga Hákonarsonar, Queen Ingibjǫrg's expectations of *Huldar saga). As I noted on an earlier occasion (1997b:231), "This story thus captures Old Norse literary history at a liminal moment, and displays, on the one hand, through the queen's remarks about manuscript-based saga entertainment and the king's commissioning of Sturla to write a saga, the extent to which the increasingly prevalent custom of written narration had eaten away at oral recitation, while, on the other hand, it demonstrates the strength of, and the court's appreciation for, the venerable tradition of orally delivered skaldic praise poetry and oral saga narration."

Furthermore, Sturla's stay with the royal couple displays a pattern of ever-more important exchanges between the poet and his host. Schematically, these reciprocal exchanges might be represented as follows:

Sturla   *Royal couple*

Sturla goes to the King →
← The King offers Sturla a place on his ship
Sturla entertains the crew by telling *Huldar saga →
← As a result, the King sends food from his table
to Sturla's table
Sturla entertains the royal couple by narrating *Huldar saga →
← As a result, the King offers Sturla an opportunity
to perform poetry

---

⁴⁰ E.g., *Monumenta Historica Norvegiae*, 1; *Gesta Danorum*, Prefatio 1.4.

>   Sturla entertains the royal couple by declaiming his panegyric
>   about the King →
>
> ← As a result, the King offers Sturla a further opportunity to perform poetry
>
>   Sturla pleases the royal couple by declaiming
>   his panegyric about the King's father →
>
> ← As a result, the King offers Sturla the opportunity to write
>   his father's saga
>
>   [Sturla composes *Hákonar saga Hákonarsonar* →]

That Sturla and the royal couple engage in a series of exchanges involving narration (especially poetry), sustenance, and hospitality seems beyond dispute, and indeed the degree to which food, poetry and narration are offered as tokens of honor is striking in this example.[41] A similar structure characterizes, it seems to me, *Sneglu-Halla þáttr* and several of the other texts under discussion here, although in several instances, what is exchanged is not honor but its obverse, ritual insult. But even this form of stylized malediction has its place in the hierarchy of verbal exchanges, representing a form of honor: Þórðr's difficulties in *Þorgils saga ok Hafliða* do not seem to derive from the nature of what is said but rather from its source, that is, from someone not of sufficient station to engage with him in this exchange of barbs. This apparently acceptable ritual behavior is interrupted when someone of the wrong—specifically lower—social status directs several lampoons at Þórðr. This contrarious behavior disrupts the orderly procession of the increasingly caustic barbs within the delicately balanced network of hospitality, stylized insult and versified rejoinder.

Conclusion

The Icelanders of the thirteenth century have, as even this incomplete review indicates, provided us with multiple opportunities to observe sagas and poetry in performance. By viewing these episodes through the prism of what Clifford Geertz, borrowing from Gilbert Ryle, calls "thick description" (Geertz 1973), and Richard Martin terms the "grammar of context" (Martin 1989, 4–10; cf. Bauman 1996), and the common ground John Foley

---

[41] On the much-discussed broader issue of the "ritual feast," see Bauschatz 1978 and Enright 1988:179, and the bibliographies there.

has sought between the "Immanent Art" and ethnopoetics (Foley 1995), interpretations emerge that differ significantly from what previous generations had concluded, working as they were within the framework of the dead, and deadening, argument of oral versus written, *Freiprosa–Buchprosa*, Freeprose–Bookprose. Of course, a fair question would certainly be whether or not this attempt to extract meaning from such scenes could not simply have been carried out in the strong light of traditional philology and mythology studies. My view is a qualified "no"—one need only look at the many decades of scholarly deadlock over whether Sturla did or did not own a manuscript to see how enervating the debate remained when it was framed by extreme views within the Freeprose–Bookprose controversy.

The advantages of this performance-oriented approach are even clearer when we remind ourselves of Bauman's tripartite dissection of such analyses (that is, *performance as practice*, of "cultural life as situated human accomplishment"; *cultural performances*, "framed, heightened, public, and symbolically resonant events"; and *the poetics of oral performance*, "performance as a mode of communication"; Bauman 1986a:132–133), all three of which are in play here in varying degrees. Through each of these performance approaches, and the occasion of performance provided by the sagas, our understanding of medieval Nordic prose and poetry is enhanced, and we are better positioned to formulate answers to the question posed above, "How do we best understand the Norse materials?" In fact, our examination of the Nordic mead of poetry underscores the reality for the Norse materials of what John Foley has so elegantly described as "the enabling event of performance and the enabling referent of tradition" (Foley 1995:208–213; cf. Foley 1992): Icelandic narrative tradition frequently portrays "enabling events," such as the declaiming of poetry at the courts; Nordic mythological and poetic tradition gives us numerous "enabling referents," such as the hydromel of praise and the effluvia of scorn; and the study of performance provides modern scholarship with the *clavis hieroglyphica* that allows us to discover the meaning in the potent combination of the two.

Chapter 4

OLD NORSE RIDDLES AND OTHER VERBAL CONTESTS IN PERFORMANCE[1]

As will become apparent, my comments here are mainly concerned with re-contextualizing possible performance contexts for riddles and other verbal, often question-and-answer, confrontations represented in Old Norse literature as part of a large group of games and competitive confrontations whose enactments are broadly recoverable;[2] thus, what I have to say is less concerned with the literary and intellectual conception of the genres than are, for example, the descriptions we usually encounter in literary histories, tomes understandably concerned with tracing hermeneutic genealogies, especially the relationship between the literary riddle and the folk riddle.[3] Or, put another way, the thumb on the scale in this brief essay favors "who" and "how" over "what," but it also attempts not to lose sight of the interconnectedness of those three interrogatives in the best tradition of John Foley's intellectual legacy.

The riddle, of course, is a special sort of conundrum or enigma, although it is much more than just that. One early specialist of the genre was largely satisfied to say that it "compares an object to another entirely different object," although, importantly, he does add that it consists of a

---

[1] Original publication: "Old Norse Riddles and Other Verbal Contests in Performance." In *John Miles Foley's World of Oralities: Text, Tradition, and Contemporary Oral Theory*, ed. Mark C. Amodio, 123–135. York, 2020.

[2] On possible oral enactments of eddic poetry, cf. the arguments in Gunnell 1993 and 1995. Of course, there exists a substantial body of literature that touches on the comparison of the Old Norse to modern traditions, including Harris 1979; Bax and Padmos 1983; H. R. E. Davidson 1983; Swenson 1991; and Pakis 2005.

[3] Cf. the applicability of the comment in Burns (1976:141), that his "study focuses not on the riddle as a generic form but on riddling as a genre of traditional behavior."

positive and a negative descriptive element, the latter being what is generally called a "blocking element."[4] In recent decades, there has been a substantial recognition of the subtleties with which riddles are constructed and deployed and proposed answers judged (see Lieber 1976); moreover, scholars have come to recognize that riddles are not subject to rigid and exclusive single-answers, but rather that their solutions often correspond to a range of potentially correct answers (see Ben-Amos 1976:249). This last point is of no small consequence when it come to the question of riddles in a competitive setting, since it allows the riddler the opportunity to deny the acceptability of the proposed answer and put an alternative in its place as the "correct" answer being looked for.

One recent scholar captures the essence of the riddle when he writes, in part, that it "can be generally characterized as a verbal game consisting of a question and answer" (Welsh 2000:824). The important characterization of the riddle as a type of "verbal game" stresses the necessarily competitive element of the genre, for as most of us will recognize, the question and answer aspect, although important, is only part of what makes a riddle a riddle. If one asks, "When does the next train arrive?" for example, and is told, "At 10:00," that is obviously *not* a riddle. Andrew Welsh goes on to refine this initial description, and amplifies this point by noting the presence of "confusing or contradictory" elements in the question and further that these elements "may be implicit in the description itself or explicitly expressed in a 'block element.'"[5] These points are all crucial to understanding what happens when riddles are encountered *in situ*, as Petsch already observed in the nineteenth century when he distinguished between "core element" (*Kernelement*) and "frame element" (*Rahmenelement*) of the riddle, and carefully placed the riddle in the context of listeners and audiences (1899:49 *et passim*).

To Welsh's estimable characterization, one would want to add, importantly, that a riddle is asked, or performed, *within a tradition of customary knowledge*; outsiders are unlikely to possess adequate familiarity with the range of possibly correct answers, so there is also an *a priori* insider quality to solving riddles correctly, as many scholars have pointed out. As another

---

[4] Taylor 1943:129. On this and other early scholarship on the riddle, see especially Georges and Dundes 1963, and Green and Pepicello 1984; for the Nordic riddle in particular, see Bødker, Alver, Holbek, and Virtanen 1964.

[5] Welsh 2000:824. Petsch (1899:49) was, to the best of my knowledge, the first to note this point when he refers to the *hemmendes Element*, that is, an element that frustrates or inhibits finding the answer.

standard reference work on folklore puts it, "The 'true riddle' [...] relies on concrete, familiar objects *in the culture*, and it equates two things through the use of a metaphor" (Noyes 1997:728 [*emphasis added*]). Understood thus, a riddle is a description or comparison, posed by one interlocutor to another, in which an intentionally ambiguous element has been inserted with the result that the description as a whole corresponds to a wide range of potentially acceptable answers but prevents the "correct" answer from being obvious.[6] The object of the game is, of course, to provide sufficient correct information styled in a sufficiently veiled form as to trick the opponent and suggest to observers, even to demonstrate, the questioner's superior mental faculty.

Old Norse Riddles and Other Genres

Once a fairly lonely area of research, and subject largely to sporadic forays into the topic (such as Finnur Jónsson 1893; Heusler 1901; and H. R. E. Davidson 1983), the early Nordic riddle seems to have come into its own in recent years. Especially important has been the publication of two books touching on the genre in northern Europe, Frauke Rademann-Veith's 2010 exploration of the early modern Nordic riddle book in relation to various German models and Jeffrey Love's 2013 *The Reception of Hervarar Saga ok Heiðreks from the Middle Ages to the Seventeenth Century*.[7]

Not surprisingly, the enigmatic nature of the riddle and the equally enigmatic nature of the Old Norse convention of the skaldic kenning make comparisons of the two types of puzzling-out forms inevitable. And, indeed, the similarity of riddles to kennings has long been noted in modern scholarship, an observation stretching back at least a century to Finnur Jónsson (1907; see also 1893), who notes in his literary history that kennings, like riddles, build on the interplay between the simultaneous similarity and disjunction of the several items involved.[8] The overlapping character of the two genres has since that time been commented on by no less than Andreas Heusler (1901;

---

[6] A point noted by most modern students of the genre, for example, Abrahams and Dundes 1972:130, who write that riddles are "framed with the purpose of confusing or testing the wits of those who do not know the answer."

[7] Of course, the vast glossary of terms developed for this folklore type and its sub-divisions in the various Nordic languages (cf. Bødker, Alver, Holbek, and Virtanen 1964) is itself testimony to the vitality of its study in modern contexts.

[8] "I enhver omskrivning ligger der en sammenligning og tillige en adskillelse, aldeles som tilfælde er med gåder," as quoted in Lindow 1975:311.

1923:131–32), Jan de Vries (1934), and Jón Helgason (1953:23); however, it is especially with John Lindow's 1975 article treating the broader, and in part extra-linguistic, relationship between these two genres that scholarship embarked on a more precise sense for the social function of these two special kinds of puzzles.

That the Old Norse poetic convention of the kenning is frequently likened to the riddle is based on the fact that the correct referents of these extended metaphors must, like the answers to riddles, be carefully worked out among the broad range of possible answers due to the frequently inherent, and sometimes manufactured, ambiguities contained in the imagery. There have, of course, been many attempts to capture the essence of the kenning, but to take two notable English-language suggestions, Jess B. Bessinger (1974:434) describes the kenning as "an implied simile in circumlocution for a noun not named," while Lindow (1975:315) offers a more subtle characterization, calling the kenning, "a traditional, verbal, poetic figure composed of one or more nominal descriptive elements (a pair of) which may be in opposition." Yet unlike the riddle, there is presumably no specific "blocking element" that looks to obscure the meaning of the kenning; however, as any modern student of Old Norse will know, that is a function which, it could be argued, is carried out by the often astronomically high levels of esoteric information used in formulating these metaphors.

Seemingly of a different sort are Old Norse wisdom confrontations, which likewise appear to be part of a game in our extant texts, and in our textual sources a deadly game.[9] The most obvious instance of such a confrontation in Old Norse literature, where the text builds on a wisdom contest between two actors, is the eddic poem *Vafþrúðnismál*, where one easily envisions the two interlocutors exchanging questions and answers; at the same time, however, this interesting exchange of questions does not directly involve what most scholars today would regard as "true riddles." Yet it is obvious that this wisdom contest would fit Welsh's view that riddles "can be generally characterized as a verbal game consisting of a question and answer" (Welsh 2000:824).

With these broad characterizations and similarities in mind, one quickly sees that a number of medieval texts, and even many medieval genres, might properly fit such parameters. Thus, for example, eleven fourteenth century Latin riddles are recorded in one of the manuscripts of the laws of the Swedish province of Västergötland, Stockholm, Royal Library (HSS), Holm.

---

[9] On which see Larrington 1993 and the literature cited there, as well as the bibliography in Poole 1998.

B59 (Wahlgren 1939). Here are posed formulaically developed queries where the line between the sort of religious question-and-answer texts common in the Middle Ages (for example, *Lucidarius* and *Viðræða lærisveins ok meistara*) and religious riddles can be seen to be quite thin. Given the fact that, as Erik Wahlgren notes, in all but one of the cases, the answer being looked for in these eleven riddles is a famous biblical person, not an object or a tale, the answers may at first appear to be easy and straightforward, yet the questions themselves clearly bear the characteristics we would associate with riddling, especially the so-called "blocking element," that dissembling data point that looks to conceal the obvious answer. So, for example, among these Latin texts, one finds,

> Quis f[uit natus et non] mortuus. helyas. et Enoc.
> Quis fuit mortu*us* [et non natus.] Adam.
>
> Wahlgren 1939:244

> (Who was born but did not die? Elijah and Enoch.
> Who died but was not born? Adam.)

Enigmas of this sort, which test the individual's knowledge of the Bible or church teaching, were part of the European-wide learned Latin clerical culture. Their purpose must have been as much to teach as to test knowledge, and, indeed, pedagogical riddles represent a recognized functional category of riddling as noted in Gachanja and Kebaya (2013).

In fact, such forms are part of a long and widespread tradition of knowledge testing, and it is not difficult to find modern counterparts, such as nineteenth- and twentieth-century American traditions of "scripture cake" and other implicit tests of an individual's knowledge of the Bible (for example, "mix half a cup of 1 *Samuel* 14:25 into a cup of Proverbs 10:26," that is, mix half a cup of honey into a cup of vinegar).[10] Yet there is much more to these medieval examples than we see in scripture cake recipes: these modern-day contests are straightforward as regards knowledge. The "blocking element" represents a paramount difference, pushing these simple questions into the area of the riddle. By contrast to "Who died but was not born?" a question like "Who did God create as the first man?" would, for a medieval

---

[10] In my experience, these recipes *qua* contests are created and executed exclusively by women belonging to small fundamentalist churches, and are always treated as being of a good-humored, even jocular, nature, if with a mildly competitive character, part of which derives from the fact that performance, whether bleak or brilliant, is entirely a matter of self-reporting at, for example, Ladies' Bible Study classes.

Christian, be more or less the equivalent of "When does the train arrive?" The quandary created by combining someone dying without having been born provides the riddle-like or blocking element.

As to why these riddles have been recorded on an Old Swedish legal document, Erik Wahlgren (1939:244) offers the picture of a dramatically stenographic moment and suggests that these enigmas may have been "noted down at the spur of the moment upon the first convenient parchment by some fourteenth-century cleric fresh from a journey or from a glad round of story-telling with his brother-monks." Some centuries later, the fifteenth-century Old Swedish *Lilla rimkrönikan*, several manuscripts of which belonged to aristocratic families, display what appears to have been a basically competitive structure, which I have suggested (Mitchell 1996:44–45) might have been used in the fashion of the *Joca Monachorum* as a pedagogical tool, in this instance for the purpose of creating a historical narrative for Sweden.

The parallel between these *Joca Monachorum*-type questions, and the sort of question typical in Nordic wisdom contests raises interesting issues.[11] Against questions of the type, "Who died but was not born?" the eddic materials place similar questions about named figures from Norse mythology but lacking the "blocking element." Thus, for example, *Vafðrúðnismál* 11, "Segðu mér, Gagnráðr [...] / hvé sá hestr heitir, er hverian dregr / dag of dróttmǫgo" [Tell me, Gagnrad [...] what the horse is called who draws every / day to mankind (41)], to which the answer is Scinfaxi.[12] *Alvíssmál* offers a more pointed comparison to the extent that it demands knowledge in the form of Þórr's repeated, "Segðu mér þat, Alvíss" (Tell me this, All-wise [109, etc.]); however, although the god may challenge the dwarf's knowledge, he never poses a question in such a way as to challenge his wit, simply giving the dwarf an opportunity to list a vast array of synonyms used among the various races of beings.

To be clear, I am *not* suggesting that the tradition we see in the eddic materials necessarily derives from the Christian religious practice—it could have, but after all, being clever and knowledgeable in word and thought must have had its advantages in many cultural traditions—but after the Conversion, the existence both in the native vernacular tradition *and* in elite

---

[11] The *Oxford Dictionary of the Middle Ages* says of the *Joca Monachorum*-type questions, "Written in the form of short questions and answers, these texts often play on biblical curiosities, and were meant to stimulate reflection and meditation via their relatively humorous presentation." For Icelandic parallels, see Marchand 1976.

[12] In citing eddic poems, all references to the original text are to Neckel and Kuhn 1983, and all translations are from Larrington 1999.

Latin culture of such mystery-oriented genres must have served to support the value of these traits in *both* traditions.

Old Norse Riddles in Context

Typically, medieval riddle traditions reflect to a high degree the writing of Symphosius, a late Classical author whose fifth-century collection of 100 riddles was deeply influential throughout the Middle Ages and formed the backdrop against which many of the so-called "literary riddles" in both Latin and the vernaculars were created. But Old Norse, as distinct from, say, Old English with which it so often otherwise shares literary characteristics, lacks any known large collection of "literary riddles."[13] Curiously, the only significant repository of "true riddles" in all of Old Norse poetry comes from *Hervarar saga ok Heiðreks*, a *fornaldarsaga* generally thought to have been composed in the thirteenth century, and preserved in a variety of fourteenth-, fifteenth-, and seventeenth- century manuscripts, but also a text with occasionally very ancient roots.[14] Some differences among the so-called H-, R- and U-traditions notwithstanding, the saga's riddle contest is placed in all versions in a judicial-like context, namely that in the kingdom over which Heiðrekr rules, trials may be decided either by the king's judges or by the accused tendering riddles to King Heiðrekr. If the king cannot solve the riddles, then the accused is to go free.

We are next told of the king's foe ("mikill óvinr Heiðreks konungs" [32]), Gestumblindi, who is called to the king's court.[15] Because he does not consider himself wise, Gestumblindi does not want to "exchange words with the king" ("skipta orðum við konunginn" [32; my translation]) and sacrifices to Óðinn, asking for help and making great promises. A stranger

---

[13] Cf. the fourteenth-c. Latin riddles noted above in Holm. B59, on which, see also Geijer and Campbell 1930 and Wahlgren 1939. In addition, sporadic riddles appear, or have been detected, in a variety of contexts, including such disparate sources as runic inscriptions (for example, Eggja, Rök), Ragnarr's challenge to Kraka that she should come neither clothed nor unclothed and so on in *Ragnars saga loðbrókar*, and the King Frothi section of Saxo's *Gesta Danorum*. Cf. Heusler 1901; Alver 1954, 1982; Mitchell 2000b; and Rademann-Veith 2010.

[14] On this late medieval Icelandic genre and its relationship to Nordic traditions, see Mitchell 1991b. The riddle contest in *Hervarar saga ok Heiðreks* has been at the center of scholarly debate on "literary riddles" and their function since at least Roger Caillois' *Art poétique* (1958), in response to which, see Abrahams 1972.

[15] Unless otherwise noted, translations of the saga refer to Tolkien's version in *Hervarar saga ok Heiðreks konungs-2*, as do references to the text.

subsequently arrives at his door, a stranger who says of himself that he too is named Gestumblindi. The two exchange clothes, and the new, recently arrived Gestumblindi makes his way to Heiðrekr, where the king and his guest engage in a wisdom contest consisting of riddles. And it is precisely in this context, that is, when Gestumblindi, the disguised Óðinn, responds to Heiðrekr's query as to whether he would rather ask riddles or leave it to the judges, that the god sets himself up to be in a position that guarantees his win: "I choose rather to propound riddles" ("'Þat kýs ek,' segir hann, 'at bera fyrr upp gáturnar'" [32]).

Understandably, much of the attention to this episode has focused on the nature of the roughly three-dozen riddles themselves, some of which appear to belong to the native tradition; in any event, at least six multiforms were later recorded from living oral tradition in Scandinavia (Alver 1982:649). For the most part, these riddles are as far from the *Joca Monachorum*-types as one could imagine, although there are variations in the texts (for example, the H-text is considerably chattier than the R-text and contains an additional seven riddles).[16]

For our purposes here, I am not so concerned with the nature and origins of the riddles themselves as much as with the frame narrative, although it should also be noted that part of the frame concerns the manner in which the contest moves from ordinary-sounding riddles, albeit mostly *not* drawn from the stock of international folk and learned riddles, to the two final questions in the riddle session, which deserve special attention as they presumably serve to bring the story back to local pre-Christian traditions:[17]

Þá mælti Gestumblindi:

"Hverir eru þeir tveir,
er tíu hafa fœtr,
augu þrjú
ok einn hala?
Heiðrekr konungr,
hyggðu at gátu!"

"Þat er þá, er Óðinn ríðr Sleipni."

---

[16] See Tolkien, *Hervarar saga ok Heiðreks konungs-2*, xviii–xxi, and, especially, Love 2013:41–80; 190–238, and his extensive review of secondary literature.

[17] The distinction is often made between "incidental riddling" and "session riddling," on which, see, for example, Goldstein 1963 and Burns 1976.

Þá mælti Gestumblindi: "Segðu þat þá hinzt, ef þú ert hverjum konungi vitrari":

Hvat mælti Óðinn
í eyra Baldri,
áðr hann væri á bál hafðr?'

Heiðrekr konungr segir, "Þat veiztu einn, rǫg vættr!" (44)

(Then said Gestumblindi:

Who are those twain
that on ten feet run,
three their eyes are
but only one tail?
This riddle ponder, O prince Heidrek!

"Thus it is," said the king, "when Óðin rides upon Sleipnir."

Then said Gestumblindi, "Tell me this then last of all, if you are wiser than any other king":

"What said Óðin
in the ear of Balder,
before he was borne to the fire?"

"You alone know that, vile creature!" cried King Heidrek [44])

The riddle section of the saga is the most frequently duplicated and best-documented portion, and at the same time, it is also the most diverse portion with respect to treatment, with the order and even the substance of the riddles themselves differing dramatically in different manuscripts. Some aspects of *Gátur Gestumblinda* do not change, however, specifically the presence of these two riddles built entirely on various elements of Óðinn's career, which serve to direct the contest toward the personality of Óðinn; neither their essential nature nor their positions among the riddles changes in any of the manuscripts of the saga, always representing the penultimate and *ultima* riddles. The function of these enigmas, as Jeff Love notes, is to underscore that Heiðrekr's demise requires supernatural intervention. And, of course, as all observers have noted, the last query is only riddle-like insofar as it poses a quintessentially occult, or secret, question amidst many true riddles;[18]

---

[18] Two opposing views on riddle function have developed of which the following may be considered representative: Abrahams 1972:196, "Thus, at the heart of riddling is the contest motive, and this means in most cases that the agon occurs in the area of wits rather than knowledge," and

moreover, it asks for exactly the same answer as the same contestant, Óðinn, poses as the *ultima* question in the wisdom contest between himself and Vafþrúðnir in *Vafþrúðnismál*, a query which by its nature is unfair, and by definition, not a normal riddle, since only Óðinn himself can possibly know the answer.[19]

In the case of *Vafþrúðnismál*, this trick question appears to trump the knowledgeable disgorging of information that has preceded it, and the giant concedes, "þú ert æ vísastr vera" (you'll always be the wisest of beings, 49). Earlier in the poem (v. 7), Vafþrúðnir suggests that his guest will not leave alive unless he proves himself to be wiser ("snotari") than his host, and Vafþrúðnir's last utterance uses the phrase "with doomed mouth I've spoken" (feigom munni mælta ec); given those comments, as well as the theme of the poem, most scholars assume that the unseen conclusion to the poem is the death of the giant (see, for example, Ármann Jakobsson 2008).

In *Hervarar saga ok Heiðreks*, the outcome is more certain, if not as immediate: on being faced with the same question, albeit packaged differently, and reaching the same conclusion, Heiðrekr attempts to kill Óðinn with his sword but fails, after which, Óðinn remarks that because Heiðrekr has tried to kill him without cause ("saklausan"), Heiðrekr will die at the hands of the worst thralls ("inir verstu þrælar") (44). And so, some time later, King Heiðrekr is indeed killed by escaping slaves whom he had earlier captured.

Wit, Wisdom and Winning:
Old Norse Verbal Duals Writ Large

It is, of course, the way in which the wisdom confrontations function in *Vafðrúðnismál* and *Hervarar saga ok Heiðreks* that excites our interest here. In one of the more interesting essays to take up the social function of kennings, John Lindow (1975) draws an analogy between skaldic poetry and what linguists refer to as a "secret language" within the *drótt*, or chieftain's retinue, showing, as he writes, that, "in folkloristic terms, skalds were active tradition bearers, other members of the *drótt* passive tradition bearers, and

---

Haring 1974:197 "African riddling is more like a catechism than a creative inquiry. Usually in African riddles the connection between question and answer is fixed by tradition and popular acceptance."

[19] This type of riddle is often referred to as a Samson riddle, as it relies on knowledge known only to that individual, or a neck riddle, since the speaker frequently "saves his neck" through its use.

the tradition itself was limited to the *drótt*: non-members were outside the tradition" (Lindow 1975:353). In other words, the peculiar diction of skaldic poetry functioned at one level as a method for communicating meaning in an aesthetic form, but it also functioned, and perhaps even primarily functioned, as a method for communicating and reifying social hierarchies and social rules, that is, who belonged and who did not, at first to the *drótt* and later to the *hirð* "court."[20]

Lindow's interesting observations about the extra-linguistic and specifically social dimensions of the practice of skaldic poetry—performances that are, for us as modern observers in any event, defined by their linguistic properties, their stylized declamations, and by such additional goals as poetic competition, and performances that are at the same time highly sociological in their purpose (see Mitchell 2001a:187–91)—encourage me to think about this situation elsewhere with regard to the Nordic riddle and its nearest kindred among Nordic literary genres. As we have seen, for a century that relationship has generally been assumed to be the province of skaldic poetry; however, we should consider the possibility that there may be Old Norse genres in addition to skaldic poetry which perhaps deserve closer scrutiny vis-à-vis the riddle, the *Joca Monachorum*, and its eddic equivalent, the wisdom contest, genres that also use "coded languages" in performances where challenges based on verbal exchanges posed serially by turns test the opponent's wits and, thus, likewise establish social hierarchies and reaffirm social rules.[21]

Although of a very different character than the riddle, two Old Norse genres, the *senna* and the *mannajafnaðr*, are, I believe, their differences notwithstanding, apt genres for comparison.[22] These ritualized forms of verbal aggression are typified by their competitive use of language in specific

---

[20] Both *drótt* and *hirð* refer to a chieftain's retinue or troops, but with an increasingly institutionalized sense over time; see Lindow 1976.

[21] Cf. Goldstein's description (1963:331) of the contest and performance aspects of a "riddling session" in the Aberdeen area of Scotland in the late 1950s: "in riddling sessions the riddler poses his riddle and usually sits back while his audience puzzles over the enigma. One or more members of the audience will make attempts at guessing the solution and, usually failing to come up with the correct answer, will turn to the riddler for the solution. The audience will then comment on the qualities of the riddle—how good, bad, or indifferent it was."

[22] For an orientation to these forms, see especially Harris 1979; Swenson 1991; and Bax and Padmos 1983 and 1993. On the application of performance and other ethnographically informed approaches to the study of Old Norse literature, see the review in Hermann (2020). I take this opportunity to thank the members of a folklore seminar at Harvard in the spring 2014 semester entitled, *Maledicta: Ritualized Verbal Abuse*, for their lively and thought-provoking discussions which helped formulate my thinking here.

marked social contexts, and are Nordic manifestations of a widely known form of competitive speech act where language can play a central role in escalating and de-escalating social conflict in structured public display venues. They offer a window on how, to whom, and under what circumstances Old Norse sub-cultures gave individuals permission to exchange powerful invectives. Parallel examples, as is well-known, come from a variety of traditions, for example medieval Italian, Middle English, Scottish, Turkish, Anlo-Ewe and other sub-Saharan African, and modern American traditions.[23]

These competitive verbal exchanges go far back in written records: in Europe that means such famous texts as the Old Icelandic *Lokasenna*, the Middle English *Owl and the Nightengale*, and Montgomerie's early modern Scottish flyting; from Africa, there are nineteenth-century reports of such traditions, as well as strong and famous living traditions of ritualized invectives among, for example, the Anlo-Ewe; and with the European slave trade of the colonial period, the tradition was apparently introduced into the New World, where it lives on under a variety of names, for example, the dozens, soundings, snaps, cuts (Dollard 1939; Abrahams 1962; Wald 2012). Already in his seminal article on *senna*, Joseph Harris (1979) suggested that we consider the genre as something of an "applied sounding."

Under the influence of John Foley's ground-breaking use of new media in the web-based corollary to his *How to Read an Oral Poem* (2002),[24] I note that in the modern globalized media environment, it is very likely that the African-American sounding or dozens will be best known to readers from its commercial successes on niche cable programming where the genre has been exploited and popularized (for example *In Living Color* or *Yo Mama*).[25] Watching these commercially produced sketches, one readily perceives the relative lack of spontaneity in the exchanges, and what these "snaps" gain in relative clarity is, I would suggest, lost by their unnatural and staged

---

[23] Much has been written on these topics, to say the least. Regarded today as essentially canonical are Abrahams 1962; Dundes, Leach, and Özkök 1970; and Labov 1973:287–353; among the very best treatments are Park 1986, 1990, while comprehensive considerations are provided in Neu 2008 and Wald 2012.

[24] http://www.oraltradition.org/hrop/, accessed July 8, 2016: "The site has been designed to offer examples and additional information that are best presented via the web, the kinds of materials that don't fit comfortably between the covers of a conventional book. In this sense we're trying to take advantage of both media—book and web—and to underline the kinship between oral poetry and the Internet (a subject discussed in HROP)."

[25] Typical of these commercial ventures was the early 1990s television show, Fox's *In Living Color* and MTV's *Yo Momma*, https://www.youtube.com/watch?v=nKTVLeUpnTw, accessed May 19, 2023.

character. By contrast, watching performances in less media-staged environments is highly enlightening: thus, a short video of two young boys, perhaps five years old or so, learning and embracing the tradition ("doing the dozens"), and being encouraged, egged on even, by the crowd listening eagerly to the formalized insults exchanged by turn, is, in my view, an excellent way to envision the type of performance contexts on which are founded all the different wit-based, enacted, formal oral competition genres we know in the North: *mannajafnaðr*, *senna*, riddle contests, *Joca Monachorum*, and so on.[26]

These playfully charged and spontaneous exchanges, if at the same time also staged and learned in a different sense, replete with shouted encouragements from the crowd ("work his ass," and so on), may seem out of place to those who want to preserve the perception of a grave dignity surrounding the performance of eddic poetry and other Norse literary forms; however, I think that the spirit of this ribald video ("doing the dozens") may be of equal significance for our understanding of competitive verbal art as are, say, the fifth-century riddles of Symphosius. In many social contexts today, riddling is a largely cerebral activity, but as has been observed of children employing riddling to test social competence and reify hierarchies in contemporary settings, what has been called "contentious riddling" can involve highly aggressive behavior (McDowell 1979). Among other things, such real-life performances underscore that the goal of competitive events of these sorts is winning, claiming victory in a competitive speech act, and a key ingredient of such triumph is the defeat, humiliation even, of the opponent, and to that extent, judgments and declarations of victory depend on audiences, onlookers, whether the gods feasting in Ægir's hall in *Lokasenna*, the members of the *drótt* envisioned as listening to a complex use of kennings in a skaldic poem, the listeners to a riddle contest between the king and Gestumblindi in *Hervarar saga ok Heiðreks*, or even young men gleefully shouting "work his ass."

Postlude

None of the suggestions above about riddling and verbal aggression in Old Norse can, as far as I can make out, be subjected to empirical testing. If,

---

[26] "doing the dozens," https://www.youtube.com/watch?v=GEZA50XB9aE, accessed May 19, 2023.

on the one hand, readers are willing to accept "argument by analogy" as a useful tool in humanistic discussions, then I believe the perspectives offered here open new avenues for understanding both the value and the operational aspects of verbal confrontations in Viking-Age and early medieval Scandinavia, a matter reflected in the heavily stylized surviving textual materials. If, on the other hand, some readers find it possible *only* to believe what can with absolute certainty be identified in the existing written words of the medieval texts rather than inferred from them, then we are left with little more to consider as regards the riddle in the medieval Nordic world than a handful of modestly interesting codicological observations on the history of the few Nordic texts that take up riddles and other relevant matters.

The price paid for that sort of absolute fidelity to the existing texts strikes me as being very, very high, and as John Foley made abundantly clear in his own research (2012), "argument by analogy" can be an extremely valuable and productive method. In contrast to a deadening intellectual minimalism, Foley's approach was one that could be characterized, as he himself once remarked in a different context, as "much less predetermined and far more interactive, emergent, and performative" (quoted in Roth 2010). Certainly, it offers a productive pathway for considering verbal aggression in the medieval Nordic world, one of which I suspect Foley himself would approve.

PART II

Myths and Memory

Chapter 5

SKÍRNIR'S OTHER JOURNEY
THE RIDDLE OF GLEIPNIR

For Scírnis—the eddic poem in which Freyr acquires Gerðr as a mate through the help of Skírnir, his *skósveinn* (messenger)—plays a central role in our understanding of early Nordic culture. So much so, in fact, that a great body of secondary literature has developed around it, encompassing virtually all theoretical approaches to myth: solar, ritual, *interpretatio christiana*, structuralist, and other contemporary mythological stances.[1] No interpretation has received more praise and attention, however, than that proposed by Lars Lönnroth (1977), who urges a socially oriented reading which decodes the central meaning of the poem as a series of oppositions between marriage and love, responsibility and desire, and so on. So important is this narrative and its interpretation to our understanding of Norse mythology, in fact, that it has generally overshadowed the role Skírnir plays in another journey, when, according to *Snorra Edda*, he is sent to acquire a bond capable of holding Fenrir, after the first two chains the gods have employed fail to hold the monster:

> Þa sendi Allfa/ðr þaN, er Skirnir er nefndr, sendimaðr Freys, ofan iSvartalfaheim til dveRga nokvRa ok let gera fiotvr þaN, er Gleipnir h(eitir); hann var giorr at vi. lvtvm, af dyn kattarins ok af skeGi konVNar ok af rotvm biargsins ok af sinvm biarnarins ok af anda fisksins ok af fogls hraka, ok þottv vitir eigi aðr þesi tiþinde, þa mattV nv fiNa skiott her savn dæmi, at eigi er logit

---

[1] Original publication: "Skírnir's Other Journey: The Riddle of Gleipnir." In *Gudar på jorden. Festskrift till Lars Lönnroth*, ed. Matts Malm and Stina Hanson, 67–75. Stockholm, 2000.
  For the poem, see *Edda. Die Lieder des Codex Regius*, 69–77, and *Edda Sn* 1:30–31, for Snorri's synopsis of the story. Cf. the works listed in von See et al. 1993; one item missed by van See and his collaborators, however, is Mitchell 1983.

at þer; set mvntþv hafa, at konan hefir ecki skeg ok engi dynr verþr af hlavpi kattarins, ok eigi erv rætr vndir biarginv, ok þat veit trva min, at iafnsat er þat allt, er ec hefe sagt þer, þott þeir se svmir lvtir, er þv matt eigi reyna. Þa mælti G(angleri): Þetta ma ec at visv skilia att satt er; þesa lvti ma ec sia, er þv hefir nv til dæma tekit, en hvernig varþ fiotvrin smiþaðr? Har s(egir): Þat kaN ec þer vel segia. FiotVRiN varþ slettr ok blavtr sem silkiræma, en sva traustr ok sterkr, sem nv skaltv heyra. Þa er fiotvRiN var færðr asvnvm, þavckvþv þeir vel sendimanni sitt eyrindi.

Edda Sn 1931:36

(High said) "Then All-father sent someone called Skirnir, Freyr's messenger, down into the world of black-elves to some dwarfs and had a fetter called Gleipnir made. It was made of six ingredients: the sound of the cat's footfall and the woman's beard, the mountain's roots and the bear's sinews and the fish's breath and bird's spittle. And even if you did not know this information before, now you can discover true proofs that you are not being deceived in the following: you must have seen that a woman has no beard and there is no noise from a cat's running and there are no roots under a mountain, and I declare now by my faith that everything I have told you is just as true even if there are some things you cannot test."

Then spoke Gangleri: "I can indeed see this is true. I can understand the things that you have given as proofs, but what was the fetter made like?"

High said: "I can easily tell you that. The fetter was smooth and soft like a silken ribbon, but as firm and strong as you shall now hear. When the fetter was brought to the Æsir, they thanked the messenger heartily for carrying out their errand."[2]

Faulkes, 28

There exist numerous international analogues to the well-known continuation of the "Binding of Fenrir," in which Týr loses his hand, and the topic has been the subject of an important debate between Georges Dumézil and his detractors concerning Týr's role in the deception of the wolf.[3] At the other extreme, however, Gleipnir itself, the remarkable restraint the gods

---

[2] Although several writers have commented on the oddity of bears' sinews, no one has satisfactorily explained why the story holds that bears did not have them.

[3] See Boberg 1966 and Thompson 1966: F864.1 *Fetter for Fenris wolf* (cf. A1072.2 *Fettered monster as ferocious animal*); and Aarne and Thompson 1961: *AT803 Solomon Binds the Devil in Chains in Hell*, which also includes the deception motif. Cf. Clunies Ross 1994:219–221, for a review of the interpretations of the myth.

have had made—and the focus of this essay—is generally all but forgotten: it has principally been of interest to philologists (e.g., Kock 1899:90–111; Sijmons and Gering 1927, 1:431), who have concentrated on the etymology of the name (e.g., *Name für Wolf, Verschlinger, der krummschließer*).

But it is useful to note that there are several points of similarity between the only two narratives in which Skírnir has an active part, well beyond the obvious central issue of his acting as messenger of the gods. In particular, the explanation in the story of Gleipnir of how women came to lack beards and so on is directly paralleled in Snorri's version of *For Scírnis*, when Freyr gives his sword to Skírnir for going to the Otherworld to woo Gerðr. This payment accounts for why Freyr does not have his sword at Ragnarǫk, and leads directly to Freyr's death.[4] Indeed, a structural outline of Snorri's accounts of the two myths in which Skírnir plays a role highlights their comparable profiles: a prominent god (Óðinn; Njǫrðr/Freyr) sends Skírnir on a journey to the Otherworld in order to acquire an object of importance to the gods (Gleipnir; Gerðr), a mission Skírnir successfully carries out and which leads to important events for the gods (the binding of Fenrir; the marriage of Freyr and Gerðr), but completing the mission also leads to the loss of other items (women's beards, the breath of fish, and so on; Freyr's sword). Or to outline this pattern more abstractly:

GOD → MESSENGER → OTHERWORLD → ACQUISITION OF SOUGHT ITEM → LOSS OF OTHER ITEM(S)

Naturally, I am making no argument here about the *meaning* of the two myths, which in my view resides in the many details of the narratives, but it does suggest that either Snorri or the tradition with which he was working ascribed to the myths connected with Skírnir, the messenger of the gods and the one mythological figure whose purpose it was to move between the gods and the Otherworld, a concomitant and mixed sense of acquisition and loss, of triumph and defeat, of joy and sorrow. It is, of course, largely impossible to know whether the similarity between the two myths is of Snorri's own

---

[4] "Þesi savk er til, er Freyr var sva vapnlavs, er hann barþiz við Belia ok drap hann með hiartar horni [...] Verþa mvn þat, er Freyr mvn þickia verr við koma, er hann missir sverþzins, þa er Mvspellz synir fara at heria" (*Edda Sn* 1931:41) (This is the reason for Freyr so being unarmed when he fought Beli, killing him with a stag's antler [...] There will come a time when Freyr will find being without the sword a greater disadvantage when Muspell's sons come and wage war) (Faulkes, 32). This point is reiterated when Snorri describes Ragnarǫk: "þat verþr hans bani, er hann misir þes hins goþa sverþz, er hann gaf Skirni" (*Edda Sn* 1931:72) (The cause of his [Freyr's] death will be that he will be without the good sword that he gave to Skirnir) (Faulkes, 54) Cf. Krohn (1911), who suggests as a Biblical model David's loss of his sword after he marries Bathsheba following Uriah's arranged death.

design, or one which existed in the materials from which he learned what he knew about pagan mythology.

The tripartite framework which leads to the making of Gleipnir appears to be a quintessentially folkloric element in the narrative: the first attempt to bind Fenrir fails, as does the second, but on the third try, the gods succeed. Of course, this pattern may be understood to ratify the story's origins in Snorri's inventive and clever use of materials or, alternatively, to suggest an origin in popular tradition. Its presence here is certainly suggestive, and conforms well with similar episodes in *Snorra Edda*, as when Loki and Brokkr make a wager over the smithing of valuable items in *Skáldskaparmál* (*Edda Sn* 1931:122–124). In this tale, two sets of three items are made by the dwarves (Sif's hair; Skíðblaðnir; and Gungnir, on the one hand, versus Draupnir; Gullinbursti; and Mjǫllnir, on the other), and Loki, in the form of a fly, tries to interrupt the forging process of the second set on each of three occasions, finally succeeding in a limited way on his third attempt. This "third time's the trick" structure is, of course, one of the most common patterns of folk literature, and no audience member then or now is surprised when the first two attempts to bind Fenrir fail and the third succeeds. The use of six non-existent materials in the making of Gleipnir finds a parallel in folk literature in the motif of six useless tasks. Thus, this story of a chain made of six impossible ingredients is reminiscent of a riddle (H871) which asks, "What six things are not worth doing?" The enumerated tasks are as nonsensical as the ingredients which make up Gleipnir are improbable, namely, sowing salt, mowing pebbles, drinking from an empty jug, making signs to a blind man, wooing at mealtime, and playing a harp at a mill.[5] These and a host of other individual motifs parallel the myth of Gleipnir, as a number of scholars have shown (for example, von der Leyen 1899:28–32), but unlike the more famous "Master Builder" story type or the myth of the "Binding of Fenrir" itself, there are no unambiguous, fully articulated parallel narratives to the forging of the fetter. How then are we to understand the Gleipnir story?

Within the Nordic tradition, the idea behind this text of impossible, unlikely, or invisible bonds has a number of analogues, including the sacrifice of King Víkarr in *Gautreks saga* (chap. 7) and the valkyries' task during battle of binding the warriors Óðinn has selected (de Vries 1956–1957, §305). Indeed, binding enemies and victims has a significant place in Norse mythology, and that the proto-typical messenger of the gods should be sent to the world of the black-elves by Óðinn—the mythological figure consistently associated with

---

[5] See Anderson 1923:227–228. Cf. AT 2014 *Chains Involving Contradictions or Extremes*.

binding—is hardly surprising. From an international perspective, this narrative, with its apparent explanation for why cats "no longer" make noise, fish "no longer" have breath, and so on, is heavily reminiscent of myths whose motifs explain the shape of the world—for example, those enumerated in A2200– A2599 *Animal Characteristics*. Amid these motifs are sundry explanations of how various animals came to have the shapes, colors, abilities, and so on we associate with them (e.g., A2326.2.1 *Why cats have no horns*, A2356.2.6 *Why bear has hump on back*). The implication in Snorri's account is that it is exactly because the various items were "used up" in the forging of Gleipnir that they no longer exist. Several later manuscripts are less ambiguous on this point and declare forthrightly that these things no longer exist since they were all used up ("því ær þat ækki æptir siþan at þat var þa allt til haft").[6] It may well be that the forging of Gleipnir should be understood as just such an explanatory myth.

The story of Gleipnir's creation also holds a well-known place as one of the eddic-style verses culled from outside the *Poetic Edda* but generally included in editions of it: most editors and commentators (e.g., Möbius, Bugge, Guðbrandur Vigfússon, Hildebrand, Sijmons, Gering, Neckel, Finnur Jónsson, Jón Helgason, Neckel and Kuhn) follow the two later medieval manuscripts (AM 748 I, 4to, ca. 1300, and AM 757a, 4to, ca. 1400) of *Skáldskaparmál* which present the ingredients that make up Gleipnir in verse, changing the "bird's spittle" of *Gylfaginning* to "bird's milk":

or kattardyn	out of the noise of a cat
ok or konv skæggi,	and out of the beard of a woman
or fisks anda	out of the breath of a fish
ok or fvgla miólk	and out of the milk of a bird
ór bergs rótvm	out of the roots of a mountain
or biarnar sinvm	out of the sinews of a bear
or því var hann glæfnir gerr.	out of these was it, Gleipnir, made.

Edda Sn 1848–1887, 2:432 (= AM 748, 4to)[7]

---

[6] *Edda Sn* 1848–1887, 2:432 (= AM 748, 4to). The other manuscript, AM 757a, 4to, differs only with respect to orthography (*Edda Sn* 1848–1887, 2:515). Holtsmark 1964:20–21, suggests that the use of the phrase "þat veit trúa mín" (by my faith) in Snorri's account points to his use of irony: "ok þat veit trva min, at iafnsat er þat allt, er ec hefe sagt þer, þott þeir se svmir lvtir, er þv matt eigi reyna" (*Edda Sn* 1931:36) (and I declare now by my faith that everything I have told you is just as true even if there are some things you cannot test) (Faulkes, 28). Of course, irony may indeed be present in Snorri's configuration of the forging of Gleipnir, but such a reading does not mean that original believers in the tradition with which Snorri was working perceived it with any less seriousness than any other portion of their mythological world.

[7] Again, AM 757a, 4to (*Edda Sn* 1848–87, 2:515) differs only with respect to orthography. Regarding the dating of the manuscripts, see Finnur Jónsson's prologue in his edition (*Edda Sn*

My purpose in taking up the question of the fetter Gleipnir derives from a sense that the continuation of the story—with its specifically causative character, i.e., that it is for this reason fish lack breath, women beards, bears sinews and so on—needs to be understood against the broad domain of Norse wisdom literature, that is, of gnomic poetry of the sort associated with *Hávamál* and other didactic poetry and, particularly, of riddling.[8] With respect to this kind of literature, the Gleipnir verse bears a resemblance to the sort of alliterative lines of wisdom with which the *Äldre Västgötalagen* (ca. 1250) is interlarded (e.g., "þæn a værgh ær vinþær / þæn a biorn ær betir") (that one owns the wolf who defeats it / that one owns the bear who hunts it), except, of course, that whereas the Gleipnir verse is elliptical and "irrational" in the way myths often are, the Swedish examples are straightforward in meaning (*SGL*, 1:65). Closer still are Óðinn's lists in *Hávamál* (st. 85) of things one should not trust: "gínanda úlfi, / galandi kráco / rýtanda svíni, / rótlausom viði" (a gaping wolf, a cawing crow, / a grunting pig, a rootless tree) (*Sayings of the High One*, 24).

Such "normative" lists notwithstanding, gnomic wisdom in Norse tradition occurs vastly more frequently in the form of dialogic confrontations, as in such famous mythological competitions as those of *Alvíssmál*, *Vafðrúðnismál*, and *Fjǫlsvinnsmál*, where didactic cosmogonic material is artfully revealed in a question-answer competition. Analogous texts are, of course, well-known in Christian (e.g., *Elucidarius*) and secular (e.g., *Konungs skuggsjá*) contexts—what distinguishes the eddic forms from these is, on the one hand, the competitive character of the confrontations and, on the other, the lack of a master-student relationship between the questioners. Still, eddic riddling, if it can be called that, is not of the same character as "true riddling" (*eigenlege gåter*, etc.). This kind of riddle—where improbable objects are *explicitly* compared and an answer to the puzzle is attempted—is an unknown form in the eddas. In fact, in Norse tradition, in contrast to, say, Anglo-Saxon, "true riddles" are rarely found at all, and outside of translated learned riddles are as good as exclusively found in *Hervarar saga ok Heiðreks konungs* (chap. 9), also known as *Saga Heiðreks konungs ins vitra*.[9] These riddles are not particularly uniform with respect to style: the 30-odd

---

1931, XIV–XVII). This instance is not the only one where these two manuscripts give poetic versions of materials in *Gylfaginning*; cf. Holtsmark 1945.

[8] de Vries 1934 and Heusler 1901 remain highly useful reviews.

[9] The exceptions to this point are mainly late medieval Icelandic and Swedish translations of collections of learned riddles (i.e., portions of *Alfræði íslenzk*, and the Swedish-Latin parallel to the *Joca Monachorum*).

riddles are presented as mostly 8-line (although some have as many as 10, others 9 and 6, and one just 3 lines) alliterative poems, both in *fornyrðislag* and *ljóðaháttr*. The frame story of *Hervarar saga ok Heiðreks konungs* places the riddles in the familiar context of a competition between two interlocutors on which a wager has been placed, and the contest includes such memorably abstract comparisons as the following:

Hvat er þat undra,	What strange marvel
er ek úti sá	did I see without,
fyrir Dellings durum;	in front of Delling's door;
ókvikvir tveir	two things lifeless,
andalausir	twain unbreathing,
sáralauk suðu?	were seething a stalk of wounds?
Heiðrekr konungr,	This riddle ponder,
hyggðu at gátu!	O prince Heidrek!

The Saga of King Heidrek, 34

The answer to this riddle is two bellows used in forging a sword.[10]

The distinction between the infrequent-in-Norse "true riddle" and other types of riddles is significant, because, of course, Norse literature excels in a different kind of riddling, namely, kennings and other forms of poetic obscurity in which equally improbable objects are *implicitly* compared to create metaphors. To the extent that kennings are a kind of riddling, a number of them are kindred forms to the type of riddle usually called the *lärogåta* or *læregåte*, sententious riddling based on acquired learning rather than general knowledge or intuition.[11] This distinction is nothing more than the obvious, if very complex, difference between a kenning such as *hráki Gleipnis tuggu* = "the spittle of Gleipnir's mouthful" = "Fenrir's saliva" = the river Vǫn, said to run from Fenrir's mouth (used in the anonymous twelfth-century *Stríðkeravísur* [*Skj*, 1:591]), which can only be solved if one possesses a knowledge of Norse mythology, and an equally good kenning, such as *vágs blakkr* = "dun-colored horse of the wave" = "ship," which can be solved by anyone with imagination. A well-known student of literature and its relationship to traditional expressive forms has noted that whereas charms lead to the "mythological universe of traditional names and mysterious powers,"

---

[10] "þat eru smiðbelgir; þeir hafa engan vind, nema þeim sé blásit, ok eru þeir dauðir sem annat smiði, en fyrir þeim má líkt smíða sverð sem annat" [Those are smith's bellows; they have no wind unless they are blown, and they are as lifeless as any other work of smith's craft, but with them one can as well forge a sword as anything else], *Saga Heiðreks konungs*, 34.

[11] Cf. the entries in Bødker et al. 1964.

riddles by contrast lead to the "actual world explored by sense experience" (Frye 1976:141). The Old Norse *lärogator* and their related kennings intentionally split the difference between these types, it seems to me, on the one hand, they have the shape and nature of the riddle, but they also display the connections to numinous knowledge often associated with charms.

This special branch of mythological knowledge is, of course, the principal purpose for the very existence of Snorri's *ars poetica*, a text which, it has been argued, elsewhere makes use of the riddle for its materials.[12] The question of Snorri's relationship to tradition, i.e., the degree to which he understood it, used pre-existing sources of it, freely invented material to supplement it, and so on, has dominated Snorri scholarship for some time. In a few instances, we have actually come closer to understanding Snorri's outlook, source materials, and methods, a task which may also be possible with respect to the Gleipnir episode.[13] The structure of *Gylfaginning* is itself patterned along the lines of such question-answer dialogues as those mentioned earlier (i.e., *Alvíssmál, Vafðrúðnismál, Elucidarius, Viðrœða likams ok sálar*), and within the meta-dialogue *Snorra Edda* represents between Snorri and his contemporaries, it may be understood to be looking to establish the answers to just such perplexing learned, numinous kennings as these. In this context, we might well look at the form in which the Gleipnir myth is given in AM 748 I, 4to and AM 757a, 4to and wonder if this permutation of the material, rather than being a later reworking of Snorri's account, might not in fact be close to the original text Snorri had as a model. Indeed, it is not at all impossible to imagine that with 1) the addition of opening and closing lines of the sort common among the *Saga Heiðreks konungs* riddles, provided here in italics, and 2) the elision of the name Gleipnir, the verse given in these later manuscripts of *Skáldskaparmál* becomes a *lärogåta* or *læregåte* in *fornyrðislag*. I take here the liberty of presenting a suggested *hypothetical* text built on the existing later verses, a reconstruction which *perhaps* approximates the sort of riddle that Snorri may have used as a source for the Gleipnir myth.

Hvat er þat undra,	*What is that wonder,*
er úlf er gott at binda?	*good for binding a wolf?*
Ór kattar dyn,	Out of the noise of a cat,

---

[12] As Holtsmark (1945:151) comments in a discussion of imagery for moonbeams and the phases of the moon, "Det verset Snorre har brukt som myte, er en ekte gåte; ikke en 'folkegåte', men en lærd gåte, laget i et skaldemiljø." (The verse Snorri has used as a myth is a true riddle, not a 'folk riddle,' but a learned riddle, created in a skaldic milieu.)

[13] Cf. the thorough review of the main trends of this scholarship in Harris 1976a:66–101.

ok ór kono skeggi,	and out of the beard of a woman,
ór fisks anda,	out of the breath of a fish,
ok ór fugla miólk,	and out of the milk of a bird,
ór bergs rótom,	out of the roots of a mountain,
ór biarnar sinom,	out of the sinews of a bear,
ór því var hann gerr;	out of these was it made;
hyggðu at gátu?	*can you guess this riddle?*

Chapter 6

THE GODDESS GNÁ

Those searching for information about the goddess Gná in reference works typically find summaries of which the following is fairly typical: *"Gnå, Asynja, Friggs budbärare färdas till alla världar på hästen Hovvarpner som löper genom luften"* (Gná, *Asynja* [Norse goddess], *Frigg*'s messenger who travels to all the worlds on the horse *Hovvarpner* which moves through the air).[1]

The fact is that Gná is found among the least known and least discussed of the deities named by Snorri Sturluson in his *edda*. In addition to *Snorra edda*, the name Gná appears in several skaldic kennings and in a *þula*, but the goddess is not otherwise mentioned in our preserved source materials. Despite the absence of bountiful evidence, I believe she represents an extremely interesting character within Nordic mythology, a character who can assist us in understanding the supernatural world Snorri describes.

Evidence of Gná

Several metaphoric uses of the name Gná are known to us from West Norse skaldic poetry:

1. the kenning *Gná hringa* from *Jómsvíkingadrápa* (st. 42) by Bjarni Kolbeinsson (d. 1222), bishop of the Orkneys, which is interpreted as:

Gnǫ́ hringa = Gná (or goddess) of rings = woman (*Skj*, 2:9)

---
[1] Original publication: "Gudinnan Gná." *Saga och Sed* (2014): 25–41.
 Hultkrantz 1999:40; cf. Simek 1995:132–133; Lindow 2002:146–147. For their valuable observations (and objections) to earlier versions of this essay, I thank Agnieszka Backman, Stefan Brink, John Lindow, and Jens Peter Schjødt.

Other skaldic testimony to Gná is generally assumed to be considerably older in origin:

> 2. the metaphor *fýris fúr Gnáar* used by Ǫlvir hnúfa, born c. 840, one of Haraldr Hárfagr's court skalds, usually interpreted as:
>
> *fyr Gnǫ́ fýris* = by the Gná (or goddess) of the pine fire = woman (*Skj*, 1:6)

To judge from just these two examples, it is difficult to say more than that Gná seems to function within the kenning system in the same way as do the other *ásynjurar*, that is to say, as a goddess name which by itself or coupled with another word—here the word "ring"— should be resolved as "woman."

A third, more complicated example also suggests the same interpretation of the name Gná. The phrase, *Glitnis gná*, occurs in *Ynglingatal* (st. 7), traditionally considered to have been composed by Þjóðólfr úr Hvini about the year 900, and which has been preserved in *Ynglinga saga* in Snorri's *Heimskringla*.[2] Snorri writes:

> 3. Dyggvi hét sonr hans, er þar næst réð lǫndum, ok er frá honum ekki sagt annat en hann varð sóttdauðr. Svá segir Þjóðólfr:

> Kveðkat ek dul,
> nema Dyggva hrør
> glitnis Gnǫ́
> at gamni hefr,
> þvít jódís
> Ulfs ok Narfa
> konungmann
> kjósa skyldi,
> ok allvald
> Yngva þjóðar
> Loka mær
> of leikinn hefr.

Ynglinga saga, 33–34 (chap. 17); cf. *Skj*, 1:8

---

[2] Lit., "Gná of Glitnir," that is, goddess of the gleaming silver and gold hall of the god Forseti. It is a kenning about which a number of suggestions have been made, including "the sun" and "Hel." Its basic sense, "goddess of the gleaming hall," might, one assumes, also, like the other cases, readily yield "woman." On the possible interpretations of the kenning, see Abram 2003:21–25, and the literature cited there. Abram draws the conclusion that "although the reliance on Glitnir's being a horse-*heiti* and thus a reference to barely attested folk-belief leaves the usual interpretation of this kenning open to doubt, it seems wise on literary grounds to assume that Þjóðólfr does mean to refer to Hel in this stanza" (25).

His son, who ruled the lands next, was called Dyggvi, and nothing is said
of him other than that he died of sickness. So says Þjóðólfr:

I call it no secret
the corpse of Dyggvi
the horse's goddess
has for pleasure,
for the Wolf's sister
as well as Narfi's
chose to keep
the king for herself,
and Loki's girl
beguiled the lord
of Yngvi's race
into her power.

Finlay and Faulkes, 19–20

Apart from these verses and a few other similar kennings, it is in *Gylfaginning* in *Snorra edda* that we are really allowed to meet this goddess.[3] Gná is named last in a long line of goddesses, but now with the difference that Snorri does not merely mention her but writes a bit more about her, although precisely what he has written, and what it means, is anything but obvious:

Fjórtánda Gná: hana sendir Frigg í ymsa heima at eyrindum sínum. Hon á þann hest er renn lopt ok lǫg, er heitir Hófvarfnir. Þat var eitt sinn er hon reið at Vanir nokkvorir sá reið hennar í loptinu. Þá mælti einn:

"Hvat þar flýgr?
Hvat þar ferr
eða at lopti líðr?"

Hon segir:

"Ne ek flýg
þó ek fer
ok at lopti líðk
á Hófvarfni
þeim er Hamskerpir
gat við Garðrofu."

---

[3] Other examples, such as the use in *Gísla saga Súrssonar* (48 [chap. 14]) of *Gnǫ́ bógar*, represent further instances of Gná-themed kennings for "woman." See the entries under "Gnǫ́" in *Lexicon poeticum*, 194.

Af Gnár nafni er svá kallat at þat gnæfar er hátt ferr.

Edda Sn 1, 30

In Anthony Faulkes translation:

"Fourteenth Gna: she is sent by Frigg into various worlds to carry out her business. She has a horse that gallops across sky and sea, called Hofvarpnir. It happened once as she was riding that some Vanir saw her travelling through the sky. Then said one:

"What is flying there? What is traveling there, passing through the sky?"

She said:

"I am not flying, though I travel and pass through the sky on Hofvarpnir whom Hamskerpir begot on Gardrofa."

From Gna's name a thing is said to tower (*gnæfa*) when it goes high up."

Faulkes, 30–31

Comparing this normalized text of *Snorra edda* against its four surviving medieval manuscripts reveals several interesting details. A certain accord exists between Regius, Wormianus, and Trajectinus, apart from orthography; however, as one might expect, Codex Upsaliensis DG 11, *The Uppsala Edda*, distinguishes itself in several respects (*Edda Sn* 1848–1887, 2:275; cf. Sävborg 2012; Bäckvall 2013).

Sometimes these differences concern word choices (*eigi* for *ne*; *mælt* for *kallat*), and in one case, Upsaliensis has an extra *eða* (*hvat þar flygr / eða hvat þar ferr / eða hvat lopti liþr*). But in some instances, the writer of Codex Upsaliensis seems to know something more, or perhaps something different, than the others. First of all, the other three manuscripts say that "some Vanir saw her traveling through the sky, then said one" (*Vanir nokkvorir sá reið hennar í loptinu. þá mælti einn*). In Upsaliensis, by contrast, it is a single *vanr* who sees her and that god's gender is clearly masculine: *vanr nockvrr* and *hann mælti*. Perhaps more meaningful is the poem's last line in Upsaliensis, *gack vm garð vorv* (usually normalized to *gakk um garð vóru*). Some editors alter *vóru* to *vórn*, and consequently translate the line as "gå genom vårt stängsel" (go through our fence). In her recent dissertation on such instances in Codex Upsaliensis, Maja Bäckvall concludes that this line represents one of the actual errors ("de egentliga felen") in the manuscript, with the sense in its preserved form, "Gå, de var kring gården (?)" (Bäckvall 2013:141–144). (Go, they were around the enclosure [?])

There are three horses in Snorri's narrative: Gná's airborne mount is named Hófvarfnir, a name usually interpreted as "Hoof-warper" (more specifically: "Hoof-caster," "Hoof-kicker," or "He who casts his hooves about"; cf. Simek 1995, Lindow 2002). All of the manuscripts call Hófvarfnir's mother Garðrofa *gärdebrytare* (fence-breaker) and Regius, Wormianus, and Trajectinus agree that his father's name is Hamskerpir. Upsaliensis, on the other hand, has Háttstrykr (ms. *hatt strykr*), "Hög vindstöt (?)" (High wind gust [?]).[4] Apart from attempts in the beginning and middle of the nineteenth century to tie the stallion's name to *hamr* "shape," etc., since Finnur Jónsson's reworking of *Lexicon Poëticum*, most people have interpreted Hamskerpir with him as "with lean hind-quarters."[5]

Etymologists have shown much interest in the goddess's name as well, although their efforts have been far from perfect. Snorri's attempt in the 1200s to join the name Gná with the verb *gnæfa* "rise high up in the air" (Fritzner's "rage høit op i Veiret") has not met with approval from modern philologists, who regard him as having been led astray by the similarity of the words.[6] Two possible derivations have been suggested that offer closely related meanings: one (which has been promoted by, among others, Hugo Gering and Albert Morey Sturtevant) sees a derivation *ga-naha*, "abundance," "affluence"

---

[4] According to Fritzner 1973, "strykr, m. *stærk Vind*" (strong wind) and Cleasby-Vigfusson 1982 [1957], "strykr, m. *a stroke, gust of wind*."

[5] *Lexicon poeticum*, 226: "harmskarpr, m, bland hestenavne, Þul IV rr 4; egl. 'med skarp, markeret hǫm lænd,' altså mager. Jfr det følgende," which is "Hamskerpir, m. er vel ensbetydende med det foregående, hest." (*harmskarpr*, m, among horse names, Þul IV rr 4; lit., "with sharp, pronounced hǫm" ["ham, haunch"]." Cp. the following entry, which is "Hamskerpir, m. the equivalent of the preceding, horse"). Cf. de Vries 1961:208: "*hamskarpr, hamskerpir* m. 'pferdname' (poet.), eig. 'mit mageren lenden.'"—vgl. *hǫm* und *skarpr*." (*hamskarpr, hamskerpir* m. horse name [poet.], lit. "with lean loins"—cp. *hǫm* and *skarpr*).

[6] Cf. de Vries 1961:177, "Das wort ist schwierig zu erklären. Der umstand, dass Snorri sagt: "nach Gná heisst es gnæfa, wenn etwa hoch dahin fährt' berechtigt uns nicht (mit Jóhannesson, Wb. 264) an *gnapa* anzuknüpfen, das führt zu einer sehr blassen Bedeutung des namens, während überdies Snorri nur lautgleichheit für etymologische verwandtschaft genommen haben kann." (The word is difficult to explain. The fact that Snorri says, "from Gna's name a thing is said to tower [*gnæfa*] when it goes high up" does not allow us (with Jóhannesson, Wb. 264) to connect it to *gnapa*, which would provide a very anemic meaning for the name, while in any case Snorri may have taken the phonological similarity for an etymological relationship.) Cf. Wiborg (1848:235) who writes, "Ordet udtales Gnaw, og findes endnu i Ordet *gnaven* (=*lynning, missmodig*) o.s.v." (The word is pronounced "Gnaw," and still exists in *gnaven* "grumpy" [= despondent, downcast]).

("Überfluss"), while the other interpretation associates the name's root with cognates in Greek, Celtic, and Balto-Slavic languages and gives the sense "einer Göttin der Fülle," or "goddess of abundance" (Holthausen 1948:91). It is difficult however to ignore the judgement of de Vries that the solution remains quite uncertain ("das bleibt doch recht unsicher").[7]

Finally, to the three skaldic kennings and Snorri's comments in Gylfaginning can be added that Gná is mentioned among 27 goddesses (*ásynjur*) in a *þula* in Skáldskaparmál (st. 433, *Edda Sn* 2, 114), and that Hófvarfnir's name also occurs in a *þula* (*Skj*, 1:676).

In short, these cases—the three skaldic poems, *Gylfaginning*'s short narrative, and citations in several *þulur*—constitute the whole of our source materials about Gná. In other words, the possibilities for interpreting Gná appear to be quite limited.

Research Survey

Already in 1835 Jakob Grimm made an important and—as things have turned out—long-lived contribution about our undervalued goddess in his indispensable study, *Deutsche Mythologie* (Grimm 1835:703; see also 387). In one of his many rich and detailed *Nachträgen*, he asserts (entirely indirectly at first) that there exists a certain similarity between Nordic mythology's presentation of a flying goddess ("eine fliegende göttin") and the attempt in antiquity to give the concept of "rumor" (alt. "renown") a human form through the goddess *Fama* (among the Romans; Φήμη among the Greeks).[8]

---

[7] de Vries 1961:177. An interesting example of a modern folk etymology perhaps lies behind the suggestion that Gná means "den outtröttliga" (the indefatigable). The claim is made, e.g., on Swedish Wikipedia (sv.wikipedia.org/wiki/Gna) [accessed February 2012]. The same information can be found at http://svenskanamn.alltforforaldrar.se/visa/Gnana, which cites Wikipedia as its source. This interpretation perhaps has its roots in yet another website, http://paranormal.se/topic/gudar_och_gudinnor_i_norden.html, from 2005, where the author writes, "Visste du att Brage var skaldekonstens gudom, att Freja var älskogens gudinna, Fulla den förtroliga, Gna den outtröttliga ryttarinnan, Vidar den tyste och starke, Uller vinterjaktens gudom...?" (Did you know that Bragi was the god of poetry, that Freyja was goddess of lovemaking, Fulla the intimate, Gná the indefatigable horsewoman, Víðarr the quiet and strong, Ullr the deity of the winter-hunt...?) Possibly this expression "Gna den outtröttliga ryttarinnan" (Gná the indefatigable horsewoman) has been shortened and misunderstood, and thereby changed into an "etymology."

[8] In 1844 Samuel Laing seems to have translated one of the skaldic verses (*Ynglingatal* 7) in *Heimskringla* with Grimm's interpretation in mind:
"What news is this that the king's men,
Flying eastward through the glen,
Report? That Dag the Brave, whose name

According to late authors, especially Virgil and Ovid, Fama was a flying figure: in the *Aeneid*, for example, one finds the expression *Fama volat*, which might be understood either as renown or rumor flies (or has wings and so on). In later editions of *Deutsche Mythologie*, Grimm develops this and related ideas such that in the end he includes Gná in the discussion as an equivalent to Fama's personification of "rumor" (alt. "renown").[9]

Aside from several attempts in the 1800s to compare Gná with different goddesses from the Graeco-Roman pantheon, very little has been written about Gná since Grimm.[10] But in *Reallexikon der Germanischen Altertumskunde* from the early 1900s, Eugene Mogk describes the goddess's characteristics and adds that the goddess is probably merely a hypotase for Frigg ("Die Göttin ist wohl nur eine Hypotase der Frigg").[11] Even Jan de Vries, who otherwise tends to have perspectives on such figures, does nothing more than to mention Gná's existence in his two editions of *Altgermanische Religionsgeschichte* (1935-37, 2:329; 1957, 2:329).

It is Bertha Philpotts who has discussed this goddess most daringly, when she suggests in *The Elder Edda and Ancient Scandinavian Drama* that the brief passage in *Snorra edda* constitutes only a minor portion of a longer poem, "an excerpt from a poem which must have dealt with Frigg much as *Skírnismál* deals with Frey" (Phillpotts 1920:52). In 2007, Ingunn

> Is sounded far and wide by Fame—
> That Dag, who knew so well to wield
> The battle-axe in bloody field,
> Where brave men meet, no more will head
> The brave—that mighty Dag is dead!"

[9] "Da sonst in der edda dieser Fama nichts entspräche, darf ihr vielleicht die göttin *Gnâ* verglichen werden, nach Sn. 38 entsendet sie Frigg 'at eirindum sînum' in alle welttheile, sie reitet durch luft und meer auf einem pferd namens *Hôfvarpnir* (hufwerfend), weder fliegen noch fahren will sie, sondern durch die luft gehn, und von allem hochfahrenden gebraucht man den ausdruck *gnæfa*," Grimm 1875:747. (Since nothing else in the edda would correspond to this Fama, perhaps the goddess *Gnâ* can be compared to her; according to Sn. 38, Frigg sends her "at eirindum sînum" (on her [Frigg's] errands) to all parts of the world; she rides through air and sea on a horse named *Hôfvarpnir* (hoof-throwing); she neither flies nor drives, yet moves through the air; and the term *gnæfa* is used of all those who go high up.) Grimm continues by noting that it is Hofvarpnir who flies, not Gná.

[10] E.g., Wiborg 1848:234–235, "*Gná* er Friggs Sendebud, og altsaa nærmæst en Parallel til Iris [...] Hun er rimeligvis en Personification af 'Dronningblikket', som Grundtvig siger, det dels Knibske og dels Majestætiske hos den sande Qvinde." (*Gná* is Frigg's messenger, and thus most nearly a parallel to Iris [...] She is probably a personification of what Grundtvig calls 'The Queen's Gaze,' the partly coy and partly majestic in the true woman.) Cf. N. F. S. Grundtvig 1832:515, with reference to both Fulla and Gná.

[11] Mogk 1913–1915, 2:263. Cf. Ingunn Ásdísardóttir 2007:50–52, who emphasizes this interpretation's continued popularity as regards goddesses.

Ásdísardóttir employed Snorri's passage about Gná as Frigg's servant in support of her view that Frigg should be regarded as "the highest goddess" (æðst ásynjanna).[12] Quite recently, Matthias Egeler has tied Gná to his views about Freyja's identity as a valkyrie (Egeler 2011:78–79).

One of the few who has discussed the passage in *Gylfaginning* in detail is Ulla Loumand, but she focuses on the horse Hófvarfnir and not the goddess. But Loumand is certainly correct when she writes that horses like Hófvarfnir and Sleipnir should be understood as "mediators" between heaven and earth, between the different worlds, and between the world populated by *mennskir menn* and the underworld (2006:133).

To the description of the goddess Gná in *Gylfaginning*, Rudi Simek adds in his handbook on Nordic mythology that he regards Snorri's etymology as doubtful and that it is unclear what the name means: "Snorris Etymologie des Namens ist nicht unbedingt richtig, aber was der Name sonst bedeuten soll, ist unsicher, auch wenn man in ihr eine 'Göttin der Fülle' hat sehen wollen" (1995:138). Doubtful too is John Lindow, who notes in his *Norse Mythology: A Guide to the Gods, Heroes, Rituals, and Beliefs* that the verse exchange is strange; moreover, he calls into question why it should specifically be Vanir deities who see her in the air (2002:146–147; see also Lindow 2016). In his *Shamanism in Norse Myth and Magic*, Clive Tolley cites Snorri's short description of Gná in his discussion of the Vanir gods, but is otherwise silent on her role in the mythology.[13]

Popular and Ecclesiastical Traditions of the Ability to Fly

As this brief review makes clear, discussions of the goddess Gná have been dominated by possible filiations to the Graeco-Roman world and etymological interpretations. However interesting these issues may be, one wonders if there are not other interpretive schemes which can help us understand this

---

[12] "Af þessu virðist mega ráða að Snorri líti svo á að ar sem Frigg er kona Óðins sem er æðstur ásanna þá sé hún æðst ásynjanna. Engin bein rök færir hann fyrir þessu utan að staðhæfa að hún sé 'æzt', að Fulla sé þjónustumey hennar, að Lofn, Hlín og Gná séu undir hana settar þó þær séu ásynjur sjálfar og að Frigg sé 'drottning ása og ásynja, Fullu ok valshams og Fensala'." Ingunn Ásdísardóttir 2007:169. (From this it would seem that Snorri looks at it this way: if Frigg is the wife of Óðinn, who is highest among the gods, then she is the highest among the goddesses. He makes no direct argument for this apart from stating that she is "noble," that Fulla is her maid, that Lofn, Hlín and Gná are placed below her even though they are themselves goddesses, and that Frigg is "queen of the Æsir and Asyniur, of Fulla and falcon form and Fensalir.")

[13] Tolley 2009, 1:212; see, however, also 224, where he takes up the metaphor "Glitnis Gná."

ásynja. If we scrutinize Gná's enigmatic answer from the perspective of the ecclesiastical and secular Old Norse text material and question what mission Gná is on, we may be able to reach a possible answer.

Naturally the most conspicuous aspect of Snorri's narrative is Gná's ability to fly—or more specifically, both to fly and not fly. In response to *Hvat þar flýgr* (What is flying there?) and so on, she says: *Né ek flýg, / þó ek ferk / ok at lofti líðk* (I am not flying, / though I travel / and pass through the sky). What can this mean? And is there a cultural background to her comment that may be important to know?

The ability to fly is not an unusual phenomenon *per se* in Norse mythology: Freyja has a feathered or falcon cloak (*fjaðrhamr*; *valshamr*) which she could even lend to others; the giant Þjazi seems to have something similar; Óðinn flies with the Poetic Mead in the shape of an eagle; and the story of Vǫlundr presents the escape of its hero through his ability to fly.[14] These examples are only the best-known cases of magical flight in Old Norse literature, but there are many such cases, so many that it is easy to ignore the importance of this ability to fly for Gná's nature. I start from the supposition that the ability to fly in the supernatural world belonged to a native Nordic tradition.[15]

But there are other traditions which can have influenced the presentation of magical flight during the Icelandic Middle Ages. We have, for example, evidence of similar popular traditions on the continent from the beginning of the tenth century. Ever since the *daemones* of antiquity, the air just above us has represented a magical space, a transitional area between *terra firma* and heaven. It has been understood as a territory where not only angels, demons, and valkyries move about, but also somewhat later as a space where even Waldensians and other heretics could be presented as flying.[16]

Parallels to this learned tradition of magical flight are to be met in discussions of the fallen angels in *De civitate Dei* by St. Augustine and the popular medieval stories about Simon Magus. Belief in such matters is reflected in a variety of Nordic texts of different types, such as, for example, *Eiríks saga*

---

[14] I am thinking primarily of texts like *Vǫlundarqviða*, but there also exists a long chain of material evidence relating to such a concept, from the so-called Franks Casket to the newly discovered figure from Uppåkra (see Helmbrecht 2012).

[15] Cf. Ingunn Ásdísardóttir's discussion (2007:64–66) of Kiviks kungagrav and other older data, such as the Gotlandic picture stones.

[16] See, e.g., Russell 1972:23 *et passim* and Flint 1991:65–66 *et passim*. Consider as well similar examples from outside of Europe: the Chinese emperor Shun, the Persian king Kai Kawus, gods like Horus and Vishnu, and so on.

víðfǫrla (36–37) and *Stjórn* (11 [chap. 2], 17 [chap. 6]), from c. 1300 and c. 1350 respectively.

But much earlier, in the beginning of the 900s, these ideas constituted part of the background to the so-called *Canon episcopi* of Regino av Prüm, which in turn built on a folk tradition. Regino writes that there are evil women who are so corrupted by the devil and by the illusions and fantasies caused by demons that they believe that they ride out at night on animals accompanied by Diana, the pagan goddess, in the company of a pack of women, and that they cover vast distances. The *Canon episcopi* is later taken up by Burchard of Worms (d. 1025), Yves av Chartres (d. 1115), Gratianus (fl. mid-twelfth century), and numerous other church leaders throughout the whole of the European Middle Ages (see Russell 1972:75–82). In this instance, folk traditions appear to have blended with ideas from antiquity and the Church and have been spread through canon law, saints legends, synodal statutes, and the like.

The Nordic world too was influenced by the *Canon episcopi*, which is in evidence in the 1200s in a paraphrase in Icelandic religious literature, even if nothing prevents this view from having been known earlier in the North. The text runs as follows in *Jóns saga Baptista*:

> þar sem finz i helgum bokum, at kveldriður eða hamleypur þykkiaz með Diana gyðiu oc Herodiade a litilli stundu fara yfir stor hof riðandi hvolum eða selum, fuglum eða dyrum, eða yfir stor lond, oc þott þær þikkiz i likama fara, þa vatta bækr þat lygi vera.

Jóns saga Baptista II, 914[17]

---

[17] See *Postola sögur*, xxviii, which dates the saga to the period 1264–1298. The section of AM 625, 4to which contains *Jóns saga Baptista II* is considered to be from 1300–1325 (cf. http://handrit.is/is/manuscript/view/AM04-0625). By comparison, Gratian presents this part of the *Canon episcopi* of Regino of Prüm as: "Illud etiam non est omittendum, quod quedam sceleratae mulieres retro post sathanam conuersae, demonum illusionibus et fantasmatibus seductae, credunt se et profitentur, cum Diana nocturnis horis dea paganorum, uel cum Herodiade, et innumera multitudine mulierum equitare super quasdam bestias, et multa terrarum spacia intempestae noctis silentio pertransire, eiusque iussionibus obedire uelut dominae, et certis noctibus euocari ad eius seruicium." (Gratian, *Decretum*, Part II, C.26, q.5, c.12 *Episcopi*; *Corpus Iuris Canonici*, col. 1030). (It is also not to be omitted that some wicked women, perverted by the Devil, seduced by illusions and phantasms of demons, believe and profess themselves, in the hours of night, to ride upon certain beasts with Diana, the goddess of pagans, [or with Herodias] and an innumerable multitude of women, and in the silence of the dead of night to traverse great spaces of earth, and to obey her commands as of their mistress, and to be summoned to her service on certain nights) (following *Materials toward a History of Witchcraft*, 178–179, with my emendations). On the *Canon episcopi* in a Nordic context, see Mitchell 2011:134, and Mitchell 2012b.

It says in holy books that "evening-riders" or "shape-shifters" (*kveldriður eða hamleypur*) believe themselves to travel with Diana the goddess and Herodias quickly over great oceans, riding whales or seals, birds or wild animals, or over great lands, and although they (*þær*, "these women") believe themselves to travel bodily, books affirm that this is a lie.

It is thus possible to envision that the ability of a supernatural entity to fly might have: 1) a foreign ecclesiastical background (albeit with roots in a popular tradition), 2) a native popular tradition, or 3) a mixture, or symbiosis, of the two types. By the end of the Nordic Middle Ages, it is easy to recognize such a symbiosis in the so-called Blåkulla myth, frequently represented in wall murals in late medieval Nordic churches (see Mitchell 1997a).

Before we return to the confusing answer Gná gives—that she is not flying but is travelling and passing through the air—let us first survey several other Old Norse cases connected to the same belief and which can help us understand her answer. The well-known scene from *Hávamál* st. 155, with its figures who "sport aloft in the sky"—*túnriðor*—provides a convenient point of departure. Óðinn maintains that he knows a charm which gives him the ability to thwart such enchanted creatures:

> Þat kann ec iþ tíunda   ef ec sé túnriðor
>   leika lopti á:
>
> ec svá vinnc   at þeir villir fara
>   sinna heim hama,
>   sinna heim huga.
>
> *Hávamál* st. 155

> I know a tenth one, if I see witches
>   playing up in the air;
> I can bring it about that they wander astray,
>   from their shapes left at home,
>   from their minds left at home.
>
> *Sayings of the High One*, 34

The choice of expression here is noteworthy: that Óðinn uses *tunríðor* (< "hedge-riders") can, of course, result from the alliterative pattern, but other terms are just as natural and less peculiar, and these would follow the poetic rules just as well, such as *trollkonur* "witches." That precisely *tunríðor* is used undoubtedly belongs to a to-us-still-hidden part of the ancient Nordic world of imagination (*föreställningsvärld*). And that these *tunríðor* in *Hávamál* are just the tip of the iceberg is pretty certain.

Indeed, that there are other figures which represent a parallel or counterpart to these *tunríðor* is seen in *Vafðrúðnsimál* st. 48. There Óðinn asks the question:

Fiolð ec fór, fiolð ec freistaðac,
    fiolð ec reynda regin:

hveriar ro þær meyiar   er líða mar yfir,
    fróðgeðiaðar fara?

Vafðrúðnsimál st. 48

Much have I traveled, much have I tried out,
    much have I tested the Powers;
who are those girls who glide over the sea,
    wise in spirit, they journey?

Vafthrudnir's Sayings, 44

Here too it is a question of female characters who can—just like Gná—"glide" (*líða*), but now over the sea, at least as most have interpreted the passage (although not the admirable Dag Strömbäck, who in a series of publications looks to make relevant a different understanding).[18] The most important point for us is that these female characters glide up in the air, and that they are described as *fróðgeðiaðar*, roughly "wisdom-glad"—in other words, they know something.[19]

In fact, there are other examples of *þær meyiar, er líða mar yfir* (lit., "those maidens who glide over the sea"), which may represent a kind of evolution within this idea cluster: namely, the corresponding compound, *marlíðendr*, in *Eyrbyggia saga*.[20] These figures are described there in a manner that suggests the author regards them as of the same character as *tunríðor*, *myrkríðor*, and other supernatural beings. The passage runs:

---

[18] As regards the original meaning of *mara*, cf. Strömbäck 1935:33–36, 157–159; 1975; 1976–1977; and 1977, who does not agree that it should mean "sea." In Strömbäck 1977:705, he characterizes *marlíðendr* as "en från en levande människa utgående gestalt, ett slags hamn eller 'sending', som företräder sin ägare och fullgör dennes önskemål och avsikter" (An entity emanating from a living person, a kind of guise or "sending" which represents its owner and fulfills the individual's desires and purposes) and in conclusion suggests that the phrase "betyder alltså 'den som svävar ut som mara'" (thus means "one who glides [or floats, soars, hovers, and so on] like a *mara*") (708).

[19] Fritzner 1973, "geðjaðr, *adj.* saadan som er efter ens Sind" (such as is after one's mind); cf. Cleasby-Vigfusson 1982 [1957], "geðjask, að, dep. *to be pleased with*."

[20] The word itself seems to be old and also occurs in Old English (e.g., *Beowulf*) and Old High German (e.g., *Hildebrandslied*), without however any supernatural character.

Ok er mjǫk leið á kveldit, mælti Geirríðr við Gunnlaug: "Þat vilda ek, at þú fœrir eigi heim í kveld, því at margir eru marlíðendr; eru ok opt flǫgð í fǫgru skinni, en mér lízk nú eigi sem hamingjusamligast á þik."

Eyrbyggia saga, 28–29 [chap. 16]

And late in the evening she said to him: "I wish you wouldn't go back home tonight, there are too many sea-spirits [*marlíðendr*] about, and there's many a fair skin hides a foul mind. Anyway, you don't exactly have the look of a lucky man about you just now."

Eyrbyggja saga 1973:60

When Gunnlaugr ignores her warning, he disappears during the night and is found the next day naked and beaten, and he remains sick throughout the winter. The rumor spreads that it is Geirríðr who has "ridden" him, although, as the saga makes clear, it is another woman, Katla (who is described as beautiful but disliked), who has done the deed (see also Strömbäck 1975, 1976–1977, and 1977; and Dillmann 2006:85–86, 244, 261).

Here we see, I believe, the influence of the church, for in *Eyrbyggia saga* the *marlíðendr* (translated by Hermann Pálsson and Paul Edwards as "sea-spirits," but also implying movement < *líða* "go, glide, pass") are presented as a kind of witch or valkyrie, a connection one finds in Old English literature (e.g., *Sermo Lupi ad Anglos*). The same image—that is, the picture of a destructive, malicious female character—appears in *Ynglinga saga* (chap. 13) when King Vanlandi is killed by the *seiðkona* (lit. "seiðr-woman," sometimes translated as "sorceress, witch"). In the verse, Þjóðólfr speaks of the king whom *mara kvalði* "the *mara* tormented" (cf. *Historia Norwegiæ*).[21]

Nordic Traditions of Supernatural Tidings

Should flying females always be understood as dangerous? This interpretation is refuted by other, perhaps more reliable, scenes, where flying characters often have other unpleasant but not directly deadly roles. In a well-known sequence in *Haralds saga Sigurðarsonar*, when the Norwegian king has decided to attack England, several poetic dream warnings occur.

In the first case, a man on the king's ship, Gyrðr, dreams that he sees a *trǫllkona* (giantess, lit., "troll-woman," "troll-wife") on a nearby island.

---

[21] *Ynglinga saga*, 29 (chap. 13). Cf. *Historia Norwegiæ*, 74 (chap. 9): *genus demoniorum Norwaico sermone 'mara' uocatur* ("a sort of demon called 'mara' in the Norwegian language").

She holds a trough in one hand and a sword in the other, and the dreamer believes that he sees birds—eagles and ravens—on every ship's prow. Among other things, she warns that "cadaver birds" (*valþiðurr*) will be able to choose whatever meat they want among the dead (*Haralds saga Sigurðarsonar*, 176 [chap. 80]). In the second, and considerably more deadly, case, a different man, Þórðr, dreams that he sees King Haraldr's fleet come to land and he sees there a *trǫllkona* riding a wolf. As quickly as the wolf greedily eats a blood-dripping corpse, he gets another from the troll-wife. She too reveals in a verse the bloodshed that awaits the Norwegian army (*Haralds saga Sigurðarsonar*, 177 [chap. 81]).

The same dreams, with variations, are found in a number of manuscripts and traditions, including *Heimskringla*, *Morkinskinna*, and *Flateyjarbók*. In *Hemings þáttr Áslákssonar*, for example, from the early 1300s, a similar scene occurs in which King Haraldr again plans to invade England.[22] In three dramatic and blood-thirsty verses here too a troll-wife prophecies about the coming battle.[23] But in *Hemings þáttr Áslákssonar* an interesting difference occurs: men awaken when they hear cantillations up in the sky. They look up and see a giantess who rides a wolf *í loftið* "in the sky" and who has a trough full of blood and human limbs. That the troll-wife is presented as being up in the air constitutes an important aspect of the narrative, and if we examine the first dream in *Haralds saga Sigurðarsonar* more closely, it seems that the dreamer himself is represented as being up in the air insofar as he imagines that he can see "over" all the ships: *Hann þóttisk ok sjá yfir ǫll skip þeira* (*Haralds saga Sigurðarsonar*, 176 [chap. 80]). Such scenes are far from infrequent and are found in other Icelandic sagas, as, for example, in *Svarfdælasaga*, and in translated classical literature (e.g., *Trójumanna saga*, 87–88]).[24]

---

[22] There is no question of these various passages being independent testimonies, as some sort of connection must exist between them, as Fellows Jensen shows. On these different traditions and their relationships, see *Hemings þáttr Áslákssonar*, cxxxvii–cxxxix.

[23] "menn voknvðv við þat er kveðit var i lofti ok þotti hverivm sem yfir sinv skipi væri. allir lita i loftið ok sia eina trollkonv riða vargi i loftinv. hon hafði trog i kníam ser fvllt með bloði ok manna lima hom qvað visvr .iij. þersar" (*Hemings þáttr Áslákssonar*, 44–45) (Men awoke at a chanting that was in the air, and it seemed to each of them as if it were above his ship. They all looked up and saw a troll-wife riding a wolf in the sky. She had a trough on her knees, full of blood and human limbs) (Faulkes, 33).

[24] In *Svarfdæla saga*, Karl looks up to heaven (*horfði ... upp í himininn*) and says that he believes he sees one of his relatives, Klaufi, with a grey horse and sled: "Ek þóttumst sjá Klaufa, frænda minn, ríða í loptinu yfir mér, ok sýndist mér hann á grám hesti, ok dragnaði þar eptir sleði; þar þóttumst ek sjá yðr austmenn mína ok sjálfan mik í sleðanum, ok skǫgðu út af hǫfuðin, ok get ek mik þá litum brugðit hafa, er ek sá þetta" (*Svarfdæla saga*, 189 [chap. 22]). Karl's comrade, Gunnarr, says that he sees the same thing, and while they discuss what they have seen, Klaufi

Sturlunga saga displays much delight in prophecies represented as dreams and so-called "warning verses." A scene of special interest comes amid the many premonitions people dream in connection with the coming Battle of Ǫrlygsstaðir. The saga tells of a man, Snæbjǫrn, who lived in Sandvík and who went outside the night before the battle. In the saga, it says that "a woman came into the homefield: she was big and strong, dreary and red of face. She wore a dark blue kirtle, and a link belt;[25] she spoke this verse, turning toward him" (Þa geck kona i tvnið mikil ok þrystilig, daprlig ok rauð-lituð; hvn var i dauck-blaam kyrtli, stocka-bellti hafði hvn um sik; hvn kuað þetta ok sneriz við honum) (*Sturlunga saga*, 1:518). The verse she recites describes future atrocities and deaths, presumably coupled to the coming battle. Then she sang (*kvað*) another verse:

Eisandi ferk unda
undrsamliga funda;
líðk of hól ok hæðir
hart sem fugl inn svarti;
kømk í dal, þars dyljumk,
dánar akrs til vánar,
harmþrungin fórk hingat
heljar ask at velja,
heljar ask ferk velja.[26]

Raging I fare away
To savaging battles.
I wing over holt, over heath
in the path of black ravens.
I come to the vale where all is dark.
The valley of death which awaits me.
Sorrow-harmed I hurry ahead

---

sings several verses in the air (*þá kvað Klaufi í loptinu*) (*Svarfdæla saga*, 190 [chap. 22]). The second verse concludes with the idea that Klaufi roams about among the clouds (*svimm ek nú við ský ... svimm ek nú við ský*). In his translation, Fredrik J. Heinemann uses "I float over the clouds" (*The Saga of the People of Svarfadardal*, 182). Cf. *svimma, svima*, v. "1) svømme [...] 2) fare vidt omkring udaf sin rette Vei eller Stilling" (Fritzner 1973, 3:623) (travel far out of one's intended way or position) and the closely related *sveima*, v. "fare frem og tilbage, hid og did uden bestemt Maal" (travel back and forth, hither and thither without a set goal) (Fritzner 1973, 3:613).

[25] Cf. Cleasby-Vigfusson 1982 [1957], which says of *stokkr*: "the single *square pieces* of a silver belt are called stokkr, whence stokka-belti = *a belt composed of several pieces clasped together*, as worn by ladies in Icel."

[26] I cite this verse following *Skj*, 2:155; for the entire text, see *Sturlunga saga* 1: 518–519, translated in McGrew and Thomas, 1:330–331.

To endure the torment of famine,
The torment of famine my fate.

I have in other contexts suggested that this passage from a so-called "contemporary saga" (*samtíðarsaga*) is more than a simple warning dream, but instead reflects aspects of much older Nordic magical practices (Mitchell 2011:100–103). This judgement depends in part on the woman's appearance, clothes, and behavior. And if we focus on the verse, it quickly becomes apparent that the expressions of movement in the poem used by the woman can be understood to reflect Gná's interest in travel-related phraseology: the woman moves in a rushing or furious manner (*Eisandi ferk*); she glides as hard and determined as a raven (*líðk* [...] *hart sem fugl inn svarti*); she fares sorrow-swollen or sorrow-harmed (*harmþrungin fórk*).

It is noteworthy that in the prose section of the text, the woman goes out in a *tún*, that is, a "corral" or "pen," or "meadow," or "enclosed field," as the word often means in Icelandic (Fritzner: "indhegnet Jordstykke"; Cleasby-Vigfusson: "the 'enclosed' in-field").[27] Ultimately, *tún*, like *kvi* (see below, n. 25), has to do with fencing, paling, railing, and hedges—with, in other words, enclosures and borders (and thus so-called *liminality*). And to this sphere belongs *Äldre Västgötalagen*'s possibly best-known phrase: "Iak sa at þu reet a quiggrindu lösharæþ. ok i trols ham" (I saw that you rode the "witch-ride" [lit., "the pen-gate"], with your hair loose, and in a witch's shape).[28] Presumably these words, along with the related Old High German *Hagazussa* and Old English *hægtesse*, terms also tied to the hedge concept, constitute a special conceptual cluster with important connections to ancient notions of magic and the supernatural in Northern Europe (cf. Mitchell 2005; Hall 2007).

A further clue is found in the much-discussed scene in Greenland in *Eiríks saga rauða*, when Þorbjǫrg "lítilvǫlva"—who is similarly clad in dark

---

[27] Cp. Swedish *kvi*, which also indicates an enclosure, pasture or meadow. The key points from *SAOB* are the following: KVI, f. [sv. dial. *kvi, kvia, kya* m. m., f., kreatursfålla, kringgärdat åkerstycke, trång körväg mellan två gärdesgårdar, motsv. nor. *kvi, kvia*, isl. *kvi*, fålla; av ett germ. *kwiō*, motsv. umbr. *bio*, inhägnad]. 1) mindre inhägnad för kreatur (särsk. får), ofta anordnad med lätt flyttbara stängsel för att underlätta ombyte av plats för inhägnaden; fålla; stundom: hage, liten äng. 2) trång väg mellan två gärdsgårdar. 3) fållgrind av flätvärk. (KVI, f. [Sw. Dial. *kvi, kvia, kya*, etc. f., pen for farm animals, fenced-in field, narrow driveway between two fences, equivalent to Nor. *kvi, kvia*, isl. *kvi*, pen; from a Gmc. *kwiō*, corr. to Umbr. *bio*, fenced]. 1) smaller enclosure for animals (especially sheep), often arranged with easily movable railings to facilitate changing the location of the enclosure; fold; sometimes: garden, small meadow. 2) narrow road between two fences. 3) pen gate of wattle.) On the connection between this word and the phrase from *Västgötalagen*, see Lidén 1914, especially 413–416, and the discussion and literature cited in Holmbäck and Wessén 1979 (1933–1946), 5:125–126.

[28] *SGL*, 1:38; see also Holmbäck and Wessén 1979 (1933–1946) 5:124–128

blue and who also wears a so-called *stokkabelti* "linked belt"—asks for and receives assistance from Guðríðr, who sings *þat kvæði, er hon kallaði Varðlokur* ("that song which she [i.e., Guðríðr's foster-mother] called Varðlokur").[29] Þorbjǫrg later thanks her and comments that "many spirits have come here and think it beautiful to hear the song so well delivered" ("Spákonan þakkar henni kvæðit ok kvað margar þær náttúrur nú til hafa sótt ok þykkja fagrt at heyra, er kvæðit var svá vel flutt") (*Eiríks saga rauða*, 208 [chap. 4]). I believe the phrase "many spirits have come here" expresses an image of magical movement or transport by the spirits similar to what is often later referred to as *magical transvection*, that is movement or floating in and through the air (cf. Mitchell 1997a, 2012b, 2012c).

Should Gná, as Philpotts suggests, be understood as a female counterpart to Skírnir? It is attractive to consider Gná in this way. Skírnir, Freyr's servant, is described as *sendimaðr Freys* (Freyr's messenger) in *Snorra edda* and as *skósvein Freys* (Freyr's page, lit. shoe-boy) both in *Snorra edda* and in the eddic poem *For Scírnis* (*Snorra edda*, 28, 31; *For Scírnis* l. 5). In the Gerðr-myth, he is sent to Iǫtunheimar to get Gerðr's response to Freyr's desire, and in *Snorra edda*, it is also Skírnir who is sent to Svartálfaheim by Alfǫðr to retrieve the restraint Gleipnir, which had been made from six "impossible" ingredients.[30]

But despite the significant similarities between Gná's and Skírnir's functions within the mythology—that is, to, as subordinates, execute errands for others—there appear to be crucial differences as well:

- First, we know what Skírnir's errands are: on one journey, he is to fetch a special chain for the gods, and on the other, he is sent to get the giantess Gerðr's approval for Freyr—what Gná's objectives might be, we, as modern readers, know little.
- Second, Skírnir's mode of travel seems to be normal. Even if the horse he is given by Freyr in *For Scírnis* has magical qualities, the trip Skírnir makes is described without the peculiarities which are attached to Gná's travels: he rode to Iǫtunheim ("Scírnir *reið* í Iǫtunheima"); he rode to where a shepherd sat on a mound ("hann *reið* at þar, er féhirðir sat á haugi"); he is said to have dismounted ("*stiginn* af mars baki"); he will "ride home" ("*ríða* heim");

---

[29] *Eiríks saga rauða*, 207–208 (chap. 4). See Strömbäck 1935:125–139, and my comments in Mitchell 2001b, where I again argue for an interpretation according to which the song called *varðlokur* should be understood as song meant to attract prophetic spirits.

[30] "Þá sendi Alfǫðr þann er Skírnir er nefndr, sendimaðr Freys, ofan í Svartálfaheim til dverga nokkurra ok lét gera fjǫtur þann er Gleipnir heitir." On this myth, see Mitchell 2000b.

and he "rode home" ("*reið* Scírnir heim").³¹ By contrast, Gná "glides" (*líð*) through the air, the same kind of motion used by the maidens who travel over the sea in *Vafðrúðnsimál* 48 and by the troll-wife in *Sturlunga saga*. Additional marked expressions used to describe these supernatural journeys include *eisandi fara* and *svimma við ský*.

- Third, Skírnir is referred to as a *sendimaðr* "messenger" and his trips as a *sendiferð* "mission." It is notable that the lexeme *erindi* "errand" occurs infrequently about his work, just once in *For Scírnis* and once in *Snorra edda*.³² In regular use, Old Norse *erindi* (*ørindi*, and so on) is most often glossed by "errand," "assignment," "business," and the like, but the word has important secondary meanings as well—"speech," "message," "tidings," "announcement"—which can be significant in this context.³³ "Speech," "tidings," "announcement" indicate something other than quotidian language use, rather something closer to formal proclamations and other so-called marked speech. Excellent examples of this kind of use are seen in ecclesiastical literature: Gabriel describes himself to the priest Zacharias in Luke 1:19, saying, "Ec em Gabriel engil. ec stænd fyri guði. ok em ec hingat sændr at boða þer þetta ærende" (I am Gabriel, that stand in the presence of God; and am sent to speak unto thee, and to shew thee these glad tidings. KJV).³⁴ When Gabriel somewhat later tells Mary that "thou shalt conceive in thy womb, and bring forth a son," the paraphrase in the Icelandic *hómilíubók* (c. 1200) says,

    gabriel bar heNe at eyrom et helgasta eyrende (4¹⁵) (Gabriel bore to her ears holy tidings)

    HaN seNde GabRiel engel til fundar við MaRío a þese tíþ. oc þat éyreNde at boþa heNe (61v¹⁴) (He [= God] sent Gabriel to meet Maria at this time and proclaim these tidings to her)³⁵

---

³¹ A possible exception perhaps comes when Skírnir says to his horse, "It is dark outside, I declare it's time for us to go / over the dewy mountain, / through giant realms" (*Skírnir's Journey*, 59) in st. 10 (*Myrkt er úti, / mál kveð ek okkr fara / úrig fjǫll yfir, / þursa þjóð yfir*) (*For Scírnis*, 71).

³² In *For Scírnis*, st. 38, where Skírnir says, *Ørindi mín vill ec ǫll vita* (All my errand will I know) (*Skírnir's Journey*, 63) and in *Snorra edda*, when Skírnir has returned to Ásgarðr and reports on his mission (*eyrendi*) to Freyr (*En er Skírnir sagði Frey sitt eyrindi þá kvað hann þetta, "Lǫng er nótt,"* etc.) (*Edda Sn* 1, 31) (But when Skirnir told Freyr the result of his errand he said this: "Long is a night," etc.) (Faulkes, 32).

³³ See Cleasby-Vigfusson 1982 [1957], *"an errand, message, business, mission," "a message, speech," "a strophe"* or *"the breath,"* and Fritzner, "1) Sag som man vil have fremmet; 2) hvad man opnaar...; 4) hvad der fremføres i Ord, Tale, Foredrag; 5) Strofe i et Digt, = vísa." (1) Case one wants promoted; 2) what one achieves...; 4) what is presented in words, speech, oration; 5) strophe in a poem = *vísa*).

³⁴ Cf. "haec tibi evangelizare," *Vulg Luc* 1,19. *Gamal Norsk Homiliebok*, 106.

³⁵ Both examples are taken from *Ordbog over det norrøne prosasprog* (http://dataonp.hum.ku.dk/).

That Snorri writes of Gná that she is sent by Frigg *at erindum sínum* into different worlds ("Gná, hana sendir Frigg í ýmsa heima at erindum sínum"), such a locution may simply mean that Gná is sent off on different errands, but perhaps with special associations, that is, she is to proclaim tidings to people. A very similar phrase is used in another passage, this one too by Snorri, and it in several key ways resembles what he writes about Gná. And also in this case the individual accomplishes the mission through a journey but without flying or travelling in a normal fashion. The description is in *Ynglinga saga* (18 [chap. 7]) when Snorri enumerates Óðinn's many characteristics:

> Óðinn skipti hǫmum. Lá þá búkrinn sem sofinn eða dauðr, en hann var þá fugl eða dýr, fiskr eða ormr ok fór á einni svipstund á fjarlæg lǫnd at sínum ørendum eða annarra manna.
>
> Finlay and Faulkes, 10[36]
>
> Óðinn changed shapes. Then his body lay as if it was asleep or dead, while he was a bird or an animal, a fish or a snake, and travelled in an instant to distant lands, on his own or other people's business [*ørendum*].

That someone should lie in repose as if sleeping while he himself or his soul—or she herself or her soul—journeyed on different errands is a motive most frequently associated around the world with witchcraft and so-called shamanism, from Regino's *Canon episcopi* to Siberia and South America in modern times, and often the sleeping individual travels through flight. The notion that a person lies sleeping while his or her spirit travels elsewhere perhaps represents a reasonable solution to what Gná means with her assertion that she is not flying yet travels and glides through the air.

Conclusion

Our only direct testimony about Gná comes from Snorri's comments in his *edda*, whereas the three skaldic kennings offer little that helps us understand her, aside from making clear that among the traditional female deities in the North was one named Gná. But we have also seen that a considerable amount of material exists belonging to the same conceptual group of which she is a part, materials we can use to understand her and, inter alia, airborne figures like the *marlíðendr*, *tunríðor*, *myrkríðor*, and *valkyrjor*—but also Christianity's

---

[36] That *erindi* also indicates "breath" seems to me to be tied to possible understanding of both Óðinn and Gná.

englar. We have seen airborne messengers who come bringing prophecies and warnings about future atrocities and catastrophes occur with some frequency in Old Norse texts. At the same time, the possibility that the influence of the Church might have been considerable cannot be ignored, even if some Church teachings (e.g., *Canon episcopi*) ultimately had popular roots.

Where does all this lead us? Is there any possibility of clearing up the issue of what role Gná had in Norse mythology? What function did Gná fill? What did Snorri mean when he wrote "hana sendir Frigg í ymsa heima at eyrindum sínum" (Frigg sends her into various worlds to carry out her business)? I believe that Snorri gives us an answer in a different part of *Gylfaginning* when Frigg—and her ability to foresee the future—are discussed. Þriði adds that the goddess knows people's fates although she does not say what they are ("ok veit hon ørlǫg manna þótt hon segi eigi spár") (*Edda Sn* 1, 21). And following directly thereafter, Þriði cites *Locasenna* 29, where Freyja observes that Frigg knows all fates even if *she does not herself reveal them* ("ørlǫg Frigg / hugg ec at ǫll viti, / þótt hon siálfgi segi") (Frigg knows, I think, all fate / *though she herself does not speak out*) (*Loki's Quarrel*, 85). My conclusion is that it is exactly such fates Gná is out to reveal on Frigg's behalf. In a very meaningful contribution several years ago, Judy Quinn (1998) raised the possibility that one could identify traces of "mythologically conceived feminine omniscience" in certain *fornaldarsögur* in the form of prophecies in eddic style which are often introduced with the phrases like "ok þá varð henni ljóð á munni" (a chant comes to her lips).

And with that we are returned to Gná's bewildering statement: what can it mean when Gná says that she does not fly, yet she journeys and travels through the air (*Ne ek flýg / þó ek fer / ok at lopti líðk*)? Several possibilities are conceivable. The simplest would be that Snorri has been deeply influenced by the *Canon episcopi* (or its ideology), and that it is glimpses of this folk-religious tradition we see in his *edda* when he describes Óðinn and Gná. In both cases he suggests that there are supernatural figures in the mythology who, so to speak, travel without traveling. A further possibility is that he recalls or has learned—heard or read—that in pre-Christian tradition one believed that supernatural spirits could be invoked and sent to convey warnings and prophecies, and that they often did so in the form of birds and other flying beings (cf., e.g., Ingunn Ásdísardóttir 2007:65, 73, 77–79 *et passim*, and Egeler 2011:66–79). As late as during the 1500s Olaus Magnus names a custom according to which ravens could reveal imminent misfortune, a belief reflected already in *Hemings þáttr Áslákssonar* and other saga presentations.[37]

---

[37] XIX, 19, 52. But cf. L. *auspicium ex avibus* and the ancient custom of augury, i.e., interpreting the behavior of birds.

And why is it specifically the Vanir who see and speak with Gná? Could the solution perhaps be tied to the assertion in *Ynglinga saga* (13 [chap. 4]) that it was the *vanadís* Freyja who taught the Æsir-gods the kind of magic called *seiðr*?[38] In order to entice the spirits to the sort of *seiðr*-ritual described in *Eiríks saga rauða*, one can easily imagine that the spirits (*náttúrur*) do not fly in the normal sense, but they nevertheless journey and travel, exactly as Gná does.

Who was Gná? The answer I suggest is that Gná was, or represented, the spirits of prophecy mentioned in the texts. To illustrate this idea with a well-known and specific depiction, could not Gná represent exactly those spirits (*náttúrur*) who are called to Herjólfsness by Guðriðr and Þorbjǫrg "lítilvǫlva" in *Eiríks saga rauða*? This interpretation would also make more rational the last line of the poem about Gná as it appears in Codex Upsaliensis: "gakk um garð vóru" ("gå, de var kring gården" [Go, they were around the enclosure] in Bäckvall 2013:144). The phrase seems to indicate that, as Þorbjǫrg maintains, the prophetic spirits had assembled. Surprising as it may be, it seems that Gná, despite the fact that she is one of the least known and least discussed of the goddesses, is perhaps a key figure in the mythology.

---

[38] "Dóttir Njarðar var Freyja. Hon var blótgyðja. Hon kendi fyrst með Ásum seið, sem Vǫnum var títt" (*Ynglinga saga* 13 chap. 4]). (Njǫrðr's daughter was Freyja. She was a sacrificial priestess. She was the first to teach the Æsir black magic, which was customary among the Vanir) (Finlay and Faulkes, 8).

Chapter 7

ÓÐINN, CHARMS, AND NECROMANCY
HÁVAMÁL 157 IN ITS NORDIC AND EUROPEAN CONTEXTS

To modern sensibilities, few images are more disturbing in Old Norse mythology than the macabre claim made by Óðinn in stanza 157 of *Hávamál*:

> Þat kann ec iþ tólpta, ef ec sé á tré uppi
>   váfa virgilná:
> svá ec ríst   oc í rúnom fác,
>   at sá gengr gumi
>   oc mælir við mic.

> I know a twelfth one if I see, up in a tree,
>   a dangling corpse in a noose,
> I can so carve and colour the runes
>   that the man walks
>   and talks with me.[1]

---

[1] Original publication: "Óðinn, Charms and Necromancy: *Hávamál* 157 in Its Nordic and European Contexts." In *Old Norse Mythology—Comparative Perspectives*, ed. Pernille Hermann, Stephen A. Mitchell, and Jens Peter Schjødt, with Amber Rose Cederström, 289–321. Publications of the Milman Parry Collection of Oral Literature, 3. Cambridge, MA, 2017.
   Note: A version of this essay was originally delivered in Zürich at the October 27–28, 2011 meeting of the Aarhus mythology conference.
   Sayings of the High One, 34. Cf. Martin Clarke's translation (1923:85):
   A twelfth I know: if I see on a tree aloft
   a corpse swinging from a halter,
   I cut and paint runes
   in such wise that the man walks
   and talks with me.

To what belief system does this grisly presentation of necromancy—if, indeed, that is what it is—refer?[2] Does this "charm" (*ljóð*) project pure fantasy or might it reflect what was once an actual practice?

The following comments review possible backgrounds of, and influences on, the text's key claim that Óðinn can make a *virgilnár* speak. They build on the work of many earlier scholars who have considered the issue of the dead and dying in Old Norse mythology, from the pioneering studies by Helge Rosén (1918), Rolf Pipping (1928), H. R. Ellis Davidson (1943), Nora Chadwick (1946), and Folke Ström (1947) to the more recent work of Kirsi Kanerva (2011, 2013), Olof Sundqvist (2009, 2010), John McKinnell (2007) and Vésteinn Ólason (2003).[3] Specifically, the essay looks to place Óðinn's boast in the comparative contexts of native and non-native traditions, exploring on the one hand the Nordic basis for Óðinn's claim, as well as, on the other hand, the more distant but possibly related European reflexes for the charm, especially those linked to classical traditions of the so-called Ferryman's Fee (Thompson 1966: P613), and various Christian saint legends. By identifying more precisely the background against which this thirteenth-century text presents the Nordic world's master of magic making an assertion of this sort, that is, that he can make a hanged man's corpse talk and walk through the use of runes, it may be possible to understand what aspect of pre-Christian Nordic religion and mythology it is that

---

English dictionaries (Cleasby-Vigfusson 1982 [1957], Zoega 1975) do indeed gloss *virgill* as "halter" but in contemporary English, this term, when used in isolation (that is, not in combination with "top" or "neck"), exclusively conveys the sense of a lead, something similar to a bridle, for securing and guiding livestock (at least in the North American dialects I know). By contrast, "noose," although technically referring narrowly to the knot (cf. its etymology), carries with it in common parlance the sense of a hangman's knot and of execution, hence, the expression, "to dangle from the end of a noose" or as Larrington has for *váfa virgilná*, "a dangling corpse in a noose." In line with this interpretation, Fritzner (1973) offers, *Strikke hvori Person hænges for at skille ham af med Livet* (knotted rope in which a person is hanged in order to separate him from life).

[2] Necromancy (< *necromantia*) properly refers to divination through the use of the dead (cf. Greek *nekros* "corpse" + *manteia* "divination"), practices associated with Óðinn in Nordic sources and with such figures as the witch of Endor (1 Sam. 28) in Judeo-Christian tradition; however, confusion, intentional or accidental, with *nigromantia* "black arts" has led to the term's more general sense of "sorcery" and "witchcraft," on which see especially Kieckhefer 1990:151–175 and Kieckhefer 1997:4, 19.

[3] Scholarship on specific topics is, of course, indicated as appropriate, but with regard to the broader, and vast, scholarship on *Hávamál*, I refer readers to the discussion in Harris 1985, the items listed in Lindow 1983, and the series *Kommentar zu den Liedern der Edda* (von See 1997–2019). As regards the literature concerned with various aspects of death and the afterlife in the Old Norse context, I refer readers to the discussion and comprehensive bibliography in Nordberg 2004:313–339.

we witness in *Hávamál* st. 157, how these views relate to pagan and Christian ideology, and just what they can tell us, both about such beliefs and, not least, our medieval religious texts.

Hávamál st. 157 in Its Nordic Setting

The significance of the dead in Nordic mythological texts has been the focus of substantial debate over the years.[4] In fact, a number of passages in extant Nordic sources allude to Óðinn interacting with the dead, occasionally in ways nearly as direct as that portrayed in *Hávamál* st. 157. Notably, on the one hand, there is the matter of postmortem conversations with Mímir.[5] On the other, there are the numerous references to Óðinn and others awakening and speaking with the dead, as presented in such poems as *Vǫluspá*, *Baldrs draumar*, *Hyndloljóð*, and *Grógaldr*.[6]

Allusions in *Gylfaginning* (*Edda Sn* 1, 17) and *Vǫluspá* (st. 28) to the story of Mímir's well, drinking from which Óðinn gains at the cost of an eye, support a general association of Mímir with wisdom and prophetic connections, but it is especially the story laid out in full in *Ynglinga saga* (chap. 4, 7), and referred to in, for example, *Vǫluspá* (st. 46) and *Sigrdrífomál* (st. 14), that excites attention in the current context.[7] According to this tale, Mímir and Hœnir are sent as hostages to the Vanir as part of the exchange that helps

---

[4] In addition to the works cited in the preceding section, cf. the argument by Andreas Nordberg with regard to the age of the *valhǫll* concept and the extensive review of related literature he provides (Nordberg 2004). Of related interest is the "mentalities" perspective Arnved Nedkvitne applies to the matter of pre-Christian Nordic views of the dead (2003:19–47).

[5] On Mímir, see the comments and overviews in Sigurður Nordal 1927:91; de Vries 1956–1957, 1:245–248, 2:82; Halvorsen 1982; Lindow 2001:230–232; and Simek 1993; on possible Celtic influence at work in the case of Mímir, as regards both his head and his well, and for a survey of the literature on the topic, see Simpson 1963–1964, as well as the recent review in Egeler 2013:85–88.

[6] H. R. Ellis Davidson, in a discussion of necromancy, brings these poems together with Saxo's account of Harthgrepa. After describing the necromantic processes of awakening and transmitting knowledge, she notes: "The wisdom which is imparted is of two kinds. Either it consists of a revelation from the future or the past of what is normally hidden—the doom of the world, the fate of the individual or the line of dead ancestors behind a man of noble rank—or else it consists of spells which give power to the possessor, which can guard him against the baleful magic of others, or give him the power to overcome certain perils in his journeyings" (H. R. E. Davidson 1943:156).

[7] The names Mímir and Mímr are both used; however, they occur in complementary distribution: "The form of the name in the formula 'Mímir's head' is always Mímr, otherwise the form is Mímir" (Simek 1993:216).

end the war between this group of gods and the Æsir. The Vanir, believing that they have been defrauded—as Hœnir, when not benefiting from Mímir's advice, proves to be less outstanding than they had thought—decapitate Mímir and send the head to Óðinn:

> Þá tóku þeir Mími ok hálshjoggu ok sendu hǫfuðit Ásum. Óðinn tók hǫfuðit ok smurði urtum þeim, er eigi mátti fúna, ok kvað þar yfir galdra ok magnaði svá, at þat mælti við hann ok sagði honum marga leynda hluti.
>
> Ynglinga saga, 13 [chap. 4]

> Then they seized Mímir and beheaded him and sent the head to the Æsir. Óthin took it and embalmed it with herbs so that it would not rot, and spoke charms over it, giving it magic power so that it would answer him and tell him many occult things.
>
> Ynglinga saga, 8

And a few chapters later, in the enumeration of Óðinn's magical abilities, the same text notes:

> Óðinn hafði með sér hǫfuð Mímis, ok sagði þat honum mǫrg tíðendi or ǫðrum heimum, en stundum vakði hann upp dauða menn or jǫrðu eða settisk undir hanga. Fyrir því var hann kallaðr draugadróttinn eða hangadróttinn.
>
> Ynglinga saga, 18 [chap. 7]

> Óthin had with him Mímir's head, which told him many tidings from other worlds; and at times he would call to life dead men out of the ground, or he would sit down under men that were hanged. On this account he was called Lord of Ghouls or of the Hanged.
>
> Finlay and Faulkes, 11

The story of Óðinn and Mímir's head holds a unique place in the mythology, insofar as in opposition to other prophetic "talking heads" in Old Norse literature (*Eyrbyggia saga*, 116 [chap. 43]), it is specifically Óðinn's charm magic that allows or induces Mímir's head to produce its utterances.[8]

---

[8] Cp. H. R. E. Davidson who suggests that the story of the *vǫlsi* in *Flateyjarbók* (*Völsa þáttr*) may be the closest direct analogue to Mímir's head in that both call for the preservation of a body part later connected to occult knowledge (H. R. E. Davidson 1943:157–158). In *Eyrbyggia saga*, a certain Freysteinn, crossing a scree called Geirvǫr late one evening, encounters a severed human head, which volunteers a quatrain (*staka*) without any manipulation from Freysteinn:

Roðin es Geirvǫr	Geirvǫr is bloodied
gumna blóði,	with the gore of men,

Clearly related to the same mythological complex that assumes that the "Lord of Ghouls" could call the dead to life are such scenes as the following in *Baldrs draumar*, where Óðinn speaks *valgaldr* "a corpse-reviving spell" (lit., "magic of the fallen or slain") in order to awaken the *vǫlva* from her postmortem sleep; she, in turn, utters *nás orð* "corpse-words":

Þá reið Óðinn	fyr austan dyrr
þar er hann vissi	vǫlo leiði;
nam hann vittugri	valgaldr qveða,
unz nauðig reis,	nás orð um qvað:

Baldrs draumar st. 4

Then Odin rode east of the doors,
where he knew the seeress's grave to be;
he began to speak a corpse-reviving spell for the magic-wise woman,
until reluctantly she rose, spoke these corpse-words:

Baldr's Dreams, 235

References in the medieval mythological texts to the summoned, prophesying dead (Thompson 1966: M301.14) naturally raise the question of whether these scenes might reflect beliefs about the dead in earlier periods. In fact, the possibility of pre-Christian traditions of such practices as ritual hanging and the gibbeting of enemies—or parts of enemies—killed in battle in northern Europe has been long bruited about. The most famous example comes half a dozen years after the battle of the Teutoburg Forest (9 CE), when a Roman army encounters the carnage left from the defeat of three of its legions:

> Medio campi albentia ossa, ut fugerant, ut restiterant, disiecta vel aggerata. Adiacebant fragmina telorum equorumque artus, simul truncis arborum antefixa ora. Lucis propinquis barbarae arae, apud quas tribunos ac primorum ordinum centuriones mactaverant.

Tacitus *Annals* 1.61

---

hon mun hylja*	she will hide
hausa manna.	human skulls.

(*Eyrbyggia saga*, 116 chap. 43)

*hylja, lit., "hide, cover." Although there is no question about the pending destruction implied by the verse, translations vary, especially as *vǫr* can also mean "lip." Thus, for example, *Origines Islandicae*, 2:124, gives "Gore-lip is red with warriors' blood / She shall cover skulls of men," whereas Hermann Pálsson and Edwards (*Eyrbyggia saga*, 137) shrewdly offer, "Geirvǫr's lips are red / with human blood; / soon she'll be kissing / human heads." Freysteinn then relates this vision (*fyrirburðr*) to Þorbrandr, to whom the episode portends important events (*þótti honum vera tíðenda-vænligt*).

> In the plain between were bleaching bones, scattered or in little heaps, as the men had fallen, fleeing or standing fast. Hard by lay splintered spears and limbs of horses, while human skulls were nailed prominently on the tree-trunks. In the neighbouring groves stood the savage altars at which they had slaughtered the tribunes and chief centurions.
>
> <div align="right">Tacitus <i>Annals</i> 348–349</div>

This scene, gruesome as the spectacle of human skulls nailed on tree-trunks must have been, lacks some of the eeriness of the scenario of revivified dead hinted at in *Hávamál* st. 157, but it does suggest a frightening range of post-proelial manipulations of the dead in Iron Age northern Europe.[9]

And with that fact in mind, it is noteworthy that this twelfth charm, the mortuary charm reference of *Hávamál* st. 157, is embedded in a martial context: both the verse preceding it and the verse following it are specifically concerned with safety in battle. *Hávamál* 156 claims knowledge of a charm with which a leader could protect his troops such that they go safely to and *from battle*, and *Hávamál* 158 is concerned with protecting a young thane (*þegn*) *in battle*. The placement of verse 157 in *Hávamál* thus fits the mold shaped by both the material and textual evidence of Germanic rituals; indeed, classical writers describe with such vehemence the terrible things the northern tribes do with defeated enemies and their corpses that they might be easily dismissed as propagandistic topoi.[10] Yet in the light of modern

---

[9] On the possibly related matter of animal skulls being ritually displayed, see the case of the Viking Age site at Hofstaðir, Iceland (Lucas and McGovern 2007) and the other examples cited there. The comments by Adam of Bremen regarding the pagan sacrifices in Uppsala bear mentioning in this context as well: "Ex omni animante, quod masculinum est, novem capita offeruntur, quorum sanguine deos placari mos est. Corpora autem suspenduntur in lucum, qui proximus est temple" (*Gesta Hammaburgensis* 4.27) (The sacrifice is of this nature: of every living thing that is male, they offer nine heads, with the blood of which it is customary to placate gods of this sort. The bodies they hang in the sacred grove that adjoins the temple [208]).

[10] Against Tacitus' emotional and elegiac tone, one may, as something of a warning against over-reading, contrast the more blood-thirsty descriptions of other writers, as in the inflamed prose of Florus describing the events in the *Teutoburger Wald*: "Nihil illa caede per paludes perque silvas cruentius, nihil insultatione barbarorum intolerabilius, praecipue tamen in causarum patronos. Aliis oculos, aliis manus amputabant, uni os obsutum, recisa prius lingua, quam in manu tenens barbarus 'tandem' ait 'vipera sibilare desisti'" (*Florus*, 340) (Never was there slaughter more cruel than took place there in the marshes and woods, never were more intolerable insults inflicted by barbarians, especially those directed against the legal pleaders. They put out the eyes of some of them and cut off the hands of others; they sewed up the mouth of one of them after first cutting out his tongue, which one of the barbarians held in his hand, exclaiming, "At last, you viper, you have ceased to hiss" [pp. 339, 341]).

Writing in a similar vein, Jordanes, in his sixth-century *Getica*, maintains that the Goths worshipped "Mars" with terrible rites, including slaying captives as sacrifices: "quem Martem Gothi semper asperrima placevere cultura (nam victimae eius mortes fuere captorum), opinantes

archaeological research (for example, Alken Enge in Jutland), scenes of the sort reported by classical writers about the north European Iron Age may not be as farfetched as once thought.[11] On the other hand, although these instances may provide some opportunity for understanding the historico-cultural context of Óðinn's claim, they should be understood as no more than broad, if highly suggestive, typological parallels to the *Hávamál* image.

Yet a remarkable passage from the twelfth- or thirteenth-century Icelandic law code *Grágás* suggests that even in the Middle Ages the corpses of the deceased (or perhaps near-dead) were not merely the discarded husks of extinguished human life but could also be meaningful sites of debate, differentiation, and classification:

> Þeir menn ero eN iiii. er náir ero kallaþir þott lifi. Ef maðr er hengðr eða kyrcþr eða settr i grof. eþa i scer. eða heptr afialle. eða i floðar mále. Þar heitir gálg nár. oc graf nár. oc sker nár oc fiall nár. Þa menn alla scal iafnt aptr giallda niðgiolldom sem þeir se vegnir þott þeir lifi.
>
> *Grágás*, 202

> There are another four men who are called corpses even though they are alive. If a man is hanged or throttled or put in a grave or on a skerry or tied up on a mountain or below high-water mark, he is called "gallows-corpse" or "grave-corpse" or "skerry-corpse" or "mountain corpse." Those men are all to be atoned for by kindred payments as if they had been killed even though they are alive.
>
> *Laws of Early Iceland*, 182

Some commentators, such as Joonas Ahola, understand this passage in practical terms.[12] An earlier observer, Viktor Rydberg, saw the text in a different

---

bellorum praesulem apte humani sanguinis effusione placandum" (*Getica* 5.41) (Now Mars has always been worshipped by the Goths with cruel rites, and captives were slain as his victims. They thought that he who is the lord of war needed to be appeased by the shedding of human blood [64]).

[11] Early reports on the project "The army and post-war rituals in the Iron Age—warriors sacrificed in the bog at Alken Enge in Illerup Ådal" suggest that here too there may have been ritual manipulations of the corpses (see Lobell 2012). Further research will undoubtedly provide a conclusive answer (cf. Holst, Heinemeier, et al. 2018), but as of the writing of this essay, that some real-world typological parallels existed to the comments made by classical writers may be more likely than once believed. See also "Alken Enge—The mass grave at Lake Mossø" (Museum Skanderborg 2013); "An Entire Army Sacrificed in a Bog" (Berg Petersen 2012); and "Barbarisk fund: Vores forfædre bar ligrester på kæppe" (Persson 2014).

[12] "For acts that were not considered to be killing and therefore did not grant the right to prosecution, such as leaving someone helplessly on a skerry, mountain, cave, or hung (*Grágás*, 265), was

light, noting that the sense of *nár* as used in this section of *Grágás* is not merely "cadaver" and so on, but rather to those who are still conscious and can, for example, suffer.[13] One certainly senses thematic filiations between this and the previously cited passages, but whereas *Hávamál* st. 157 uses *virgilnár* "halter corpse" or "noose corpse" (cf. n. 1 above), *Grágás* here uses the term "gallows corpse" (*galgnár*).[14]

Gallows in non-mythological medieval Nordic contexts generally show them being used for execution, as when in *Magnúss saga berfœtts* (216–218 [chap. 6]), Egill and Þórir are hanged for raising forces against the king. But, of course, once the execution phase of the process was over, hanged corpses, so positioned, transformed into highly effective and tactile warnings for others and could be left gibbeted, hanging—and visible—until they rotted off the rope, thus becoming public spectacles and expressions of authority visible for long distances, which, of course, accounts for the fact that they were often placed on heights like Galgberget [lit. "Gallows Hill"] in Södermalm, overlooking late medieval Stockholm, and near highly trafficked areas, such as crossroads.

Beyond the gallows' function in daily life as the ultimate legal sanction and as a potent demonstration of centralized power, gallows and the hanged are frequently mentioned in mythological and semi-mythological contexts that suggest that they also provided the means of torture, pain, and, as in the previous case, spectacle, both as an end in itself and as part of Odinic rituals of varying interpretations, such as initiation.[15] An example of the first type

---

likewise to be paid compensation (*wergild*), and the one at fault was responsible for that compensation" (Ahola 2014:82).

[13] "Här tillämpas ordet *nár* således på varelser med medvetande och förmåga att lida, men under den förutsättning, att de äro sådana, som hemfallit under straff afsedda att icke upphöra, så länge de äro i stånd att förnimma dem" (Rydberg 1886–1889, 1:324). (Here the word *nár* is applied to beings with consciousness and the ability to suffer, but with the understanding that they are those who have incurred punishments not meant to cease, as long as they are able to perceive them.)

[14] In addition to the probable synonymy of the two "corpse" terms, I note that even the devices from which they were suspended were likely to be thought of as equivalent: *galgtré* "gallows tree" is a relatively common collocation, used interchangeably with *galg* "gallows" (see *Magnúss saga berfœtts*, chap. 6). Although *tré* principally indicates arboreal organisms, it can also mean the products of them, such as "beam"—exactly what is needed to construct an H-shaped *galgtré*. On the other hand, Old Swedish and Old Danish sources tend to say that a thief should be hanged on either of the alliterative pair, *galgha æller gren* "gallows or limb," suggesting perhaps a perceived need for more immediate satisfaction of the death penalty than a constructed gallows would allow. Cf. the term *vargtré* "wolf [i.e., outlaw]-tree" for "gallows" in *Hamðismál* st. 17.

[15] Cf. Jens Peter Schjødt, who argues for the social reality of such a practice as a *rite de passage* within pre-Christian cultic practices (Schjødt 2008:173–206; see also Sundqvist 2009, 2010). As

Chapter 7. Óðinn, Charms, and Necromancy   133

Figure 7.1. Scene of sacrifices? Detail from Lärbro Stora Hammars I. (Bunge Museum, Gotland). Photo by the author.

is found in *Hálfs saga ok Hálfsrekka*, when Hjǫrleifr is hung by his shoelaces between two fires. When he eventually escapes, Hjǫrleifr in turn hangs his enemy on the same gallows (*gálg*) which had been intended for his death.[16]

In other instances, such as *Gautreks saga*, when the mock sacrifice of King Víkarr turns real (chap. 7), the scene strikes most readers as being informed by a series of surviving narratives about those "hanging" between life and death: Óðinn's self-sacrifice on the World Tree; the comments in Saxo about sacrificial practices at Uppsala; the thanatological ritual in which Óðinn spouts numinous knowledge between the fires in *Grímnismál* (albeit a non-hanging image).[17] It is, of course, scenes of these types that many believe we see on one of the panels of the Lärbro Stora Hammars I stone on Gotland (figure 7.1).[18] Whatever else the picture stone is meant to depict, it

---

Sundqvist notes, citing Bugge 1881–1889:291–293, the picture is far from clear, as the medieval Latin *pendente in patibulo* "hanging in the gallows" was a common expression for the Crucifixion.

[16] "Hjǫrleifr konúngr var uppfestr í konúngs hǫll með skóþvengjum sínum sjálfs, millum elda tveggja" (King Hjǫrleifr was hung up in the king's hall with his own shoe laces between two fires) and, after being stabbed to death, "Reiðar konúng lèt hann hengja dauðan á gálga þann, er hann hafði honum ætlat" (He [King Hjǫrleifr] had King Hreiðarr hanged on that gallows which he [King Hreiðarr] intended for him [King Hjǫrleifr])(*Hálfs saga ok Hálfsrekka* 1829–1830:34 [chap. 8]). I read these two locations as being the same, although I recognize that the wording does not absolutely demand it. Cf. the "hanging" in *Hrafnkels saga Freysgoða* (chap. 5).

[17] As Hans-Joachim Klare suggests, the dead could know things even an otherwise all-knowing god would be eager to discover: "Die Toten wissen alles, was geschieht, sie sehen in die Zukunft, drum haben sie ein Wissen, das den nach Allwissen dürstenden Gott immer aufs neue reizt, sie zu befragen" (Klare 1933–1934:16) (The dead know everything that happens, they see into the future, and thus they possess knowledge that excites that god thirsting for omniscience to question them). The literature in this area is vast: Ström 1947; Kragerud 1981; and H. R. E. Davidson 1988 remain useful portals into it; important recent studies include Schjødt 2008:173–224; Patton 2009:213–236; and Sundqvist 2009 and 2010.

[18] See the discussion in McKinnell 2007.

clearly means to show a warrior figure hanging from a tree in the context of a ritual.

Also significant in *Hávamál* st. 157 is the gallows-corpse (*virgilnár*) which Óðinn claims to be able to control: such a person might be a criminal or a sacrificial victim (perhaps even both). In fact, we meet not-quite-actually-dead cadavers in a variety of forms in the Old Norse world.[19] One type of undead dead populating Old Norse literature is the *haugbúi*, the mound-dweller, essentially always male, who seems to live in an almost human-like way, occasionally in the company of others, within his mound. Among mound-dwellers, there seem to be a variety of types: at one extreme, there are the malicious, terrifying ones like the *haugbúi Kárr inn gamli* in *Grettis saga Ásmundarsonar* (56–59, [chap. 18]) who frightens all the farmers off the island until Grettir dispatches him (Vésteinn Ólason has called this type "the ungrateful dead"). At the other extreme are the benevolent undead like the mound-dweller Brynjarr in *Þorsteins þáttr uxafóts*, who significantly helps Þorsteinn. In between lie morally neutral types like the mound-dweller in *Kumlbúa þáttr*.[20]

Apparently, a different category comprises the awakened dead female seeress or *vǫlva*, perhaps the best-known type to modern audiences, as in *Grógaldr*, *Vǫlospá*, and *Baldrs draumar*. The division of these two types, the male *haugbúi* and the well-informed female *vǫlva*, although not absolute, is fairly consistent, with some important exceptions, as in *Hyndloljóð*, which features an awakened giantess who does not spew forth numinous knowledge in the manner of the *vǫlur* but rather engages, formally at least, in a wisdom contest with Freyja on their ride to Valhǫll (*Sennom við ǫr sǫðlom!*, etc. st. 8) (Let's contend from our saddles!) (*The Song of Hyndla*, 246). Another exception, in this case of stunning proportions, comes in Book I of Saxo's *Gesta Danorum*. Here, in a gender-reversing scene, we witness a recently dead man being used by a female worker of magic, when the giantess, Harthgrepa (significantly, perhaps, dressed as a man), and Haddingus come upon a house

---

[19] This topic has attracted much attention over the years; see Klare 1933–1934; Ohlmarks 1936; H. R. E. Davidson 1943; and Chadwick 1946.

[20] On these types, see my comments in Mitchell 2009b. In his fine, wide-ranging discussion of death and the dead in Icelandic literature, Vésteinn Ólason notes of the ungrateful dead, the sort we see in Kárr, that "they are resentful of the living, or some of them, and a strong desire to cause damage and destruction binds them to earthly life" (Vésteinn Ólason 2003:169; on related concepts in Old Icelandic, such as the *draugr*, see Ármann Jakobsson 2011).

where the funeral of the master of the place, who has just died, is occurring.[21] Then, Saxo continues, Harthgrepa calls his spirit in this manner, with the following results:

> Ubi magicę speculationis officio superum mentem rimari cupiens, diris admodum carminibus ligno insculptis iisdemque linguę defuncti per Hadingum suppositis hac uoce eum horrendum auribus carmen edere coegit:
>
> > Inferis me qui retraxit, execrandus oppetat
> > Tartaroque deuocati spiritus poenas luat! *etc.*
>
> Gesta Danorum 1.6.4–1.6.5

Desiring to probe the will of the gods by magic, she inscribed most gruesome spells on wood and made Hading insert them under the corpse's tongue, which then, in a voice terrible to the ear, uttered these lines:

Let the one who summoned me, a spirit from the underworld, dragged me from the infernal depths, be cursed and perish miserably, *etc.*

The History of the Danes, 23

This "spirit" eventually foretells their fate, but most of all he curses in direst terms "the one who summoned me ... dragged me from the infernal depths."[22]

This scene is perhaps the closest we come to a literary presentation of what Óðinn suggests in *Hávamál* st. 157, when he says of the *virgilnár* that "I can so carve and colour the runes / that the man walks / and talks with me" (*Sayings of the High One*, 34). In Saxo, the dead man responds to Harthgrepa's use of runic magic, not only speaking with her but also journeying back to the world of the living. Other loquacious corpses occur in Old Norse literature, of course, such as Guðríðr's deceased husband, Þorsteinn Eiríksson, in *Eiríks saga rauða* (chap. 6) and in *Grænlendinga saga* (chap. 6). He too prophesies, but unlike the dead man in Saxo, his supernatural feats are generally understood to relate to the Christian-themed tone of the saga, and in any event, he is not responding to the manipulation of a magician.[23]

---

[21] I note here the similarity of this scene to that in *Hervarar saga ok Heiðreks konungs* (chap. 3), when Angantýr's daughter, looking to fulfill a male warrior's role, goes to his mound and awakens him.

[22] On this passage, see further the comments in *Saxo Grammaticus: The History of the Danes* 2:30, as well as my remarks in Mitchell 2008a.

[23] Perhaps a more proximate example comes through the manipulations of Þrándr in *Færeyinga saga*, when he apparently causes three dead men, or their apparitions, to appear in order to

Figure 7.2. The one-eyed figure from the stave church at Hegge, Norway. "Hegge stavkirke, maske på stav - 1" by John Erling Blad—Own work. Licensed under CC BY-SA 3.0 via Wikimedia Commons. http://commons.wikimedia.org/wiki/File:Hegge_stavkirke,_maske_p%C3%A5_stav_-_1.jpg#/media/File:Hegge_stavkirke,_maske_p%C3%A5_stav_-_1.jpg.

The rune-awakened corpse in Saxo does not walk, as Óðinn's comments might lead us to expect, at least not in a normal sense, but he does move from the underworld to our world, the world of the living. And certainly he talks, if reluctantly and with ire, once the rune stick has been placed under his tongue. Saxo's presentation is then not that distant from what *Hávamál* st. 157 suggests.

That this charm, among others, focuses on the tongue of the dead is not surprising: after all, Old Norse *tunga* refers to the physical entity, as well as to the general concept of a language (as in the expression *á danska tungu*), that is, both to one of the busiest muscular organs in the human body, the one necessary for the production of speech, *and* to the resulting product of such activity. It has been conjectured that Óðinn's cognomen, "god of the hanged," a name that comes to us in a variety of forms, including *hanga-Týr, hangaguð, hangadróttinn, heimþinguðr hanga*,[24] should be understood in relation to sacrificial hanging of the sort pictured on figure 7.1 (Lärbro Stora Hammars I), especially where asphyxia (rather than breaking the cervical vertebrae) is understood as the cause of death. Hanging in this way typically causes a protruding, purplish tongue, just the sort of image useful, necessary even, for forced thanatological revelations of great secrets, of being "between two worlds" in Jens Peter Schjødt's evocative phrase (2008). It is also one of the reasons scholars have been inclined to believe that the one-eyed figure from the stave church at Hegge, Norway, should be understood with reference to Odinic belief systems (figure 7.2).

I note, however, that Saxo's reluctant, revelatory corpse is not the only case where tongues play an important role in stories involving interactions between the living and the dead. In fact, we have something of an inversion of Saxo's story pattern in *Þorleifs þáttr jarlsskálds*; here it is the dead poet, Þorleifr's *haugbúi*, who comes out of his mound, on which the aspiring but inadequate poet, Hallbjǫrn, regularly sleeps. Hallbjǫrn's attempts at

---

discover the causes and places of their deaths. The description of his preparations includes setting a large fire in the fire pit, making four trellises or frames, drawing nine squares, and requesting that no one speak to him: "Þrandr hafde þa latit gera ellda mykla j ellda skala ok grindr fiorar lætr hann gera med fiorum hornnum ok íx ræita ristr Þrandr alla uega vt fra grindunum en hann setzst astol mille elldz ok grindanna hann bidr þa nu ekki vid sig tala ok þeir gera suo" (*Færeyinga saga*, 88 [chap. 40]). (Thrand had had big fires made in the hearth-room, and he had four hurdles [*frames*] set up with four corners, and he scratches nine squares all around out from the hurdles, and he sits on a stool between the fires and the hurdles. Now he gives orders that nobody is to talk to him, and they do as he says) (*The Faroe Islanders' Saga*, 81).

[24] *Víga-Glúms saga*, 95 (chap. 27); Hávarðr halti ísfirðingr st. 14 in *Skj* 1:182; *Ynglinga saga*, 18 (chap. 7); *Heiðarvíga saga*, 291 (chap. 26). Cf. the additional *heiti* enumerated in Falk 1924:59–61, and his discussion concerning *haptaguð* "god of fetters" (?) (62).

composing poetry never go further than the opening line, "Here lies a poet" ("Hér liggr skáld"). Þorleifr pulls the tongue of the would-be poet ("togar hann á honum tunguna"), recites a verse for the aspirant to memorize, and instructs Hallbjǫrn to compose a poem praising Þorleifr and to be certain that the poem is complex with regard to both meter and metaphor. Hallbjǫrn succeeds and goes on to become a great skald (*Þorleifs þáttr jarlsskálds*, 222–229 [Chs. 5–8]). Here, the tongue as the generative organ of speech, and thus of poetic production, is essentialized and its manipulation by the dead poet, Þorleifr, is the turning point in Hallbjǫrn's endeavor to acquire poetic ability.[25]

The tongue and its relation to the production of speech also plays a key role in *Þorsteins þáttr uxafóts*. This story tells of how the hero of the *þáttr* enters a grave mound, where he finds there two fraternal *haugbúar* and their retinues. The helpful brother, Brynjarr, explains that his brother Oddr, the evil one, has a special piece of gold that, when placed under the tongue of an aphasic person, gives them the power of speech.[26] Importantly, Þorsteinn's mother, Oddný, had been born without the ability to speak and must respond to others by writing on a rune stick or *kefli* ("Oddný reist rúnar á kefli, því at hon mátti eigi mæla"). Þorsteinn wrests the gold piece from Oddr and gives it to his mother; when it is shortly thereafter placed

---

[25] Without wishing to strain the soup too thin, I note that Hallbjǫrn's poem specifically praises Þorleifr's libeling of Earl Hákon and that the story, which is, after all, about Þorleifr, follows with the comment that his brothers go to Norway the summer after his death, but it was not in the cards for them to kill Hákon, that is, "to have his head [lit., scalp; "head-skin"] at their feet" (En þeim varð eigi lagit þá enn at standa yfir hǫfuðsvǫrðum Hákonar jarls (*Þorleifs þáttr jarlsskálds*, 229 [chap. 8]). When in *Óláfs saga Tryggvasonar*, Hákon is dispatched, is it then mere coincidence that the following scene takes place: "Þá fór Óláfr konungr ok fjǫlði bónda með honum út til Niðarhólms ok hafði með sér hǫfuð Hákonar jarls ok Karks. Sá hólmr var þá hafðr til þess at drepa þar þjófa ok illmenni, ok stóð þar gálgi, <u>ok lét hann þar til bera hǫfuð Hákonar jarls ok Karks</u>. Gekk þá til allr herrinn ok œpði upp ok grýtti þar at ok mæltu, at þar skyldi níðingr fara með ǫðrum níðingum. Síðan láta þeir fara upp í Gaulardal ok taka þar búkinn ok drógu í brott ok brenndu" (*Óláfs saga Tryggvasonar*, 298 [chap. 50]; emphasis added). (Then King Óláfr and a large number of farmers with him went out to Niðarhólmr, taking with him the heads of Jarl Hákon and Karkr. This little island was at that time used for executing thieves and criminals on, and a gallows stood there, and he had the heads of Jarl Hákon and Karkr taken there. Then the whole army went there and shouted out and threw stones at it, saying that there should a villain go with other villains. Afterwards they got people to go up into Gaulardalr and get the body and dragged it away and burned it) (Finlay and Faulkes, 298).

[26] "Oddr hefir at varðveita gull þat, er sú náttúra fylgir, at hverr maðr, sem mállaus er ok leggr þat undir tunguraétr sér, þá tekr þegar mál sitt, ok af því gulli má móðir þín mál fá" (*Þorsteins þáttr uxafóts*, 353 [chap. 6]). (Odd keeps a piece of gold whose nature is that whatever dumb person puts that gold under the root of his or her tongue will then gain the power of speech and by means of that gold your mother will be able to speak (*The Tale of Thorstein Bull's-Leg*, 346).

"under the root of her tongue" ("undir tungurætr henni"), Oddný acquires and retains the power of speech.[27]

These plays on "tongue-power"—the gold object that cures Oddný, said to have been placed "undir tunguraetr henni"; the gift of mantic speech in Saxo's *Gesta Danorum* that comes with the insertion of a rune charm under the tongue of the corpse; and so on—suggest that the various authors had degrees of familiarity with the same tradition from which *Hávamál* st. 157 derives. Of related interest to these later literary sources are examples of actual "tongue objects," or "Charon's obol" as archaeologists often term them (on which see below).

Such mortuary practices, although not common, are in evidence in early Scandinavian graves from, for example, Gotland and Sjælland. In fact, instances of the "Charon's obol" have been documented in Scandinavia dating back to at least the late Roman Iron Age (see Almgren 1903; Shetelig 1908; Stjerna 1912:101-102; H. R. E. Davidson 1943:37; Gräslund 1965-1966). Summarizing much of this research, Signe Horn Fuglesang writes, "the best evidence for the custom in the Viking period comes from eastern Sweden, while it seems to have been rare in Denmark and the evidence from Norway and Finland is inconclusive" (Fuglesang 1989:21-22). She notes further that "graves of the 13th and 14th centuries have documented [the practice] from Sweden, Scania and Norway" (Fuglesang 1989:22). The tradition arguably continued even into modern folk beliefs, as there are graves from the 1700s that reflect the continuity of the practice.[28]

---

[27] Noteworthy here are the Philomela-like aspects of the story line in the *þáttr*—the inability to speak, pregnancy, and so on.

[28] See especially Gräslund 1965-1966. The recent excavation of an early eighteenth-century site in which 14 small silver coins were found in 13 graves suggests the possibility that this practice continued up to modern times: "Myntfynden för tanken till den grekiska mytologin, som omtalar att färjekarlen Charon. [...] Att denna hedniska sedvänja kan ses i gravar från tidigt 1700-tal är ovanligt, och har möjligen att göra med att begravningarna inte ägde rum på den vanliga kyrkogården, och att de som begravts avlidit i en fruktad farsot. Mynten kan således ha fått följa de döda i graven som en extra försäkran om att man trots detta skulle få komma till himmelriket."(Jacobsson 2002:17). (The discoveries of coins makes one think of Greek mythology, which speaks of the ferryman Charon [...] That this pagan custom is to be seen in graves from the early 1700s is uncommon, and may be connected to the fact that the burials did not take place in a normal cemetery, and that those buried died in a dreaded plague. The coins may thus have followed the dead in their graves as extra assurance that one would despite that enter Heaven.)

Hávamál st. 157 and the Learned and Ecclesiastical Tradition

As we have seen, there exists a rich native tradition that touches, or appears to touch, on the images suggested by *Hávamál* st. 157. But is that sufficient to explain the background against which Óðinn formulates his claim to know how to reanimate the dead and make them talk? Perhaps, but certainly there is more to the medieval cultural tapestry concerned with the dead and dying than these native traditions alone. In the end, we may decide that the influence of foreign learned and ecclesiastical materials is slight and favor instead the domestic traditions, but let us first examine the external materials and assess the effects they might have had.

As literature and as homily, a striking Judeo-Christian parallel to *Hávamál* st. 157 in which a dead person is raised and speaks specifically, like Mímir, for the purpose of prophesying, is the so-called "witch of Endor" (I Sam: 28), a narrative known to have been used in sermons in northern Europe by, for example, Ælfric (*Macarius and the Magicians, Saul and the Witch of Endor*). In this necromantic narrative, the spirit of the dead prophet Samuel is raised by a female medium; the shade converses with Saul and, like the spirit of the dead man in Saxo, he complains of having been disturbed and of having been "brought up," apparently out of the world of the dead.[29]

On a related issue, namely the role of the severed head, the story of John the Baptist's decapitation (Matt. 14:1–11; Mark 6:14–29) naturally meant that trunkless heads often played a key role in medieval Christian iconography. The Baptist is the most obvious figure of this sort to modern eyes; however, medieval hagiology includes a large number of saints whose legendary martyrdoms include decapitation. And among these, there are dozens of particular interest in the current discussion, such as the cephalophoric saints, that is those saints who, after being beheaded, pick up their detached heads and carry them, sometimes speaking as they go.

Very likely the most famous of such saints in the Middle Ages was St. Denis, the first bishop of Paris and one of the city's patron saints, who was

---

[29] On this scene and Nordic mortuary beliefs, see H. R. E. Davidson 1943:168–169. Cf. the comparison Clive Tolley makes between the biblical scene and *Vǫluspá*, in which he concludes that the echoes of the Bible in the poem are "clear and intentional" (Tolley 2009:485–486). He goes on to say, in an excellent statement about the full range of purportedly pre-Christian materials, that this view "does not mean that the pagan elements […] are not genuine, but it suggests these elements are being structured and perhaps interpreted in a way which may not have taken place in earlier, more purely pagan times."

martyred in the mid-third century CE. Over time, the legend of St. Denis developed considerably (cf. Spiegel 1983) and by the thirteenth-century *Legenda aurea* of Jacobus de Voragine, it acquired the form in which it is best-known today: having been beheaded, St. Denis picks up his head and walks several miles to the site of the present cathedral basilica of Saint Denis, accompanied by the singing of angels (*Legenda aurea*, 685).[30] Some later versions of the legend add that the head of St. Denis preached throughout the journey.[31] The point is, in other words, that there existed a notable emphasis in the Middle Ages on cephalic imagery in religion and law: this theme, as Esther Cohen argues, intensified over time, and by the high Middle Ages there is, as she writes, "a gradually growing shared perception of the head as the most important organ for life and identity, which derived from different fields of action and influenced different fields of knowledge" (Cohen 2013:73).[32]

A similar type of decapitation narrative as that which came to signify St. Denis can be seen in the story of St. Edmund. According to the tenth-century *Passio Sancti Eadmundi* of Abbo of Fleury, the East Anglian king, Edmund, is martyred by the Danish army; according to the legend, he is tortured and beheaded due to his unwillingness to reject his Christian faith. The severed head of the martyr is deposited in a forest by the invaders and when the locals finally venture forth, they discover his headless body and begin a search for the missing head. In response to their cries, the head identifies its location by yelling, "Here, here, here!"[33]

---

[30] This part of the legend is faithfully reproduced in the Old Swedish translation of *Legenda aurea*, *Ett fornsvenskt legendarium*, here from Codex Bildstenianus (early 1400s): "Sidhan ledhis han ther wt ater (at / for) hedhan domara (mz sinom kompanom) at thola manga nya pinor: Ok halshuggus mz yxe. The thre. vm sidhe. Dyonisius ok hans compana rusticus ok eleutherius widher mercurii monster. Sancti dyonisii (liikir / licame) reste sik wp siælfuir. Ok grep howdhit mz armomin. Ok gik æpter ængla ledsagh(ara) Ok himna liuse. thwo mila wægh fra halshuggeno som nu kallas martyrium biærgh til thæn stadh han ligger nu" (*Sagan om Sankt Dionysius* 1:344) (Then he was led before a heathen judge with his companions and suffered many new torments. And the three, Dionysius and his companions, Rusticus and Eleutherius, were beheaded with an axe at the temple of Mercury. The body of Saint Dionysius raised itself up and grasped its head with its arms and followed angels and heavenly light for two miles from the place of the beheadings which is now called the hill of martyrs (Montmartre) to that place where he now lies).

[31] I note, however, that I have not been able to identify this particular embellishment in any of the medieval sources.

[32] Cf. the many examples and themes covered by the essays in Tracy and Massey 2012; Gardeła and Kajkowski 2013 (many of which concern Old Norse topics); and Baert et al. 2013.

[33] "Vispillonum sane more pluribus pedententim invia perlustrantibus, cum jam posset audiri loquens, ad voces se invicem cohortantium, et utpote socii ad socium alternatim clamantium, Ubi es? illud respondebat, designando locum, patria lingua dicens, *Her, her, her*. Quod interpretatum Latinus sermo exprimit, Hic, hic, hic." (*Passio Sancti Eadmundi*, 40) (A number of the

This well-known motif (Thompson 1966: V229.25, "Severed head of saint speaks so that searchers can find it") appears to have had recognizable resonance in medieval Scandinavia, if in a modified version: in a legend first recorded ca. 1200 in the officium *Celebremus karissimi*, the eleventh-century English missionary, Sigfrid, undertakes conversion activity in Swedish Småland, at Växjö, accompanied by his nephews, Unaman, Sunaman, and Vinaman, all of whom are also ecclesiastics. They are engaged in the construction of a church at Växjö, dedicated, appropriately as it turns out, to John the Baptist. While Sigfrid is away in Västergötland, purportedly in order to baptize King Olof Skötkonung at Husaby, a group of pagans kills and beheads the three nephews. Their heads are placed in a wooden tub which is then weighed down with an enormous stone and sunk in the middle of the nearby lake. When Sigfrid returns, he is miraculously led to the heads' location in Lake Växjö when he sees three lights over the lake. The heads are floating on the water and speak to him. This legend gained traction quickly, and already by the end of the thirteenth century, the severed, and seemingly still bleeding, heads of the three nephews formed the seal of Växjö cathedral chapter.[34]

Thus, the idea of the recently dead being reanimated and regaining their capacity for speech and locomotion might not have been as farfetched or macabre to a medieval audience as it seems to us today. But these scenes apparently play out within the lives of saints as demonstrations of God's will, miracles with which to show the extent of God's power and love. Moreover, as noted above, there exists a long-standing Mediterranean tradition of "tongue objects," generally referred to as the "Ferryman's Fee" or "Charon's obol," special articles placed in the mouths of the dead. "Charon's obol" is, of course, a name that invokes the most famous classical example of this practice, but it is a tradition by no means limited to the world of the Greeks and Romans.[35] Indeed, the same practice of placing objects (often but

---

party, like corpse-searchers, were gradually examining the out-of-the-way parts of the wood, and when the moment had arrived at which the sound of a voice could be heard, the head, in response to the calls of the search-party mutually encouraging one other, and as comrade to comrade crying alternately "Where are you?" indicated the place where it lay by exclaiming in their native tongue, Here! Here! Here! In Latin the same meaning would be rendered by Hic! Hic! Hic! [41]). Cf. subsequent reworkings of the passion, such as Ælfric's *Life of St Edmund*, which build on this scene (2:324–325).

[34] See the image in L-O. Larsson 1975:13. On the legend, see T. Schmid 1931; Lundén 1967; L-O. Larsson 1975; and *Celebremus karissimi*, 9–17.

[35] "Charon's fee: putting coin in dead person's mouth to pay for ferry across Styx" (Thompson 1966, P613). In her wide-ranging review of the literary and archaeological evidence for the practice in the classical world, Susan T. Stevens summarizes the phenomenon thus: "According

not always coins) in the mouths of the dead was already known among the Egyptians, Phoenicians, and others from periods anterior to its use by the Greeks (see Grabka 1953:3, 6; Wolff 2002:136).

It should be noted too that this concept, or at least something that looks very much like it, is not limited to the Old World but is also found in the pre-Columbian New World, as in the case of the Cañete valley of South America, where, for example, small copper discs were found in the mouths of Peruvian mummies.[36] Noting the existence of these cases is not, of course, meant to be an argument about *function*, which, to the extent we understand it, would likely have been quite discursive in these various instances; rather what interests us are the similar techniques, methods, operational elements, and outcomes of such practices.

From the perspective of our medieval data-points, perhaps the single most important aspect of the "Charon's obol" tradition is how it influenced Christian tradition, specifically, the Church's adaptation of the "Ferryman's Fee" into the so-called Last Rites, where the Eucharist is administered to the dying, the so-called *Viaticum*. The history of the relationship of the pagan *viaticum*, the provisions for the journey (< *via* "road") into the afterlife, and the Christian *Viaticum*, is complex, and it is a history not without its disputes (cf. Grabka 1953). In the early Church, such provisions or preparations might include baptism, prayers, or any other means that could help the dying in their transition into the next world. It could also refer to the Eucharist generally, until, in the words of the *Catholic Encyclopedia* in their entry on *Viaticum*, "finally it acquired its present fixed, exclusive, and technical sense of Holy Communion given to those in danger of death" (*Catholic Encyclopedia* 2003). It was, as Grabka has argued, *both* a Christian bulwark against the need to employ "Charon's obol" and an adaptation of

---

to ancient authors, the custom of 'Charon's obol' has four characteristics, though there are some variations in their discussions: (1) a single low-denomination coin (2) is placed in the mouth (3) at the time of death (4) to pay Charon's fare" (Stevens 1991:216). Among other motifs connected with this tradition are: A672.1.1, "Charon exacts fee to ferry souls across Styx"; E431.11, "Coin placed in mouth of dead to prevent return"; and E489.3, "Forgetting Charon's fee" (Thompson 1966). On the many, widely dispersed manifestations of the tradition, see Grinsell 1957.

[36] Regarding Peruvian practices in the Cañete valley, Kroeber and O'Neale write: "Most mummies had copper or occasionally silver sheets or ornaments bestowed about the head, most frequently perhaps in the mouth, but also about the ears or elsewhere on the face. Where the metal is entirely corroded it shows in green stains on the bone or teeth, as previously mentioned. This burial habit prevails for the Late period of all parts of the Peruvian coast which I have visited, from north of Trujillo to south of Nazca, frequently even as regards the graves of the poor. The most frequent disposal is of a round or oval sheet of thin metal about the size of a coin, apparently laid on the tongue—a sort of Charon's obol." (Kroeber and O'Neale 1926, 4:247)

that same tradition to Christian ritual.[37] But either way, whether the custom was preemptive or adaptive, it was also about inserting something highly symbolic into the mouths of the dead and dying.

A final, further "learned" parallel to *Hávamál* st. 157 comes from the medieval world of natural magic, specifically the lapidary tradition. In this tradition, certain stones, when placed in the mouth, possessed the occult power to make the speaker reveal truths, including prophecies. Compendious works detailing the power of stones and gems are known already from antiquity, but the best-known example in medieval Europe was the eleventh-century *De Lapidibus* by Bishop Marbod of Rennes.[38] The earliest Nordic example I have found of this tradition of stones with prophetic properties being placed under the tongue comes from an Old Danish translation of Marbod (ca. 1300), which reads in part:[39]

> Haldær man hanum [*Celonites*] undær ren tungæ. tha ma han spa.[40]
>
> *Stenbog*, 191
>
> If one places it under a clean [alt., pure] tongue then he may soothsay.

---

[37] The wide-ranging learning displayed by Grabka in his review of the traditions which led to the *Viaticum* does not, however, prevent him from seeming to hold two contradictory views of this history. Cp. "The ancient funeral rite of placing the *viaticum* coin in the mouth of the corpse was responsible for the superstition in Christian burials of administering the *Viaticum* to the dead" (Grabka 1953:42) *versus* "the pagan custom of placing a coin into the mouth of the dead as a *viaticum* for the journey of the soul to its after-life never gained a firm foothold among the Christians. They had their own *Viaticum* with which they provided their departing brethren: the Holy Eucharist" (Grabka 1953:27) and "Seen in its essentials, the ancient Christian custom of providing the dying faithful with the Eucharist as their *Viaticum* for the journey to eternity was neither derived from nor inspired by the pagan *viaticum*; it was based on the revealed truths of Christianity" (Grabka 1953:42).

[38] On the learned tradition of magic in the Nordic world—lapidaries, alchemy, and so on—see esp. Mitchell 2008c, as well as Mitchell 2011.

[39] On these translations, see *Stenbog*, LXVIII-CII, and Brix 1943:38–39.

[40] The complete entry under the heading Chelonites runs: "Silenites hetær en steen. oc føthæs af en snæghæl .i. brittani land. Han ær blalyk røth. Haldær man hanum undær ren tungæ. tha ma han spa. Thænnæ steen ma æi eld skathæ." (There is a stone called 'Silenites' which comes from a snail in Brittany. It is blueish[?] red. If one places it under a clean [alt., pure] tongue, then he may soothsay. This stone cannot be harmed by fire.) I take this opportunity to thank Henrik Jørgensen of Aarhus University for his advice on the treatment of *blalyk røth*. Ny. kgl. Samling 66, 8vo is a composite manuscript, which makes its dating difficult, but it is usually set to ca. 1300. In this instance, the description, although based on Marbod's lapidary poem, has been altered: India has become Brittany, and tortoise (*testudo*) has become a snail. Cf. Jespersen 1938:164. Other manuscripts, such as Sth. K4, are fragmentary and do not contain an entry for "Chelonites/Silenites." For a facsimile (and text) of Ny. kgl. Samling 66, 8vo [136v], see Det

The same belief later appears in Peder Månsson's Old Swedish translation of the late medieval *Speculum lapidum* of Camillus Leonardi, which similarly says that by taking *Celonites* and placing it under the tongue one can speak many prophecies about things that will come to pass.[41] Although we cannot know with certainty whether this tradition exercised influence on the way Óðinn's powers are presented in our texts, it is likely that the existence of this parallel belief system would have been known among the clerics who possessed Latin learning and the other requirements necessary for engagement with natural magic.

Raising these points about the cephalophoric saints, the Ferryman's Fee, and the *Viaticum* and its history is not the same as claiming that these aspects of learned lore necessarily shaped the traditions we see in Saxo, *Hávamál*, or the other Nordic materials, but given the tendency to adduce parallels between the pre-Christian and Christian worlds, and to see in such analogues, prefigurations, and revelations of the Almighty's power, that such a parallel existed may well have reinforced the pre-existing concept and even allowed for its easier acceptance within clerical culture.

Conclusion

If we consider this problem operationally, as a ritual performed at some point in time, how was such a belief as that suggested by *Hávamál* st. 157 practiced, or believed to have been practiced? After all, we possess, so far as I know, no *kefli* "piece of wood" or other materials on which appropriate runic inscriptions have been carved to suggest such charms were ever used.[42] Even though there may exist no surviving recognizable runic inscriptions, we do have Church edicts and synodal statutes condemning the use of runes, listed in collocations with such things as magic, witchcraft, and superstitions. Presumably, mundane runic use was of little interest to the Church but precisely such things as charms to awaken the dead would have been what

---

Danske Sprog- og Litteraturselskab's online site, *Tekster fra Danmarks middelalder 1100–1515*, at: http://middelaldertekster.dk/harpestreng-nks66/3/58.

[41] "Celonites är en sten som taks vth aff storom skölpaddom. [...] Hwilken som honom bär wndy twngonne han talar mangan spaadom som komma skal oc ske" (*Stenbok*, 466). (Celonites is a stone taken from large turtles [...] Whoever bears it under his tongue can speak many prophecies of things that will come to pass.)

[42] Cf. modern narratives concerning "uppvakningar eða sendingar" in *Íslenzkar þjóðsögur og ævintýri* (1:304–339), on all aspects of which see especially Gunnell 2012.

the bishops looked to eradicate. But, of course, this point is nothing but an inference.

We perhaps get a bit closer when we examine the provincial laws. Here, for example, the Older Law of Frostaþing speaks of those who are killed for various deeds, including witchcraft, visiting soothsayers, or sitting out in order to awaken spirits [lit., trolls] and thereby promote heathendom ("fordæðu scapi oc spáfarar oc útisetu at vecia trǫll upp oc fremia heiðni með því," *NGL* 1:182). This is just one of nearly a dozen such laws in Iceland and Norway specifying prohibitions against "sitting out." Sometimes the laws go one step further, as in "So also those who attempt to awaken spirits (*draugar*) or mound-dwellers (*haugbúar*)" ("Sua oc þeir er freista draugha upp at ueckia æða haughbua," *NGL* 2:326–327). This asserted practice brings to mind such developments in the mound as those presented in *Þorsteins þáttr uxafóts*, for example, as well as the commands used by saga characters that the seeresses and others should "awaken" (*vaki þú*).

Still, it is highly unlikely that anything like the sort of practice referred to in *Hávamál* st. 157 was ever practiced in the Christian Middle Ages and thus, our best presentation of such a performance derives from the surviving mythological materials. With respect to the poetry, *Baldrs draumar* provides the fullest information about how Óðinn accomplishes his task of compelling the dead to awaken and speak, as well as expressions in this instance of the *vǫlva*'s reluctance to be awakened and cooperate with the magician.[43] He rides to Hel and then to the seeress's resting place, where he undertakes a relatively detailed performance (at least compared to the general rule): Óðinn speaks, or more narrowly, chants or intones (past tense, *qvað*), various corpse-related items of word-power: *valgaldr* and *nás orð*, that is, literally,

---

[43] How the dead person is raised in *Grógaldr* is unclear. Klare (1933–1934:16) assumes that in awakening his mother from death and getting her willing assistance, Svipdagr does nothing more than speak ("er hatte nicht einmal Zaubermittel gebraucht. [...] Nun genügt ein Wort, sie kommt und hilft bereitwillig") (he does not even use a magic spell. [...] With just a word she comes and helps willingly). Although the poem gives no explicit information other than his command to "awaken," the audience here, and elsewhere, may, of course, have assumed other operations were in play. In the famous scene in *Hervarar saga ok Heiðreks konungs* between live daughter and dead father (NB: gender-reversed compared to *Grógaldr*), referred to earlier, Hervǫr too appears to do no more than command that the dead man awaken (*vaki þú*) to begin their dialogue but there may have been much more to it. *Vǫlospá* is, if anything, even less clear than these other cases: the poem begins with the *vǫlva*'s calls for attention, not any act of Óðinn's. It is from the *comparanda* and such clues as her addresses to *Valfǫðr* about what he wants to know and her repeated phrase, "vitoð ér enn, eða hvat?" (do you want to know more: and what?) (*The Seeress's Prophecy*) that scholars draw the reasonable inference that it is indeed cut from the same cloth as the others. And, in fact, rhythmically repeated questions of the "do you want to know more: and what?"-sort characterize most of these poems.

"slain-magic" and "corpse-words."[44] The vǫlva responds by asking who it is that has forced her to travel such difficult paths. The extant text does not specify that Óðinn does more than to vocalize these powerful charms in order to bend her to his will, but we cannot know for sure. It would not be difficult to envision the carving of a *kefli* during the performance of such a charm, just as Harthgrepa does in forcing the corpse to speak in *Gesta Danorum* or as other characters do in performing rune magic, such as Skírnir in *For Scírnis* (see Mitchell 2007b).

What happened when Nordic prophetic practices involving the dead encountered similar beliefs from the classical world or Christian interpretations of them? Nordic tradition could easily accommodate these views to its own, where the tongue object was not for the purpose of accompanying the dead into the afterlife but for the use of the living to look into the *arcana coelestia* which could only be known within a certain narrow mantic framework. Given the extensive *comparanda* over time and space, the practice of placing something in the mouth (and under the tongue) of a corpse need not be envisioned as having been borrowed from elsewhere, either the practices of the classical world or the Church, or indeed from adepts of natural magic. It is possible that these necromantic practices and belief systems had evolved in northern Europe over a very long time with ongoing reticulations between vernacular and learned belief systems.

Accusations of *Hávamál* being overly consistent are few for good reason. Certainly, in one respect, the earlier part of the poem may have even been *very* wrong: in st. 71, *Hávamál* claims "nýtr manngi nás" (a corpse is of no use to anyone) (*Sayings of the High One*, 22). As we see from st. 157 and its cognate materials, apparently there existed a tradition according to which nothing could be further from the truth.

---

[44] Cleasby-Vigfusson 1982 [1957], for example, glosses *valgaldr* as "*charms*, a kind of *necromancy* ascribed to Odin" and *nás orð* as "necromancy."

Chapter 8

MEMORY, MEDIALITY, AND THE "PERFORMATIVE TURN"
RECONTEXTUALIZING REMEMBERING IN MEDIEVAL SCANDINAVIA

Scandinavia's longest runic inscription, the visually and textually imposing early ninth-century Rök stone, opens in a way that serendipitously illustrates the memory, media, and performance triad of this essay—"In memory of (*aft*) Vémóðr stand these runes (*runaR*). And Varinn colored (*fāði*) them, the father, in memory of his dead son. I say the folktale (*sagum mōgminni*)."[1]

Of course, this is only the beginning of an inscription consisting of more than 750 characters, but on the face of it, Rök, just like several thousand other rune stones, is concerned with memory in a most basic and obvious sense, in that many stones were expressly carved and erected as memorials to—"in memory of" (*aft*)—dead people.[2] Expanding the sense of what is remembered at Rök, however, is a phrase that appears repeatedly throughout

---

[1] Original publication: "Memory, Mediality, and the 'Performative Turn': Recontextualizing Remembering in Medieval Scandinavia." *Scandinavian Studies* 85:3 (2013): 282–305.

In Old Swedish, "Aft Wæmōð/Wāmōð stąnda rūnaR þāR. Æn Warinn fāði, faðiR, aft fæigjąn sūnu. Sagum mōgminni." See the entry for Ög 136 in *Samnordisk Runtextdatabas* whose translation I cite here (NB: unless otherwise noted, translations throughout this essay are my own).

I take this opportunity to note the obvious, namely, that an essay on a topic as sweeping as the current one cannot hope to provide anything like a complete account, much less a complete bibliography, of all the work on these topics; my strategy has generally been to provide references to recent works that will in turn steer interested readers to additional literature.

[2] The relationship between commemoration, media and performance is one of the central themes of Judith Jesch's admirable 2001 study of runic monuments and skaldic poetry, which begins with perfect pitch by examining the Karlevi stone, uniting, as she writes, "in one monument, oral and literate ways of commemorating the dead" (9).

its text—both verbatim and implied—*sagum mōgminni*, usually translated as "I tell the folk memory."³ Clearly, a compound of the "folk memory" sort evokes, not the individual memory of a bereaved relative for a dead kinsman, but rather a different sort of memory, memory that is shared, memories that are at once cultural and communal, what we might more readily recognize with a different appellation—tradition.⁴ And, indeed, the Rök text alludes time and again to narrative traditions largely unknown to us now.

The inscription's other repeated formulation *sagum*, "I say," "I tell," and so on, emphasizes the highly performative nature of the text, performances acted out both by its fictional (or perhaps historical) "I," and, more notably, by what must have been the repeated reading aloud of the text by each new viewer of the stone capable of the task.⁵ One quickly understands, too, that the public declarations of sorrow and respect such memorial stones represent, are specifically meant as lasting elegiac "performances," acts to honor the dead that, given their lithic nature, are inherently frozen in time. Yet these proclamations are also, as in the case of *sagum*, but now for the text in its entirety, re-enacted with each new attempt by a passerby to read the inscription. And it is not difficult to imagine that further performances—rituals or ceremonials of various sorts—accompanied the erection and dedication of such stones; it would be perverse to imagine that the stones were silently tipped into position without the accompaniment of familial or local ritualized behaviors of one sort or another.⁶

Finally, one cannot help but be struck by the obvious self-conscious mediality of the monument. Not only does the text note its own corporeal existence—"stand these runes"—but the father's, Varinn's, role in the physical production of the monument is expressly referred to. Knowledge of runic writing, or runacy (a neologism meant to capture for runic writing the same sense "literacy" has for alphabetic writing; cf. Spurkland 2004), and thus of the written word as a medium for preserving, even enshrining, memories and thoughts, had been used in Scandinavia for half a millennium

---

[3] The scholarship on the Rök stone is vast, but for insightful and recent views of the text, especially with regard to the issues at stake here (including an alternative reading of *mōgminni*), see, for example, Harris 2006, 2010b and the literature cited there.

[4] As a discipline, folklore has a long and evolving view on tradition; for orientation, see, for example, Ben-Amos 1984 and Bronner 2000.

[5] Morphologically, *sagum* represents both the first person singular and plural, and thus can be translated as either "I say" or "we say"—or, if one envisions the phrase having a role in a public ritual, perhaps both at the same time.

[6] Cf. Harris 2010a, and the literature cited there by,for example, Ottar Grønvik (1981, 1982).

at the time the Rök stone was carved. Although the epigraphic system associated with Christianity would in time become the principal vehicle for the written word in northern Europe, beginning roughly at the time of Rök, even exemplified by Rök, runic writing entered into an era of enormously expanded use.[7]

Throughout the Viking and the Middle Ages, Scandinavians were acutely aware of runic mediality, as they would also in time be about Latin and manuscript culture: the relationship between the self-conscious written text and its narrative was much more diverse and complicated than simply the fact of the story or sentiment being recorded, as a number of recent studies have emphasized, and as the example from Rök suggests.[8] In fact, it is anything other than happenstance that the Rök stone's opening focuses on memory, mediality and performance: these functions were at the heart of such monuments, their production, and their performance.

The paradigm shift we have witnessed in recent decades in Old Norse studies away from formalist approaches, which were long in vogue, and toward so-called performance and media studies, premises well-suited to the contextualization of our inherited goods to their cultural moments, was long in coming (cf. Lönnroth 1980, 2009; Clunies Ross 1997). To those approaches to the medieval Norse world the addition of the formidable field of memory studies has created new interpretive possibilities, as we will see, enhancing the opportunity to re-create or re-contextualize performance contexts.[9]

Memory and Old Norse Studies

Medieval Scandinavians were acutely aware of memory, both as a useful tool in their cultural kits and as an abstract concept. That this is so may be seen in their use of language, both its lexical inventory and its poetic confections, each of them richly stocked with various ways to give shape to the idea. This

---

[7] A late medieval charm expressly notes the fact that it is in runes: "[you] shall neither sleep sweetly nor wake warmly until you pray this cure which I have proclaimed in runic words" (in Old Danish: skulæ huærki søtæn sofæ æth uarmæn uakæ førr æn thu thæssæ bot bithær, thær ak orth at kæthæ ronti). See DR EM85;493 M in *Samnordisk Runtextdatabas*.

[8] For example, Glauser 1994, 1998, 2007, 2009, 2010; Harris 2000, 2010a; Jesch 2001; the essays in Zilmer and Jesch 2012.

[9] See the key surveys in Hermann 2009, 2010; for examples, see Harris 2010a and Zilmer 2009, as well as the essays in Hermann, Mitchell, and Agnes S. Arnórsdóttir 2014.

fact is readily seen, to use two Old Norse avian images, when memory is represented by, and even as, Óðinn's news-gathering raven, Muninn (from *muna* "to remember"), a mythological beast woven into the indigenous religious system (see Hermann 2014 and Mitchell 2022c), as well as its opposite, "the heron of forgetfulness" (*óminnis hegri*), a product of their poetry.[10] And, of course, with the arrival of Christian learning and its traditions, perspectives on memory among the Nordic peoples were further shaped through contact with older European rhetorical practices, methods dating back at least to the Classical period, according to which memory was regarded as a talent that could be enhanced through training.[11]

Some Nordic genres were themselves specifically geared to the notion of marking, and making, memories, such as the Nordic tradition of elegy, the *erfikvæði* (also: *erfidrápa, erfiljóð*).[12] Such poetry is, in essence, the public memorialization of private grief, and there are some particularly well-known examples of these laments (e.g., *Eiríksmál* about Eiríkr blood-axe; the memorial poem in honor of King Magnús berfœttr by Gísl Illugason; for additional examples, see Holtsmark 1982a). This was not, however, a memorial rite reserved for royalty alone: *Landnámabók* records that at the death of Hjalti Þorðarson, his sons arranged the most magnificent funeral ever held in Iceland, at which Oddr Breiðfirðingr declaims the *erfikvæði* he had composed in honor of the deceased, a public, perhaps even professional, dirge to memorialize Hjalti's life.[13]

How personal, even familial, memories can be deployed rhetorically to represent larger, communal visions of the past is well-documented in the Old Icelandic materials. Thus, in one of its most dramatic episodes, *Óláfs saga helga* (chap. 80) portrays the Swedish lawspeaker, Þorgnýr Þorgnýsson, rising to speak at an assembly in Uppsala. After much commotion among those present, he addresses the king of Sweden, appealing to him, on behalf

---

[10] On *glemselshejre* see *Lexicon poeticum*, 235, and Heslop 2014.

[11] See the review in Hermann 2014. Naturally, we do not know that the Scandinavians did not have practices of their own in this regard; given the amount of skaldic poetry preserved over the centuries, Occam's razor would suggest that they did.

[12] This and related topics have been examined with great care and insightfulness in studies by Judith Jesch, for example, 2001, 2005, and Joseph Harris, for example, 1988, 2000, 2008 (1996), 2010a.

[13] "Þat hefir erfi verit ágætast á Íslandi, er þeir hafðu fǫður sinn [...] At <því> erfi fœrði Oddr Breiðfirðingr drápu þá, er hann hafði ort um Hjalta" (*Landnámabók*, 238 [S207, H174]). (The most magnificent funeral feast ever to be held in Iceland was the one his sons celebrated in honour of their father [...] At this feast Odd of Breidafjord declaimed a dirge he'd composed in honour of Hjalti) (*The Book of Settlements*, 93).

of the farmers, to make peace rather than war with the king of Norway. Þorgnýr begins by noting how different things are now with Swedish kings than had previously been the case. He then launches into a recitation of the conduct of earlier kings, in which, as part of his jeremiad's rhetoric, Þorgnýr invokes the memories of his grandfather, his father, and himself, and the various regents they had known: "My grandfather Þorgnýr remembered Eiríkr Emundarson of Uppsalir, and said this of him" (Þorgnýr, fǫðurfaðir minn, munði Eirík Uppsalakonung Emundarson ok sagði þat frá honum); "My father Þorgnýr was with King Bjǫrn for a long period" (Þorgnýr, faðir minn, var með Birni konungi langa ævi); "I remember King Eiríkr inn sigrsæli [the victorious] and I was with him on many warlike expeditions" (Ek má muna Eirík konung inn sigrsæla, ok var ek með honum í mǫrgum herfǫrum).[14] Þorgnýr notes, moreover, that many of the works of these kings are still to be seen (e.g., "Ok mun enn sjá þær jarðborgir ok ǫnnur stórvirki, þau er hann gerði"), transforming the landscape into a form of visible memory. And, finally, he reminds the king that the Swedes had in the past killed no fewer than five kings who were filled with the same overwhelming pride (*ofmetnaðr*) this king now demonstrates. Following Þorgnýr's speech, and the din from the throng it foments, the Swedish king artfully agrees to follow the farmers' wishes (*Óláfs saga helga*, 116 [chap. 80]). Whether these events are being accurately remembered or not is beside the point: what is key is that the saga represents this form of recollection as a persuasive tool in the speaker's arsenal.

Another intersection between literary form and memory is in evidence in skaldic verse, namely, its social role as a means of shaping, codifying, and fixing official memory. Thus, just before the critical battle at Stiklastaðir, King Óláfr tells three court skalds to stand within the shieldwall, in order to see everything that will take place, so that they can later give their own accounts and compose poetry about the battle ("því at þér skuluð frá segja ok yrkja um síðan").[15]

Within memory studies, with its strongly Durkheimian intellectual roots, there is an understandable tendency to focus on socially constructed

---

[14] *Óláfs saga helga*, 115–116 (chap. 80); *Óláfr Haraldsson (The Saint)*, 74. On this sort of "Oratorical Structure" in the kings' sagas, see Knirk 1981:51–73.

[15] "'Skuluð þeir', segir hann, 'hér vera ok sjá þau tíðendi, er hér gerask. Er yðr þá eigi segjandi saga til, því at þér skuluð frá segja ok yrkja um síðan'." (*Óláfs saga helga*, 358 [chap. 206]). (You [pl.] shall be here and see the events that here take place. You will then not have to rely on verbal reports, for you will report them and compose about them later) (*Óláfr Haraldsson (The Saint)*, 239). On this scene and the question of authenticity, see Poole 2001:185–186.

memories, as we will see. Yet the memories individuals possess based on their own firsthand experiences are also highly relevant. We see this, for example, in the capacity of individuals to recall facts, details, events, and word patterns, in other words, rote memorization. An individual's relationship to this kind of memory can be seen in the careful overnight composition Egill undertakes when at tenth-century York, he must compose his so-called *hǫfuðlausn* "head ransom," a poem through which he was able to win his freedom by praising Eiríkr blood-axe. Despite various attempts by the queen to interrupt his somnambulistic work, the saga says, "þá orti Egill alla drápuna ok hafði fest svá, at hann mátti kveða um morgininn" (then Egill composed the entire poem and had fixed it [in his memory] such that he could recite it in the morning).[16] This ability to fix a poem in one's memory is clearly a critical skill, and saga literature even provides an excellent counter-example to Egill's ability in *Morkinskinna*, when Einarr Skúlason makes a wager with King Eysteinn to see if the monarch and his men can remember a poem he composes. As it turns out, the king only manages to recall its first and last lines, and the saga notes that he and his men could not remember at all what had been in the middle ("Aldregi munðu þeir þat er í milli var") (*Morkinskinna*, 2:225 [chap. 105]). One implication of this story is that skalds were especially good, by training or by nature, at remembering the results of their craft.

Both Egill and Einarr are working out entirely new and original works of art; in Egill's case, the poem is based partially on events from Eiríkr's life, partially on the commonplaces and tropes of traditional skaldic art. The process results in a complicated poem which he in turn commits to memory in order to present it at court the following day. What is easy to lose sight of in this narrative is the larger context of Egill's work, namely, that although his composition is his own, that is, the product of his personal inventiveness and constructed by him according to his personal design, his composition and its performance occurs *within* a larger skaldic tradition, which he has learned during his own years of informal apprenticeship as a young skald.[17]

---

[16] *Egils saga Skalla-Grímssonar*, 183 (chap. 59); my translation. Cf. Cleasby and Vigfusson 1982 (rpt. 1957), 15, "festa e-t í minni, *to fix in the memory*, Edda (pref.), Fms. iv. 116, hence minnisfast; also absol., festa kvæði, *to fix a poem in the memory, learn it by heart*."

[17] Although dealing with traditional, as opposed to newly minted poetry, the remark made by Albert Lord (1953:316) regarding the relationship between singers and their traditions is useful to consider here: "Everything in the poem belongs to the group, but the poem itself and the formula in which it happens in a particular performance is the singer's. Every item is the tradition. But when a great singer is sitting in front of an audience, his music, the expression of his face, and his particular version of the poem at the time is his."

So although the poem is in one sense a reflection of Egill's memory, that is, his knowledge of events in Eiríkr's life (whether personal or acquired from others), that information is transformed into art within a social performance, that is, the poem's declamation at court, an ability Egill possesses due to his acquisition of "skaldship" (*skáldskapr*).

Skaldic ability points then to the key role of apprenticeship, understood broadly—and here it is useful to bear in mind that our word *tradition* derives from *tradere*, "to bequeath," "to hand over," "to deliver," 'to consign," and so on. All of these meanings suggest the image of new practitioners learning their skills from the more experienced and more knowledgeable. Apprenticeship as a socially bounded form of education is in some cultures very formal and highly structured; conversely, it can elsewhere also be relatively informal. I suggest that we consider as an example of the latter form the case of skalds like Egill Skallagrímsson who are not portrayed as having been apprenticed in the normal sense, but who clearly undergo a period of learning during which their skills are acquired and tested.[18]

Perhaps the most famous episode suggesting informal apprenticeship in medieval Scandinavia, although now with respect to sagas, comes in the thirteenth-century *Morkinskinna*, when King Haraldr Sigurðarson is visited by a young Icelander who asks for the king's hospitality.[19] Given the opportunity to provide entertainment, the young man succeeds but eventually grows despondent as his store of tales runs low and he must admit that the only narrative he has left is one about his host's foreign adventures.

To his surprise, the young raconteur discovers that the king approves of his narration, and asks the Icelander who taught him the story.[20] In response, the Icelander describes his custom of going annually to the Alþing ("hvert sumar til þings"), where "every summer I learned something of the story from Halldór Snorrason" (namk hvert sumar af sǫgunni nǫkkuat af Halldóri Snorrasyni). The king responds, saying it is not surprising then that he knows the story well.

---

[18] The story of the three-year-old Egill composing a skaldic verse is nonsense as biography, but enlightening as an attempt to demonstrate the young boy's precociousness, and the episode perhaps suggests that informal poetic "training," if it can be called that, may indeed have begun early.

[19] "Svá barsk at eitthvert sumar at einn íslenzkr maðr, ungr ok fráligr, kom til konungs ok bað hann ásjá" (*Morkinskinna*, 1:235 [chap. 44]) (It happened one summer that an Icelander, who was young and nimble, came to the king and asked for hospitality) (Andersson and Gade, 222).

[20] "Konungr mælti: 'Mér þykkir allvel ok hvergi verr en efni eru til, eða hverr kenndi þér sǫguna.'" (*Morkinskinna*, 1:236 [chap. 44]) (The king said: "I am very pleased with it. It is perfectly faithful to the actual events. Who taught you the story?") (Andersson and Gade, 223).

This brief description, its repeated "every summer" (hvert sumar) emphasizing the gradualness with which the young Icelander learned the tale, is, of course, an excellent allusion to an apprentice-like relationship with a raconteur whose narrativized memories of events have been passed on to someone who was not personally present on those occasions. Naturally, that King Haraldr, the narrator's host and patron, who is at the same time the subject of this story, likes the tale and finds it "perfectly faithful to the actual events," speaks to a sequence of important reciprocity dualisms at play in the story (e.g., host-guest, sponsor-entertainer, ruler-ruled), as well as to how memories can be packaged, passed on, and influenced by such factors as patronage.

The phrasing used at the beginning of this story is worth considering as well: "Konungr spurði ef hann kynni nǫkkverja frœði, en hann lézk kunna sǫgur" (*Morkinskinna*, 1:235 [chap. 44]) (The king asked him if he had any sort of learning, and he said that could tell stories) (Andersson and Gade, 222). As Preben Meulengracht Sørensen noted some years ago, the opposition referred to may not be so much a distinction between different genres, between historical knowledge (*fræði*), on the one hand, and saga literature (*sǫgur*), on the other, as is sometimes argued, as it is the more subtle distinction between historical knowledge, that is, public memories, and the same materials presented in narrativized form. As Meulengracht Sørensen writes, this was "the knowledge that the bearers of tradition, the wise men and women, thought it important to pass on unchanged to their inheritors" (Meulengracht Sørensen 1993:108). These same items, he sensibly reasons, were then manifested in different ways over the centuries, at first in oral forms, and later in written saga forms.

The vignette from *Morkinskinna* parallels the criteria Snorri Sturluson cites in the prologue to *Heimskringla*, where he expresses the view that historical events publicly performed before chieftains in the manner described in *Morkinskinna* are to be preferred over other forms of information, as he assumes that no one would affront the chiefs by telling stories in front of them not in keeping with *their* memories.[21] In fact, the introductory remarks to Nordic historical writing are often quite direct on these points, where memory, equated with various expressions for knowledgeability, is the key element: for Ari Þorgilsson, it is "lore, both old and new" (*frœði, bæði forna ok nýja*); for Saxo, "a faithful image of the past" (*fidelem uetustatis notitiam*);

---

[21] *Heimskringla*, 1:3–4. On the performance of such materials and the various dyads implied in such a context, see in Mitchell 2001a.

for Theodoricus Monachus, "relics of our forefathers" (*majorum nostrorum memoriæ*). Medieval Scandinavian authorities place a high value on the authenticity of their materials and the mirror-like memories they purport to preserve.[22] The author of *Historia Norwegiæ* goes further than most in proclaiming the verisimilitude of the memories he uses when he remarks: "For I am neither eager for praise as a historian nor fearful of the sting of censure as a liar, since concerning the course of early times I have added nothing new or unknown but in all things followed the assertions of my seniors."[23]

As is apparent from these examples, even when memories are, in the first instance, private remembrances, the recollections of individuals, eventually they involve a degree of social context: they are repeated to others, employed rhetorically, or form parts of shared narrative traditions. Pertinent to this point are the influential works on memory and constructions of the past by the French sociologist Maurice Halbwachs.[24] Fundamental to his views is the idea that the social frameworks of memory, *les cadres sociaux de la mémoire*, or at least of so-called "lived memory," is at its heart an exchange between people, as we have seen (cf. Halbwachs 1925, 1950). This socially situated proposition means, as it has been formulated by Pernille Hermann, that "due to its social and communicative components, cultural memory is not to be considered something that is *inside* individuals; rather, it exists *between* individuals" [*emphases added*; Hermann 2009:288]. In that sense, all memories, to the extent they are recorded, become collective and institutional rather than individual and experienced.

---

[22] *Heimskringla, Prologus*, 5; *Gesta Danorum*, Praefatio 1.3); *Monumenta Historica Norvegiae*, 3. The concept of authenticity, and its pursuit, has a long and vexed history within folkloristics; on this chimera and the hunt for it, see Bendix 1997.

[23] *A History of Norway*, 1–2. *Neque enim laudis avidus ut chronographus existo neque vituperii stimulos ut falsidicus exhorreo, cum nihil a me de vetustatis serie novum vel inauditum assumpserim, sed in omnibus seniorum assertiones secutus* (*Historia Norwegiæ*, 72). On the significance of the prologues to questions of mediality and the authors' self-consciousness as writers, see especially Sverrir Tómasson 1988:149–260, and Glauser 2010.

[24] As important as Halbwachs' views are, his is only one voice in what has become a very rich field; my focus here on Halbwachs is not meant to slight the other important perspectives on the topic (e.g., Assmann 1992; 1995). For a survey of memory studies and Old Norse, see especially Hermann 2009 and 2014; more generally, see Erll and Nünning 2005; and Erll 2008.

Performance and Mediality

If memory—collective, cultural, or of whatever sort—is primarily a phenomenon that exists between individuals, rather than inside them, it must naturally be communicated, either, to borrow Ruth Crosby's still useful framing of the issue, with the eye or the ear (Crosby 1933:88 *et passim*). Given those realities, both the manner and mode of such communication—that is, performance and mediality—are key considerations. And due to the important functional relationship between the two, although they often represent differing areas of theoretical concern, I will attempt to address them, and their relationship to memory, together as much as possible.

Of the many varieties of performance and mediality that bear on our considerations of how memory was packaged and communicated, we may begin with performance as understood, for example, within the field of dramatic arts: in fact, excellent arguments have been put forward in recent years about how the nature and presentation of the medieval materials might be better understood within such a paradigm (e.g., Gunnell 1995, 2008). Scholarly attention has also been drawn toward performance studies of a related but different kind, one I would characterize as being especially close to the so-called ethnography of speaking, where a recognition of, among other leads, the key roles of linguistic anthropology and folkloristics have been pronounced.[25] One of the more prominent results of melding this ethnographic approach with medieval studies has been to lift the words of our materials off the vellum and to recognize that medieval texts are first and foremost communicative acts (cf. Kiening 2003:26), a simple empirical recognition of fact, but one with far-reaching ramifications as the thinking about medieval texts has shifted from fixity to flexibility.[26]

Several of the examples above have already touched on performativity as it relates to memory expressed and exchanged through the medium of runic or manuscript writing. The problematization of these areas has spawned a

---

[25] The beginnings of this "performative turn" stretch back at least to the 1950s, and include scholars coming from several diverse fields, for example, John Austin, Richard Baumann, Clifford Geertz, Erving Goffman, Dell Hymes, John Searle, Richard Schechner, and Victor Turner. On the approaches I intend here, see, for example, Bauman and Sherzer 1975; and Bauman 1977.

[26] Cf. Glauser 2007:4, who writes: "A new interest, often associated with the New Philology, in the material processes of transmission in medieval manuscript culture has meant abandoning the notion of a stable text and instead foregrounding the lack of fixity, the variance and seriality (*mouvance, variance*) of the medieval text."

sub-discipline concerned with questions of mediality.[27] Speaking to other medieval traditions and invoking Paul Zumthor's idea of "vocality," the embodied voice, Almut Suerbaum and Manuele Gragnolati write of the opening lines of the *Nibelungenlied* that they represent, "a complex form of fictional orality—the creation of a spoken, collective voice evoking poetic presence, but doing so by means of a consciously literate and literary written text" (Suerbaum and Gragnolati 2010:1), words equally apt to the Old Norse situation.

Yet however modern and forward-thinking our views about these matters have become in recent years, there is no escaping the significant shadow cast by arguments concerned with medieval Scandinavian literature's oral versus written background.[28] Since the beginning of modern scholarship on medieval Nordic life and literature in the nineteenth century, the question of oral performances of the texts has readily attached itself to the Icelandic sagas and other narrative forms, and it is not difficult to see that memory would, in fact, have had a key part in the construction and preservation of a wide variety of pan-national genres, including charms, legends, and genealogical lore, as well as the areas of greatest interest to modern scholarship, the sagas, and eddic and skaldic poetry. What all of these genres share is a fascination with history, even deep history; thus, inherently, all of them have important ties to memory functions.

Now, whether such texts as the Old Icelandic sagas are to be seen principally as the products of well-established traditions of an oral culture,[29] or works inspired and shaped in important ways by written texts from elsewhere in Europe, or some compromise between the two, that is, written texts borrowing at times from foreign models but also using much native (sometimes equated with "oral") tradition, has been the focus of a great

---

[27] For excellent examples of these intersecting approaches, see the works of Jürg Glauser (e.g., 1994, 1996, 2007, 2009) and Joseph Harris (e.g., 2000, [1996] 2008, 2010a), as well as the review in Lönnroth 2009. More broadly on the medieval era, see Kiening, 2007, and the literature cited there.

[28] See, for example, Andersson 1964; Harris 1983; Mitchell 1991b:1–6, *et passim*; 2001a; and Hermann 2017.

[29] The sagas have been the main, but by no means only, focus of this discussion. While the topics of the sagas vary from historical, legendary, religious, and contemporary themes to the completely fantastic (and as such, they offer an inclusive and panoramic view of medieval Nordic cultural life, narrative imagination, and attitudes toward the past and the heroic), eddic poetry principally concerns itself with mythological and heroic themes, while skaldic verse tends toward praise, memorial, and occasional poetry. Of course, these genres could also be highly contemporary as well: skaldic panegyrics, for example, also take up Christian religious themes.

deal of scholarly debate.[30] At the turn of the twentieth century, the labels "Free-prose" (*Freiprosa*) and "Book-prose" (*Buchprosa*) were attached to these views. It is, however, impossible from a modern perspective to call the nativist view "Free-prose," since it was far from free, built instead on belief in a word-for-word fixed text. "Book-prose," for its part, although readily acknowledging the importance of the oral tradition, was so heavily focused on the written perspective that, as one scholar noted some years ago, one could almost believe that material from one saga manuscript moved to another manuscript without ever being influenced by, or moving through, the surrounding social environment.[31]

Much has changed since these debates dominated the work of earlier generations. Perhaps the greatest shift in the study of medieval Nordic literature and lore over the past century has been an enhanced appreciation for the cultural context of these materials, that is, such questions as those of patronage, social context, and political dimensions, and not least, performance and mediality, which have re-oriented our attention. Recognition of these critical questions, together with a broader consideration of the nature of medieval culture, has simultaneously led to fewer fixed positions and more interesting analyses.[32]

Because we are provided with occasional portrayals of Old Norse poetry and prose being performed—as, for example, in such famous cases as the scene in *Þorgils saga ok Hafliða* (composed ca. 1237), which tells of how at a wedding at Reykhólar in 1119, several prosimetrical sagas are narrated—these descriptions have played a particularly prominent role in discussions of performance and mediality in medieval Scandinavia, but as we shall see, they are far from our only available ingresses to such questions in Old Norse

---

[30] See, for example, T. M. Andersson 1964; Gísli Sigurðsson 2004:17–50; and Hermann 2017. Although new models occasionally emerge (e.g., Lönnroth 1976), it is clear that the weight of the nativist–anti-nativist arguments remains a powerful influence on academic treatments of the topic.

[31] "From his [Sigurður Nordal's] survey of literary causes and effects one would think that sagaw-riting existed in a social vacuum, that written sagas were influenced only by other written sagas" (Lönnroth 1976:207).

[32] In attempting to break with this past and move away from these polarities, I wrote some years ago: "Once such wonderful works had been wrenched from the hands of a desiccating formalism dedicated to a fixed text and an equally alkaline literary criticism which saw only words on a page, an understanding of the Norse materials' potential as ethnic textual photograph *and* literary wonderwork was available, a synthetic view which exhibits allegiance to neither extremist position, but understands the potential for developing a much-needed symbiosis between them." Mitchell 2003b:204. Cf. Gísli Sigurðsson (2002), who challenges many older assumptions about medieval orality and the sagas' oral background.

(e.g., Bauman 1986a; Harris 2000a; Mitchell 2001a). Indeed, amid the often-complicated genres of the medieval Scandinavian literatures, it is easy to forget the significance of memory, the substantive character of memory, and the performance of memory in cultural monuments beyond the celebrated sagas and poetry of the Old Norse world.

As an illustration, let us consider the monument associated with the so-called Ramsund runic inscription (Sö 101), which reads in its entirety: "Sigríðr, Alríkr's mother, Ormr's daughter, made this bridge for the soul of Holmgeirr, father of Sigrøðr, her husbandman."[33] There is much to be read out of this text, even when taken in isolation: obviously, the monument first and foremost commemorates a man named Holmgeirr; less obviously, the text suggests the coming of Christianity, since the terms for "soul" (OSw *siæl*, OIce *sála*) are part of the foreign lexicon that arrives with the Saxon and Anglo-Saxon missionary efforts; even more to the point, the monument speaks to the status of this woman, Sigríðr, who is defined genealogically in the inscription entirely in terms of her relationships to males (her son, her father, her father-in-law, her husband), yet who, one infers, must also be seen as a person who controlled sufficient authority and resources to have caused such a monument to be made; and so on.

But far more so than the inscription itself, Ramsund is famous for its large and complex carvings related to the story of Sigurðr the Dragon-Slayer, executed on a huge slab of stone located precisely next to the path that led to the bridge celebrated in the inscription (the bridge abutments are still visible, although the bridge itself has long since disappeared).[34] If we envision the monument as a complete unit, or ensemble, in its contemporary setting, every person who walked along the path and was about to cross, or had arrived from the opposite direction and had just crossed from the other side, would encounter and engage this astonishing monument.[35] Those who possessed the capacity to read runes—by the eleventh century time of the monument, perhaps a relatively common skill—would surely work the text out. But even for those who did not have this ability, the impressive ornamentation of the site on such a grand scale would have drawn their attention. Moreover, we cannot discount the likelihood that for some considerable time,

---

[33] "siriþR kiarþi bur þosi muþiR alriks tutiR urms fur salu hulmkirs faþur sukruþar buata sis." See *Samnordisk Runtextdatabas*, from which this translation comes.

[34] Some estimates put the bridge at ca. 75 meter in length; on it and Sigríðr's family, see Lindqvist 1914.

[35] See Anders Andrén's comments on "places, monuments and objects" (2013), as well his observations on the relationship between images and runic texts (2000).

local memories about the construction of such a monument, its dedication, and, especially, about the people celebrated on it, must have circulated and been noted and discussed by passersby.[36]

In other words, this entire complex—the inscription, the artwork, and the bridge—represented an elaborate and regularly repeated *performance* in honor of Holmgeirr and the others. As each traveler was spared the necessity of circumambulating the body of water and consequently passed by the inscription and the decorations, and over the bridge, he or she would have recalled, perhaps even mentioned aloud, the names of those celebrated on the slab. It is not difficult to imagine that however else we understand the site, given the monument in its totality—its inscription, its artistic references to heroic ideals, the monument's placement, the bridge-building project, everything they knew about the *kumbl*'s memorial and practical functions—we must necessarily decode this "cultural monument" as a meeting place of many different strands of Norse memory culture. In this view, the memorial at Ramsund is a performance writ large—very large, indeed.

If Ramsund and other memorials (e.g., Karlevi) suggest one kind of performance, it is not difficult to see that other sorts of ritual behaviors would also intersect with questions of memory, as, for example, in the case of magical practices like prophecy and cursing.[37] A well-known example will suffice to illustrate this connection, the story of Þorbjǫrg lítilvǫlva [little sibyl] from *Eiríks saga rauða*. In the famous case of a *seiðr* ceremony, when Þorbjǫrg is ready to begin her soothsaying ceremony,

> ...she was supplied with the outfit she needed to perform the witchcraft [*seiðr*]. She asked for the aid of women who had that knowledge which was necessary to the witchcraft called Warlock-songs (*Varðlokur*). But no such women were found. Then an inquiry was made among the household to see if anyone there knew them. Guðríðr says then, "I am neither a sorceress nor a witch, but in Iceland my foster-mother Halldís taught me a song which she called the Warlock-songs."[38]

---

[36] Grønvik (1982:9), for example, writes that "the funeral feast was the central cultic and juridical proceeding of the inheritance of property," a description that would help explain this monument and contextualize its construction.

[37] A recent article argues this very point; see Søndergaard 2011. A possible avenue for further exploration comes in the work of Foley (1981), and others on the South Slavic *bajanje* and other curse forms, where the density of hapax legomena would argue for the importance of memorization.

[38] "var henni veittr sá umbúningr, sem hon þurfti at hafa til at fremja seiðinn. Hon bað ok fá sér konur þær, er kynni frœði þat, sem til seiðsins þarf ok Varðlokur hétu. En þær konur fundusk eigi. Þá var at leitat at um bœinn, ef nǫkkurr kynni. Þá segir Guðríðr: 'Hvárki em ek fjǫlkunnig

Guðríðr's memory serves her well, and she goes on to perform the songs to Þorbjǫrg's complete satisfaction. Certain facts about these songs stand out: they are presented as a special kind of knowledge with limited distribution, since none of the other women know them; their use apparently required that they be sung by someone other than the main practitioner (since otherwise Þorbjǫrg might just as well have sung them herself); they are understood to be gender-restricted, since only women are presumed to have familiarity with them and to be capable of providing them for the *seiðr* ceremony; and they are teachable (*kenndi... mér*). And although these pagan songs are used by the author as a device to underscore with favor Guðríðr's Christian faith, one senses an *ubi sunt* quality to the comment by Guðríðr that her stepmother back in Iceland had taught them to her. Guðríðr's singing of such songs, seen within the framework of the tiny tenth-century famine-plagued Greenlandic colony at Herjólfsnes reflected in the saga, can also be understood to be a special kind of performance, a performance of things past, of a world far away, of nostalgia, of memories. By singing these special songs, the settlers connect, not only, as presented in the saga, with the spirit world, but, through the *seiðr*'s ritual form, with the memory of the world and the people these colonists living on the edge of the world had left behind them.

Thus, the social dimension of this performance of a song taught to Guðríðr long ago—not just that she knows the words, but that she performs it well, beautifully, and publicly—is a significant aspect of her expertise. A similar connection to the past and to the public domain is apparent in other episodes relating to the magico-religious world of the medieval Norsemen, such as the curse performed by Egill Skallagrímsson against King Eiríkr and Queen Gunnhildr, or the curse used in the real-life case of Ragnhildr tregagás in early fourteenth-century Bergen. Ragnhildr's attempts to thwart the marriage of her former lover to his new bride apparently require an explicitly public performance. Importantly, Ragnhildr learned the curse formula already as a youth (*in juventute*), meaning she remembered the curse formula for some time (see Mitchell 2011:57–58, 68–72, *et passim*).

---

né vísendakona, en þó kenndi Halldís, fóstra mín, mér á Íslandi þat kvæði, er hon kallaði Varðlokur'" (*Eiríks saga rauða*, 207–208 [chap. 4]). My translation. On this scene, see Mitchell 2011:96–97 *et passim*, and the literature cited there.

Conclusion

Two saga scenes provide useful final illustrations of this interplay between memory, mediality, and performance: one, the colophon to *Yngvars saga víðfǫrla*; the other, the story of Sturla Þórðarson's entertainment of a ship's crew and its royal couple in *Sturlu þáttr*.[39]

In the case of *Yngvars saga víðfǫrla*, a saga reporting a historical—albeit heavily embroidered—eleventh-century journey into the Russian hinterland, we are provided with an extraordinarily complete explanation of the text's evolution: Ketill, one of the participants in this remarkable trip, returns home to his native Iceland, where he is said to be the first to tell tales about his experiences ("sagði fyrstr frá þessu"). At this point, the saga notes that there are other multiforms of the story that look to privilege certain aspects of the characters, and it also queries if there might not be confusion between Yngvarr and a similar figure known from "Gesta Saxonum," and then helpfully provides the appropriate citation about him in Latin. Later, the saga says that *this* story ("þessa sǫgu," i.e., this *version* of the story) was written following an existing book that had been made according to the "forsǫgn fróðra manna" "accounts of wise men." The author of that first written account had heard the story from three different sources, from which he made the selections used in the text. One of those sources claimed to have heard the story from a merchant, who in turn said he had gotten it ("hafa numit hana") at the Swedish court. The second claimed to have the tale from his father, and the third had heard it from his relatives (*Yngvars saga víðfǫrla*, 458–459 [chap. 14]).

With regard to the modes and means of the story's earlier existences, it is apparent that it had, or we are to believe it had, a variety of different embryonic manifestations, quite a few that seem to be oral and at least one earlier written iteration.[40] The main thrust, however, of the colophon is less to emphasize the many different types of narrative art that existed than it is to ratify the scheme suggested by Meulengracht Sørensen, according to which knowledge was *selectively* passed along by tradition bearers, at first in oral forms, and subsequently in written saga forms (1993:108). The saga's concluding statement, although information-laden, is largely unconcerned

---

[39] The literature on *Yngvars saga* is, to say the least, vast; cf. the remarks and literature cited in Mitchell 1991b:89–90, and Phelpstead 2009; my comments here on this aspect of *Sturlu þáttr* build on and expand my remarks in Mitchell 1991b:98–102; 2002.

[40] Hofmann 1981 has made the strongest case thus far for crediting the saga's account.

Chapter 8. Memory, Mediality, and the "Performative Turn"   165

with the discursive methods of communication by which, it seems, Ketill first relates his memories of the voyage in Iceland, followed, as it is, by further memories and tales about the voyage. What the statement especially wants to emphasize, I believe, is the author's discernment in making selections amid these many possibilities ("Af þeira frásǫgn hafði hann þat, er honum þótti merkiligast"). Amid all the verbiage about sources, the key thing is that a synthesizing genius must make order, and a tale, out of them.

Sturlu þáttr also describes a journey, albeit a much more sedate one from 1263, when the Icelander Sturla Þórðarson visits King Magnús Hákonarson. The king refuses to receive him, but does allow Sturla to join the ship's party. Sturla is asked by the men if he will entertain them, and he obliges, telling (*sagði*) *Huldar saga*, better and more cleverly than anyone had heard (*heyrt*) it before, so much so that a crowd gathers wanting to hear (*heyra*) it. This arouses the queen's interest and she asks what is happening and is told: "The men there want to hear (*heyra*) the saga that the Icelander is telling (*segir*)." Inquiring about the saga, she is told that it is about a troll-woman, "and it is a good story and is being well-told" (vel frá sagt). Thanks to the queen's interventions, things improve somewhat between Sturla and the king, and the queen asks Sturla to come to her and bring with him the saga about the troll-woman ("bað hann koma til sín ok hafa með sér trǫllkonu-sǫguna"). When he arrives, the queen asks him to tell that same story ("segja þá sǫmu sǫgu") that he had told earlier. He does so, telling the saga for much of the day ("sagði mikinn hluta dags sǫgu"). When he is done, the queen and many others thank him, acknowledging that he is a knowledgeable and wise man.[41]

There has been much debate about what this story says about mediality in the Old Norse context: does Sturla have a manuscript with him from which he is reading, or is he narrating orally without the use of a manuscript? Partisans, even modern ones (but often with lingering filiations to the old Bookprose-Freeprose debate), have tended to promote readings that vouchsafe their favored interpretation. I think both sides are right but asking the wrong question. After all, we know that by the middle of the thirteenth century, various models of literary activity, oral and written, were in play. What this story illustrates is that the queen, Danish born and bred, and coming from a world that had already participated in its own "performative turn," that is, from oral delivery and toward medieval manuscript culture (cf. Mitchell 1997b), assumes that Sturla's performance is writing-based, and thus she asks that he "bring the saga with him," imagining that he has a

---

[41] *Sturlunga saga*, 2:325–326. The compilation as a whole probably dates to ca. 1300.

physical tome. It is also a request in keeping with her character: after all, the story later goes out of its way to note how she wants to appear to understand the nature of the Norwegian court, and of orally declaimed skaldic verse, even when she does not.[42]

Other characters in the tale, by contrast, constantly emphasize that Sturla is an Icelander (thus playing on the medieval stereotype of Icelanders as better at such archaic forms of entertainment than other Scandinavians) and that the story is told, heard, and done better and more cleverly than they ever heard it before. Because he is so good at narrating, Sturla is allowed to declaim the praise poems he had composed in honor of the king, and of the king's deceased father. And because these are so well-received, he is asked to write *Hákonarsaga Hákonarsonar*.

This brief *þáttr* allows its readers to witness virtually all the available literary possibilities of that era: oral saga narration (Sturla's two recitations of *Huldar saga); declaimed skaldic poetry (the panegyrics to Magnús and Hákon); and the written and read saga (*Hákonarsaga Hákonarsonar*, Queen Ingibjǫrg's expectations of *Huldar saga). It is a tale that captures Old Norse literature at an inflection point, a liminal moment.[43] It is, to be sure, a narrative that wants to prove how clever Sturla is, both as a man of arts and as a knowledgeable figure; at the same time, it gives us an impression of the evolution Nordic literature was experiencing, as it moves from predominantly orally performed forms of art toward a culture where written sagas and recorded skaldic poetry also have their important, and eventually hegemonic, parts to play.

As we have seen, memory, mediality, and performance lie in one way or another behind every text we have from the Nordic Middle Ages, whether commemorative and literary, as has been the focus here, or of a different sort—letter, charter, deed, court protocol, or synodal statute. Untangling and reconstructing the meaning of such data inevitably depends on our ability to perceive and engage these three issues, each of which has in its way shapes the construction of our cultural monuments from the Nordic Middle Ages.

As we consider how to approach the interdependence of memory, mediality, and performance in medieval Scandinavian culture, a useful observation

---

[42] After the queen praises Sturla's declamation, the king asks if she could really understand it; she responds that she wants him to think so.

[43] Cf. the implications of the evolution from *Verschriftung* (transcription) to *Verschriftlichung* (textualization) in Ehler and Schaefer 1998:2–4, and Harris 2010a, and the literature cited there. On the further possibility of secondary oralization, including improvisation during the reading of a saga, see, for example, Mitchell 1987:414–415; Driscoll 1996; and Glauser 1996.

comes, not from medieval studies, but from ethnography. Writing of his experience studying witchcraft among the Azande in sub-Saharan Africa, E. E. Evans-Pritchard, summarized his findings by noting, "Witchcraft, oracles and magic are like three sides to a triangle." (Evans-Pritchard 1937:387). So likewise do memory, performance, and mediality form the trifold mechanism that made possible, produced, and preserved narrative art in the Old Norse world, a reality which already our ninth-century rune master at Rök appears to have fully understood.

Chapter 9

MEMORY AND PLACES THAT MATTER
THE CASE OF SAMSØ

The Ruin, a fragmentary Old English poem from the tenth-century Exeter Book, famously projects a central concern for "pastness" and the transient nature of life by describing in detail the decaying remnants of a once proud Roman settlement (often thought to be Bath).[1] Its elegiac tone, although subject to many different modern interpretations, remains unmistakable in such lines as *burgstede burston / brosnað enta geweorc*, "the city-steads are broken / the work of giants crumbles."

How very different the situation of Viking Age Scandinavians, at least as regards their own longhouses and pit houses, constructed as they mostly were of perishable organic materials, and leaving behind very few traces, apart from discolored soil indicating postholes and other human activities. On the other hand, of course, the public-display monuments (memorial stones, gravemounds, ship settings) raised during the Viking Age, as well as the landscapes inherited from the Bronze Age and other earlier periods, remained highly visible to them and their heirs. But what of once-important so-called "central places," or "places of power," when these sites were

---

[1] Original publication: "Erindring og steder af betydning: Samsø som eksempel." In *Samsø: et sted af betydning*, ed. Andreas Nymark, 49–79. Studier i Samsøs Historie og Arkæologi, 1. Tranebjerg, 2022.

Many people have helped make this essay possible: Andreas Nymark for his steady hand as editor; Pernille Hermann, Jürg Glauser, and Stefan Brink for their inspiring writings on landscapes and memory; Peter Jensen, Peter Hambro Mikkelsen, and other excellent colleagues at Moesgaard Museum and Samsø Museum for literally showing me Samsø "from the ground up"; Pia Kleis, Lis Nymark, Jens Jørgen Øster-Mortensen, and numerous other residents of Samsø for their gracious attitudes and welcoming ways over the course of many summers; and in the case of the original published Danish version, "Erindring og steder af betydning: Samsø som eksempel," to Karen Bek-Pedersen for translating it.

sometimes no longer conspicuous on the horizon?[2] Or perhaps even more intriguing, when they were, but were ignored nevertheless? Perhaps we should not be surprised that places that once mattered so much were often, but far from always, well-remembered in the narrative traditions of the North, even in the absence of substantial tangible presence.[3]

In fact, a feeling for "pastness," and past places, runs strong in the works of medieval Nordic writers; that is, not just that they knew something about the events and places of the past, but, more importantly, that they recognized the emotions and the sensibilities evoked by this awareness of the past and of the landscapes of the past, frequently referred to with nostalgic memory of former greatness. For the Scandinavian Middle Ages, the many monuments—runestones and grave mounds, for example—dotting the landscape suggested cultural continuity across time, connections to a deep and mythical past. Thus, Saxo's preoccupation with visible history dominates much of his introduction to the *Gesta Danorum*. In the same spirit as *The Ruin* and its *enta geweorc* (the work of giants) and, especially, the testimony of Genesis (6:4)—that in those days, there were giants on the earth (that *gigantes autem erant super terram* in the Vulgate)—Denmark had once, Saxo writes, been populated by a race of giants.

How does Saxo know that? Because, as he writes, of the enormous stones attached to caves and barrows which can still be seen, as well as the boulders carried to the tops of the hills (*Danicam uero regionem giganteo quondam cultu exercitam eximię magnitudinis saxa ueterum bustis ac specubus affixa testantur*, *Gesta Danorum* 3,1). And Danes of an earlier era, he observes, carved letters onto rocks proclaiming the feats of their ancestors celebrated in popular songs. It is such narratives, he claims, that he has translated into his chronicle, proof that his work "should be recognized not as something freshly compiled but as the utterance of antiquity" (*quia pręsens opus non nugacem sermonis luculentiam, sed fidelem uetustatis notitiam polliceur*, *Gesta Danorum* 1, 3). Similar writing elsewhere, he suggests, has been silted over and is no longer readable.[4] It is an apt metaphor for how such "places that matter" are discussed, valo-

---

[2] "Central places" are generally conceived of as continuously used, multi-functional, regional centers, perhaps also, as Helgesson 1998 argues, connected to a special individual.

[3] Explorations of "the past in the present" are numerous, of course. For Denmark, excellent starting points are Adriansen 2011 and Hermann 2018a, b.

[4] "Unde conspicuum est etiam petrinę soliditatis rimas diutino madore complutas aut sordium colluuione aut irrigua nimborum instillatione concrescere." *Gesta Danorum. Praefatio* 2,5. (It is obvious that even the crevices of solid rocks will choke up when exposed to the continued wash of silt and rainfall.)

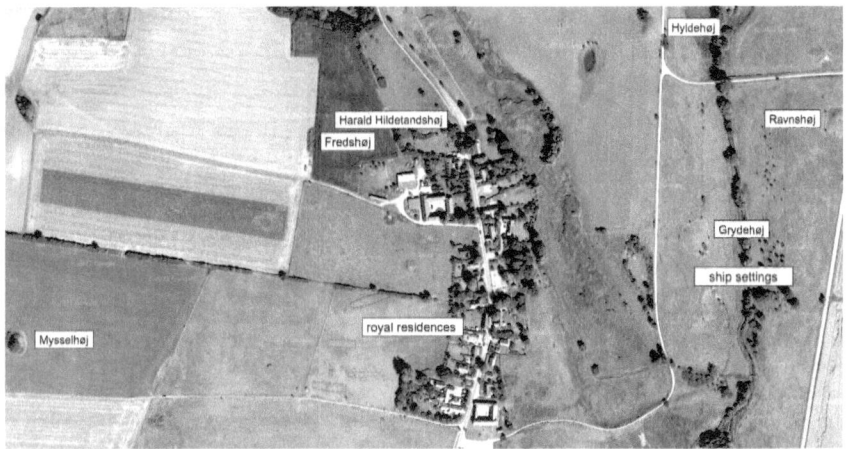

Figure 9.1. Map of selected monuments at Gammel Lejre, showing grave mounds from the Bronze and Iron Ages (Mysselhøj, Grydehøj, Ravnshøj, Hyldehøj, Fredshøj); a long barrow from the Neolithic (Harald Hildetandshøj); remains of at least four ship settings; and large ("royal") residences in use from the seventh to tenth centuries. Map data: Bilder ©2021 Aerodata International Surveys. CNES / Airbus. Maxar Technologies, Scankort. Kartdata ©2021.

rized, memorialized, and recorded in—and fade from—the narrative traditions of the North, the topic of the present essay, with particular attention to Samsø.

Remembering and Forgetting "Central Places": Samsø in Context

There is perhaps no better example of a remembered South Scandinavian "central place" than Lejre [figure 9.1], frequently noted as it is in Danish historiography and in Icelandic literature (for example, *Lejrekrøniken*, Saxo's *Gesta Danorum*, Sven Aggesen's *Brevis Historia Regum Dacie*, *Hrólfs saga kraka, Ragnarssona þáttr*, and Arngrímur Jónsson's paraphrase of *Skjöldunga saga*, as well as in kennings in skaldic and eddic poetry).[5] Writing in the twelfth century, for example, Sven Aggesen notes, "Huic in regno successit filius Rolf Kraki, patria uirtute pollens, occisus in Lethra; que tunc famosissima regis extitit curia, nunc autem Roskildensi uicina ciuitati inter abiectissima ferme uix colitur oppida" (*Brevis Historia Regvm Dacie* 1:97). (His

---

[5] Steinn Herdísarson's kenning *atseti Hleiðrar* "ruler, resident of Lejre" for the Danish king; *Grottasöngr*'s *Hleiðrar stóll* "seat of Lejre" for "royal residence."

successor as king was his son, Rolf Kraki, who became powerful through his inherited valour, and was killed at Lejre. This was then the king's most famous residence, but now, near the city of Roskilde, it lies scarcely inhabited among quite the meanest of villages.) (Christiansen 1992:49).

From these comments, it is apparent that whatever the possible reality of Lejre's former position, the growth of medieval Roskilde had largely come at Lejre's expense. That "most famous residence" was in Aggesen's day obviously a rather pathetic little hamlet.

A similar recollection of a grander Lejre is reflected in *Hrólfs saga kraka*, when the saga reports that Lejre—Hleiðargarðr—was a magnificent king's seat:

> Hrólfr konúngr setti þar höfuðstað sinn, sem Hleiðargarðr heitir, þat er í Danmörk, ok er mikil borg ok sterk, ok meiri rausn ok hoffrakt var þar, en nokkrs staðar, ok í öllu því, sem til stórlætis kom, eða nokkr hafði spurn af.
>
> *Hrólfs saga kraka,* chap. 23, p. 46

> King Hrolf established his capital at a place in Denmark called Hleiðargarðr [Lejre], a large and strong fortification, and there was more splendor and pomp there in all that related to greatness than at any other place.

But for at least some eight centuries, the village of Lejre (now Gammel Lejre) has been anything but the sort of residence envisioned in these texts. Yet due to the prestige reflected in these medieval sources, the symbolic significance for Danes of this humble if charming village, today consisting of perhaps a dozen homes, lived on through the Middle Ages, right into modern times. It was at Lejre, in Herthadalen, for example, that several nineteenth-century folk meetings (*folkemøder*) in connection with the debates about the establishment of a Danish *grundlov* (constitution) took place.[6] As recently as 2007, the local branch of Venstrepartiet held a public meeting in the same location ("Venstre i Lejre genopliver fortidens tradition for politiske folkemøder"), attesting to its continuing role in public consciousness.[7]

And as even the earliest excavations in the 1850s began to confirm, this location had indeed once had an economic and political significance that did not remotely correlate with its modest standing in medieval and modern times. With increasing frequency, the archaeological work of past

---

[6] The post-medieval uses of Lejre and Jelling, official and unofficial, are carefully detailed in Adriansen 2003, 2:165–192. See also Warring 2005.

[7] See Hornemann, "Folkemøderne i Herthadalen genoplives," *Kristeligt Dagblad*, June 4, 2007. https://www.kristeligt-dagblad.dk/danmark/folkemøderne-i-herthadalen-genoplives. Cf. Hermann 2018b on the similar valorization of Glavendrup.

Figure 9.2. The best preserved of the ship settings at Gammel Lejre, with Grydehøj and Ravnshøj in the background. Photo by author.

decades has revealed the existence of imposing Viking Age buildings of significant size, organized with halls measured in dozens of meters in length, and surrounded by smaller workshops;[8] high status objects in precious metal of the sort one would associate with the apex of Charlotte Fabech's model of settlement hierarchy, such as the so-called "Odin fra Lejre";[9] and an earlier site a few hundred meters further north at Fredshøj that has pushed the Iron Age continuity of the site yet further back, so much so that the principal archaeologist of the site, Tom Christensen, suggests it is likely that for more than five hundred years Lejre was a royal residence.[10]

In short, at least in the identification of Lejre as a magnate farm, a "place of power," or a "central place," the sagas and other medieval sources had the historical significance and character of ancient Lejre broadly correct, noticeably so, even when that imposing legendary status did not match the existing medieval hamlet—apart, of course, from such impressive monuments as the

---

[8] See, e.g., the press announcement, "Porten til 'Skjoldungernes Kongsgård' i Lejre Fundet," October 8, 2019, Museumskoncernen ROMU = https://www.mynewsdesk.com/dk/romu/pressreleases/porten-til-skjoldungernes-kongsgaard-i-lejre-fundet-2924105.

[9] Fabech 1999. On the silver figurine, see T. Christensen 2010c.

[10] "Gennem næsten 500 år var Lejre måske en kongelig residens. Stedets tidsmæssige kontinuitet er imponerende" (For almost 500 years Lejre may have been a royal residence. The location's temporal continuity is impressive), T. Christensen 2010b:186.

ship setting and the various grave mounds in the area.[11] In some instances then, the sagas and other medieval texts can know what they are talking about—they can contain, preserve, perform and pass on memories, cultural memories, of what once was.

But caution is clearly in order. Even if our texts can offer us memories, that is a far cry from wanting to return to the uncritical days when scholars thought it possible to reconstruct, even impose, history from later literature.[12] And a nearby counter-example serves as a useful warning, where popular culture has interpreted the inherited landscape within the frameworks of their own knowledge: a Neolithic long barrow at Lejre has, since at least the early modern era, been known as "Harald Hildetandshøj" (Harald Wartooth's mound).[13] Thus, writers of every period can inventively imagine and chart these landscapes, and imagine they do, even when there is little or no tangible evidence—one's mind readily envisions, for example, the many New World stories of El Dorado, and the supposed "Viking city of Norumbega" in New England.

Considering several other famous "central places" as they are, or are not, treated in narrative tradition, can help us contextualize how Samsø is remembered. The case of Jelling is instructive: it is, after all, the area specifically known as "Jalangrsheiðr á Jótlandi" (Jelling heath on Jutland), but notably not the stunning Jelling memorial and ritual complex, which is mentioned in Icelandic sources: *Knýtlinga saga* (258 [chap. 95]) and several of the Icelandic annals cite the heath as the site of a battle in 1131. And that same heath is cited again as the place where a gold ring could lie without being stolen during the Fróðafriðr (peace of Fróði; *Upphaf allra frásagna*, 40).

In Denmark itself, Saxo, with all of his extensive knowledge, refers only once in the long narrative about Athislus to the royal estate at Jelling (*Ialunga*

---

[11] On Lejre, older Germanic legendary traditions, and archaeology, see especially the excellent contributions in Niles, Christensen, and Osborn 2007, as updated by T. Christensen 2010a, b, c, as well as Bruce 2002, which surveys medieval materials relating to Lejre. On the development of royal manors in northern Europe, see Iversen 2009 and the literature cited there.

[12] A representative case of this sort of thinking is M. G. Clarke's *Sidelights on Teutonic History*, with the important sub-title *Studies from* Beowulf *and other Old English Poems* (cp. Stanley 2000:43). Of course, the ability of tradition to keep alive the political, cultural, and economic importance of Lejre is hardly the same as arguing that there was an actual historical occasion on which, for example, a supposedly historical Böðvarr pulled a cowardly Höttr out of a hastily built bone fortification in one of the halls at Lejre.

[13] La Cour 1921:154, notes that in the seventeenth century, Ole Worm and Stephen Hansen Stephanius refer to it as "Sepulchrum (Monumentum) Haraldi Hyldetan." For similar examples, cp. Brink 2018.

Figure 9.3. Proposal for how Jelling may have appeared in the tenth century (NB: The gray structures have not been confirmed archaeologically). Graphics: Gert Gram. Data: Peter Jensen, Arkæologisk IT, Aarhus Universitet.

uilla, 4, 3, 4), but without displaying any acknowledgement of the Jelling complex we think of today. On the other hand, Sven Aggesen expressly incorporates the built landscape at Jelling, as well as its history, into his narrative, writing,

> Ut autem precluis illa regina cum rege marito omnes etatis sue annos complesset, Haraldus Blaatand filius superstes, qui et regni extitit heres, iuxta ritum gentilium in tumulis gemellis et paribus, quasi illustribus mausoleis, secus regis curiam in Jelling utrumque parentem fecit humari.
>
> *Brevis Historia Regvm Dacie*, 7:117
>
> And when that famous queen and the king her husband had completed their span of years, leaving a son, Harald Bluetooth, who was also the heir to the kingdom, Harald had both his parents buried according to heathen rites in almost identical mounds of equal size by the king's residence at Jelling, to serve as glorious mausoleums.
>
> *The Works of Sven Aggesen*, p. 61

And Sven Aggesen's knowledge of Jelling appears to be extensive and specific: his use of the phrase *Decus Datie Tyræ* (*Brevis Historia Regvm Dacie*, 114 [chap. 6]ª) ("Thyrwi, the Ornament of Denmark," p. 74) has long been interpreted as a reflection of the runic expression "þurui [...] tanmarkaR but" (Þorvé [...] Denmark's adornment) on Gorm's runestone at Jelling (DR 41).[14]

---

[14] What is meant by "tanmarkaR but"—Denmark's adornment or salvation—has been much debated over the years. On the formulation on DR41 and similar phrases in Old Norse literature, see L. Olsen 2013, who argues that the expression on DR41 should be understood as "Danmarks utbetring" (Denmark's improvement).

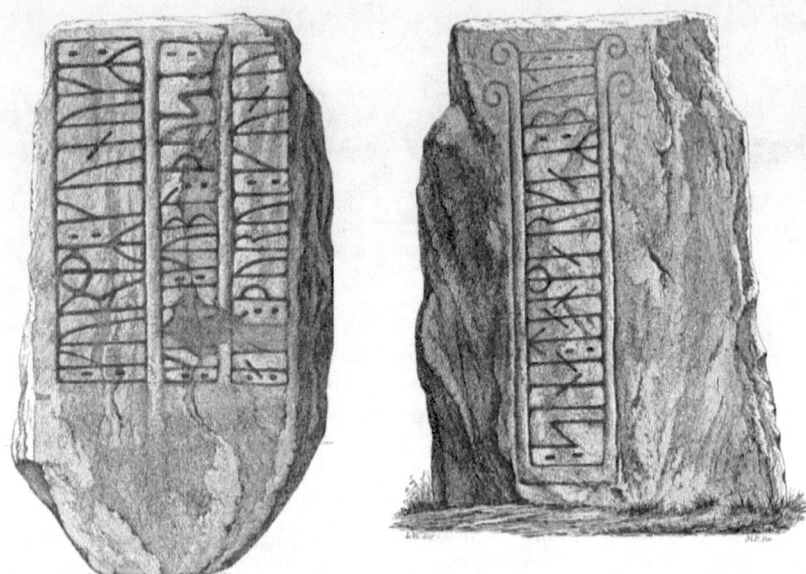

Figure 9.4. The so-called "Gorm ſtone" (DR 41) at Jelling with the inscription, "§A Gormr kunungr gærþi kumbl þøsi æft Þorwi, kunu §B sina, Danmarkar bot" (§A King Gormr made this monument in memory of Þorvé, §B his wife, Denmark's salvation). Illuſtration by J. Magnus Petersen in Wimmer's *De danske Runemindesmærker* (1893).

Jelling thus represents a conflicting data set—generally speaking, it appears to be remembered as a royal residence and the site of important not-too-distant events, but, with the notable exception of Sven Aggesen, not a place recalled for its monumental runestones and grave mounds.

Other South Scandinavian landscapes can serve as useful examples of a different kind of memory, of erasure, intentional or not, a radical instance of a once significant site being entirely lost to tradition: Tissø is an impressive case, as is the cult site at Uppåkra in Skåne. There, in an area inhabited throughout the entire first millennium, a ritual building was built and rebuilt numerous times from about 200 CE to about 800 CE (L. Larsson 2007). In this cult structure, as in many other ways, such as the numbers of gold foil figures, so-called *guldgubbar*, found there, Uppåkra is now known to have been a true "central place"—but with what appears to be a move of activity from Uppåkra to Lund (cf. comparable developments, such as Birka to Sigtuna, Hedeby to Slesvig, etc.), Uppåkra itself disappeared entirely from memory. Its remarkable continuity as a "central place" notwithstanding, there is no identifiable reference to Uppåkra anywhere in our preserved cache of Nordic texts (cf. Andrén 1998).

Against these instances, what are we to make of the case of Samsø? References to Samsø/Sámsey are frequent in a variety of medieval materials.[15] They appear in several Icelandic sagas, in Saxo, and in eddic poetry, references which for ease of presentation I divide here into three groups:

1. geographical and administrative notes;
2. narratives connected with kings and bishops; and
3. the mythical-heroic tradition.[16]

Occasionally, as in Adam of Bremen's eleventh-century *Gesta hammaburgensis ecclesiae pontificum* (4, 16), Samsø simply appears in a geographical list (*quarta est Samse*). Likewise, in *Göngu-Hrólfs saga* (chap. 37), Sámsey is enumerated geographically as one of several points on a mental map ("Milli Jótlands ok Skáneyjar liggja mörg stór eylönd. Þar er Sámsey, Álsey, Láland, Langaland"). Similarly, the island sometimes appears as part of a catalogue, as when *Knýtlinga saga* specifies in its episcopal overview that Samsø is part of the Århus bishopric (p. 152, "Sámsey er undir Áróss biskup").

References of a similar cartographical type are to be found in a number of documents among the late medieval Danish *diplomataria* (cf. *Diplomatarium Danicum*: 1401. 27. August, Helsingborg; 1402. 9. December, Stralsund; etc.). And that a list in an Icelandic *þula* of a number of well-known islands (Falster, Hankø) to be used as a designation or substitute for "island" in general (*eyja heiti*) includes Sámsey is yet another indication of the island's continuing notoriety. Similarly, when we are told in *Árna saga byskups* that an army wanted to return to Norway from Falster and sailed northwards off of Sámsey (chap. 141, p. 198 "sigldi norðr um daginn undir Sámsey"), the audience is to understand that the island represents an important and recognizable location on its mental map.[17]

Of a very different character are those occasions when authors use Sámsey as sites for specific activity, rather than as a mere geographical marker. This expanded attention is perhaps due to correctly recalled historical realities, or

---

[15] Regarding the spelling variation Samsø/Sámsey, I have tried to use the two forms in language- and period-appropriate ways.

[16] The medieval sources on Samsø are carefully detailed in Etting 2018a; cf. Poulsen 1902.

[17] A similar tendency to use the island as a geographic "memory peg" is to be seen in the ballad tradition in the Icelandic and Danish refrains of *Ásu kvæði* [D412] (*Íslenzk fornkvæði* [SG], 226–234): "fögrum tjöldum slógu þeir undir Sámsey," "fagr tjælde sloge de under Samsø" (fair tents they raised on Samsø).

perhaps due to the likelihood that such activities might logically take place on an island so well-known and so strategically well-situated. Thus, as examples of the first possibility, in several of the later books of his *Gesta Danorum*, Saxo places the Danish king on Sámsey: on one occasion (15, 4, 11), King Valdemar is said to be hunting on the island and calls for Absalon to consult with him there, and on another (16, 4, 2), King Knútr is said to have called for a meeting on the island of the kingdom's leading men.

Possibly the most extensive such event is an episode involving the Norwegian king, Haraldr harðráði, a tale known to several of the great synoptic histories of the north, *Morkinskinna* (1:201–203 [chap. 34]) and *Fagrskinna* (258–260 [chap. 55]). These rather foggy accounts seem likely to be examples of the second possibility, that is of Sámsey's fame overwhelming other factors. In this story, Haraldr raids throughout Denmark, including Hedeby, and according to both *Morkinskinna* (1:203 [chap. 34]) and *Nóregs konunga tal* in *Fagrskinna* (259 [chap. 55]), sails north off Thy (Þjóð), then sails further north [!] and turns east into the Limfjord, and when the wind fails, rows *north* to Sámsey [!].

In a corresponding—and geographically more coherent—account, *Haralds saga Sigurðarsonar* in *Heimskringla* (115–116 [chap. 35]) has the Norwegian king sail further north from Thy, around Skagen (Vendilskaga), and on to Læsø (Hlésey). The landscape flaws in the two earlier narratives prove, one suspects, the point that Samsø's notoriety in the Nordic "mindscape" trumped historical accuracy. *Morkinskinna* (1:174 [chap. 30]) also offers another glimpse of the island, when Einarr þambarskelfir is transporting the corpse of King Magnús north to Norway, he comes to Sámsey and sails into the harbor where King Magnús always anchored when he came to the island ("í einni hǫfn sem jafnan hafði legit Magnús konungr fyrr þá er kom við eyna"). A miracle story of a blind man who regains his sight then unfolds.

At other times, Icelandic tradition associates Sámsey with dark, pagan activities, as when Loki slanders Óðinn by saying that he practiced magic on Sámsey (*Locasenna* 24). And in *Ragnars saga loðbrókar*, Sámsey is presented as a cult site, when a ship anchors off it in Munar Bay (*í Munarvági*) and the crew encounters a very tall wooden idol. Taken together with other materials, these factors lead Eldar Heide (2011) to argue for Samsø's special significance within the Norse mythological landscape.[18] But the Sámsey event best remembered today is a story of lust, love, comradery, and various forms of parricide, a narrative widely known as *Slaget på Samsø* (the Battle on Samsø).

---

[18] On Sámsey as a so-called "textscape," see Larrington 2017.

Chapter 9. Memory and Places That Matter 179

Figure 9.5. The encounter on Samsø (insulam Sampse) of the sons of Arngrímr with Hjálmarr and Örvar-Oddr according to the retelling of Saxo's story in Olaus Magnus, *Historia de gentibus septentrionalibus* (Book V, Chap. 14). Source: https://litteraturbanken.se/f%C3%B6rfattare/OlausMagnus/titlar/Historia/sida/179/faksimil.

This story is testified to in many texts which possess an exceptionally vexed set of relations one to the other: the E90 ballad materials ("Angelfyr og Helmer kamp"), Book V of Saxo's *Gesta Danorum* (repeated in an altered form again in Book VI), the eddic *Hyndluljóð* preserved in the late fourteenth-century *Flateyjarbók* (but whose composition is widely ascribed to earlier periods), and two late medieval *fornaldarsögur—Örvar-Odds saga* and *Hervarar saga ok Heiðreks konungs*. It is the concatenation of the *Männerbund* motif and the contested love story, told from differing points of view, that tends to be maintained in all of the medieval Sámsey texts.

Using the multiform from *Hervarar saga ok Heiðreks konungs* (420–437 [chaps. 5–7]) by way of example, the story runs broadly as follows: a viking and his wife have twelve sons, all berserks. One of the sons makes a vow to marry the daughter of the king of Sweden. Hjálmarr, one of the Swedish king's retainers, offers to marry her as well, and a duel is arranged on an island. When the brothers' leader, Angantýr, and his eleven siblings arrive at Sámsey, they find ships belonging to Hjálmarr and his companion Örvar-Oddr, whose men they slay. Hjálmarr and Örvar-Oddr are themselves in the forest and return to fight the berserks. Oddr is protected by a magical silk shirt, but Hjálmarr dies from his wounds, and all twelve of the berserks are dispatched. They are laid in a mound with their weapons, but when Örvar-Oddr carries the news of Hjálmarr's death back to Sweden, the grief-stricken princess takes her own life. And it is on Sámsey that Angantýr's daughter,

Hervör, engages in a dialogue with her dead father in his grave mound, requesting his famous sword, Tyrfing.

Although lacking the episode with Hervör, *Örvar-Odds saga* (chap. 14) tells a similar story highlighting glory and fame as part of the motivation for the vikings' attack on Hjálmarr and Oddr.[19] It is quite specific in its references to Samsø (chap. 14, p. 210), saying "ok halda þeir at ey einni, er heitir Sámsey. Þar eru vogar þeir, er heita Munarvogar [ms var. Mínnívogar]" (they anchored at a certain island called Sámsey. Those bays are there which are called Munar Bays). This same name is used in verse when Örvar-Oddr sees the berserk brothers going *frá Munarvogum* (chap. 14, p. 212). Importantly, Munarvogar in some manuscripts has the variant Mínnívogar (Memory Bay), raising interesting questions in the context of the present essay: despite the usual etymology (< *muna* "to long, desire," thus, *længslens bugt* "bay of longing [love, desire]"), taken together the forms suggest that in popular thinking the name was instead being interpreted as deriving from semantic categories of remembering (*muna* "to mind, remember"; *minni* "memory").

Saxo's treatment of the Battle on Sámsey in *Gesta Danorum* is similar to *Örvar-Odds saga* and includes most of the familiar elements, and even mentions Sámsey by name (*Sampso insula*; 5, 13, 4), but lacks the romantic conflict in Book V, although this conflict is present in Book VI. For its part, *Hyndluljóð* preserves the names and the association with the *Männerbund*, but otherwise divulges little else about the materials.[20] The E90 ballads and related materials, such as the "Angelfyr og Helmer kamp" complex, best known from the Danish versions, DgF 19 A-D, collected ca. 1570-1616, are described in *Types of the Medieval Scandinavian Ballad* as follows:

> D, F: The brothers Helmer and Angelfyr both ask a king for his daughter's hand. The princess is consulted and chooses Helmer. The two brothers fight, and Helmer is mortally wounded. D: Their father arrives, and when he finds Helmer dying he kills Angelfyr. F: Helmer kills Angelfyr. Before Helmer dies from his wounds he asks his friend Orvaroddur, who has helped him in the fight by killing Angelfyr's brothers, to give his ring to the princess. She dies from sorrow.

---

[19] The Sámsey episode is only known from the M tradition (AM 344a, 4to, etc. See FAS 1829–1830 II:ix–xii), due to a lacuna in the earlier fifteenth-century S manuscript (Sthlm. Perg. 7, 4to). See Mitchell 2003a.

[20] The name-lists concerned with the sons of Arngrímr in *Hyndluljóð* are discussed extensively in Gurević 1992 (esp. pp. 76–82).

S: Tyreson's proposal to the king's daughter is rejected, and he and his ten brothers fight the king. The king is wounded and asks his manservant Otte to help him. Otte kills all of the eleven brothers. (TSB E90)

The DgF 19 tradition appeared in print already in Anders Vedel's 1591 anthology of one hundred Danish ballads, and in the eighteenth century, Jens Christian Svabo encountered aspects of this same ballad complex in the Faroes (CCF 16 A: 58–113; B: 1–59).

As a number of scholars have argued, the printed materials of the complex raise serious questions about the independent source value of the Faroese texts, the most obvious effect being for the printed version to exercise a corrective tendency on the ballad texts (cf. Mitchell 1991b:157–158). Although far from certain, the possibility of a related existence in Iceland of the same tradition is suggested by a refrain from among the post-medieval *vikivakakvæði*.[21]

Lost to many of the ballads (and to some of the other texts) is the aftermath of the battle, with its news of the protagonist's death and the death of the maiden; so too has the identity of Sámsey as the site of the battle, dropped out of the E90 ballad tradition. Yet the notoriety of Sámsey in relation to the story line in Iceland is well-attested by, for example, nineteenth-century riddle traditions on Iceland that include references to the riddler having been buried "í haug á Sámsey forðum" (in a mound on Sámsey long ago).[22] And Sámsey as the specific location of the battle is carefully preserved in the manuscript traditions of *Örvar-Odds saga* and especially *Hervarar saga ok Heiðreks konungs*. And local onomastic tradition, documented since at least the seventeenth century, assigns to various monuments on the island identities associated with this narrative—there exist, for example, several mounds known as Angantyrs Høj (Angantýr's mound) on modern Samsø.[23]

---

[21] "Angantýr og Hjálmar, / hjuggust þeir í ár / sundur var í brynjunni / hringurinn blár" (Angantýr and Hjálmar, they fought this year, broken was in the byrnie the blue ring) (*Íslenzk fornkvæði* (JH), 8:127).

[22] *Íslenzkar gátur* 1:103. A text cluster of special importance that has largely been left out of these discussions is the so-called "S-group," consisting primarily of a seventeenth-century Swedish text, on which see Mitchell 2003a.

[23] See Knudsen et al. (1922:6–7) regarding Angantyrshøj (Angantyr's Mound): "Ikke et gl. folkeligt Navn, men af sen, litterær Oprindelse og dannet i 19. Aarh. under Indflydelse af Sagnet i Hervararsaga" (Not an old traditional name, but of later literary origin, formed under the influence of the legend in *Hervarar saga*). Boberg (1932:9) relates that the Icelandic historian, Thormodus Torfæus (Þormóður Torfason), in a manuscript from 1664 (AM 864, 4to, fol. 57) "omtaler den berømte Høj, »tumulus ille præsignis«, der for ham er et Bevis paa Ørvarodds Sagas Historiskhed" (mentions the famous mound, *tumulus ille præsignis*, which for him

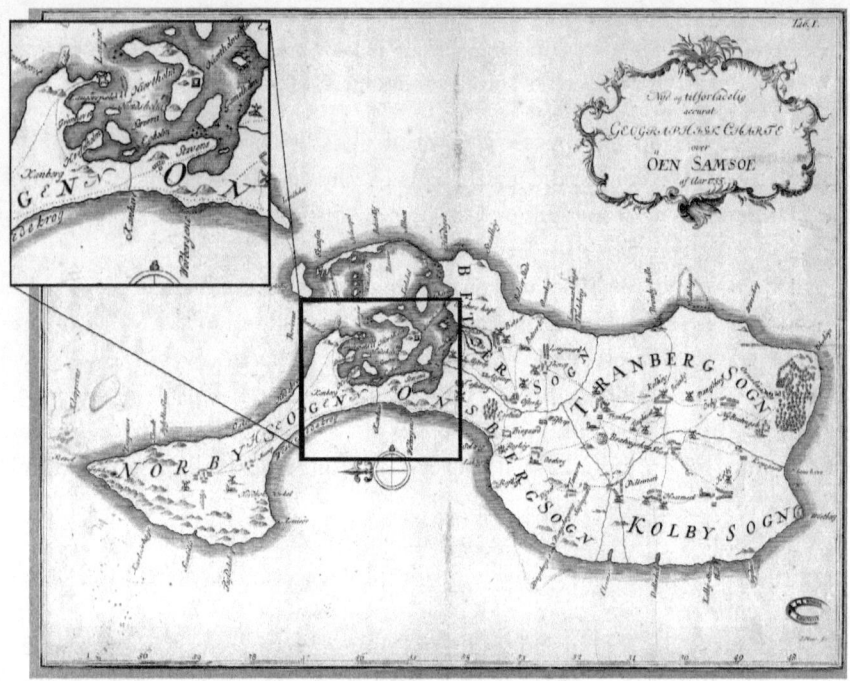

Figure 9.6. Map of Samsø from 1755, with the placename "Kanhave" used for the border between Nordby Sogn and Onsbjerg Sogn. *Nye og tilforladelig accurat geographisk Charte over Öen Samsoe af aar* 1755, Thurah 1758. Source: http://www5.kb.dk/images/billed/2010/okt/billeder/object396722/da/.

Yet the real mystery of Samsø might just be that while we have many references to events that did, or that purportedly did, take place on it (but which we can only rarely confirm *did* take place on it), we do not get any unambiguous references to the one feature we can be sure *should have been* the most significant and memorable feature of the island's ancient history, the construction and use of the early eighth-century Kanhave canal across the neck of the island, an engineering feat of no small account, requiring

---

offers evidence of the historicity of *Örvar-Odds saga*). The first map to indicate an "Angantyr's Mound" appears to be one with a handwritten note ("Monument. Angantÿri") on a copy of Jacob Langebek's 1770 *"Selandiæ, Fioniæ ducatuumve Samsø, Falster, Laland, Langeland..."* (see http://www5.kb.dk/maps/kortsa/2012/jul/kortatlas/object71709/da/ and later versions, http://www5.kb.dk/maps/kortsa/2012/jul/kortatlas/object71712/da/). See also Knudsen et al. 1922:6, 51, 116; Boberg 1932:7–10; Andersen 1981:161; Mitchell 2020c; and *Danmarks Stednavne* (http://danmarksstednavne.navneforskning.ku.dk/). Also highly relevant are such place names as Banehøj ("killer [slayer, etc.] mound"), attached to an Iron Age mound just off the Sælvig coast, opposite Stauns (see Nymark and Nymark 2018:10 and the photo in Etting 2018b:25).

massive labor, substantially altering the island's landscape, and enabling the swift transfer of ships from one side of the island to the other.[24] Yet that accomplishment appears nowhere in the various references we possess to the island, so that from the point of view of what is recalled within the various genres that take up Samsø as a "place of memory," the one that never seems to appear is the historical reality that must have been one of the most important aspects of the island's position in early Danish history from both an economic and military perspective. The canal's name is itself something of a puzzle: the initial element clearly derives from an older form for "boat" (often of a simple type).[25] The second element, however, has a rather wide range of possible meanings relating to enclosing something, including the object doing the enclosing or the area thus enclosed. The object marking or enclosing the area might take one of many forms, such as an embankment, fence, ditch, or dyke (see figure 9.6).[26]

This brief essay is naturally not the place to rehearse Samsø's history in the light of archaeology, but it could fairly be said that from that perspective, the island is far better known for its place in studies of the Mesolithic and Neolithic than the archaeology of the Viking Age. Still, excavations focused on the Viking Age at Søby, Besser, Endebjerg, Tønnesminde, and elsewhere certainly suggest industriousness, and have even yielded some impressive cultural goods.[27] Yet to date, there are no indications of anything comparable to the famous South Scandinavian "places of power." This state of

---

[24] See Adamsen 1995, as well as the comparative study of two early northern canals, Kanhave kanal and the Migration Era Spangereid kanal in Norway, by Del Rio 2020. The eminent Danish archaeologist, Olaf Olsen, summarizes the possible uses of the canal as follows: "The task of the king's ships in Stavns Fjord would be a triple one: to protect the coastal areas of East Jylland and Fyn against attacks from seafaring enemies, probably mainly from Norway, to diminish the threat to peaceful shipping—merchantmen and fishermen alike—from native and foreign pirates operating in the Kattegat, and to uphold the unity of the Danish kingdom through a demonstration of the king's power, strong enough to suppress the traditional quarrels and fighting between the inhabitants of the former petty kingdoms within the Danish realm" (1989:30).

[25] Following Knudsen et al. (1922:104), the first element derives from ODa *Kane*, "Baad, Knubskib, Ege" (boat, dugout canoe [monoxylon], flat-bottomed boat) (according to *Kalkars Ordbog*, *knubskib* = "en båd udhuggen af ét stykke træ" [a boat hewn from a single log] and *ege* = "en båd af en udhulet træstamme (egestamme), en fladbundet båd" [a boat hewn from a single tree trunk, a flat-bottomed boat]). Regarding the historical data in Knudsen et al. 1922, cp. K. Christensen 1995:104.

[26] The second element, according to Knudsen et al. (1922, VIII), derives from ODa *haghæ*, "Gærde" (fence), "Indhegning, Vænge" (enclosure, field/paddock).

[27] See, e.g., Nancke-Krogh 1978; Adamsen 1995; P. B. Christensen 1983; Christiansen et al. 2014, 2015; and the *Tønnesminde* website (https://en.wikipedia.org/wiki/T%C3%B8nnesminde). Cf. the excellent table of finds in Adamsen 1995:87–91.

affairs can strike observers as odd, given how the periods immediately before and after the Viking Age bracket that period with indications of the island's prominence. Thus, in the immediate pre-Viking Period, signs of such significance are more than hinted at by the activities around the construction of the Kanhave kanal.[28] Moreover, in the Middle Ages, there were no fewer than five *borge* (fortresses, castles) on the island.[29] Medieval Samsø was the site of several assemblies of leading men from around the kingdom, and, according to the early thirteenth-century *Kong Valdemars Jordebog*, it was a royal possession.[30] These cultural indices, together with Samsø's geographically strategic location, argue loudly for the fact that Samsø was indeed a place that mattered.

Places of Memorable Pastness

In his ground-breaking works on memory and constructions of the past, the French sociologist, Maurice Halbwachs (1925, 1950), like Pierre Nora and many others since, stresses the role of physical space, of places and objects of memory, and their function in the process of constructing memory.[31] That built landscapes also help negotiate the nature and meaning of memory in the North is central to what Jürg Glauser calls "spatial modes of thought," noting that "Graves and barrows (*legstaðir* and *haugstaðir*) are the media from which memory is constituted" (Glauser 2007:19).

[28] Although we do not know how far back in time they may reach, I note too the fact that there are at least eight placenames on Samsø which incorporate *snekke*- (Snekkebæk, Snekkebjerg, Snekkeballe, Snekkehøj, Snekkeholm; see http://danmarksstednavne.navneforskning.ku.dk/). *snekke* derives from ON *snekkja*, a term for the smallest of the Viking Age longships, with a typical crew of around thirty men. Heide (2012:89) argues that the term is younger than generally thought ("The first quite certain Old Norse example is from 1014 and it is recorded a number of times in contexts from the mid- eleventh century") and replaces the earlier term *skeið*.

[29] See the various essays in Etting 2018b:63–184, where in its English summary, "borg" is glossed with "castle."

[30] Cf. Etting 2018a:26: "Den såkaldte 'Kong Valdemars Jordebog' er en opgørelse fra 1231 over Kronens gods med taksering af diverse skatter for hvert område i landet. På side 11v står Samsø opført, og det er tydeligt, at hele øen har tilhørt Kronen" (The so-called "Kong Valdemars Jordebog" is an inventory from 1231 of the Crown's estates with miscellaneous taxes from every region in the land. On fol. 11 verso, Samsø is listed, and it is clear that the entire island belonged to the Crown).

[31] Halbwachs's insights on memory reoriented Western thinking about this key cultural category, but since his original post-WWI observations many other important perspectives on the topic have developed (e.g., Assmann 1995). For a survey of memory studies and Old Norse, see especially Hermann 2009 and the entries in *Handbook of Pre-Modern Nordic Memory Studies*

Also fundamental to Halbwachs's work (1925, 1950) is the idea that so-called "lived memory" is socially constructed, that is, an exchange between people. As Pernille Hermann formulates this socially situated proposition, "due to its social and communicative components, cultural memory is not to be considered something that is *inside* individuals; rather, it exists *between* individuals" [emphasis added].[32] Thus, memory tends to be collective and institutional (or socially constructed, at any rate) rather than individual and experienced, and in the case of physical locations, it represents what Stefan Brink, speaking of the human capacity for turning our surroundings into shared language, calls "a transfer of *landscape to mindscape*" (Brink 2018:565 [emphasis added]): as one might rephrase that idea, landscapes are narrativized as part of cultural memory.

The significance of landscapes holds a venerable status in scholarship on the past, especially in the modern era of international memory studies.[33] A key advance in recent years has been understanding the use of space in less marked, even ordinary scenarios, not just in awe-inspiring royal monuments like those at Jelling.[34] Even so, there are differences: the once great cultural and political positions of places like Lejre and Jelling were reflected in the tangible landscape even after their eras as active and significant central places had passed—later pre-modern visitors to these grand sites, on seeing imposing ship settings, massive grave mounds, and other majestic markers of human activity, must have nostalgically wondered, like the author of *The Ruin*, who made such monuments. By contrast, every indication suggests that although Uppåkra once possessed cultural significance similar to, if not greater than, Lejre, once its cultural moment had passed, this central place left no clearly altered landscape behind by which it could be recognized—it was in essence silted over like the hieroglyphs Saxo refers to in the preface to *Gesta Danorum*, hidden from view by the passage of time.

What factors led, then, to the cultural memory of certain places in this world being maintained between individuals, not just inside of them, as Hermann writes? And, to extend her formulation, what factors led to cultural memory being maintained between the written tradition and the

---

[32] Hermann 2009:288. The issue of what happens when memory is no longer exchanged in face-to-face communication, but is now exchanged through the medium of the written word has spawned an entire sub-discipline concerned with questions of mediality. For additional studies, see Glauser 2007, 2009, and the literature cited there, as well as the relevant essays in *Handbook of Pre-Modern Nordic Memory Studies*.

[33] See Andrén 2018, esp. pp. 141–144, and the literature cited there.

[34] Cf. Hållans Stenholm 2018; Bennett 2018; Zachrisson 2018, as well as Hermann 2018b.

Figure 9.7. Kanhave canal to the east, summer 2021. Photo: Lis Nymark.

oral tradition, not just inside the one or the other?[35] Certainly, functional factors play an important part in those sites which are heavily memorialized. Some of them, such as Lejre, were associated with successful royal dynasties and their founding, circumstances where patronage likely played a key role in establishing cultural memory. This explanation is, of course, important, but such dynastic sponsorship cannot explain everything or every situation—that seems to be the case at Jelling, at least in the case of Sven Aggesen. His knowledge of the striking characteristics of Jelling's monuments, and its specific ties to important royal personages (Gormr inn gamli, Haraldr blátönn, et al.), stands in marked contrast to the treatment of Jelling in other medieval texts.

Without impressive physical monuments, direct, identifiable references to even once-important sites like Tissø and Uppåkra seem to be entirely missing in subsequent literary tradition. And Saxo's image of the past being obscured by silt may in the case of Samsø's Kanhave Kanal be much more than just a metaphor: one wonders just when this relatively shallow channel

---

[35] There exists a massive literature on this issue in the Old Norse context; my own views are expressed in, inter alia, Mitchell 2003b and 2018b.

Chapter 9. Memory and Places That Matter   187

Figure 9.8. Kanhave canal to the west, summer 2016, with a replica "snekkja" and reconstructed planking along the canal bank. Photo by author.

(ca. 1.25–1.5 meters; see K. Christensen 1995:109) lost its economic and/or military value through silting and land rise (cf. see K. Christensen 1995:102–103), and perhaps also its place in tradition.

Another functional aspect of importance and one that would help explain Samsø's enduring presence over time results from advances in the study of oral tradition and its role in cultural memory. In his wide-ranging and influential examination of how an understanding of oral contexts enhances and sharpens what can be had from the preserved Old Icelandic texts, Gísli Sigurðsson (2002; 2004) examines among other issues how "orally derived knowledge" provided mental maps to saga audiences with the location of Vínland. Gísli's point is not to attempt to reconcile the saga accounts against historical events, but rather to demonstrate how the sagas were able incorporate knowledge alive in oral tradition and "pass on an overall picture of the new lands for others to reconstruct in their own minds." The analogous situation for Samsø in our surviving texts is quite compelling, especially if we consider how frequently mentions are made not just to the island itself but to much more specific locations, especially the references to Munarvág-r/ar.

Despite the obvious need for caution, these examples raise perplexing questions about the relationship of places, central places, and how they were remembered, or not, in Nordic tradition. On the one hand, such references as those to Lejre suggest that we might consider the reports of key central places in the sagas, chronicles and other sources with more introspection and greater confidence; on the other hand, cases like Uppåkra make it apparent that this is not always the case. On several occasions, Pernille Hermannn has reminded Nordicists of the value of the "memory as a storehouse" metaphor referred to earlier as used by the Dutch literary scholar, Ann Rigney, where memory is compared to a leaky bucket which slowly runs dry of water (2005:12). In Hermann's paraphrase (2009:288), "The basic components of this view of memory are firstly that it is something that was in the beginning complete and secondly that in the course of time it becomes diminished and incomplete."

This is, of course, a valuable way to conceptualize memory, and it is an image that accepts that such "leaks" are of different sizes, with the result that the storehouse runs dry at different rates according to such factors as the landscape's significance to prevailing political, economic, and social hierarchies. Lejre, Jelling, Uppåkra, and Samsø were among a number of important South Scandinavian sites that played their roles in the evolution of Denmark, yet they are remembered differently. Lejre and Jelling, with their built monuments, have always been remembered throughout history. Uppåkra, which I nostalgically recall as consisting of broad fields of sugar beets between Staffanstorp proper and Lund when I was a student fifty years ago, held then, as we now know, very important secrets under its green sward, but was largely unremembered by tradition.

Samsø seems to occupy a place somewhere in-between these antipodes; moreover, that the island and its important harbor(s) are maintained by name in Icelandic oral and literary tradition over many centuries, yet interestingly disappear in the nearby non-insular Nordic ballad tradition about *Slaget på Samsø*, is noteworthy. Perhaps this cloven geographic distribution fits and adds strength to Gísli Sigurðsson's views about the value of mental maps of distant lands in maritime cultures. But that Kanhave Kanal plays no recognizable role in the various memorializations of the island remains an enigma; perhaps the various otherwise unidentifiable references to Munarvágar and so on might in ways we do not fathom today refer to this remarkable man-made feature.

Alternatively, perhaps the significance of this man-made waterway was neither as profound nor as long-lasting as we moderns are inclined to imagine. *Brosnað enta geweorc*, indeed.

Chapter 10

THE MYTHOLOGIZED PAST

MEMORY IN MEDIEVAL AND EARLY MODERN GOTLAND

By examining the way several historical episodes are treated diachronically in the traditions of the Baltic island of Gotland, this essay looks to explore interrelated questions about the role of constructed memories, specifically: how empirically knowable facts are treated by the shapers of the island's history, its "men of memory," in order to make these events fit larger schemes, that is, how the past is mythologized. Of special importance with respect to Gotland are the means by which the community refers to and recalls this history—that is, with what references to (by which I generally mean "uses of") popular culture, texts, monuments, the natural and built landscapes, heritage objects, and other mnemonic aids to (or, if not aids, then proofs of) "history," real or imagined.

In addition to how certain events are remembered and memorialized, emerging as equally significant have been the seemingly collective, corporate, or popular decisions about which events to incorporate into the fabric of the community's history and which to leave out. And, one wonders, what factors condition such choices: are they responses to political expediency, philosophical decisions by elites working within a high-status media culture (i.e., writing), popular, serendipitous recollections or re-workings of history, or, perhaps, some combination of these possibilities? How, for example, does this relatively small, increasingly heterogeneous, insular community shape its identity over time? And how does it do so in relation both to larger political situations, and to, and in part through, its well-documented, and sometimes turbulent, past? And, finally, were those people making these competing choices consciously struggling with the issues facing them about how to remember the past and what to remember from it?[1]

The answer to the last question would appear to be "very much so," if we consider the theoretical treatments of this question by intellectuals already in the classical and medieval periods, as well as the empirical data reflecting the views of those confronting the issue of memory in practical situations.[2] A revealing example from the Nordic Middle Ages of the pressures that were felt about preserving the past, and of the remedies being applied, is reflected in a letter from the Archbishop of Lund in the early 1200s to one of the Swedish bishops. It concerns previous agreements about episcopal visits to Gotland. In his missive, the prelate offers his reasoning for the need to record such arrangements in writing. He laments, for example, that such things as forgetfulness and competing interests can cause quarrels to arise as long as the regulations are not written down (*dum scripta non habentur*). Moreover, he assures the bishop at some length, written texts will aid memory (*succurratur memoriæ*).[3] Through its very explicit references, indeed, among the most explicit we know of in the medieval North, the archbishop's letter exemplifies the problem of memory, control, and the need for writing.

Although far from unique in medieval Europe, the archbishop's logic in preferring the comforting, presumed stability of writing stands in stark contrast to the signs we find elsewhere in medieval Scandinavia of a preference for the authority of the spoken, oral tradition as a source of facts and as a truth filter.[4] It is this preference, for example, that famously informs Snorri's prologue to his history of the Norse kings, *Heimskringla*, and is to be seen in such phrases as that in the Old Swedish *Laws of Hälsingland* (*Hälsingelagen*),

---

[1] Original publication: "The Mythologized Past: Memory and Politics in Medieval Gotland." In *Minni and Muninn. Memory in Medieval Nordic Culture*, ed. Pernille Hermann, Stephen A. Mitchell, and Agnes S. Arnórsdóttir, 155–174. Acta Scandinavica, 4. Turnhout, 2014.

    On these and related issues in an Old Norse context, see the reviews and arguments in Hermann 2009 and 2010, as well as the essays in Hermann, Mitchell and Agnes S. Arnórsdóttir 2014. A parallel situation, in which popular memories and narratives are selectively preserved and shaped by elites, may be adduced from nineteenth- and twentieth-century traditions of folklore collecting, archiving, and publishing, the subject of Skott's 2008 *Folkets minnen*.

[2] See, for example, the views expressed by Hugo of St. Victor, Albertus Magnus, Thomas Aquinas and others in Mary Carruthers and Jan M. Ziolkowski, eds, *The Medieval Craft of Memory*.

[3] *SD* no. 832, 1:690–691.

[4] For examples of this view in both Old Norse literature and medieval Scandinavian historiography, see Glauser 2007 and Hermann 2009.

minnugha mæn, the "men of memory" on whom it relies for truth.[5] The archbishop's concerns, and his remedy, are of general interest to us because they pointedly raise the question of mediality in the North; however, what makes his letter of *particular* interest to this discussion of Gotlandic history is that it has been argued that *this* letter is itself connected in important ways with the very idea of writing out Gotland's history in a narrative form.

The Sources

Gotland distinguishes itself in the East Scandinavian area for the existence of an early prose history of the territory, the so-called *Guta saga*. Written in Old Gutnish, *Guta saga* is a brief (ca. 1,800 words) narrative encompassing the legendary events of the island's past: how its first settler brought fire to the island, thus preventing its magical disappearance into the water during the day, and how the island was then settled by his three sons, each taking one third of the island from north to south, how it was Christianized, and so on. One cannot help but suspect that the surviving medieval text represents something of a collective précis of more elaborate, independent narratives, purpose-written in this instance to support a distinctively Gotlandic view of the island's history.[6]

The oldest text of the "saga" survives in a fourteenth-century manuscript (Cod. Holm. B64) mostly devoted to the so-called provincial laws (*landskapslagar*) of the island.[7] Most researchers have concluded that the extant *Guta saga* was shaped in the thirteenth century.[8] The possibility that it may

---

[5] "þa witi þæt II minnungæ mæn af aþrum soknum ok II præstir huru þæt hawr wærit" (*Hälsingelagen*, 9) (then two "men of memory" from a different parish and two priests shall establish how it has been). Cf. Le Goff (1992:73), "The Middle Ages venerated old men above all because they were regarded as memory-men, prestigious and useful." See also his discussion of the institution of the *mnemon* on pages 56 and 63.

[6] Or so, at least, I have argued in Mitchell 1984.

[7] The text was described by Carl Säve in the nineteenth century as "En verklig Gotlands-Saga eller liten Gutnisk Landnamabok" (A veritable Gotland Saga or a little Gotlandic Books of Settlements), and has at various times been called *Gutasaga, the Legendary History of Gotland, Historia Gotlandiæ, Gullandskrønike*, and *Gotlændinga saga*. Its designation as a *saga* is not at all out of place insofar as the term fundamentally means an account, history or narrative but, of course, insofar as it has come to imply a tale of some length associated, in Scandinavia, at least, with composition in Iceland, is misleading.

[8] Whether the date is early or late in the century has been a matter of some debate. Among those arguing for an early date is Läffler 1908:167. On the more general assessment of a thirteenth-century origin, see Wessén 1982 [1956–1978]; Naumann 1968, but cp. Sjöholm 1976, who

have been composed early in the thirteenth century has largely centered on the perceived connections, both historical and verbal, between the Gutnish narrative and the letter referred to above from Archbishop Andreas Suneson of Lund to the Bishop of Linköping sometime between 1220 and 1223. The letter's discussion of episcopal visitation to the island, it is argued, shows strong verbal ties to the section of *Guta saga* also dealing with that topic.[9]

In addition to the Old Gutnish original, *Guta saga*, or parts of it, also exists in a number of translations into the major languages in the island's history. These include a fifteenth-century Swedish translation (Cod. Holm. D2), and three partial Danish translations, all now generally held to be late medieval and reformation era works independent of one another.[10] A German translation, the only complete rendering of the text into another tongue, dates to 1401; importantly, it was executed exactly during the period (1398–1409), when control of the island was in the hands of the Teutonic Order.[11] Like the B64 manuscript, the German *Guta saga* follows immediately after the translation of the island's provincial laws into German in Cod. Holm. B65. Thus, the text's connections, both functional and codicological, with the medieval laws of Gotland need to be understood as deep and significant, and it is likely this symbiotic relationship between the narrative and the legal traditions of the island that accounts for the fact that the various translations, Swedish, German, and Danish, generally follow the B64 text closely as regards content.[12]

---

argues for a date roughly a century later. In a recent assessment of the dating question, Peel notes in her commentary in *Guta saga* 1999, lii–liii, "It thus seems reasonable to propose a *terminus ante quem* for the composition of *Guta saga* of 1275 or very shortly thereafter, with a *terminus post quem* of 1220 as agreed by the majority of scholars." Stobaeus 2010:79–80, the most recent review of the dating question, forwards new, and to my mind, convincing, evidence to suggest that the text came about in the second half of the thirteenth century.

[9] Cf. the analysis in Läffler 1908:162–169, who notes that the relevance of this correspondence was argued already in J. H. Schröder (and C. A. Weström) 1848:2–3. The possibility of this relationship has awakened considerable debate, including in recent years the question of whether the archbishop's letter might possibly be a medieval forgery, itself built on *Guta saga*. See the discussion and bibliography, including rejections of this theory, in Stobaeus 2010:79.

[10] For brief introductions to the texts, see Wessén 1982 [1956–1978]; Mitchell 1993a; and Naumann 1968; for a comprehensive review of the literature, see *Guta saga* 1999, x–xiv. Detailed commentaries and editions of the later texts are provided in Jacobsen 1911 and *Guta saga* 1959.

[11] See H. U. Schmid 2006:62.

[12] Scholarly opinion about the *Guta saga* stemma varies, but generally holds that a now missing thirteenth-century original gave rise to three branches, of which the mid-fourteenth century B64 manuscript is the oldest surviving text; however, the differences between the texts as regards narrative content are slight. See *Guta saga* 1999, xiii.

Chapter 10. The Mythologized Past   193

Augmenting our knowledge of the history of the island, and apparently independent of the *Guta saga* materials, are the annalistic materials from the Franciscan monastery in Visby, contained in Cod. Holm. B99.[13] Gotland's story continued to be a subject of interest for history writers well into the post-medieval world, especially in the sweeping narrative provided in Hans Nielsson Strelow's *Cronica Guthilandorum* (1633). Also of interest is *Cimbrorum et Gothorum origines* by Nicolaus Petreius (alt., Niels Pedersen), written in the period 1573–1579, but not published until 1695.[14] But whereas Strelow's work represents an expansive—and native Gotlandic—view of all things connected with the history and traditions of Gotland, Petreius has a goal that is much narrower. Crudely summarized, he is a Danish functionary briefly stationed on Gotland arguing for an identification of the Gotlanders with the Goths of history, and, thus, ultimately looking to legitimize the Danish king's connection to these famous brigands of history. Among many other resources, both authors make much use of *Guta saga*, but neither of them shows the sort of fidelity to that text exhibited by the *Guta saga* translators. At the same time, both authors footnote or document their versions of history by multiple references to various "objects of memory," not just to the *Guta saga* text but to the monuments, onomastics, traditions, and the natural and built landscape of Gotland.

As these comments suggest, my main concern here is, of course, not in the earlier traditions that inform *Guta saga*, but rather in exploring the ways Gotlandic history in and after the thirteenth century is shaped. In other words, what results do we see from the call by Archbishop Andreas Suneson for a firm written form of the past? His position is rational, but as we will see, the apparent fixity of the written text shows itself to be every bit as susceptible to manipulation and the vagaries of selective recollection, whether intentional or not, as the oral tradition he fears. More than simply a demonstration of the capacity of authors working in a written medium to treat their materials as malleably as their oral counterparts, I am also curious about what has been included and what has been left out of the Gotlandic historical narrative as it is massaged (= translated, embellished, retold, rewritten, and transformed) over four centuries.

As a means of exploring the way the past is selectively preserved, memorialized, elided, and so on, in the context of this new medieval media culture,

---

[13] *Visbyfranciskanernas bok*, 52–69; facs. 43–49; the main text, covers the years 815–1444.

[14] On, and for, Petreius, see Körner 2008. One of the Danish translations of *Guta saga* is bound with a manuscript of *Cimbrorum et Gothorum origines*; see *Guta saga* 1999, xi.

I focus here on two key episodes in the history of medieval Gotland and how they are represented, if at all, in the island's history over time, from the thirteenth century through the seventeenth, namely, 1) Gotland's conversion to Christianity, and 2) the mid-fourteenth-century bubonic pandemic.

Conversion Narratives

In histories almost entirely written and recorded by churchmen (both before and after the Reformation), it is hardly surprising that the Christian conversion of pagan Gotland is painted quite vividly in *Guta saga*, with a description of the Gotlanders' lamentable and lurid heathen practices, rituals which are said to have even included human sacrifice.[15] *Guta saga* then offers detailed information about how the island is transformed from this heathen state into a Christian world. Like the famous dual creation myths of the biblical Genesis (1:1–2:3, 2:4–2:25), *Guta saga* provides two versions of the Christianization process, one directly tied to the figure of St. Olaf (Óláfr inn helgi Haraldsson) as an outside agent of change, the other lacking this historical figure and emphasizing the Gotlanders' own initiatives in promoting Christianity.[16] Quoting Christine Peel's translation, *Guta saga* relates the following about Olaf's role in the process:

> Later, after this, King Olaf the Saint came fleeing *from Norway* with his ships, and laid into *a harbour, the one called Akergarn*. St. Olaf lay there a long time. Then *Ormika of Hejnum*, and several other powerful men, went to him with their gifts. Ormika gave him *twelve yearling rams along with other valuables*. St. Olaf then reciprocated and gave him in return *two round drinking vessels and a battle-axe*. Ormika subsequently received Christianity according to St. Olaf's teaching and built himself *an oratory at the same location as Akergarn church now stands*. From there St. *Olaf travelled to visit Jaroslav in Novgorod*.[17] [emphases added]

---

[15] "Blotaþu þair synum ok dytrum sinum ok fileþi miþ mati ok mungati. Þet gierþu þair eptir vantro sinni. Land alt hafþi sir hoystu blotan miþ fulki" (*Guta saga* 1999:4) (They sacrificed their sons and daughters, and cattle, together with food and ale. They did that in accordance with their ignorance of the true faith. The whole island held the highest sacrifice on its own account, with human victims, otherwise each third held its own) (*Guta saga* 1999:5).

[16] See the review of literature in *Guta saga* 1999, xxxvi–xl, and Pernler 1977:11–19. As a practical matter, I will use the personal name form Olaf except in quoting other texts or in reference to their usage.

[17] *Guta saga* 1999:9. The original reads in full, "Eptir þet siþan quam helgi Olafr kunungr flyandi af Norvegi miþ skipum ok legþis i hamn, þa sum kallar Akrgarn. Þar la helgi Olafr lengi. Þa for

To some extent, this story intersects with West Norse traditions about this missionary king-turned-saint, insofar as Olaf is said to have been on Gotland in 1007 as a twelve-year-old, where, according to his court skald, Óttar, he forced the Gotlanders to pay him tribute.[18] There may be a suggestion in the conflicting West Norse accounts of Olaf's journey in 1029–1030 to Russia that he again stopped at Gotland but certainly nothing that would directly account for the story as it is developed in Gotlandic tradition. Still, some sort of presence on Gotland by this famous missionary king is indicated.

Notably, the *Guta saga* author frames his story by having the king flee from Norway to Gotland and then, at the end of the narrative, Olaf departs from the island for Novgorod. Thus, Gotland is situated in the middle of the "mental map" sketched by the saint's journey. If the typical medieval *mappa mundi* places Jerusalem at its center, the image sketched here looks to do something similar for Gotland. It should be noted too how well this brief narrative, and its projection of truth value (however fabulous its composition

---

Ormika af Hainaim ok flairi rikir menn til hans miþ giefum sinum. Þann Ormika gaf hanum tolf veþru miþ andrum klenatum. Þa gaf helgi Olafr kunungr hanum atr agin tua bulla ok aina braiþyxi. Þa tok Ormika viþr kristindomi eptir helga Olafs kennidomi ok gierþi sir bynahus i sama staþ, sum nu standr Akrgarna kirkia. Þeþan for helgi Olafr til Ierslafs i Hulmgarþi," *Guta saga* 1999:8.

[18] According to *Óláfs saga helga*, "Óláfr konungr sigldi um haustit til Gotlands ok bjósk þar at herja. En Gotar hǫfðu þar samnað ok gerðu menn til konungs ok buðu honum gjald af landinu. Þat þekkðisk konungr ok tekr gjald af landinu ok sat þar um vetrinn. Svá segir Óttarr:

Gildir, komtu at gjaldi
gotneskum her, flotna.
Þorðut þér að varða
þjóðlǫnd firar rǫndu.
Rann, en maðr of minna
margr býr of þrek, varga
hungr frák austr, an yngvi,
Eysýslu lið, þeyja."
(*Óláfs saga helga*, 9 [Chap. 7])

(King Óláfr sailed in the autumn to Gotland and started to lay it waste. But the Gotlanders met together there and sent men to the king and offered him tribute from the country. The king accepted it and took tribute from the country and spent the winter there. So says Óttar:

From the troops of Gotland, tribute
you took, sailors' supporter;
mean dared not defend from you
the folk's land with the shield-rim.
They ran, Eysýsla people;
plenty possess less daring
than the king; I heard wolves had their
hunger, in the east, lessened.)
(*Óláfr Haraldsson (The Saint)*, 6–7)

may in the end prove to be) is enmeshed in the geography and onomastics of northeastern and north central Gotland: the king anchors in a harbor called Akergarn, where a chapel is built in honor of the king, "i sama staþ, sum nu standr Akrgarna kirkia" (at the same location as Akergarn church now stands). Subsequently renamed St. Olafshamn (St. Olaf harbor), the church there—a St. Olaf church, naturally, one of many on the medieval island whose patron saint he became—apparently enjoyed a significant income by the thirteenth century.[19] Importantly, the saga specifies that Ormika accepts Christianity "according to St. Olaf's teaching" (eptir helga Olafs kennidomi), a phrase widely, although only with uncertainty, assumed to suggest a break with the influence of other Christian traditions, such as the Orthodox church's.[20] The ritualized exchange of gifts—Ormika's twelve rams to Olaf and Olaf's gift of two drinking vessels and a battle-ax, the saint's most important physical attribute in later iconography (and providing a connection between the text and his image in subsequent Gotlandic church art)—simultaneously conveys to the audience the sense of medieval traditions of christening gifts, of Gotland as a trading nation, of the reciprocal respect being shown by the saint and the Gotlanders, and perhaps of the stories about Olaf having received tribute from the islanders in order to halt his harrying there.

For a variety of reasons, not least the degree to which the *Guta saga* version clashes with other sources, it has been reasonably suggested that the scenario in which Olaf is portrayed as "Gotland's apostle" is a narrative developed in response to the growing Olaf-cult of the thirteenth century from information about the royal saint's eleventh-century visits to Gotland.[21] This version thus places Gotland's Christianization squarely at the center of one of northern Europe's fastest growing cults and builds on historical events, events memorialized in part by the landscape: the harbor, the chapel, Akergarn church, and the prominence in the process of the Hejnum region, whose parish church conspicuously displayed its historical connections with St. Olaf.

Having thus established the key role in Gotland's conversion process for one of medieval Scandinavia's great cult figures, the saga then goes on to say, ignoring the previous tale about Ormika's conversion, that when they were pagans, the Gotlanders had gone on trading voyages to other countries, both

---

[19] Cf. *Guta saga* 1999:38–39.

[20] See, for example, Blomkvist, Brink, and Lindkvist 2007:184.

[21] See the excellent reviews of secondary literature in Pernler 1977:11–19, and Pernler 1981:101–114.

Christian and heathen. Some consequently became Christians and brought priests back with them. What follows in this second conversion narrative, apparently untroubled by its juxtaposition with the first, is a vastly less placid version of the island's Christianization than the one surrounding Olaf's activities. Here we get a tale of native Christian converts being set upon by native pagans—after the initial comment about foreign priests, these figures simply fade away and are nowhere to be found later in the tale. Here again, but with vastly greater profusion, the story's factuality is undergirded by a plethora of still identifiable place-names: Botair of Akebäck builds the first church, "in that place which is now called Kulstäde." The pagan islanders burn it, for which reason (apparently) the location is known as *Kulstäde* ("charcoal place"?). Botair builds a second church at Vi, where a sacrifice is taking place, and he defends it by going into the church and saying that if people want to burn it, they will have to burn him as well. Because of his status, and that of his powerful father-in-law, who lives at a place called Stenkyrka "stone church," and who reminds the pagans of the sacred nature of the location (Vi), the church is left standing. This man, Likkair, is said to have had great authority, and he is reported to have said: "Do not persist in burning the man or his church, since it stands at Vi, below the cliff."[22]

Although scholars have argued at length about the name *Vi* and the degree to which the text here may or may not refer to the location of medieval Visby, it is obvious from the references both to the cliff and to the specific site called St. Peter's (but formerly known as Allhelgona) that whatever the "real" historical situation may or may not have been, within the narrative we are to understand that this location is indeed at the very heart of the emerging commercial capital of the island. It is surely not irrelevant that this church is said to be the first—St. Olaf's earlier oratory notwithstanding—to survive on the island ("Han var fyrsti kirkia i Gutlandi, sum standa fikk"). From this centrally located house of worship, others descend: Liccair's church, at the place "now called Stenkyrka," is the first church in the northern third of the island. The author then assures his audience that Gotlanders begin becoming Christians of their own will and without duress, and that a second church is built at Atlingbo, in the middle third of

---

[22] "Botair af Akubek hit þann sum fyrsti kirkiu gierþi, i þan staþ, sum nu haitir Kulasteþar. Þet vildi ai land þula utan brendu hana. Þy kallar þar enn Kulasteþar. Þa eptir þan tima var blotan i Vi. Þar gierþi kirkiu aþra. Þa samu kirkiu vildi land ok brenna. Þa for hann sielfr upp a kirkiu þa ok segþi: 'Vilin ir brenna, þa skulin ir brenna mik miþ kirkiu þissi.' Hann var rikr sielfr ok *rikasta manz dotur hafþi hann, sum hit Likkair *snielli, boandi þar, sum kallar Stainkirkiu. Hann reþ mest um þan tima. Hann halp Botairi, magi sinum, ok segþi so: 'Herþin ai brenna mann ella kirkiu hans, þy et han standr i Vi, firir niþan klintu.'" *Guta saga* 1999:8–9.

the island. And then in the southern third of Gotland, a church goes up in Fardhem. And from these churches, others spread everywhere in Gotland.

It is obvious here that the mythology of the growth of the church on Gotland mirrors, and I suggest is meant to mirror, exactly the origin legend of the island: just as the first settler must bring fire to keep the island above water, the first Christian must brave fire in order to assure the survival of the island's first church. And just as from that original settler, three brothers descend who divide the island up into thirds and populate it with their descendants, so too does the growth of churches on the island follow the same process, beginning in the northern third, and moving to the middle third, and then to the southern third.[23] Here the author of *Guta saga* has, I think, used a highly traditional pattern, well-documented throughout the Germanic world, and certainly an intimate aspect of the island's mythology, to present the conversion of the island.

The *Guta saga* translations carefully follow suit, of course. On the other hand, *Chronica Visbycensis* does not discuss this process at all, contenting itself with simply noting St. Olaf's martyrdom. Writing in the sixteenth century (but a text not printed until a century later), Petreius specifically mentions that he wants to avoid the sense that he is focused on the pagan past and has forgotten Christianity. In his telling of the story of Olaf and Ormika, the gifts from Ormika are because Olaf lacked foodstuffs; in return, Ormika is given an ax and two silver chalices. But the greatest gift to Gotland is that Olaf converts Ormika. A chapel is subsequently built, and Ormika lives at the place called *Krekebol* (= *kirkebol* "church dwelling"), which, it is noted, still exists in Hejnum parish.

Strelow's 1633 account, as is so often the case, is more detail-rich than these earlier tales and differs, in fact differs substantially, from them. It is generally assumed that, particularly as a native of the island, he is mirroring the folk traditions of his own day. In Strelow's version, Olaf is on a mission to Gotland precisely because he has heard that they are heathens. He explains how Olaf had arrived at locations which are now no longer by the water and how the remains of his ship's mooring rings were visible in the cliff until recently ("huor nu er tørt Land oc store Fyrreskofue for faa Aar /

---

[23] "Þair skiptu siþan Gutlandi i þria þriþiunga, so et Graipr, þann elzti, laut norþasta þriþiung ok Guti miþal þriþiung. En Gunfiaun, þann yngsti, laut sunnarsta. Siþan af þissum þrim aukaþis fulk i Gutlandi so mikit um langan tima, et land elpti þaim ai alla fyþa." (They later divided Gotland into thirds, in such a way that Graipr the eldest inherited the northern third, Guti the middle third and Gunfiaun the youngest inherited the southernmost. Subsequently, from these three men, the population of Gotland increased so much over a long period of time that the land was not able to support them all.) *Guta saga* 1999:2–3.

siden ere de store Jernringe seet i Klippen / huor ved hans Skibe skulle været fested / nu udhugne").[24] And now follow entire episodes not known to other traditions, including Olaf's going ashore and spying *in cognito* as a beggar, only to be recognized by his royal undergarments when a servant girl at the home where he is staying watches him through a keyhole. His host reveals himself to be a Christian and Olaf in turn explains to him his goal of converting the Gotlanders. A great battle takes place then between the pagans and Christians, complete with people, place names and a miracle in which the imprint of Olaf's knee and arm—which had sunk into the stone as he prayed—are said to still be visible. Having won the victory, Olaf then harries widely and forces the Gotlanders to become Christians, all the while accepting tribute (*Brandskatt aff Siølff oc Guld*).[25]

Olaf overwinters and has *Ackergaarns* church built on *S. Olufs Holm*, which Strelow notes is now desolate, although some of the church's walls are still visible. Ormika of Hienum, now referred to as a woman, and others, visit Olaf, presenting him with a wide array of foodstuffs, and she is baptized (but no longer is there any reference to "according to Olaf's wisdom" or the like). Olaf travels to Kirkeby where he has built "the large stone building where his bed, his chair, his washbasin" (det store Stenhuus / huor hans Seng / hans Stoel / hans Haandfad) are still visible. Olaf then—in 1029—sails to Russia. In certain ways, specifically, the battle between Olaf's forces and the Gotlanders and the matter of tribute, Strelow's presentation of Olaf's visit stands in better accord with *Heimskringla*'s account and since there is little likelihood of the West Norse text having been known so early to Strelow, it seem possible that his version reflects folk traditions uninflected by the tendentious elite version of *Guta saga*.

Strelow then follows the account of the second conversion process as it is given in *Guta saga* fairly carefully, complete with its many identified people and places, until we get to another strange change in the identity and gender of one of the saga's characters. In the thirteenth-century text, Botair is married to the unnamed daughter of Likkair Snielli ("the wise"), who lived at a place called "stone church." In Strelow's account, Botair's wife is named *Lickersmella*, the daughter of Tyssi of "stone church." Whether this amalgamation of the names given in *Guta saga* into a single name is the result of a misreading of the manuscript or part of some tradition outside the manuscripts is not easy to say. In any event, it did not start with Strelow. One of

---

[24] Strelow, *Cronica Guthilandorum*, 130.

[25] Strelow, *Cronica Guthilandorum*, 131.

the Danish translations, Ny Kgl. Saml. 408 8:o, from c. 1500, has the same configuration as Strelow: Botiar [!] "had a rich man's daughter who had most authority at that time and she was called *lickher snalle*."[26]

I suspect that what we do *not* see in these histories of Gotland is the scenario where one written text gives direct rise to another, but rather a heavily reticulated stemmata, one suggesting a complex relationship between written texts coming from the hands of the clerical culture, on the one side, and oral traditions from *all* elements of Gotlandic society, on the other.[27] In the stories of Gotland's conversion, two different and partially opposed forces are at work: medieval Christian thinking and traditional Germanic mythological patterns.

In the first case, we see a story shaped by Christian considerations aimed at giving the island a role in one of the region's best-known saint's lives, indeed, the saint who becomes the island's patron saint. In this way, the Olaf story responds to, shapes, and perpetuates two important local myths: 1) the independent, uncoerced, free nature of major changes in the island's governance and political life, and 2) a myth in which Gotland stands at the center of the northern world as evidenced by the "fact" that its conversion through the martyred Christian king, St. Olaf, represents his very first missionary achievement while still only a youth.

In the second conversion narrative, we see this same basic experience, of how the Gotlanders came to be Christians, shaped according to very traditional Germanic modes of thought, not only in terms of the Gotlanders' own island history but paralleled by the roughly contemporary presentation of Norse pagan cosmography in *Snorra edda* and traceable as far back as the story provided by Tacitus (AD 98) of the Germanic progenitor Tuisto, with his son Mannus, who in turn sires three sons.[28] Casting the conversion story in this way, parallel to traditional Germanic origin legends, thus places the rather mundane tale of foreign commercial contacts leading to Christianity

---

[26] The ambiguity of whether it was the father or daughter who had the authority is implicit in the manuscript form. *Guta saga* 1959:23, "Ok haffdhe righæ mantaz dotther / som rodhe mesth oppaa then tidh / Ok hwn heth lickher snalle."

[27] Cf. the comment by Le Goff 1992:68, that "the most characteristic traits of memory in the Middle Ages" are "the Christianization of memory and mnemotechnology" and "the division of collective memory between a circular liturgical memory and a lay memory little influenced by chronology."

[28] On this topic, see the summary of materials in Schütte 1926–1934. Cp. Gutenbrunner 1936 and Avis 2009.

into a mythic mold known to the audience. It was part and parcel of the Gotlanders' so-called "ethnic memory."[29]

Clearly, both conversion narratives are responding to, and contributing to, traditions, but traditions of different sorts.

The Fourteenth-Century Plague

Against these multiple, popular, creative, vibrant and competing myths of the island's conversion, with their many references to the memorial landscape of the island, its churches, places, prominent families and so on, I want to set a different kind of memory, the empty set, that is, when there is, by accident or planning, *oblivion*, that is, *no memory*. The absence of memory, although not lending itself to lengthy description or multiformity, also tells a tale. A lack of memory, or more specifically, the erased memory, can also be a conscious social construct every bit as meaningful as the more obvious forms of memory, where we would use terms like retention, recollection, and memorialization.[30] An easy-to-miss yet important example of this sort of empty set from Gotland comes from an incident connected to the great fourteenth-century pandemic, known as the Black Death (or *digerdöden*), which is frequently said, although with uncertain factuality, to have hit Gotland with particular ferocity.

In addition to the deaths resulting directly from the bubonic plague itself, a number of innocent people across Europe, Jews in particular, are killed amid rumor panics that follow the spread of the plague and the suggestion that people outside "normal" society—Jews, Muslims, lepers—are conspiring to undermine Christian society by poisoning wells and other water sources.[31] Gotland does not escape this rumor panic, and according to information preserved in the archives of several north German cities, an uncertain number of people, perhaps as many as nine—one of whom we know by

---

[29] Cf. Le Goff 1992:55–58. I employ "ethnic memory" here but note that students of culture coming from many disciplinary directions—history, folklore, anthropology, to name some of the most prominent—have over the decades looked to explain the nature of such memories and their continuity over time; in the process, they developed an array of terms to describe the phenomenon, terms often freighted with theoretical orientations, such as superorganic, cultural memory, ethnohistory, mentifact, tradition, and mnemohistory.

[30] Burke 1997:57, refers to such erasures as "social amnesia" and "acts of oblivion," and asks (p. 58), "Can groups, like individuals, suppress what it is inconvenient to remember?"

[31] On this point, see, for example, the excellent discussion in Ginzburg 1991:33–86, as well as, more generally, Harrison 2000.

name, Tidericus—have supposedly poisoned wells and also murdered people through even more ingenious forms of poisoning throughout Sweden (i.e., in Stockholm, Västerås, and Arboga, as well as Visby); moreover, they are supposedly in the pay of the Jews. Some of them, perhaps all nine, are burned at the stake in Visby in July 1350.[32]

Several aspects of this event are striking: one is the fact that one of the condemned men maintains that it is the Jews and "we villains" who are poisoning all of Christendom (*sed tota christianitas est per Judeos et pessimos nos intoxicata*). What group he means by the "villains" phrase is unclear and has understandably caused considerable puzzlement.[33] Because he is identified as an *organista* "organist," the inference is made that this man may be an itinerant organ builder, but in any event, an outsider to Visby and Gotland in several different ways. Of a very different sort are the identities of two of the other condemned men: they are both priests and said to be guilty of worse offences than the others. One of them confesses that when he celebrated mass in St. Olaf's church in Visby on the second day of Pentecost (*secunda Penthecostes*), he infused the *mapula* (a napkin, or maniple) with poison such that those who kissed it died within a day or two. He also warns, as he is about to be burned, that all of Christendom may be doomed and that "you should beware of priests and other religious [persons]" (*quia vobis cavere debetis pro sacerdotibus et religiosis aliis quibuscunque*).[34]

But while the ferocity of the plague itself is mentioned in passing in contemporary and later documents,[35] and the term for the pandemic, *digerdöden*, is even famously memorialized in a late medieval runic inscription in

---

[32] The events are recounted by the council in Visby to the council in Rostock, from whence copies were further distributed to other various Hanseastic cities. For the texts of the two extant letters, see *Codex diplomaticus Lubecensis, Lübeckisches Urkundenbuch*, No. 110 A-B, 103–106. The more interesting communication with regard to events on Gotland is the 'B' letter, also published in *SD* no. 4655, 6:259–260, as well as in *En giftmordares bekännelser*, in both the original Latin and in modern Swedish translation, with a note on the letter's textual history on page 20. See also Myrdal 2003:87–88.

[33] The clause is translated in *En giftmordares bekännelser*, 19, as "men hela kristenheten är förgiftad av judarna och oss uslingar."

[34] *Codex diplomaticus Lubecensis, Lübeckisches Urkundenbuch*, No. 110 B, 196.

[35] For example, *Visbyfranciskanernas bok*, 50: "Anno Domini mcccl fuit maxima pestilencia per totum mundum" ("AD 1350 there was the greatest pestilence throughout the whole world"); Strelow, *Cronica Guthilandorum*, 162: "Aar 1350 / var en swer Pestilenße / kalledis den dyre død / der om er giort saadan it Verß: *Rystram triustrum Spid longum tunc mala pestis.*" (In the year 1350 there was a terrible pestilence called the great death (*dyre* for *diger*), about which this verse is made: *Rystram* (= M) *triustrum* (trevurstum? = CCC) *Spid longum* (= L), i.e., 1350 then evil plague). On this verse and parallel examples, see Mansa 1873:68–69.

Lärbro church, these horrific executions by burning find no place, none at all, in the medieval and early modern histories of the island. In fact, whether by design or accident, we only know about the event from references in documents preserved in various north German cities.

Perhaps it was a crime against the senses so great that it had to be actively erased, or, conversely, an act so banal and inconsequential, that it was simply forgotten, although this is difficult for the modern imagination to comprehend. Then again perhaps the violent events a dozen years later, when in 1362 the city is conquered by King Valdemar Atterdag of Denmark, have so overshadowed the plague conspiracy and executions that no one remembers them. A further possibility is that the event's consignment to the dustbin of history should be connected with the active roles in the events of the two clerics as poisoners found guilty of the most heinous crimes. It may not be unreasonable to imagine that the clerical conspiracy theories of the mid-fourteenth century offended later ecclesiastics such that they actively erased the narrative from the island's history. The fact that the gruesome spectacle is not recorded in, for example, the contemporary entries in *Visbyfranciskanernas bok* suggests that already at the time of the executions, there was a vested interest in not remembering the awful occasion.

In any event, unlike the conversion narratives, with their elaborate references to families, genealogies, and the homesteads and churches dotting the landscape, this fiery event—apparently involving at least some foreigners without these kinds of complex local connections and whose deaths were not subject to the sort of elaborate memorialization to which, for example, Valdemar Atterdag's 1361 invasion of the island gave rise—slips, or is erased, from memory.[36]

Conclusion

This essay began by asking how socially constructed memory contributes to the mythologizing of the past, that is, how the identity of a small insular community is shaped over time, and with what references to its history and that history's associated texts, monuments, landscapes, games, songs, and other mnemonic aids?[37] This brief foray into Gotland's constructed past

---

[36] This event and the question of its treatment was the basis for an excellent recent conference presentation. See Cole 2012, as well as his 2020 monograph on this episode.

[37] Strelow, *Cronica Guthilandorum*, for example, makes elaborate allusions to the built landscape and to island traditions: he notes and reproduces monuments commemorating calamities (p. 171)

suggests that all of these means—and more (such as the rituals and celebrations on St. Olaf's day, July 29)—played their parts as members of the island's population selected, shaped and valorized their visions of its past, but perhaps nowhere more so than when its communal historical narrative, both the canonical *Guta saga* text and its many unrecorded multiforms, was performed (a term meant to include every occasion on which the story was read, told, referred to, or formed the basis for further elaborations).[38]

At first blush, as many have noted, the word "memory" tends to conjure a sense of what individuals personally recall from their own lived experiences, the remembrances, recollections, and so on of particular people; when we transfer the idea of memory from the individual to a broader social level, to a Halbwachian sense of "collective memory," agency naturally continues to matter. Who "remembers" and what they "remember" counts, especially when such memories are given shape as narratives, plastic arts, rituals, and so on. By reference to various objects of memory, Gotland's "men of memory," a term I intend here in a non-technical sense to include all those who contributed to the island's proto-national narrative, gave their versions of Gotlandic history sustenance, making plausible their projections of the island's "memories."[39] But as the treatment in Gotlandic tradition of Tidericus and the others at the time of bubonic plague suggests, it was also possible for inconvenient or unpleasant memories to be elided, an erasure behind which one suspects a studied act of commission and thus oblivion of a different character than merely forgetting.[40] In this sense, willful forget-

---

and carefully records games and songs mocking Valdemar Atterdag before his conquest of the island in 1361, performances which he says were enacted everywhere throughout the island (pp. 168–169). As Zachrisson 2003:119, notes in her exploration of memory, folklore and landscape, the relationship between the built and natural surroundings and those memories we ascribe to them by way of names, events and narratives are both reciprocal and vital: "The immaterial and material memories give landscape its character."

[38] One senses the degree to which Strelow himself recognized the importance of this point when in his foreword, he quotes *Psalm* 78. st. 2 "Jeg vil udøse mørck Tale om Ting fra gammel tiid. st. 3 den som vi hafue hørt oc vide / oc vore Fædre fortellede os" (King James English translation, st. 2. I will utter dark sayings of old: st. 3. Which we have heard and known, and our fathers have told us.)

[39] The matter of agency, that is, whether Halbwachs's notion of collective memory is *of* the group or one shaped *for* the group by active tradition bearers within the group, has been an object of debate almost since the beginning. See the discussion and review of critical theories in Wertsch 2008.

[40] Memory studies sometimes use a leaky bucket analogy, in which the originally complete storehouse of information is drained over time of its contents; on this concept, see the review in Hermann 2009:288–290.

ting can be viewed as simply another form of remembering, or of actively constructing the past.

The synergy between Gotland's "traditions" (or to the extent that term is occasionally conceived in popular imagination as static and fixed, one might understandably prefer such dynamic terms as "cultural memory") and the goals of its "men of memory" was clearly profound.[41] The Gotlandic history that synergy has bequeathed to us provides a valuable lesson in how "memory studies" may in time finally lead to a realization of "tradition studies."[42]

---

[41] Cf. the comment by J. Assmann (1992:34) rejecting what he takes to be the usual understanding of tradition, but conceding that, "Gewiß läßt sich manches von dem, was hier mit den Begriffen *Erinnerungskultur* oder *kulturelles Gedächtnis* beschrieben wird, auch Tradition oder Überlieferung nennen. (Of course, some of those elements described by the terms "memory culture" or "cultural memory" may also be called tradition.) (*Cultural Memory and Early Civilization*, 20). Notably, Assmann uses the locution *Tradition oder Überlieferung* (elided in the translation), which adds in the original a sense not only of what is customary lore or habitual usage, but also a survival from the past. One assumes that Assmann has in mind something akin to the nineteenth century's fondness for the analogy of tradition to a fossil found in a field (and here I am especially thinking of Andrew Lang), rather than the view in modern folklore that tradition is by definition a dynamic process, or as the view is sometimes phrased, all tradition is change.

[42] Cf. the discussion of this idea, tradition research and traditions science in Bronner 2000, who notes, "There is yet to be conceived a program in tradition studies or traditionology. But there may well be one in the future if multidisciplinary efforts to engage continuities and themes of culture grow further."

PART III

Traditions and Innovations

Chapter 11

HEROIC LEGEND AND ONOMASTICS
HÁLFS SAGA, *DAS HILDEBRANDSLIED* AND THE LISTERBY STONES

Several years ago, Gregory Nagy, referring to epic heroes from Greek, Indian, Hittite and other traditions, commented, "These constructs—let us call them simply 'characters' for the moment—are in some ways radically dissimilar from each other. Even within a single tradition like Homeric poetry, heroes like Achilles and Odysseus seem worlds apart. In other ways, however, 'epic heroes' are strikingly similar to each other, sharing a number of central features. The question is, how to explain these similarities?"[1] In answering this question, Nagy demonstrates how the similarity of epic heroes to each other can be accounted for by integrating three comparative methods, which he describes as (1) typological, (2) genealogical, and (3) historical. Nagy explores this idea in several specific cases (e.g., Herakles, Achilles), and underscores in his discussion the cult hero as epic hero (and the reverse), a figure whose career is marked by unseasonality, extremism, and antagonism toward the god to whom he bears the closest resemblance.

---

[1] Original publication: "Heroic Legend and Onomastics: *Hálfs saga, Das Hildebrandslied* and the Listerby Stones." In *Donum natalicium digitaliter confectum Gregorio Nagy septuagenario a discipulis collegis familiaribus oblatum / A virtual birthday gift presented to Gregory Nagy on turning seventy by his students, colleagues, and friends*, ed. Leonard Mueller and David Elmer. Washington, D.C., 2012. https://chs.harvard.edu/book/donum-natalicium-digitaliter-confectum-gregorio-nagy-septuagenario-a-discipulis-collegis-familiaribus-oblatum/

G. Nagy 2006. I take this opportunity to note that the present essay builds on and extends ideas I first outlined in Mitchell 1991a. I also want to thank the members of a recent graduate seminar at Harvard on the Germanic epic—Nicole Burgoyne, Leonard Neidorf, Seth Peabody and Frederick Reece—for their invaluable remarks on a draft of this essay.

One senses immediately that Nagy's observations have important implications not only for Hellenists but also for scholars engaged with other traditions. Inspired by his insights, the following comments look to extend Nagy's findings by applying his ideas and methodological innovations to a medieval northern Europe heroic complex, especially as it is articulated in the story of Hálfr Hjǫrleifsson, a Nordic champion known to us mainly as the eponymous hero of the legendary saga called *Hálfs saga ok Hálfsrekka* "the saga of Hálfr and Hálfr's warriors."[2]

Hálfs saga and Hálfr in Nordic Traditions

Preserved in a fifteenth-century manuscript (with numerous later copies), this tale has deep roots in the Nordic world and intersects with a number of other legendary traditions, in each case understood as referring to the hero of the saga.[3] In addition to the saga itself, his tale is mentioned in the thirteenth-century *Skáldskaparmál* of *Snorra Edda*, where the phrase *Hálfs bani* (Hálfr's bane) is cited as a *kenning* (metaphor) for "fire" (*Edda Sn* 2, 39). This metaphor was already used in describing the death of King Dómarr in the *Ynglingatal* of Þjóðólfr ór Hvini, traditionally dated to the ninth century.[4] Similar references to this same *Hálfr* dot the landscape of medieval Icelandic literature, often with references to his genealogy, his *berserkr* (pl. *berserkir*) status, and his warrior band: he is mentioned, for example, in *Geirmundar þáttr heljarskinns*, *Hversu Noregr byggðist*, and the lists of "sea-kings" in *Snorra Edda*.[5] He is also the king to whose court Guðrún flees in the *Poetic Edda* (*Guðrúnarqviða ǫnnor*) and in *Vǫlsunga saga*.[6] A recurrent theme in Old Icelandic literature portrays Hálfr and his warriors as valorized

---

[2] The text cited here is generally the normalized edition in *FAS* 1954, 2:93–134; for the diplomatic edition, consult *Hálfs saga ok Hálfsrekka* 1981.

[3] On this saga, see especially *Hálfs saga ok Hálfsrekka*; on the genre to which it belongs, see Mitchell 1991b.

[4] Quoted extensively in the *Ynglingasaga* of Snorri's *Heimskringla*, the dating of *Ynglingatal* has traditionally, but not without objection, been accepted as the ninth century. For the arguments in favor of this view, as well as a review of the extensive literature on the topic, see Sundqvist 2002. Cf. *Hóalfs galla* in the eleventh-century *Sexstefja* of Þjóðólfr Arórsson.

[5] Cf. Seelow's comments in *Hálfs saga* 1981:157–166. *Geirmundar þáttr heljarskinns* forms part of the saga but is also known from other texts; see Mitchell 1987.

[6] "Guðrún fór, unz hún kom til hallar Hálfs konungs" (*Vǫlsunga saga*, chap. 32) (Guðrún traveled until she came to the hall of King Hálfr); cf. *Guðrúnarqviða ǫnnor* 13$^{1-4}$ (*Edda. Die Lieder des Codex Regius*, 226).

ideal heroes from, and representing, the past. Thus, *Tóka þáttr Tókasonar* explicitly juxtaposes Hálfr and his warriors with one of Scandinavia's most renowned legendary kings and his champions, Hrólfr kraki.[7] The Hálfr image is employed in a similar way in *Magus saga jarls* (28–29, 31–32 [chaps. 15, 16]), where his size, strength and prowess are presented as legendary.

Hálfs saga ok Hálfsrekka itself consists of a series of narratives held together in the first instance by the genealogical ties of its heroes, but certain recurrent themes—such as the over- and under-valuation of familial bonds, ideas of manliness and honor—also provide connective threads binding the episodes together into a single entity.[8] In the first of these narratives, King Alrekr resolves the bickering of his two wives through a beer-brewing contest. The successful wife accomplishes this goal when Óðinn appears in disguise and she unwittingly agrees to give him, in exchange for his help, her unborn child, who will as an adult be sacrificed to Óðinn.[9] A series of killings, including a "burning-in," follows, the conflict precipitated, as so often in *Hálfs saga ok Hálfsrekka* and the other mythical-heroic sagas, by struggles over, and between, women.

The next section of the saga reports the story of Hjǫrleifr inn kvensami, "the Womanizer" or "the Amorous." A long series of adventures, including encounters with an ogre and a merman, traces the smoldering conflict between Hjǫrleifr's two surviving wives, Æsa and Hildr. When Hjǫrleifr's home is attacked, his wives and goods are taken by the attacker back to Denmark. Hjǫrleifr counter-attacks and enters his enemy's house, in which everyone is asleep except his first wife, Æsa, who is to show him the way to the Danish king. Instead, she treacherously locks Hjǫrleifr up and he is then, at her suggestion, hung between two fires. Once the household has feasted itself into a drunken stupor, Hjǫrleifr's second wife, Hildr, cuts him down. Hjǫrleifr hangs his enemy on the same gallows on which he himself had been strung up and takes his wives back to Norway with him, where, at an assembly, it is decided that Æsa should be drowned in a swamp. This is

---

[7] "Konungr mælti: 'Muna muntu þá Hálf konung ok rekka hans eða Hrólf kraka ok kappa hans'" (*Tóka þáttr Tókasonar*, 137 [chap. 1]) (The king spoke: Then you will remember king Hálfr and his warriors or Hrólfr kraki and his champions).

[8] And as is often the case with the Icelandic sagas, this one frequently traces the progeny of its legendary actors to specific lineages in Iceland. On this point, see Mitchell 1991b:122–126.

[9] The end of this narrative is related in *Gautreks saga* (chap. 7).

a retribution the king declines to take, with the result that their progeny are known in Iceland as the family of the Reyknesingar.[10]

The sons of Hjǫrleifr and Hildr are Hjǫrólfr and Hálfr. Hjǫrólfr, the eldest, mounts an expedition that stands as a paradigm for ill-prepared journeys: he takes all men regardless of their qualifications and they use all manner of weapons, with predictably disastrous results for Hjǫrólfr's prestige. Hjǫrólfr plays a very small role in the saga, being primarily a foil for his brother, Hálfr, and a vehicle for explaining a "fools go a-journeying" phrase in Icelandic.[11] Hálfr, determined not to make the same error, prepares his forces more carefully and the various champions who join him, after passing tests of strength and bravery, are enumerated. They become a great and renowned band of warriors and their code of heroic conduct is detailed. When King Hálfr arrives home from a voyage, he is met by his stepfather, Ásmundr, who invites him to his hall, along with "half" his troop. Hálfr's counselor, Innsteinn, advises him not to accept the invitation, because he suspects treachery, but the king rejects his words of warning. Hálfr and half his men go to the hall, and are fêted with strong drink. Once they are asleep, the hall is set aflame by Ásmundr's men. One of Hálfr's warriors awakes, smells the smoke, comments on it and falls asleep again. A second warrior does the same, this time remarking on the heat. Finally the king awakens, rallies his men, and they break through the walls to face their attackers. A battle ensues and eventually nearly all of the men, including Hálfr, are killed.[12] A long section on the fortunes of two of the survivors of Hálfr's warrior band, Útsteinn (Innsteinn's brother) and Hrókr the Black, follows.

The final section of the saga relates how Hálfr's son, Hjǫrr, and his queen have two sons. Hjǫrr is away at the time of their birth, and the queen,

---

[10] Icelandic sagas, including those based on heroic materials, often write leading families (presumably patrons) into the genealogies.

[11] *Hjǫrólfsfæri*, "Hjǫrólfr's opportunity (or shot, etc.)." "Hann hafði hvert skip, er hann fekk, smá ok stór, ný ok forn, ok hvern mann, er hann fekk, frjálsan ok nauðgan. Þeir hǫfðu margt til vápna: stengr ok stafi, klumbur ok kraka. Fyrir þá sǫk er þat kallat síðan Hjǫrólfsfæri, er ófimligt er. En er hann kom til orrostu við víkinga, þá treystist hann liðsfjǫlda ok lagði til orrostu. Hann hafði lið ókænt ok vápnlaust, ok fell margt lið hans, en sumt flýði, ok kom við þat aptr at hausti, ok varð hann lítill maðr fyrir sér." (*Hálfs saga* 1954:106 [chap. 9]). (He [Hjǫrólfr] took every ship he could get, small and large, new and old, and every man he could get, willing and levied. They had many weapons: poles and staffs, clubs and pales. For that reason that which is awkward is called a "Hjǫrólfr's opportunity." When he went into battle against vikings, he trusted in his great host and set to war. He had untrained and unarmed troops, and many of his men fell, but some fled, and on returning in the autumn, he had become a man of little account).

[12] This part of the plot has had a generous legacy in the ballad traditions of the Faroe Islands and Sweden; see Mitchell 1985.

finding them unattractive, exchanges them with the more comely son of a maid. When the children are older, the two brothers attack the "changeling" and reclaim their positions. Their mother confesses her misdeed to the king, but he refuses to acknowledge them as his sons, and asks that they be taken away, as he has never seen such "dark-skinned" children (*heliar skin*), by which name they are known thereafter. The text concludes by saying that the genealogies of the residents of Espihóll and Meðalfellsstrǫnd in Iceland can be traced back to these two brothers.[13]

Even this brief review of the saga's contents indicates that emphasis on two themes—the virtues that constitute manliness, and the proper, and improper, observation of familial ties—provides thematic unity to the saga, a unity strengthened by the generational linkage between the various forebears and descendants of Hálfr, who are the protagonists of the individual episodes, aspects of the saga to which we shall return.[14]

As the synopsis indicates, by the late medieval period, the name Hálfr was phonologically indistinguishable from the adjective "half" (e.g., *hálfr mánuðr* "half a month," "a fortnight"). That the word's synonymy was apparent to medieval saga writers and audiences is clear in the saga and played on several times, as when Hálfr fatefully accepts the invitation to the feast for himself and "half his troop."[15] The actual Proto-Scandinavian etymon of the name Hálfr is, however, quite different and of special interest, namely, Haþu-wulfR "battle-wolf" (< *haþu-* "battle" [cf. Old Norse *hǫð*, Old English *heaðo-*] + *wulfR* "wolf").[16]

This earlier dithematic name-form, HaþuwulfR, is documented on three famous, interrelated runestones from near Sölvesborg, Blekinge, in modern southern Sweden dating to the sixth to seventh centuries CE: Stentoften

---

[13] On the relationship of several of these episodes to Icelandic oral tradition, see Mitchell 1987.

[14] Cf. *mandómr* "manliness," "prowess"; *drengskapr* ("Tænkemaade, Opførsel, der gjør en til et saadant Menneske, som han bør være") (Fritzner 1973, 1:264) (*drengskapr*—mode of thinking, behavior, which causes one to behave as he should), etymologically derived from "young male" made into an abstract concept by the addition of the suffix (cf. virtue < Latin *virtūs* "manliness," "goodness").

[15] Both the poetry and prose of the saga refer to this play on words: "Vér skulum hálfir / herjar þessa / sáttir sækja / frá sjó neðan"; "ok bauð honum til veizlu ok hálfu liði hans," (*Hálfs saga* 1954:109, 108 [chap. 11]) ("One half shall / From shores below / To these lords / Go in peace"; "and invited him and half his followers to a feast").

[16] *HaþuwulfR > Hálfr* is widely accepted (e.g., Lind 1905–1931:452–453; de Vries 1962:204; Müller 1970:179; Hald 1971:33; Krause 1971:150–151). Without objecting to this development, Janzén (1948:76) suggests an alternative reading, but his views have generally remained unembraced. Sundqvist and Hultgård 2004:584–585, the most recent treatment of the question, includes an extensive review of the research literature and accepts the "battle-wolf" etymology.

(DR 357 U); Istaby (DR 359 U); and Gummarp (DR 358 U).[17] A further runic attestation to a later form of the name appears on a Christian runestone from Swedish Södermanland (Sö 270), hauIf (acc.), the sole runic reference to the name Haþuwulfar not associated with the Blekinge stones.[18] In fact, it would seem that, Sö 270 aside, all other known uses of the Nordic figures named Haþuwulfar, Hálfr, and so on are either connected to the Blekinge stones or refer to the legendary hero of *Hálfs saga ok Hálfsrekka*.[19]

These runic inscriptions, the so-called Lister- and Listerby-stones, are generally dated to the seventh, possibly as early as the sixth, century, with Istaby placed to ca. 625. It reads:

  A: 1. AfatRhAriwulafa
      2. hAþuwulafRhAeruwulafiR

  B: warAitrunARþAiAR

That is, "§A In memory of Hariwulfar. Haþuwulfar, Heruwulfar's son, §B wrote these runes."[20] In other words, Haþuwulfar (Old Norse *Hálfr*), descended from Heruwulfar (Old Norse *Hjǫrólfr*), raised the monument in honor of Hariwulfar (Old Norse *Herjólfr*). Like Haþuwulfar, the other two names build on "wolf" as their second elements: in addition to Haþuwulfar "battle-wolf," the inscriptions show Heruwulfar "sword-wolf" and Hariwulfar "army-wolf." These facts have naturally excited much curiosity, especially given that we have in these monuments the use of dithematic names built on a shared second element ("wolf"), showing familial relations, from a temporally bounded group of inscriptions, found in close proximity to each other.

---

[17] Since the seventeenth century, Blekinge has been part of Sweden but was earlier part of the Danish cultural sphere. In addition to these three inscriptions, a fourth, Björketorp (DR 360 U), also forms part of the so-called Lister- and Listerby-stones; however, its inscription is not directly relevant to this discussion. Gummarp mentions only Haþuwulfar ("§PA Haþuwulfar §PB placed §PC three staves §PD fff." Alternatively, "§QA [In memory of] Haþuwulfar §QB [...] placed §QC [these] three staves §QD fff."). Stentoften contains both Haþuwulfar and Hariwulfar ("§AP(To the) <niuha>dwellers (and) <niuha>guests Haþuwulfar gave full year, Hariwulfar ... ... I, master of the runes(?) conceal here" [Alternatively, "§AQ nine bucks, nine stallions, Haþuwulfar gave fruitful year, Hariwulfar ... ... I, master of the runes(?) conceal here"] §B runes of power. §C Incessantly (plagued by) maleficence, (doomed to) insidious death (is) he who this §D breaks.") The standard work on the Danish runic materials is *Danmarks runeindskrifter*.

[18] Cf. *Södermanlands runinskrifter*, 233–234. For ease of reading, following *Samnordisk Runtextdatabas*, I normalize the name to Haþuwulfar.

[19] Cf. Reichert and Nedoma 1987.

[20] Alternatively, "§AQ Haþuwulf(a)r, Heruwulfar's son, in memory of Hariwulfar §B wrote these runes," following here, and in all other runic cases, the translations in *Samnordisk Runtextdatabas*. The transliteration follows *Danmarks runeindskrifter*.

Importantly, the three names alliterate, the metrical requirement of all early Germanic verse.

Onomastic Tradition and Parricidal Heroic Legends

What then to make of these inscriptions and the names on them? In a wide-ranging review of the inscriptions and the *comparanda*, described by the authors as the "... ritual contexts of lycanthropy and religious wolf-symbolism," Sundqvist and Hultgård (2004) make a compelling and insightful case for understanding the ritual and ideological context of these three stones and their names within a tradition of war-bands and fertility rituals, concluding that the inscriptions are "... related to ritual practices and religious ideas that refer to both initiations of young warriors and seasonal community festivals to ensure divine support and protection."[21]

Expanding on these conclusions, I note that the three south Scandinavian inscriptions have a special connection by way of "anthroponymic bundling" to a number of heroic legend complexes in the Germanic world, including *Hálfs saga ok Hálfsrekka*, a fact that, although it has been noted in passing on occasion in the past, has never to my knowledge been explored.[22] In addition to *Hálfs saga*, related legendary materials of onomastic interest include the Baldr story and its reflexes elsewhere in Nordic tradition (*Gesta Danorum*) and in Old English (*Beowulf*), and the Old High German (*Hildebrandslied*), as well as such cognate stories as the Old Icelandic *Ásmundar saga kappabana* and a corresponding section of Saxo's *Gesta Danorum* (7.9.12–7.9.16).[23]

The underlying broken taboo shared in all these stories is parricide, the failure to respect familial ties, as when these rules are subordinated to

---

[21] Sundqvist and Hultgård 2004:597. See this essay for complete coverage of the relevant secondary literature relating to these stones.

[22] The possibility of a relationship between these runic monuments and the medieval legend complex has been noted previously by Lukman 1982, 6:425 and Nielsen 1968:46, although neither pursues the question further than to suggest a similarity between the names used in the two sets of monuments. Years ago, I raised the issue in the pre-prints of a conference paper (Mitchell 1991a), but to date the question has remained unaddressed.

[23] There are numerous other related texts, including Saxo's account of the tale in *Gesta Danorum* and the Old Norse (but Low German-derived) *Þiðreks saga*. On the Nordic traditions, see especially Ciklamini 1966. It should be noted that the resolutions of the various *Hildebrandslied* stories differ, with such later Continental traditions as those in *Þiðreks saga* and *Das jüngere Hildebrandslied* showing a non-lethal victory for the father, followed by a reconciliation between the pair. For a very complete attempt to account for the filiations among the traditions, see Gutenbrunner 1976.

competing cultural codes, (e.g., honor). Among the various traditions, three types of incidents can be adduced: one in which the combatants transect generational boundaries (i.e., involving fathers and sons); another concerning inner-generational homicide (i.e., involving brothers and half-brothers); and a third category in which both types, cross- and inner-generational violence, are present.[24] Presented tabularly, the names, organized within these broad categories of parricide, appear in Table 11.1. For comparative purposes, the naming traditions witnessed on the Listerby-stones are also provided, although naturally we cannot postulate anything about the nature of the relationships beyond what the inscriptions themselves reveal.

There are, of course, many acts of parricide in older Germanic literature, just as there are abundant alliterating genealogies which build on such elements as *hildi-* "battle" (for example, the various Hildibrandr's, Hilde's and so on of such texts as *Sǫgubrot af fornkonungum*). It is, however, the intersection of these two patterns in the traditions that interests us here—one a pattern of *frænd-víg* "parricide," the other a pattern of alliterative names built on a common second element ("wolf," "sword") with a first element related to warfare.

The most prominent, and earliest, of the first category, the father-son type, is the Old High German *Hildebrandslied*, of course, and some of the later traditions related to it.[25] The second type (father-son and brother-brother) is represented by the reflex of the Hildebrand story in *Ásmundar saga kappabana* and *Gesta Danorum*, where the innovation of one half-brother killing the other has been added to the tale of father killing son.[26] The vitality, strength and notoriety of the legend complex is fully on display in both *Ásmundar saga kappabana* and *Gesta Danorum*, when the Hildibrand

---

[24] This motif, N731.2. *Father-son combat* (cf. N349.2. *Father kills his son in battle rage*) is well-documented in, e.g., Celtic, Germanic, and Persian traditions but extends well-beyond these historically related groups. The vast, comprehensive study of the father-son conflict by Potter (1902), taking the famous Persian example as its starting point, but including many other Indo-European and non-Indo-European traditions, remains a solidly useful starting point on this topic. Given the obvious Oedipal character of this narrative type and its analogues, it has naturally attracted much attention over the years from scholars with psychoanalytic perspectives as well (e.g., Róheim 1945:68–79).

[25] E.g., *Þiðreks saga*; *Das jüngere Hildebrandslied*. Of course, that the *Hildebrandslied* manuscript breaks off before the battle is fully engaged means that the attribution to it of the father slaying his son is conjectural. In holding this opinion, however, I note that I enjoy the company of most scholars.

[26] Cf. *Gesta Danorum*, 7.9.12–7.9.16. It is noteworthy that both here and in *Hálfs saga*, another name pattern seems to emerge with a half-brother and stepfather named Ásmundr (cp. *Hervarar saga ok Heiðreks konungs*).

Table 11.1. Onomastic traditions, parricide and Germanic heroic legends

	?	FATHER-SON		FATHER-SON and BROTHER-BROTHER		BROTHER-BROTHER		
First element of name*	Istaby, etc.	Hálfs saga	Hildebrandslied	Ásmundar saga kappabana	Gesta Danorum	Snorra Edda, etc.	Gesta Danorum	Beowulf
'army'**	Hariwulfar		Heribrant					Herebeald
'war'†	Haþuwulfar	> Hálfr	Hadubrant			Hǫðr	Høtherus	Hæðcyn
'battle'††			Hiltibrant	Hildibrandr	Hildigerus			
'sword'‡	Heruwulfar	> Hjǫrólfr (Hjǫróleifr)						

* The glosses used in this column are merely convenient labels for the purposes of this chart and indicate but do not give complete expression to the full semantic ranges of each name element, some examples of which are provided below (on which, see esp. Naumann 1911 and Schramm 1957, as well as the standard dictionaries).
** *her–* cf. Old Norse *herr* 'host,' 'multitude,' 'army'; Old English *here* 'army,' 'host,' 'multitude,' 'large predatory band'; Old High German *heri* 'Schar,' 'Heerschar,' 'Heer.'
† *haþu–* cf. Old Norse *hǫð* 'war,' 'slaughter'; Old English *heaðu–* 'war,' 'battle'; Old High German *hadu–* 'fight,' 'battle,' 'Kampf.'
†† *hild–* cf. Old Norse *hildr* 'battle'; Old English *hild* 'war,' 'battle'; Old High German *hiltia* 'Kampf.'
‡ *heru–* cf. Old Norse *hjǫrr* 'sword'; Old English *heoru* 'sword.' Cf. the Old High German name Heruprecht.

figure, who has just been mortally wounded by his half-brother, refers in passing (*only!*) in his death-song to the fact that he has killed his own son. This dramatic parricidal act plays no substantive role in the extant story but appears to have been a sufficiently integral part of the tale complex—and the expectations of the audience—that it finds a place, however fleeting, in the extant texts. The original tale is now little more than a narrative "survival,"[27] with the father's reluctance to kill his son apparently transferred to Hildibrandr's attempts to avoid fighting his half-brother Ásmundr. In the third category, brothers slay brothers (e.g., *Beowulf*, *Gesta Danorum*, *Snorra edda* [also in *Vǫlospá*]).[28] Perhaps the most renowned example of this last type is the Baldr story in Norse mythology, a case famously paralleled in *Beowulf* (ll. 2432–2443):

> næs ic him tō līfe   lāðra ōwihte,
> beorn in burgum,   þonne his bearna hwylc,
> Herebeald ond Hæðcyn   oððe Hygelāc mīn.

---

[27] I use this term advisedly, but in this instance it really is of the type beloved by the British Anthropological School of the nineteenth century.

[28] *Beowulf*, lines 2432–2489; *Gesta Danorum* 3.3.2; *Gylfaginning* in *Edda Sn* 1 (cf. *Vǫlospá* sts. 31–32, 62; *Baldrs draumar* sts. 8–9).

> Wæs þām yldestan   ungedēfelīce
> mǣges dǣdum   morþorbed strēd,
> syððan hyne Hæðcyn   of horn-bogan,
> his frēawine   flāne geswencte,
> miste mercelses   ond his mǣg ofscet,
> brōðor ōðerne   blōdigan gāre.
> Þæt wæs feohlēas gefeoht,   fyrenum gesyngad,
> hreðre hygemēðe;   sceolde hwæðre swā þēah
> æðeling unwrecen   ealdres linnan.
>
> Beowulf, 92

> In no way was I,   a man of his stronghold,
> more hateful to him   than his own sons,
> Herebeald, Hæthcyn,   of Hygelac my lord.
> For the eldest brother   a death-bed was strewn,
> undeservedly,   by his kinsman's error:
> Hæthcyn shot him,   his brother, his leader,
> with an arrow from his bow   curved and horn-tipped
> missed his mark   and struck his brother,
> one son's blood   on the other's shaft.
> There was no way to pay   for a death so wrong,
> blinding the heart,   yet still the prince
> had lost his life,   lay unavenged.
>
> Beowulf 1977:195

Noteworthy of this third type is the fact that the figures whose names are based on *haþu-* are either killed by the father figure—as in the cases of Hadubrand and Hálfr—or perpetrate fratricide under tragic circumstances—as in the cases of Hǫðr and Hæðcyn (who kill, respectively, Baldr and Herebeald). Nor is the distribution haphazard: where the *haþu-* warrior is the son in a father-son relationship, he is the victim; where he is one of two brothers, he is the killer of his unwitting sibling.[29]

---

[29] One wonders if the negative overtones of this association might be reflected in the inventory of Old English *kent heiti* for "warrior": although the other proper names under discussion constitute possible substitutions for military men (*herewulfas, hildewulfas, heorowulfas*) in Old English, there is no evidence of a corresponding **heaþuwulfas*.

Social Codes and Social Realities

What sorts of social realities lie behind these interlocking patterns? That is, what moral codes, underlying social fears, and cultural norms are projected by them, and what historical realities explain the naming patterns and the larger frameworks to which they belong?[30] Of great interest in this regard is the evidence adduced by Sundqvist and Hultgård (2004:586) that just this sort of alliterative naming practice involving dithematic animal names, in this case, Hariulfas (cp. Hariwulfar), son of Hanhavaldus, is in evidence on a stela from Trier already in the fifth century.[31] This custom is reflected in many of our cultural documents, as is the possibility of a tradition of warrior bands, groups bonded together in part through shared naming conventions. A tradition of induction- or initiation-related taking of names, perhaps corresponding to the totemic symbol of the band (e.g., "wolf," "bear"), would certainly explain much.[32]

The data regarding the existence of warrior bands in early northern Europe, both in the Celtic and Germanic worlds, is overwhelming, and the circumstantial evidence for a warrior cult in the Blekinge case is strong: certainly the Istaby names themselves, "army-wolf," "war-wolf," "sword-wolf," conjure up images of the *úlfheðnar* "wolf-clad warriors [i.e., *berserkrir* in wolf skins]" known from Old Norse literary sources.[33] A parallel to the warrior band of "wolves" suggested by the Blekinge inscriptions is in evidence in Saxo's *Gesta Danorum* (6. 2. 1–6. 2. 9), where he describes twelve "brothers" (*duodecim fratrum*, 6. 2. 1) from Norway who harry and

---

[30] I note that I do *not* by this phrase mean to resuscitate the so-called fact vs. fantasy discourses sometimes conjured by such terminology.

[31] Of course, compound personal names, as well as simplexes, built on "wolf" are attested in a wide range of Indo-European language families, including Greek, Slavic, Indic, and Germanic (e.g., Müller 1970:4). Indeed, they may be among the most common of early Germanic names (Schramm 1957:77–82), and are, in addition to the Old Norse forms, attested in this type, "army" + "wolf," as attested in Visigothic (Ariulf), Frankish (Chariulf), Bavarian (Hariulf), Alamannic (Herolf), Old Saxon (Heriulf), Burgundian (Hariulfas), Langobardic (Ariulfus), and Old English (Herewulf).

[32] On the question of initiations in Old Norse tradition, and of such warrior figures as Sigmundr and Sinfjǫtli, see Schjødt 2008, especially 271–327, and 352–355.

[33] The literature in this area is vast, but excellent points of departure include, e.g., J. Nagy 1985 and Weiser-Aall 1927 and Höfler 1934, especially as updated by Meier 2001. For an orientation to the berserkr, see Blaney 1993, and for a thorough review of the relevant archaeological data (set against the literary sources), see Price 2002. Näsström 2006 provides a wide-ranging recent review of the evidence, concluding (*pace* Klaus von See and others) that the *berserkr* is no mere literary confection but existed in reality.

pillage Denmark from the safety of a fortress they have built for themselves on an island. His description leaves little doubt that these men constitute a warrior band of some sort: "These young men were of fierce temperament, stalwart in their early manhood, pre-eminent in physique, famous as the conquerors of giants, renowned for triumphs over defeated peoples and rich with their spoils."[34] Significantly, the seven names Saxo cites demonstrate that the brothers are joined together by a shared animal designation, in this case, the bear, -*biorn*: Gerbiorn, Gunbiorn, Arinbiorn, Stenbiorn, Esbiorn, Thorbiorn, and Biorn. The famous inscription at Rök in Swedish Östergötland (Ög 136) from the early 800s includes what in this context is the tantalizing patrilineage, "which twenty kings sat on Sjólund for four winters, of four names, born of four brothers: five Valkis, sons of Hráðulfr, five Hreiðulfrs, sons of Rugulfr."[35] Such "wolf" groupings are surely as likely to be "brothers," that is, members, of theriomorphic warrior bands, as actual siblings.

The literary image of "wolf warriors" has numerous iconographic corollaries as well.[36] Certainly the most clear-cut instance of a therianthropic presentation is that on the sixth-century helmet die from Torslunda (Öland), which shows what could only be a warrior (he bears a sword and a spear) wearing an animal skin; given the portrayal of its snout and long bushy tail, it is almost certainly a wolf's skin (cf. Beck 1968). Likewise the so-called "Long Horn" from Gallehus (ca. AD 400) depicts several figures who appear to have wolf-heads (or other animal heads) on men's bodies bearing swords and axes. A similar animal-headed (wolf-headed?) warrior is represented on a seventh-century sword-sheath from Gutenstein. It should be noted that all of these materials, including Istaby, fall within a relatively narrow pre-Viking Age timeframe. The identification of *berserkir* with wolves (and other animals, especially bears) in Old Norse is multidimensional; in addition to

---

[34] "Fuere autem iuuenes hi acres animis, robufti iuuenta, pręstabiles habitu corporis, giganteis clari triumphis, tropheis gentium celebres, spoliis locupletes," *Gesta Danorum*, 6.2.3. The translation is from H. R. E. Davidson 1979:163.

[35] "huariR tuaiR tikiR kunukaR satin t siulunti fiakura uintur at fiakurum nabnum burniR fiakurum bruþrum ualkaR fim raþulfs| |suniR hraiþulfaR fim rukulfs suniR," *Samnordisk Runtextdatabas*.

[36] This point has naturally been one of great moment within the older Germanic field, and I offer here only a few of the more salient struts that support the argument. On the theriomorphic significance of the *berserkir*, see Dumézil 1970:139–144.

the evidence adduced above, *berserkir* were said to "howl" and the very word *berserkr* itself refers to "bear sark" (i.e., bear-shirt, wearing a bear skin).[37]

A further analogue to these patterns exists in the extant mythological materials as well. Importantly, it too is a reflex of these two interlocking schemes, if seen somewhat hazily, contained in the one eddic poem specifically dedicated to father-son conflict, *Hárbarðzlióð*. The poem is fundamentally a catalogue of exploits, adventures and mythological information set into the framework of Nordic traditions of ritual confrontation, verbal abuse, and manly one-upmanship (i.e., the *senna* and the *mannajafnaðr*) between Þórr and a ferryman who calls himself Hárbarðr "grey beard," a known cognomen for Óðinn. It is then a verbal duel between the disguised father and his son in which the son, Þórr, is left frustrated and humiliated. It may be objected that Þórr's paternity is frequently subordinated in the mythological materials, but it should be noted that in *Hárbarðzlióð*, when Þórr is asked for his identity, Þórr is at some pains to place himself into the context of his family pedigree, at least of the males, saying that he is the son of Óðinn, the brother of Meili, and the father of Magni: "ec em Óðins sonr, / Meila bróðir, / enn Magna faðir" (*Hárbarðzlióð* 9).

It is worth noting too that as in, e.g., *Hildebrandslied*, we must assume that the father possesses knowledge of the father-son relationship but the son does not. When Þórr calls to the disguised Óðinn to help him across the river, Þórr asks who owns the boat. Óðinn's response deserves scrutiny, because he says that he has gotten the boat from a hero wise-in-counsel (*reccr inn ráðsvinni*) named Hildólfr. Hildólfr in Old Norse literary tradition is Þórr's (half-)brother, another of Óðinn's sons, mentioned in several manuscripts of *Snorra Edda*.[38] If the name in *Hárbarðzlióð* had associations for its audience external to the poem itself, it would have conjured up the possibility of this conflict involving not only father and son, but also brother against brother.

If, as some have thought, Óðinn's naming of Hildólfr is self-referential, the tie between *Hárbarðzlióð* and other texts treating father-son conflicts, such as the *Hildebrandslied*, becomes even more striking. In either case,

---

[37] This point has been at the center of a long controversy, but few have improved on the arguments in Noreen 1932.

[38] *Edda Sn* 1848–1887, 2:473 under the rubric *heiti sona oðins* (the names of Óðinn's sons) couples a Hildólfr together with Þórr as one of Óðinn's offspring: "Bvrir ro oðins / balldr ok mæili / viðarr ok næpr / vali áli / þórr ok hilldolfr / hermoðr siggi / skiolldr ok olldnir / ok itræks ioð. / hæimdallr sæmingr / hoðr ok bragi" (Óðinn's sons are Baldr and Meili, Vidar and Nep, Vali, Ali, Þórr and Hildolf, Hermod, Sigi, Skiold, Yngvi-Freyr and Itreksiod, Heimdall, Sæming) (Faulkes, 156). So also *Edda Sn* 1848–1887, 2:556, 616.

Óðinn's reference to Hildólfr importantly provides an example of the thus-far "missing" Nordic member of the name paradigm, *Hildi-wulfar "battle-wolf."[39] It is not the name alone that raises our expectations, naturally, but the matrix in which it is embedded: it comes in the midst of a father-son conflict in which the relationship is known to the father but of which the son is unaware.

Although Þórr's defeat in Hárbarðzlióð is merely symbolic and spiritual rather than literal and lethal, it nevertheless represents the dominance of the son by his more experienced father, and certainly it has overtones of the "treacherous blow" found elsewhere in the Hildebrand tradition (e.g., Þiðreks saga) in Óðinn's deceptive behavior. Moreover, the reduplicated association of Hildólfr with sagacity and wise counsel, a figure who resides in "Counsel-island sound" ("reccr inn ráðsvinni, er býr í Ráðseyiarsundi" [that warrior wise in counsel / who lives in Counsel-island sound]), and the claim by "Hárbarðr" that *he* is the wisest in counsel (thus solidifying the connection between the characters), further associates Hildólfr with his continental counterpart, Hildebrand.[40] This famous warrior was, after all, well-known for his age, his prowess, and his cunning, a kind of Germanic Odysseus.

Heroic Patterns and Warrior Initiations

Several patterns characterize and unite these legends, and it is useful to re-examine them, following Nagy (2006), with regard to their (1) typological, (2) genealogical, and (3) historical relationships, and with respect to Nagy's observations on the careers of heroes. A strict typological comparison of our northern European heroes, of the sort described by Nagy, is very telling.[41] A neutral review of the evidence shows the following: the literary and mythological traditions of various Germanic peoples in northern Europe held in common tales characterized by parricide and other acts of familial disloyalty (or subordination of family ties and so on); further, they display recurrent and shared anthroponymic features. Specifically, many of the names show multi-generational dithematic structures according to which the first element

---

[39] Cf. Petterson 2002:95.

[40] "Hildólfr sá heitir, / er mic halda bað, / reccr inn ráðsvinni, / er býr í Ráðseyiarsundi" (Hárbarðzlióð 8) (Hildolf he's called / the man who ordered me to keep it, / that warrior wise in counsel / who lives in Counsel-island sound), and "varð ec þeim einn ǫllum / efri at ráðom" (Hárbarðzlióð 18) (only I was superior to them all / with shrewdness).

[41] "Parallelisms between structures as structures pure and simple, without any presuppositions," G. Nagy 2006:72.

of the name is drawn from the common lexical inventory of Germanic military terms and compounded with a second element indicating either totemic animals or further military items (e.g., "wolf," "sword"). To such narrative sources, we may add the historical evidence of a limited number of runic inscriptions showing the same onomastic features.

The fundamental genealogical connection (in Nagy's terms) between these narratives derives from the fact that they violate the manifold injunctions in Germanic sententious literature concerning parricide, that is, the killing of kinsmen, specifically, filicide and fratricide.[42] Taboos against the slaying of a kinsman must surely be something of a human universal but they seem to have held a special place in Germanic thinking, as evidenced by the fact that in Norse mythology, it is Baldr's death at the hands of his brother, Hǫðr, that marks the beginning of the apocalypse, of the gods', and the world's, demise. It is this crime that epitomizes the outbreak of moral decadence in the sibyl's précis of the history of men and gods, where the world in decline is characterized by assorted social calamities—adultery, whoredom, strife, violence. But the unfathomable crime that introduces this descent into the moral abyss is that of kinsman slaying kinsman.[43] And this association of parricide with a Germanic apocalyptic worldview is by no means limited to Norse mythology, but also permeates such Christian texts as Wulfstan's *Sermo Lupi ad Anglos*.[44]

The narratives discussed here use that association in order to cast their characters into the famous "double-bind," the choice between honor and family, and force their actors into choosing which of their culture's most fundamental precepts they will violate. This dilemma draws its strength

---

[42] Cf. Old Norse *frænd-víg* "slaughter of a kinsman," "parricide"; Old English *mægcwealm* "death of a father or kinsman," [equated with *parricidio*], *mægmorðr* "murder of a kinsman," etc.; Old High German *magslaht* "parricide." With regard to the runic inscriptions, we cannot know, of course, what the situation was.

[43] "Brœðr muno beriaz / oc at bǫnom verðaz, / muno systrungar / sifiom spilla" (*Vǫlospá* st. 45^(1-4)) (Brother will fight brother and be his slayer / sisters' sons will / violate their kinship-bond) (*The Seeress's Prophecy*, 9).

[44] Wulfstan begins this sermon (AD 1014) by seeing the coming end of the world (*& hit nealæcð þam ende*) and then, seemingly at every turn, identifies this eschatological view with the undervaluing of family ties. Thus, for example, he specifies as part of this moral decline the fact that kinsmen do not spare kinsmen, nor fathers sons, nor children fathers, nor brothers brothers ("Ne bearh nu foroft gesib gesibban þe ma þe fremdan, ne fæder his bearne, ne hwilum bearn his agenum fæder, ne broþor oþrum"). Throughout the sermon, he uses such depravities as attacks on kinsmen (*mægræs*) and the selling of family members into slavery to further illustrate this view. I cite the text from "The Electronic Sermo Lupi ad Anglos" of Melissa Bernstein Ser, ed., at http://english3.fsu.edu/~wulfstan/, last accessed on October 14, 2011. I especially want to thank Len Neidorf for bringing this analogue to my attention.

in each of the traditions from a shared *Weltanschauung* and demands that we at least consider whether these narratives might have derived from a common source,[45] the sort of proto-structure envisioned by de Vries (1953), who suggested that the *Hildebrandslied* is to be understood against a background of warrior cults and initiation rites displaying a filiation with Indo-European mythic archetypes. One way to understand this parricidal theme in the context of an initiation rite, naturally, is that it represents the "double bind" in which the initiate finds himself, that is, bound to honor his family in one direction and bound to honor the group in the other.

Nagy's third method, the historical, involves, as he writes, "comparisons of parallels between structures that are related to each other by way of *intercultural contact*" (2006:72), a point with much relevance to the socially, linguistically, and narratively cognate groups that comprised the Germanic world of northern Europe. One possible source of contact would, of course, be the shared background of these northern European tribes from the period when the differentiations between the various groups were not especially pronounced and the migration era had not yet begun in earnest, centuries before our earliest texts. In addition, the continued proximity, trade relations, and so on of the people who display these parallel structures over the succeeding centuries was such that ongoing episodes of sharing cultural goods was by no means outside the realm of possibility.

To take one possible example, much has been made over the years of the fact that there may be a direct connection of some sort (either codicological or stemming from shared traditions) between the Old High German *Hildebrandslied* and the Old Icelandic *Ásmundar saga kappabana* based on the fact that the two traditions both offer descriptions of Hildibrand as "hoary" or "old" and in each case use the etymologically "identical" simplex: in the *Hildebrandslied*, Hildibrandr is called as "the older man" (*hêrôro man*) and in *Ásmundar saga*, we find the cognate phrase "the hoary [i.e., old] Hildibrand" (*inn hári Hildibrandr*). Naturally, the historical relations between and among the various West and North Germanic peoples suggest manifold opportunities for such ongoing reticulations of these story lines and their unusually named characters.

Of course, with regard to the possible connections between and among these materials, there is an argument that their origins are rooted in deep

---

[45] "The second method involves comparisons of parallels between structures related to each other by way of a common source. I describe this comparative method as *genealogical* because it applies to parallelisms between *cognate* structures—that is, structures that derive from a common source or proto-structure," G. Nagy 2006:72.

history. Generations of scholars have noted the similarities between the ultimate Oedipal conflict in Germanic tradition with cognate Celtic, Russian, and Persian texts, a comparison that led, for example, to de Vries's conclusion that the pattern we see in *Hildebrandslied* and the other texts is mythic, stretching back to the world of the Indo-Europeans, a view that has been challenged over the years.[46] That conclusion, it has been argued (Hatto 1973), relies too much on the similarity of basic plot elements and plays out in too dimly lit a world to be fully proven one way or another. It is also a search for origins which, barring further evidence, is likely to remain a matter of frustrated cogitation for scholarship.[47] Yet the recent reevaluation of these materials against the naming, *Männerbunde*, and religious traditions in Greek, Celtic, Indo-Iranian and Germanic by Sundqvist and Hultgård (2004) has yielded a balanced and very interesting appraisal: on the one hand, it offers further support for some of the ideas in de Vries and elsewhere, especially the possibility of rituals and initiations forming the appropriate framework within which to understand the Listerby stones; on the other hand, it argues against other notions (e.g., a Scythian tribe known as the Saka haoma-wolves). And the shared lycanthropic rituals Sundqvist and Hultgård adduce among the various historically connected peoples, for example, certainly re-open for our consideration the de Vries hypothesis about the possible Indo-European background of such traditions.

An additional point raised by Nagy's discussion seems to me to have relevance in this matter as well, *viz.*—the relationship of the hero to the god he most resembles.[48] Although the Christianization of the West Germanic groups generally means that we have little data to work with from Old High German and Old English traditions, the considerably later conversion of Scandinavia and the deep historical interests of the medieval Icelanders provides us with rich materials from this area. And these data certainly point us in interesting directions.

---

[46] "Das Ergebnis ist also, daß der Archetypus der Hildebrandsage letzten Endes ein Mythus ist" (de Vries 1953:272) (The result is that in the end the archetype of the Hildebrand legend is a myth.) Cp. the objections in, e.g., Hatto 1973.

[47] Cf. de Vries 1953:257, "Unter den zahlreichen Problemen, die das Fragment des Hildebrandsliedes der Forschung aufgibt, gehört die Frage nach dem Ursprung des darin auftretenden Sagenmotives zu den am meisten umstritten." (Among the many problems the fragment of the *Hildebrandslied* offers scholarship, the question of the origin of the legendary motif is one of the most controversial.)

[48] Specifically, G. Nagy writes that the hero "is antagonistic toward the god who seems to be most like the hero" (2006:87).

The manifold connections of the *Hálfs saga* and other figures discussed here to Óðinn are suggestive, to say the least. Óðinn involves himself in the dispute between Alrekr's wives; Víkarr is promised to the god (a pledge redeemed by his mock-sacrifice in *Gautreks saga* suddenly turning real [Ch. 7]); and Hjǫrleifr is tortured by being suspended in a gallows in a way that strongly resembles aspects of Óðinn's career.[49] In addition, the Baldr-Hǫðr episode is, in its Nordic context anyway, intimately connected with Óðinn and the key events in his life. And, of course, the Óðinn-Hildólfr identification in *Hárbarðzlióð* underscores the significance of the deity to the theriomorphically derived warrior figures who populate our parricidal narratives.

And as we shall see, the Óðinn-*berserkr* connection also plays an important role, for another of Nagy's observations about heroic attributes applies here as well, and that is that heroes are often extreme, extreme in their positive behaviors when they look to achieve *kleos* "glory," but also extreme in their negative behaviors, especially when martial fury possesses them, an identification that readily brings to mind the behavior of a *berserkr*.[50] In the later Nordic traditions, *berserkir* are generally presented as troublesome outsiders, opponents whose chief role in the story line is to provide a foil for the hero of the saga and to be heroically dispatched by him. The possibility, however, that a real and historical institution of warrior bands is reflected in these later literary traditions has generated much debate over several generations of scholarship.[51]

Importantly, the *berserkir* are presented as fighters specifically connected with the figure of Óðinn. Thus, for example, *Ynglingasaga* refers to such warriors—acting mad like dogs or wolves ("váru galnir som hundar eða vargar"), biting their shields, as strong as bears or bulls ("váru sterkir sem birnir eða griðungar"), the animal imagery glaringly suggestive—as "his men" (hans menn), that is, Óðinn's men.[52] This association between the *berserkir* and Óðinn is deep and may have played a significant role in pre-Christian

---

[49] Cf. Schjødt 2008:173–224 *et passim* and Patton 2009:220–229.

[50] "He is extreme, mostly in a positive sense, since he is 'best' in many categories, and 'best of the Achaeans' in the Homeric *Iliad*; occasionally, however, he is extreme in a negative sense, as in his moments of martial fury. In war, the warrior who is possessed by the god of war experiences this kind of fury, which is typically bestial. For example, martial fury in Greek is *lussa*, meaning 'wolfish rage'. Comparable is the Old Norse concept *berserkr* and the Old Irish concept of *ríastrad* 'warp spasm' or 'distortion'," G. Nagy 2006:88.

[51] The secondary literature on this topic is vast. For an overview, see Schjødt's careful review of the literature (2008:22–57).

[52] *Snorri Sturluson. Heimskringla*, 17.

views of the afterlife.⁵³ The fact that Óðinn's name (< *Wōþanaz) is clearly connected with a range of meanings indicating to be "mad," "frantic," "vehement" (cf. Old Norse óðr; Old English wōd; Modern German wut), an etymology apparently recognized in the eleventh century by Adam of Bremen when he writes "Wodan, id est furor" ("Wodan, that is Fury"), has naturally been seen as highly relevant, especially when set against the idea of the *berserkir*'s battlefield fits of frenzy, the *berserksgangr*.⁵⁴ These battle-mad moods play an important role in the parricidal materials reviewed here, as the act of filicide is sometimes carried out exactly when the father is in a *berkerskr* fury: thus, in *Ásmundar saga kappabana*, we are told by way of explanation that "[Hildbrandr] went into a berserk rage [...] This rage was on him as he went on his way and saw his son and immediately slew him."⁵⁵ It is also worth recalling that Icelandic tradition is very keen to note that Hálfr is a *berserkr*, as well as that he is always seen as part of a group of warriors, men who have had to prove their courage and strength before joining his band.

Moreover, the possibility that Óðinn had a role in the initiation of young warriors into war bands, secret societies and the like has long been bruited about. In his masterful study of initiation in the Old Norse world, Jens Peter Schjødt (2008:454) offers a fine summary judgment on this point: "in his relationship to the world of human beings [Óðinn] is characterised by being the one who, *as initiator*, gives certain social categories a range of numinous knowledge [...] It is, therefore, as the god of initiation that Óðinn's role in relation to his chosen heroes becomes understandable and meaningful."

One of the most discussed instances where the later literary texts have been understood to echo such processes is the story in *Hrólfs saga kraka* of Hǫttr, the timid weakling who is transformed into a doughty warrior through the intervention of the heroic Bǫðvarr-Bjarki ["little bear of war"].⁵⁶ Part

---

53   Cf. the view that "...having been a berserk in one's life (having been initiated into a warrior band) means that one has got a special relationship with Óðinn which again implies that one become[s] one of the *einherjar* after death," Schjødt 2008:353.

54   I emphasize here the association of Óðinn with the fury of the battlefield, but it is also the case that the etymology indicates the mental excitement of poetic composition and other functions (cf. Latin *vātes*, Old Irish *fáith*); for a brief review of the theories, see Mitchell 1993b. For recent detailed discussions, especially with respect to the question of warrior bands, see Kershaw 2000 and Schjødt 2008:22–57.

55   "þá kom á hann berserksgangr [...] En í vanstilli þessu, er á honum var ok hann var á ferðina kominn, þá sá hann son sinn ok drap hann þegar" (*Ásmundar saga kappabana* 1:404–405 [chap. 9]).

56   This story has been much commented on by Georges Dumézil (1970:154–158) and others, none more so than Schjødt 2008:311–326 *et passim*, who also provides an excellent review of the secondary literature.

of the process (explicitly tripartite, involving separation—liminality—and reintegration) involves the dispatching of a monster and the drinking of its blood.[57] The result of these procedures is to show that Hǫttr will become a noble and valiant youth (*goðr drengr ok hraustr*).[58]

To underscore this transformation, "the new man" also gets a new name. Formerly called Hǫttr "hood," "cowl," a designation often used in various collocations by Óðinn as a means of hiding his identity, he is now to be called Hjalti (< *hjalt*, the boss of a sword or its guard), explicitly said to be a name taken from that of a famous sword.[59] The image of an initiate undergoing a trial through which he achieves an enhanced status and is provided with a new *military name* plausibly reflects past cultural behaviors among the Germanic tribes. As Sundqvist and Hultgård (2004:597) note with regard to the naming practices on the Listerby stones, "These names might have been used as some kind of insignia received after the ceremonies, i.e. the *rite de passage*, at the time of entering or leaving an age group or warrior confraternity."

Conclusion

Where does this review of the data lead us? By applying Nagy's hero paradigm and its comparative methodology to these highly discursive materials from northern Europe—runic inscriptions, legendary and mythological texts, onomastic conventions—plausible outlines of the past begin to emerge. The relationships among the various Germanic parricidal narratives taken up here, with their particular naming traditions, paralleled in turn by historical evidence of the same onomastic practices, represent, of course, only the sober collocations of facts, pure and simple.

But they also represent hard data we should not fear to subject to informed speculation. Going then beyond the proven testimonials of our materials, I would like to suggest a way of interpreting the details and patterns, one that I readily admit is necessarily speculative, but also one that fits the facts. It overlaps in a general sense with de Vries (1953) and like Sundqvist and

---

[57] These phases are examined in depth in Schjødt 2008:311–326.

[58] *Hrólfs saga kraka ok kappa*, 68 (chap. 36).

[59] "Ok skal hann heita Hjalti upp frá þessu. Skaltu heita efter sverðinu Gullinhjalta" (*Hrólfs saga kraka ok kappa*, 69 [chap. 36]) (from now on he will be called Hjalti. You will now be called after the sword Golden Hilt, *The Saga of King Hrolf Kraki*, chap. 23)

Hultgård (2004) locates the ideas to a specific time and place proximate to the materials and ties these patterns to known cultural phenomena.

Is it too much to imagine that, in a Durkheimian spirit, what we witness in such texts are reflections of lived lives within a tradition of military bands (whether called secret societies, *Männerbunde*, age groups, or *berserkir*) at some early point (e.g., the Roman Iron Age) and which continued as a cultural practice for long periods in Scandinavia? The particularities of the alliterating and semantically tied onomastic patterns repeated in the various narratives, as well as the parricidal themes employed, would in turn reflect the initiation rituals or age group inductions associated with such warrior groups.

In these naming practices, it is the second element—"wolf," "bear," and so on—that apparently signifies the institutional part of the name, that is, the war band's identity to the outside world, sometimes with totemic associations. The first unit of the dithematic name, on the other hand—"army," "battle," and so on—provides the individual's identity, perhaps even status or rank, within the group. These names would have been, as in the case of Hǫttr-Hjalti, provided for, or by, the initiate after having passed whatever tests or introductory rites the group used, a practice broadly paralleled in many cultures, including the traditions of the Christian church (see Boniface).

That the heroic narratives are centrally concerned with acts of parricide is intimately related to this process: just as the various kin-slayers in the texts must choose between codes relating to family and codes relating to personal honor, demonstrations of military prowess and so on (which may run up against, or even afoul of, family obligations), so the initiate is compelled to make choices within the hierarchy of ideals between fidelity to the war band, on the one hand, and fidelity to the family, on the other. As part of this new association, they vow to honor their obligations to the confraternity over all other calls to duty.[60] Seen in this context, the filicidal and fratricidal deaths presented in the texts reflect metaphorical, perhaps even ritually enacted, severing of the initiate's bonds to the family, and the concomitant valorization of his ties to his new "family," the war band.

I realize that these comments push the data vary hard, of course. On the other hand, if we are not to allow some such reading of the evidence, how

---

[60] Such a practice would also fit Stentoften's wording, one interpretation of which is that the last part of the text—"Incessantly (plagued by) maleficence, (doomed to) insidious death (is) he who this breaks"—refers not to the monument but rather to the oath associated with the ritual conjured on the inscription.

instead should we would explain the shared naming and behavioral patterns drawn from the traditions of the Continent, Anglo-Saxon England and the Nordic world? The war band initiation theory I have proposed here, although perhaps daring, does not violate the evidence; indeed, it appears to fit the data very well. And what alternative explanation accounts for the common naming and narrative patterns we find in the various Germanic traditions?

Chapter 12

COURTS, CONSORTS, AND THE TRANSFORMATION OF MEDIEVAL SCANDINAVIAN LITERATURE

Medieval Scandinavian literature is justly celebrated for the sagas produced by thirteenth-century Icelandic authors, yet realistically the Nordic "center of gravity" in this period—economically, politically, demographically, and culturally—was Scandinavia itself, that is, Denmark, Sweden, and Norway. But whereas native traditions concerning viking activities and the era of Icelandic colonization retained their vitality in Iceland and fed into the production of saga literature, the Norwegian, Swedish, and Danish courts were increasingly responding to the cultural rhythms of European developments.[1] In fact, already in the late eleventh century, the Nordic courts set about the business of imitating Continental fashions with dispatch, as is reported, for example, at the court of Óláfr kyrri (d. 1093) (*Óláfs saga kyrra*, 204–206 [chaps. 2-3]), and it was to these courts that the Icelandic skalds looked to declaim their art, and where they hoped to be remunerated for it. As an indication of the changes that occur in elite Scandinavian society, it should be noted that by the turn of the fourteenth century—the "cultural moment" of this essay—knighthood in something like its European sense had been established in all three kingdoms, and within a few decades, the Nordic courts turned from the traditions of the past (i.e., in declaimed

---

[1] Original publication: "Courts, Consorts, and the Transformation of Medieval Scandinavian Literature." In *Germanic Studies in Honor of Anatoly Liberman*, ed. Marvin Taylor, 229–241. North-Western European Language Evolution, 31/32. Odense, 1997.

 I do not mean to suggest that Iceland was immune to such influences, only that literature with connections to the past seems to have enjoyed particular prestige there. Iceland too had its responses to developments in Europe.

skaldic praise poetry) to foreign literary models (i.e., the rhymed chronicle).[2] The following essay looks to explore this issue on three fronts: 1) the preconditions necessary for such a change, factors which develop over a long period of time as the skalds struggled to keep their positions of prominence at the courts; 2) the increasingly international character of the courts, especially as such multi-culturalism, with the inherent linguistic and cultural diglossia such a term implies, brings with it literary sponsorship by foreign-born royal consorts; and 3) the fact that, although skaldic poetry is displaced only over the course of many generations, the innovation in cultural and literary norms, and especially in poetic idiom, that revolutionizes Scandinavian literature turns on the influence of a very small number of individuals at the Norwegian court around the year 1300.

The degree to which by the middle of the thirteenth century there already existed distinctly different models of literary activity—rather than a single uniform model, as is sometimes assumed—is well illustrated by the story of Sturla Þórðarson in *Sturlu þáttr* and its famous scene of saga narration, a diversity made apparent by Queen Ingibjǫrg's expectations and role. The text reports events which took place in 1263, when the Icelander Sturla Þórðarson comes to Mágnus Hákonarson, the Norwegian king, to whom he has been maligned, in the hopes of gaining his support.[3] The king refuses to hear him, but does allow him to accompany the royal party on board ship:

> And when men lay down to sleep, the king's forecastle-man asked who should entertain them. Most remained silent at this. Then he asked: "Sturla the Icelander, will you entertain [us] [*skemta*]?"
>
> "You decide," says Sturla. Then he told (*Sagði*) *Huldar saga, better and more cleverly (*betr ok fróðligarr*) than any of them who were there had heard (*heyrt*) before.
>
> Many thronged forward on the deck and wanted to hear (*heyra*) it clearly, so that there was a great throng there.
>
> The queen asked, "What is the crowd of men on the foredeck?"

---

[2] See especially Löfqvist 1935. The earliest specific reference to knights in Norway is 1277, *Islandske Annaler*, 140 (see also 29, 50); for Denmark 1287, SRD, 3:314; and for Sweden ca. 1280, SD 1:652.

[3] The argument presented here builds on my comments in Mitchell 1991b:98–102.

A man says, "The men there want to hear (*heyra*) the saga that the Icelander is telling (*segir*)."

She said, "What saga is that?"

He replied, "It is about a great troll-woman, and it is a good story and is being well told (*vel frá sagt*)."

The king told her to pay no heed to this but to sleep. She said, "I think this Icelander must be a good fellow and much less to blame than he is said to be."

The king remained silent. People went to sleep for the night. The following morning there was no wind, so that the king['s ship] was in the same place. When the men were sitting at table during the day, the king sent to Sturla some dishes from his table. Sturla's companions were pleased at this, and [said], "Things look better with you here than we thought, if this sort of thing goes on."

When the men had eaten, the queen sent a message to Sturla asking him to come to her and bring with him the saga about the troll-woman (*bað hann koma til sín ok hafa með sér trǫllkonu-sǫguna*), Sturla went aft to the quarterdeck then and greeted the king and queen. The king received his greeting curtly but the queen received it graciously and easily. The queen then asked him to tell that same story (*segja þá sǫmu sǫgu*) that he had told in the evening. He did so, and told the saga for much of the day (*sagði mikinn hluta dags sǫgu*). When he had told [it] (*hafði sagt*), the queen and many others thanked him and understood that he was a knowledgeable and wise man (*fróðr maðr ok vitr*).[4]

Certain key aspects of this all-important presentation of the changed multi-layered media environments of the Nordic Middle Ages call for comment:[5]

- First of all, readers infer that Sturla arrives at the royal couple's ship with a strategy in hand, a strategy very much built on his skill as a poet and a raconteur.

---

[4] *Sturlunga saga*, 2:325–326. The compilation as a whole probably dates to ca. 1300.

[5] Given the central role of this scene from *Sturlu þáttr* in discussions of orality, performance, manuscripts, and court culture in the Nordic Middle Ages, I have revisited it often, including in Chapter 3 "Performance and Norse Poetry: The Hydromel of Praise and the Effluvia of Scorn," where it is given an extended treatment. As a historical matter, however, it was in this chapter, the outgrowth of a paper titled "Social Notes from Christmas 1302 and the Transformation of Scandinavian Literature," presented to the CLCS Seminar on Cross-Cultural Poetics, Harvard University, directed by Gregory Nagy, in April of 1991, that I first began to tease out the relevance and meaning of this pivotal saga episode.

- This strategy Sturla pursues carefully, moving from his narration of a troll saga, well-told before the crew, to his declaiming of a panegyric he has composed in honor of the king, to his eventual delivery of a praise poem in honor of the king's father, both declaimed before the king and queen. Paralleling this rise in social status at the court is his physical movement from the forecastle (the forward, and rougher, section of the ship used by the crew) to the aft section where the royal couple spend their time.
- Sturla's successful series of performances ingratiate him to the king, and eventually the king grants Sturla what must have been the great literary commission of the age, the responsibility for composing the king's father's saga, *Hákonarsaga Hákonarsonar*.
- A fundamental aspect of the episode is its serial staging of oppositions—Icelander :: Norwegian, disempowered :: empowered, poor :: rich, active tradition bearer :: non-native admirer of the tradition, and so on. These points are made when, for example, Sturla has with him no provisions, but must instead live off the victuals sent to his table by the king; when the king asks whether his Danish queen can really understand the Icelander's poem, and she responds that she wants him to think that she can; and when the Norwegian forecastleman asks, "Sturla inn íslenzki, viltu skemta?" ("Sturla the Icelander, will you entertain us?"). This comment about the Icelander being asked to *skemta* reflects an old stereotype in Scandinavia that emphasizes the Icelanders' knowledge of tradition and their narrative skill, a view noted by various twelfth-century Danish and Norwegian historiographers.[6]
- How modern observers elect to interpret the nature of Sturla's troll saga performance largely depends on their dispositions toward the possibilities. Thus, discussions of this episode are generally binary in nature: either the narration of **Huldar saga* is to be understood as a case of saga reading ("bring the saga with him" = a manuscript) or of oral saga narration ("better and more cleverly" = an unfixed text).[7] But I am confident that a reasonable and revealing solution to its apparently contradictory information is to hand, as I shall lay out below.

The author's treatment of the scene builds on a series of distinctions between his Icelandic hero, the Norwegian king and court, and the Danish queen, now living at the Norwegian court, an institution which has been the center of an active translation industry for at least thirty-five years and which possesses a noteworthy library. When she calls for Sturla to entertain them on board the becalmed ship, the cultural frame established by her background (i.e., the

---

[6] E.g., Theodoricus Monachus, *Historia de antiquitate regum Norwagiensum*, 1; *Gesta Danorum*, Prefatio 1.4.

[7] E.g., Stefán Einarsson 1957:158; Hermann Pálsson 1962:52; Hofmann 1971:135–175; Lönnroth 1976:172; Clover 1982:194.

royal courts of Denmark and Norway) anticipates an entertainer who will come forward with a manuscript from which he will read. In fact, Sturla has no such manuscript. His obviously oral narration of *Huldar saga, contrasts sharply—and is fully intended to contrast—with the queen's request that Sturla "bring the saga" with him. Here the author sets the "old" and "new" forms of entertainment (i.e, "unaided narration" and "manuscript-based narration"), physically associated with the ship's forecastle and its quarterdeck, against each other, while at the same time, the text underscores the national, social, and aesthetic differences between the two types. Thus, the full range of literary possibilities at mid-century are placed on display: oral saga narration (Sturla's two recitations of *Huldar saga); declaimed skaldic poetry (the panegyrics to Magnús and Hákon); and the written and read saga (*Hákonarsaga Hákonarsonar*, Queen Ingibjǫrg's expectations of *Huldar saga).

Sturlu þáttr thus catches Old Norse literary culture at a transitional moment, and shows, on the one hand, through the queen's remarks about manuscript-based saga entertainment and the king's commissioning of Sturla to write a saga, the extent to which the increasingly dominant practice of written narration had eroded the tradition of oral narration, while, on the other hand, it demonstrates the strength of, and the court's appreciation for, the venerable tradition of orally delivered skaldic praise poetry and oral saga narration.

The story also hints at another sea-change in the nature of court literature: against the tradition of skaldic praise poetry, in which a system of reciprocating honors was paramount, the commission Sturla receives to compose *Hákonarsaga* demonstrates the increasing importance of contractual sponsors in the creation of court literature. Within a generation, the native practice of praise poetry passes into oblivion as far as the courts are concerned: the last recorded instance of a poet receiving favor from the Norwegian court for such poetry comes in 1296, when the Icelandic annals record that Guðmundr is given the governorship of Iceland's North Firthing by Magnús's son Eiríkr in recompense for a skaldic poem ("skipadr Nordlendinga fiordungr Gudmunde skalldstikle," *Islandske Annaler*, 385 [see also 261]). Yet, as Einar Ól. Sveinsson (1953:41) notes concerning this delivery, those at the court must have been more perplexed than pleased by this obscure verse form.

One important component in the erosion of skaldic poetry's status was the change in the character and composition of the courts themselves, and perhaps especially foreign-born royal consorts for whom this poetry must have been nearly incomprehensible. Sturla's story hints at this point as well. When he finishes the first of two praise poems, the saga relates the following scene:

> Drottning mælti: "þat ætla ek, at kvæðit sé vel ort."
> Konungr mælti: "kanntu mjǫk gerla at heyra?"
> Hon mælti: "ek vilda, at yðr þætti svá, herra."
>
> Sturlunga saga, 2:326
>
> The queen said, "I think that the poem is well-made."
> The king said, "Could you really understand it?"
> She said, "I want you to think so, Lord."

Here the king clearly calls into question the queen's ability to understand a form of praise poetry which must by now have been an almost exclusively West Norse preoccupation. The queen is portrayed as being interested in forwarding Sturla's case at every turn, perhaps even when his poetry is less than crystal-clear to her Danish ears, as the king's critical—and probably bemused—query suggests. The queen's own retort certainly strengthens the impression that she has understood little of what she has heard, but does recognize the honor being paid. How much less then must her successors (and daughters-in-law), the Scottish-born Margaret and the German-born Eufemia, have understood of such linguistically demanding and subtle encomia?

Queen Ingibjǫrg's consternation over Sturla's poem no doubt results both from linguistic realities and from literary differences that were emerging between the various regional and socioeconomic divisions of the Norse population. Furthermore, it is yet another indication that at the Norwegian court of the thirteenth century, despite the queen's interest in this instance, skaldic poetry was ripe for being displaced, and was increasingly marginalized to a quaintly archaic and provincial Icelandic preoccupation, just the situation which seems to have obtained a century earlier at the Danish court. There in ca. 1149, Sveinn svíðandi Eiríksson refuses to compensate Einarr Skúlason for a poem.[8] The preference the Danish king displays for professional performers with their pipes and fiddles over traditional praise poetry gives rise to Einarr's testy lament:

Ekki hlaut af ítrum	Einarr got no gift
Einarr gjafa Sveini,	from the glorious Sveinn
ǫld lofar ǫðlings mildi	for the poem, [yet]
æðru styggs, fyr kvæði;	men praise the fearless prince's generosity;

---

[8] "Hann [Einarr] orti kvæði um Svein konung ok fekk engi laun fyrir" (Knýtlinga saga, 275 [chap. 108]). (He composed a poem in honor of King Svein, but received no reward for it.) (Knytlinga saga, 148.)

Danskr harri metr dýrra,	the Danish king values more highly
dugir miðlung þat, fiðlur,	fiddles and pipes—
ræðr fyr ræsis auði	inadequately does it suffice—
Rípa-Ulfr, ok píspur.	Ribe-Ulfr governs the king's wealth.

Knýtlinga saga, 275 (chap. 108)

Yet another confrontation between skalds and professional entertainers is portrayed in *Sverris saga* in the story of the skald Máni at the Norwegian court (ca. 1184), who wins King Magnús Erlingsson's favor through his own poetic skills, his ability to deliver the poetry of others (Halldórr skvaldri's "Útfarardrápa"), and his handling of two "jesters" (*leikarar*) (*Saga Sverris konúngs*, 206–208 [chap. 85]). The entertainers have been amusing the court by having two dogs hop over a rod held before men of high station; the higher the status of the man, the greater the jump demanded of the dogs. Máni delivers several scathing verses:

Slœgr ferr gaurr með gigju,	The crafty ruffian manages the fiddle and pipes;
ginn's hér komit inni,	a 'jester'[9] has come in here,
(meiðr hefr skjaldar skóða	(the fellow
skrípalǫt) ok pípur;	possesses buffoonery);
rekkr lætr rauða bikkju,	the man has a red bitch jump
rækið skvaldr, fyr aldir	over a rod before the men; refuse the twaddle!
skulut hlýða því þjóðir,	people shouldn't listen to such;
(þat's skaup) of staf hlaupa.	it's mockery.
Gígja syngr, þars ganga	The fiddle sings, where
grípa menn til pípu,	men take up the pipe's course,
fœra fólsku stóra	great foolishness do
framm leikarar bleikir;	the pale 'jesters' produce;
undr's, hvé augum vendir	it's a wonder, how he rolls his eyes,
umb sás þýtr í trumbu;	the one who blows on the horn;
kníðan lítk á kauða	I see the rascal's
kjapt ok blásna hvapta.	hard-pressed yap and puffed-out mouth.

Skj, 1:520

---

[9] *ginn* is glossed as "a juggler, jester" specifically for this passage in Cleasby-Vigfusson 1982 [1957], 200, and similarly translated (*gögl*) by Finnur Jónsson in *Skj*, 520; however, Finnur glosses it as "deception, falsehood" (*svig, falskhed*) for this passage in *Lexicon Poeticum*, noting its origins in the verb *ginna* "to dupe, fool one."

Máni's lampoons are well received by the company, and Mani becomes a member of the court. Thus, Máni's predicament at the Norwegian court in the twelfth century results in an outcome altogether different from that of Einarr at the Danish court—when the antics of jesters and their ilk, *leikari* and *ginn*, are placed against the tradition of skaldic poetry at the Norwegian court, the native poetic institution is victorious: Máni becomes a "king's man" and it is the professional fools who are displaced by a practitioner of the indigenous arts.

In the various representations of skaldic performance, the impression occasionally emerges that a king's largess in rewarding such tributes was connected more with the honor of such an encomium being composed (i.e., process and pageantry of such a gesture), than with the meaning of the work. Eiríkr blóðøx, for example, accepts the honor of Egill's multi-layered "Hǫfuðlausn" in tenth-century York without fully comprehending the sense of it at a time when the art was flourishing and the distance between the Nordic regional dialects very small indeed (*Egils saga*, 185–192 [chap. 60]). A similar image is presented when Sneglu-Halli boasts—using a verse in one tradition—to Haraldr harðráði in the eleventh century that although he composed a poem in honor of an English nobleman, likely Harold Godwinsson (and despite the fact that in one tradition the English king's own court poet had approved of the poem), it contained intentional faults not perceived by the English court.[10] What then, one wonders, must the situation have been by the thirteenth century, when Nordic tastes, as well as tongues, were growing further apart? In the 1260s, the Swedish ruler, Birger Jarl, accepts as an honor Sturla Þórðarson's twelve-verse poem (*flokkr*) about him and rewards Sturla with magnificent gifts, and when Sturla later flatters him with another poem (*drápa*), Birger Jarl asks Sturla to accompany him to Sweden, where, the Jarl promises, he will lack for neither good horses nor money ("skal þik hvárki skorta góða hesta né gangsilfr") (*Sturlunga saga*, 2:327). Although the honor of such compositions was something the Jarl

---

[10] This same story is referred to and outlined in both the *Morkinskinna* and *Flateyjarbók* traditions, although in somewhat dissimilar forms. *Sneglu-Halla þáttr* M (282–283) recounts the tale (minus the verse) in some detail, making it clear that the king's poet approves of Halli's *þula*, even if the king himself does not and that the sovereign is outwitted by Halli as to the reward he earns. *Sneglu-Halla þáttr* F (425–426), although it contains such elements as the trick reward, is more sly in its presentation of Halli's visit to the English court, yet also quite specific about the nobleman being Harold Godwinson. And when he returns to Norway in *Sneglu-Halla þáttr* F, Halli is asked by the king if he has composed poems about other kings. He responds with a poem detailing the failings of his work for the English Harold. Upon hearing the poem, we are told that the Norwegian king *brosti* (smiled) and says that Halli is always entertaining.

apparently understood, one wonders with Noreen whether Birger Jarl would have comprehended very much of poems so delivered (Noreen 1926:255). Indeed, one can with reason question just how distant this kind of poetry must have seemed to individuals reared outside its West Norse orbit, in areas where its poetic form and diction may by the late thirteenth century have seemed remote indeed.

The decline of skaldic poetry and the triumph of end-rhymed poetry within elite Scandinavian society was a direct result of cross-cultural contacts, of Scandinavians travelling and studying abroad and of foreigners travelling and living in Scandinavia. The important role played by foreign-trained Scandinavians, a large number of whom studied in Italy, France, and Germany during the thirteenth century, in this process is underscored by the fact that among the oldest specimens of Nordic end-rhyme poetry is one written on the Continent ca. 1270:[11]

| iac wet en frugha i wærældet wære | I know of a lady in the world, |
| hænna lif tha wil iac æra[12] | her life ("form") I would honor. |

The transfer of Continental tastes to Scandinavia was also served by the presence of foreigners in Scandinavia, especially the growing Hansa populations, and one can unfortunately only speculate about the possible influence of such figures as Rumelandt von Sachsen, a Minnesinger who plied his trade at the Danish court in the late thirteenth century (cf. Panzer 1893:16–17). Both the Norwegian and Swedish courts had German-born queens at the end of the thirteenth century (Eufemia and Helvig), and they and their retinues, together with political developments in Sweden and Norway at the close of the thirteenth century, increasingly made these courts microcosms of the north European elite—and correspondingly made them ever more important factors in transforming Nordic aesthetic sensibilities. In 1276 Magnus Ladulås (Birgersson) married Helvig, daughter of Count Gerhard I of Holstein. Their three sons were Birger, Erik and Valdemar. Hákon V Magnússon married Eufemia in 1299, the same year in which he succeeded

---

[11] See, for example, Lindroth 1989 [1975], 1:53–63, and the essays in Jokipii and Nummela 1981, as well as the entries under "Studiesresor" in *Kulturhistorisk leksikon for nordisk middelalder* 1982 [1956–1978] by Sällström, Laugesen, Gallén, Jakob Benediktsson, and Johnsen.

[12] Bartsch 1872:444. Brøndum-Nielsen 1929:65–71, argues that the verse must be Danish, not Swedish. Interpretation of *lif* as "form" or "life" is, of course, tied directly to the question of whether the text is to be understood within the *Minnesang* tradition, or, as Weibull 1932:86, suggests, the Marian tradition. It was certainly the case that rhyme in such native Latin religious works as Anders Sunesøn's *Missus Gabriel* or Brynolf Algotsson's *In festo spinee corone* may have further promoted its use, but here I refer only to end-rhyme in its vernacular contexts.

to the Norwegian crown (*Islandske Annaler*, 145; see also 72, 199, 262, 386). According to Icelandic sources, Eufemia was the daughter of Count Gunther of Ruppin, the maternal granddaughter of Prince Witzlaf of Rügen, and the great-granddaughter of Duke Otto of Braunschweig (d. 1252). Her uncle was a well-known poet, also Witzlaf of Rügen (I. Andersson 1959:9). Princess Ingibjǫrg was born to King Hákon and Queen Eufemia in 1301, and married to Duke Erik in 1312.

The literary works that developed as a result of the arrangements for the marriage, and of the visit by Duke Erik to the Norwegian court during Christmas 1302, were the three so-called *Eufemiavisor*. These reworkings of Continental literature represent a grand gesture from the future mother-in-law to her future son-in-law, as well as the first full-scale introduction in form and spirit of chivalric literature into Scandinavia. *Herr Ivan Lejonriddare* was followed by *Hertig Fredrik af Normandie*, and finally *Flores och Blanzeflor*, the last not being completed in all probability until 1312, the year of the wedding itself.[13] All three texts are at some pains to emphasize the role of their patroness. *Hertig Fredrik af Normandie*, for example, closes around the following information:

Thenne bok j her høræ	The book to which you've listened
hona loth keysær Otte gøra	Kaiser Otto had made
och wendhæ aff walsko j tytzt mall;	and turned from French into German,
gudh nadhæ thæss ædhlæ førstæ sial!	God bless that noble prince's soul!
Nw ær hon annan tiidh giordh til rima	Now it's again been done into rhyme,
nylikæ jnnan stuntan tima	lately, in a short time,
aff thyzko och j swænskæ thungo,	from German into Swedish,
thet forstanda gamble och vngæ.	[as] old and young understand.
Hona loth wændæ a thetta mall	Queen Eufemia had it translated
Eufemiæ drøtning [...][14]	into this language

The author-translator of these works has never been identified with certainty, although the poem's language indicates an individual with a background in southern and western Sweden.[15] One prominent candidate is Peter Algotsson,

---

[13] Jansson 1945:304, assesses the various theories and concludes that the only conceivable order is *Herr Ivan Lejonriddare*, *Hertig Fredrik af Normandie*, and *Flores och Blanzeflor*. His widely accepted argument concerning the chronology stresses metrical considerations above all else.

[14] *Hertig Fredrik av Normandie*, 169. My translation. Cf. *Herr Ivan*, 407–408, and *Flores och Blanzeflor*, 136–137.

[15] See Jansson 1945:313–319, on previous arguments concerning the author, and especially on the "pan-Nordic" aspects of the author's language (i.e., Swedish, with significant Danish and Norwegian features). *Contra* Noreen 1923–1929, 22:2, 22:7, and 26:1 and Sawicki 1939, Jansson

brother of Brynolf Algotsson, Bishop of Skara, a hymnist of renown. The brothers belonged to a powerful "law man" family from Västergötland, and Peter's personal history conforms well with what one might anticipate as requirements for the task: he had studied in Paris and had been sent on diplomatic missions to the English and Scottish courts by King Magnús. Of critical importance, he was in exile at the Norwegian court, as a result of having been implicated in the bride theft of Ingrid Svantepolksdotter by his brother Folke Algotsson in 1288.[16]

Whoever the author-translator was, there can be little doubt but that, as the romances themselves suggest, Eufemia exercised considerable control over the selection of the materials, with their emphasis on "bride quests," on young lovers who are parted and reunited, on fidelity, and on knightly virtues. With respect to the question of patronage and Eufemia's authority over the selection of materials, *Hertig Fredrik af Normandie* is of particular interest: although the poem claims to have come from a French original, it has been cogently argued that this attribution is an amiable fiction designed to lend the tale authenticity and that this text, preserved only in Scandinavia, was in fact commissioned by "keysær Otte" (i.e., Duke Otto of Braunschweig; Lütjens 1912). Whether Eufemia's great-grandfather commissioned its composition or its translation, there seems to be little doubt but that the text was intimately tied to Eufemia's family, and may even have come to Norway with her in 1299. That these three texts could have come about at all was made possible by the fact that there already existed a tradition of ballad song in Scandinavia from which the author-translator could draw, an essential component to the background of the *Eufemiavisor*.[17] In the *Eufemiavisor* themselves, the presence of the ballad

---

1945 holds that all three texts were translated by the same individual; moreover, he argues that all three texts were original translations into Swedish (against the view that they were originally done into now lost Norwegian verse translations).

[16] Peter Algotsson's possible role as author-translator was first raised by Beckman (1947:63–67), who suggested that Peter had been the translator of *Hertig Fredrik*. Ståhle 1967, 1:65–66, endorses the possibility and expands on the rationale for viewing Peter as the author-translator of the Eufemiavisor. This otherwise attractive identification must, however, be reconciled with the information in the Icelandic annals for 1299 concerning "θ [= dauði] Petrs biskups af Skávrum i Gavtlandi" [the death of Bishop Peter of Skara in Götaland] (51) and that "and*adiz* Petr bys*kup* af Skaurum" [Bishop Peter of Skara died] (386). Peter Algotsson is not elsewhere identified as Bishop of Skara (although he was *kanik* there at the time of his brother's elevation to bishop), and, in fact, most documents, including several letters from Edward I of England written in the winter of 1293, refer to him as *magister*. See *DN* 19:420–422. In 1299, Peter's brother, Brynolf, was still Bishop of Skara.

[17] See, for example, Wessen 1928:43–69; Jansson 1945:213–217; and Colbert 1989:76–87. Ingvar Andersson (1959:13) surely overstates the case when he describes the end-rhyme of the *Eufemiavisor* and *Erikskronikan* as perhaps "en mer överraskande och chockerande estetisk modernitet" (a more

tradition is indicated most strongly by the appearance of the ballad idiom, as in *Arla om morghin* (Early in the morning). Yet, while the concept of end-rhyme poetry has precedents in the North well before the *Eufemiavisor*, the execution of end-rhyme as the sole poetic mechanism for lengthy narration is completely original with these three works.[18] In medieval Swedish literature, end-rhyme (*knittelvers*) becomes the dominant literary form, and is often used for the same purposes to which the other major poetic innovation of this period, the Icelandic metrical romances, or *rímur*, was put, namely creating historical works (e.g., OSw *Erikskrönikan*; OIc *Ólafsríma Haraldssonar*), translating foreign texts (e.g., OSw *Konung Alexander*; OIc *Rímur af Amíkus ok Amilíus*), and recasting prose texts (e.g., OSw *Historia Sancti Olaí*; OIc *Ólafsrímur Tryggvasonar af Indriða þætti ilbreiðs*). About the earliest history of the *rímur* little is known, but already in the late fourteenth century the Icelandic metrical romances are documented as a fully developed genre, suggesting that the *rímur*'s origins may be roughly contemporary with the appearance of *knittelvers* in Sweden.[19]

Experimentation in the West Norse area with end-rhyme and alliteration apparently led to the Icelandic *rímur* meters.[20] Similar attempts appear to have been made in Old Swedish as well, but failed to develop. An intriguing indication of such an "experiment" is present in four lines of the oldest surviving Swedish-language Christian poem, *Kristi lidande* (or *Kristi pina*, "Christ's Suffering"), which incorporates aspects of the old and new poetics; it is preserved in a manuscript of *Fornsvenska legendariet* (ca. 1350), and believed to have been composed earlier in the fourteenth century:

ihesu guz son ihesu goþe	Jesus, God's son, Jesus good,
bløt mit hiærta mæþ þino bloþe	soften my heart with your blood
at þænkia mz þakom þina pino	that I may gratefully recall your suffering
af allom hugh ok hiærta mino[21]	with all my thoughts and all my heart

---

astonishing and shocking aesthetic modernity) than most other developments in Swedish poetry (although one suspects that the ballad had already laid the groundwork for the reception of rhymed epics). Cf. Frandsen 1935, who suggests a lost East Norse tradition of *Minnesang* by ca. 1300.

[18] See the review in Jonsson 1978:9–15.

[19] Cf. Mitchell 1991b:163–168, and the discussion of end-rhyme in Mitchell 1996:19–28, amplified here. In the years since this essay was written, important contributions on these issues have been made in Layher 2008, 2010.

[20] See the competing views in Vésteinn Ólason 1978 and Hughes 1978, as well as the overview in Hughes 1982–1989. Earlier views by Jón Þorkelsson, Eugen Mogk, Finnur Jónsson, Knut Liestøl, and others are summarized in Noreen 1921–1923, 3:52–54.

[21] On *Fornsvenska Legendariet* generally (including the manuscripts), see Jansson 1982. On *Kristi lidande*, preserved only in Cod. Holm. A 34 ("Codex Bureanus," 1350–1370), see Pipping

This experimental case of alliteration (g-g, b-b, þ-þ, h-h) combined with end-rhyme (a-a-b-b) is highly reminiscent of the *rímur*. Yet while poetry of this sort becomes the mainstay of Icelandic literature for the next five hundred years, it never develops further in Sweden, where *knittelvers* becomes the dominant aesthetic form, perhaps best realized in the Swedish rhymed chronicle *Erikskrönikan* (written sometime between 1317 and 1332).

Scandinavian literature at the close of the thirteenth century was subject to a variety of forces—cultural, literary, and linguistic—which called for the development of a "new" form of poetry: yet the breakthrough of *knittelvers* on such a grand scale undoubtedly derives from the specific influence of one patroness (Queen Eufemia) and one author-translator (Peter Algotsson?) working to create what had never before existed in a Scandinavian language, *viz.*—lengthy end-rhymed narratives. A further change in the nature of Nordic literature is indicated by the evidence as well: in 1263, King Magnus, admittedly much influenced by Queen Ingibjǫrg, commissions Sturla Þórðarson to write *Hákonarsaga*; some forty years later, it is openly and decidedly Magnús's daughter-in-law, Queen Eufemia, who sponsors the translation of the works so appropriately named after her, *Hertig Fredrik av Normandie*, *Herr Ivan*, and *Flores och Blanzeflor*. Once introduced, end-rhyme became the primary literary vehicle of Swedish letters throughout the Middle Ages, and an important literary model in Denmark.[22] And one may well wonder if female patronage does not also become an important component of court literature after this date as well. Although the introduction and acceptance of the rhymed chronicle takes decades, requiring the introduction of ballads, a taste for chivalric texts, and a period of poetic experimentation, the transformation of Scandinavian literature can at the same time be localized to a few important years: in 1296, it was still possible to win acclaim and reward at the Norwegian court with a skaldic poem. Not long after Christmas 1302, the Danish, Swedish, and Norwegian courtiers who made up the remarkably multinational Norwegian court undoubtedly listened with rapt attention to a rhymed Nordic version of the story of Ivain, Knight of the Lion, signaling a change in taste that would alter Scandinavian literature for the remainder of the Middle Ages.

1943:101, and Klockars 1967, 1:158. See also the parallel case of U 214 (Vallentuna kyrka).

[22] In line with Jonsson 1991, concerning the introduction of the ballad to Scandinavia through Norway, it should be noted that Continental poetry in end-rhymed translations, such as the *Eufemiavisor*, appears last in Denmark: the manuscripts of the Danish translations from the Old Swedish *Hertig Fredrik af Normandie* and *Herr Ivan Lejonriddare* date to the mid and late fifteenth centuries, for example.

Chapter 13

ON THE OLD SWEDISH *TROLLMÖTE* OR *MIK MÖTTE EN GAMUL KERLING*[1]

The Old Swedish poem with the opening line, "I met an old crone" (*Mik mötte en gamul kerling*), perhaps better-known by the supplied title, *Trollmöte* (troll meeting, or encounter), exists in a single, unique text, part of the impressively large Vadstena miscellany, Uppsala universitetsbibliotek (UUB) C 4.[2] The poem was first edited and published by the indefatigable Robert Geete in 1902 as one of a pair of poems from the Swedish Middle Ages (the other text is *Jungfru Marias sju fröjder*). The name under which Geete brought the poem to the attention of the members of Svenska fornskriftsällskapet, *En allegorisk dikt (dröm eller saga)* [An allegorical poem (dream or story)], is perhaps less a title than an attempt at a categorization, perhaps even an appeal for comment.

Some years later, Emanuel Linderholm, in the context of his life-long labor to provide for Swedish an anthology of charm texts to match such national editions as Bishop Bang's *Norske Hexeformularer og magiske Opskrifter*, apparently encountered the poem as he was examining UUB C 4 and edited it anew, with the assistance of Otto von Friesen, seemingly unaware at first that it had already been published by Geete.[3] Linderholm

---

[1] Original publication: "On the Old Swedish *Trollmöte* or *Mik mötte en gamul kerling*." In *Beyond the Piraeus Lion: East Norse Studies from Venice*, ed. Jonathan Adams and Massimiliano Bampi, 171–187. Selskab for østnordisk filologi, 2. n.p., 2017.

[2] I note that the title "trollmöte" retains a high degree of popularity among Swedish poets. There exist a number of modern texts on that topic and bearing that name, as well as any number of contemporary accounts of such encounters. Except where noted, quotations of the poem follow Geete's edition.

[3] "Å samma blad, som har täxten till 'Den signade dag'. Svårläst. Sedan jag avskrivit täxten direkt efter handskriften, kom genom Erland Hjärne till min kännedom, att den förut tryckts av R.

publishes the slightly improved text of the poem again amid his anthology of more than 1200 Swedish charms and conjurations;[4] moreover, it is Linderholm who first suggests an answer to Geete's implied query about the poem's character. This he accomplishes most prominently when he gives the poem the title *Trollmöte*, as well as when he comments in a footnote that the text deserves attention not only for its complicated rhyme scheme but also for its contents, which he says seem to him to refer to a troll-like creature (*ett trolskt väsen*).[5] It is precisely toward a better understanding of the poem's place in the two areas Linderholm mentions in that note that this essay is directed, namely, 1) the text's impressively complex rhyme scheme and 2) its content, that is, the cultural context that arguably inspires and explains the poem and its allegory.

The manuscript context of the poem, the heterogeneous UUB C 4, is described in Andersson-Schmitt and Hedlund as containing materials from the fourteenth and fifteenth centuries, and that the specific gathering containing *Trollmöte* and several other poems and hymns (folios 276–279) dates to the late fourteenth century.[6] These folios are made up of, using Andersson-Schmitt and Hedlund's terms (1988, C 4, 59), the following groups and texts:

276^r	Vagantenverse = *Ad terrorem omnium surgam loquturus*
276^v–277^r	Altschwedisches Gedicht über die freuden Mariae = *Then første frigh marie mø at hende*
277^{r-v}	Altschwedisches Gedicht über Trinität und Maria [e.g., *Then signadhe dagh*]
277^v–279^r	[De laetita u.a.] *Dies est leticie*
279^{r-v}	Altschwedisches allegorisches Gedicht [i.e., *Mik mötte en gamul kerling*]

Trollmöte thus appears at the end of a discrete section that includes a Goliard poem and such hymns as *Then signadhe dagh* and *Dies est leticie*. Briefly

---

Geete," *Signelser ock besvärjelser*, 86. (On the same leaf as 'Den signade dag'. Hard to read. Since I copied the text directly from the manuscript, it has come to my attention through Erland Hjärne that it was previously published by R. Geete).

[4] The differences between the two texts are slight but significant, especially the reading *ey* for *en* in the eleventh line of verse 3. See the appended text.

[5] "Såsom ytterst märkligt ej blott till sin konstnärliga form med dess invecklade rimflätning utan också till sitt innehåll, som synes mig avse ett trolskt väsen," *Signelser ock besvärjelser*, 86.

[6] Andersson-Schmitt and Hedlund 1988, C 4, 51, 52, 59. "XII. 276–279. 14 × 10,5 cm. 4 Einzelblätter. Schriftraum 13 × 9 cm. Kursive von einer Hand des späten 14. Jh. Schweden." Cf. Geete 1903:39, who dates the manuscript and poem to the first half of the 1400s.

summarized, the first-person narrative voice of the poem says that he once encountered an old crone (*Mik mötte en gamul kerling*), whose gait was remarkable (*henna färdh war swa underlik*).[7] With one foot she stepped high and groans (*hon stegh swa hoght oc stunde*), with the other she stepped low (*medh annan fot stegh hon nidh*), so that she looked like someone on crutches (*som thæn a styltom gaar*), and was like a "stumbler" (*som een rumfelling*), that is, a horse that habitually falters. She later refers to herself as standing in a "wobbly" or "unsteady" manner (*hwi jak swa löslik staar*). She says that if he would know what she knows (*Vil thu vita hwat jak kan*), he should follow her on the road (*tha gak thän vegh jak gangir*). Thus, they travel together and she relates the enormous longevity of her journey, more than a thousand years, as well as the great and precious burden she bears in a sack, which, through her counsel, he eventually carries for her, groaning when it is placed on his back. The crone laughs at him, saying "Thus have I fooled many a man with the same trick (or art or deception)" (*swa haffwir jak darath mangin man / medh thesse ssamu list*), noting that all others have missed out on the bag's gold and silver.[8] And she adds, "Now I would not corrupt you, I give you a portion" (*Nu vil jak e[y] fordarva thik / jak giffwer thik aff eet stykke*).[9] Her parting words appear to echo the closing statements of many Nordic charms, something like, "it is [thus?] fully shown [or proved?]" (*thet a ... ful vist*).

What are we to make of this unusual and apparently supernatural encounter and its elaborate meter?

Metrical Considerations

Against the Nordic *comparanda* of such renowned genres as eddic poetry, on the one hand, with its apparent window onto the world of the pagan Norse, and skaldic poetry, on the other, with its sophisticated metrical designs and intricate metaphors, against those standards, Old Swedish poetry, with only rare exceptions, has generally been consigned by literary scholarship to an aesthetic category only ever so slightly above doggerel and nursery rhymes—such is the unfortunate fate of the elite poets who under the influence of the German-speaking courts apparently abandoned traditional alliterative verse in favor of the more modish *knittelvers*. Looking beyond such simplistic

---

[7] NB: I include a rough translation as an appendix.

[8] Cf. the discussion of *list* in Mitchell 2014b:68.

[9] NB: Linderholm here importantly corrects with *ey [not]*, Geete's reading of *en [a]*.

bromides, however, one perceives that there is much more to East Norse literature than such derogatory and hasty appellations suggest.

One such area has to do with what would appear to be purposeful attempts to create for Old Swedish poetry, or mimic in it, highly complex rhyme schemes, metrical patterns which bear little if any resemblance to the seemingly undisciplined character of the so-called "free *knittelvers*" which Swedish poets otherwise so happily embraced (cf. Mitchell 1996; 1997b; 2008c; Layher 2008). Indeed, given the many secular Old Swedish works in *knittel*, it is easy to lose sight of the interest that existed for more complex verse forms, as well as of learned figures like Brynolf Algotsson (d. 1317), for example, who had studied in Paris. Later, as Bishop of Skara, Brynolf famously wrote a number of complex liturgical works, such as *Elinsofficiet* ([c. 1288] *Brynolf Algotssons samlade diktverk*, 78–86), some of which, as Piltz (1987:71) notes, adopt a Goliard verse form ("använde [...] genomgående en eljest ovanlig versteknik, den sk vagantstrofen *cum auctoritate*"). Similarly noteworthy in this regards is a text like the early-fourteenth-century *Poetria* by another former Paris student, Magister Mathias (Matts Övidsson, d. 1350), a treatise that offers a detailed assessment of poetic composition, exemplified in its poem about Uppsala.[10]

What is the relationship of Latin texts such as these to the creation of the small number of extant vernacular religious poems exhibiting similar complexities, such as *Trollmöte* and *Den vises sten*, a poem that can be dated to 1379? As early as the beginnings of the fourteenth century, *Kristi pina* demonstrates impressive complexity, albeit admittedly only in a few lines, where the poet incorporates both alliteration and end-rhyme in a way reminiscent of the soon-to-emerge Icelandic tradition of *rímur*.[11] Even more complex is the rhyme scheme of *Den vises sten*: uncanny degrees of poetic complexity are executed throughout the poem, where each of the twelve verses consists of thirteen lines in the pattern *aa bccb dede ffe* (see Mitchell 2008c).

---

[10] *Magister Mathias Lincopenis*, 82–89; however, it should be noted that Mathias's concerns in *Poetria* are less focused on meter as such than on such topics as visualization, allegory, periphrasis, personification and other aspects of locution and rhetoric.

[11] Cf. Mitchell 2008b:98, "Kristi pina incorporates in 4 of its lines both end-rhyme and alliteration [...]: "ihesu guz son ihesu goþe / bløt mit hiærta mæþ þino bloþe / at þænkia mz þakom þina pino / af allom hugh ok hiærta mino" (Jesus, God's son, Jesus good, / soften my heart with your blood / that I may gratefully think of your suffering / with all my thoughts and all my heart). It is hard to escape the impression that this case of alliteration (g-g, b-b, þ-þ, h-h) combined with end-rhyme (a-a-b-b) echoes qualities we elsewhere associate with the Icelandic rímur."

The metrical pattern of *Trollmöte* is comparably complex, described by Piltz (2012:61) as *abcde abcde fgfghe*, to which one might add that the poem contains further refinements, including, for example:

- the final word in the *f* and *e* lines is consistently monosyllabic;
- the final word in the *g* lines is consistently bisyllabic; and
- in sections 1 and 3, lines *abc* of verse 1 rhyme with lines *abc* of verse 2, whereas in section 2, lines *abcd* of verse 1 rhyme with lines *abcd* of verse 2.

Thus, the rhyme scheme of *Trollmöte* is generally reminiscent of sonnet structure, and is clearly related in its complexity, and very probably, its date of composition and ecclesiastical background, to *Den vises sten*. In an earlier context, I noted, with some timidity, that the verses of *Den vises sten* are "broadly reminiscent of Dante's development [...] of *terza rima* (consisting of iambic tercets in a rhyme scheme of *aba bcb* and so on), and its subsequent adoption not only by his countrymen Boccaccio and Petrarch, but also by Chaucer in *A Complaint to his Lady* in the years around 1370" (Mitchell 2008c:98). Simply stated, the so-called Petrarchan sonnet, developed in Italy in the fourteenth century, typically shows *abba abba cdcdcd* (by contrast, the later English sonnet, as executed by Shakespeare and generally more familiar to us today, shows *abab cdcd efef gg*).

One naturally suspects that, in addition to those clerics who studied at Continental universities, the Birgittine mother house at Vadstena played a key role in the poetic experimentation these works represent. The Vadstena connection was manifestly the case with *Den vises sten* (1379), and almost certainly so in the current instance, especially given the codicological context of the poem. The multiple connections within the Birgittine order between its mother house at Vadstena and the cultural world of fourteenth- and fifteenth-century Rome, especially to the extent that the Birgittine footprint (at, for example, "Palatium Magnum") remained strong, makes a conduit between Petrarchan innovations and medieval Östergötland seem unproblematic. Whatever conclusions specialists in the area of meter eventually draw about the emergence of these Old Swedish poetic texts in the corpus, they clearly developed in a learned and cosmopolitan milieu and stand in stark contrast to the prevailing mode of *knittel*. And here, beyond versification, it is useful to bear in mind the view that the sonnet is more a matter of outlook and intent than of rhyme schemes. With that in mind, let us turn to the substance of the poem.

Content

Although we are able to make some conjectures about the poem's sophisticated and intricate meter, can the same be said about its contents? Indeed, in the most basic sense, what is this text about, what is it meant to do, and to whom is it addressed? Is it really meant to portray "a poetic encounter with the supernatural"? Linderholm's own rationale for providing the title *Trollmöte* depends heavily, as he writes, on his perception that the poem refers to the poem's "narrative I" having had a meeting with a "troll-like" creature (*ett trolskt väsen*). But what led him to this conclusion? After all, the poem never overtly identifies the nature of the figure encountered on the road, other than to call her an old woman, a *kerling*, roughly comparable to old crone, or even hag, in English. None of the many possible Old Swedish terms for monstrous beings (e.g., *trwll*, *iätun*, *trollkärling*) appear in the poem, and yet most modern readers quickly formulate, as did, one suspects, the medieval audience of such a poem, the view that the text opens with a meeting between a human and some sort of otherworldly being.

Such an interpretation is largely predicated on our socialization to the norms of Nordic story-telling, for encountering a troll while traveling in the forest is perhaps one of the most stereotypical scenarios in all of Nordic literature.[12] Indeed, it is likely more than a coincidence that the oldest known reference to a troll in the North is the report of the ninth-century meeting between Bragi and a troll woman in a Norwegian forest (although not in evidence before Snorri's thirteenth-century *Skáldskaparmál* [*Edda Sn* 2, 83]). As John Lindow quite rightly notes of the scene, "The exchange between Bragi and the troll woman forms a paradigm that will often recur: a threatening encounter, in a place far from human habitation, between troll and human, with the human emerging unscathed in the end" (Lindow 2014:17).

Mindful of the recent debates about the wide semantic coverage "troll" may imply in the medieval north—Ármann Jakobsen, for example, lists no fewer than fourteen categories for Icelandic (2008a, 2008b; cf. Hartmann 1936; Schultz 2004; M. Arnold 2005; Lindow 2014)—and of some of the differences in the physical attributes that exist within and between various regions, whether national in a modern sense or regional in then-contemporary medieval senses, one may well ask, is such a description, as Linderholm

---

[12] For a detailed analysis of cross-gendered encounters in myth and legend, frequently between characters representing different groups, including trolls, in the West Norse materials in particular, see McKinnell 2005.

believed, sufficient to suggest and encounter with a "troll-like" creature? In a brief but convincing note, Terrence Wilbur (1958) reviews the etymological theories regarding *trwl, troll, tröll*, and so on, and offers evidence to support the view, building on, e.g., the insights of Eduard Sievers,[13] in particular, and such works as the etymological dictionary of Hjalmar Falk and Alf Torp,[14] that a complex that comes to refer to so many different things in Germanic vernaculars, from fishing methods to prostitutes to deception to monsters, had its origins in a verb of locomotion meaning "to roll." If the many different links to movement noted by Sievers, Falk-Torp, and Wilbur are indeed the key to the history of the term, it is easy to see that the references in this poem to the old crone's bizarre locomotion are intended to build on this connection.

It is clear from the poem that we are meant to understand that the most characteristic feature of the old crone is her unusual gait and posture (or stamina)—her bizarre high and low steps, her appearance as though she is on crutches, her resemblance to a "stumbler," and her comment that she stands in a "wobbly" or "unsteady" (*löslik*) manner. Thus, to the extent that movement, marked movement, was part of the cultural kit that triggered the image of a troll figure, the poem's opening appears to fit nicely with narrative conventions in Scandinavian tales. Indeed, late medieval and early modern narratives about trolls often play up, and on, the monstrous physical characteristics of trolls, that is, their peculiar size, large or small, their appearance, and so on, as they evolve from those otherworldly entities which the earlier medieval laws prohibit being ritually awakened toward the comically monstrous figures of later Nordic lore.[15]

We possess, as modern readers are certainly aware of, some quite vivid images from the West Norse region of trolls portrayed in this fashion, such as the description of the loathsome *tröllkona* [trollwife] Gríðr in *Illuga saga Gríðarfóstra* (Ch. 4), the earliest extant text of which is from ca. 1600, with

---

[13] "Bei an. *troll* 'Zauberer, gespenstisches Wesen' und seiner Sippe (mhd. *trolle, trulle, trülle*) möchte man an Zusammenhang mit got. *trudan*, an. *troða*, ahd. *trëtan* usw. denken: an. *troll* N. aus ursprünglichem **troð-lá-*, **trol-lá-* 'das Treten'...", Sievers 1894:339 [For Old Norse *troll* "wizard, ghostly creature" and its cognates (Middle High German *trolle, trulle, trülle*) one might consider a connection with Gothic *trudan*, Old Norse *troða*, Old High German *trëtan* and so on: Old Norse nominative *troll* from an original **troð-lá-*, **trol-lá-* "the treader"...]

[14] "...so muß *trold* zu germ. **trullôn* 'kugeln, rollen' zu stellen sein," Falk-Torp 1910–1911, vol. 2, p. 1286 [*trold* must be formed from Germanic **trullôn* "trundle, roll"].

[15] The phrase, *útisetur at vekja troll upp ok fremja heiðni með því...* ("sit out" to awaken trolls and thereby promote paganism) occurs frequently in the earliest Norwegian laws. See *NGL*, 1:19, 182, 265; 2:51 and 212.

her flaring nostrils, claw-like hands, beard, bald pate, overly short and ill-fitting tunic, snot dripping from her nose, and so on.[16] It is less frequently remembered that Old Swedish possesses a similarly hideous description of "troll-like" figures. In the mid-fifteenth-century *Namnlös och Valentin*, we are presented with "en stor iætte j græseligin skipilsse" [a large giant in a terrifying form] whose head is described as frightful, large and bald, with a long nose and a mouth as wide as a barn door, bad breath and ears that hang down to his shoulders; his eyes are black as pitch, his arms large and thick, his hands broad, his body large, his legs long and his feet wide. And at the end of the description, in a brief verse, the author adds "aff hans skipilsse kan iach ey mere sighiæ / wtan han war trullom lik*er*" [of his guise I can say no more / except that he was "troll-like"] (*Namnlös och Valentin*, 39–40). An equally repulsive description is provided in a short, late medieval miracle tale, *Om S. Bartholomei moder, eller folk-sagan om Qvinnan utan Händer*, a legend translated (*wænt*) by the general confessor at Vadstena, Karolus Benedicti, ca. 1500 and preserved in Cod. Linc. B 70 a.[17] This story, published in the nineteenth century as part of the Old Swedish legendary, consists of a tale-type known as AT 706 "The Maiden without Hands." In it, we are given one of the most compelling verbal images of what trolls might look like in the mind of a late medieval Swedish cleric. There the author writes that the woman gives birth to a troll (*haffwer føth eth trol*), "something like a devil, with an enormous head, a crooked neck, twitching (?) hands and feet, donkey ears, [and] hideous eyes, the one above the other" (*diäfflenom likast hwilket som haffwer stort hwffudh krokotan hals, oc obeqäma händher oc föther, asna öron, rädhelikan öghon eth owan för thz andhra* [219]).

A late medieval ecclesiastical text from the Continent, one that came to have widespread popularity, offers important perspectives on our topic: first of all, it indicates that knowledge of Nordic trolls was, as such, of interest to clerical circles outside of Scandinavia already during the later Middle Ages, and, second, it demonstrates that not only was the existence of these creatures

---

[16] en honum þótti sem hríð eða hregg stæði ór nǫsum hennar. Horrinn hekk ofan fyrir munninn. Hún hafði skegg ok skǫllótt um hǫfuðit. Hendr hennar váru sem arnarklær, en ermar báðar brenndar, en sá stakkr, er hún var í, tók henni eigi lengra en á lendar á bakit, en allt á tær í fyrir. Augu hennar váru græn, en ennit bratt, eyrun fellu víða. Engi mátti hana kalla fríða (*Illuga saga Gríðarfóstra*, 418 [Ch. 4]). (It looked to him as if snow and hail were storming out of her nose. Drool dripped out of her mouth. She was bald, but had a beard. Her hands were like the claws of an eagle, and both sleeves were burned. She wore a coat which hung only to her buttocks in back, but to her toes in front. Her eyes were green, her forehead steep, and her ears stuck way out. No one was going to call her pretty! [*The Saga of Illugi, Grid's Foster-Son*, 68]).

[17] On the career of Karolus, see Silfverstolpe 1898:97–98, 166.

known in Europe but so too was the same narrative paradigm identified by Lindow (above)—"a threatening encounter, in a place far from human habitation, between troll and human, with the human emerging unscathed in the end"—a fact that would seem to confirm the relative age and continuity of this belief about their behavior.

The text is the *Malleus maleficarum* "the hammer of the witches," the infamous inquisitorial handbook from 1486 by the German inquisitor, Henrik Institoris Kramer (and possibly co-authored by Jakob Sprenger). In its discussion of otherworldly beings, this deeply influential manual underscores how within religious circles in the later Middle Ages, the supernatural vernacular world had been, and was being, amalgamated with other traditions of demonic beings among demonologists and other theologians. In the context of a discussion of demons and "unclean spirits" (building on St. John Cassian in his *First Collation* 7.32), the author-inquisitor(s) of this witch-hunting manual write(s) that the lower order of such spirits are unable to harm anyone, but, in essence, merely play jokes:

> Nam nonnullos eoru, quos etiam paganos vulgus appellat, nos verò Trollen. et abundant in regno Norueye, aut Schretel. Ita seductores et ioculatores esse manifestu est, vt certa quæque loca vias iugiter obsidentes, nequaquam tormentis prætereuntes lædere possunt, de risu tantummodò et illusione contenti, fatigare eos potius studeant, quàm nocere.
>
> *Malleus maleficarum.* Part II, Question I, Chapter III

> This is corroborated without any doubt by the manifest fact that some of them, whom the common people call pagans (*paganos*) but we call trolls (*Trollen*) (these are plentiful in the Kingdom of Norway [*abundant in regno Norueye*]) and fairies (*Schretl*) are misleading tricksters with the restriction that while they constantly haunt certain places and roads, they cannot harm passers-by in any way. Instead they are content with derision and deception and strive to harass rather than harm them.[18]

Echoes of this same combination of trolls and demonic spirits, typified by the desire to deceive and fool Christians in association with roads, pilgrimages,

---

[18] *Malleus maleficarum*, 296. Cf. Montague Summers's translation of the key section, "...which the common people call Fauns [*Schretel*], and we call Trolls, which abound in Norway." In translating *Schretel* as "fairies," Mackay stresses the Otherworldly character of these spirits; with "fauns," Summers emphasizes the word's original woodland associations, although by the late fifteenth century, it was likely to be understood as a more terrifying demonic spirit. Relevant in this context is the section of the witch's curse (*Bulsubæn*) in *Bósa saga ok Herrauðs* that reads, *en gǫtur allar / ok gagnstígar, / troðist allar / í trǫllhendr fyrir þér* (*Bósa saga ok Herrauðs* 1954:293), with the sense that "all roads and paths will lead you right into troll-hands."

and other travels, are to be heard in the mid-sixteenth century: the encyclopedic ethnography by Olaus Magnus published in 1555, *Historia de gentibus septentrionalibus* (History of the Northern Peoples), refers to this concatenation several times, surely meaning trolls, although without using the term.[19]

The remainder of *Trollmöte* sketches how the crone invites the narrator to accompany her and her willingness to share with him her knowledge. She refers to the heavy burden she must bear, calls the narrator a remarkable fool (*än vndirlik gek*), and then offers to share the valuable treasure in her sack which he now bears for her, saying, *swa haffwir jak darath mangin man / medh thesse ssamu list* (Thus have I fooled many a man with the same trick [or art or deception]). The term she uses is *list*, which, of course, includes exactly such meanings as deception and subterfuge, what I have tried to express with the term "trick." The poem as a whole is followed with the benediction, "Mary, Jesus, Blessed Trinity" (*maria jhesus o beata trinitas*).

Now the reader-hearer, whether medieval or modern, must early on decide whether this narrative portrays, to use Elizabeth Hartmann's bifurcated characterization of the troll figure in Nordic folklore (1936:144–176), "Der Troll als übernatürlicher Gegner" (the troll as supernatural opponent), or "Der Troll als übernatürlicher Helfer" (the troll as supernatural helper). Given the character of the crone's remarks, making this choice may not seem to be an overly burdensome task: I note that, in addition to the obvious references to deception, the imagery of the poem also tilts our interpretation in the direction of "opponent." The images of sacks and burdens and the condition of being weighted-down most often refers in medieval religious literature to demonic behavior.[20] One of the Old Swedish sermons, for example, says that "It is written that the devil called out to a condemned soul, saying 'Come, accursed soul, heavy as stone'" ("Thy är scrifwat at dyäfla ropadho mot enne fordömde siäl sighiande Kom forbannat siäl thung som sten," *Svenska medeltids-postillor* 1:219 [cf. 1:297]). Moreover, the notion of sinners as those who stumble on life's road—and recall that the crone is described as a stumbler—is an old one, with many biblical attestations (such as Proverbs 4:12 and 1 Peter 2:8), and one attested in Old Swedish works from the translation of *Stimulus amoris* to homiletic literature.[21]

---

[19] *Historia de gentibus septentrionalibus*, 2.15; 6.10; 6.19.

[20] In *Index exemplorum*, no. 4188, Tubach notes, *Scholar given stones by devil*. "A student wishing to be rich, calls forth the devil and agrees to worship him; he later discovers that the devil has given him stones instead of gold." Cf. no. 1630, no. 4249, and no. 5181.

[21] "Ok aff the stora frygdhinne gar tha människian swa som staplandis som thän som drwkkin är," *Stimulus amoris*, 30. (And from these great joys people walk with faltering step like a person who is drunk).

And, indeed, all indications suggest that this poem takes its inspiration from the sort of "life's journey" literature which in later centuries will produce such well-known works as Stiernhielm's *Herkules vid skiljo-vägen* (Hercules at the crossroad) in Sweden and Bunyan's *Pilgrim's Progress* in England, yet the predicate for these famous works was the earlier medieval exploitation of the journey monomyth, as some have called it. Carol Zaleski notes that "... one of the central religious conceptions of the Middle Ages [is] the idea that life is a pilgrimage [...] Christian pilgrimage became a symbol for the individual's journey through life and death" (Zaleski 1985:479; cf. Dinzelbacher 1988, 2005). Among the most renowned visionary travel narratives of the Middle Ages are Dante's early fourteenth-century *Divine Comedy*, composed between 1308 and 1321, and *Pèlerinage de vie humaine (Life's Pilgrimage)*, by Guillaume de Digulleville, a description of a journey to Paradise, composed between 1330 and 1332. But perhaps the text of this sort that resonated most loudly in the North was the twelfth-century *Visio Tnugdali* (The Vision of Tundale), known in an Icelandic translation, *Duggals leiðsla*, and extant in a number of vellum and paper manuscripts. Certainly less well-known in the modern period, however, is the fact that *Visio Tnugdali* was also given separate treatment from Latin into Old Swedish, the earliest two manuscripts of which date to 1457 and 1467.[22]

Clearly there was an appetite for the life's pilgrimage narrative in late medieval Sweden. Do these facts, together with our poem's codicological position in UUB C 4, point us toward a fuller understanding of the poem and its context, that is, what is it about, what is it meant to do, and to whom is it addressed? Here the recent work by Anders Piltz plays an important role: in a major review of texts related to *Den signade dag*, Piltz notes that the mid-fifteenth-century manuscript in which *Trollmöte* is found, UUB C 4, is also the oldest evidence for the text of this psalm (*Den signade dag*) in Swedish. He further demonstrates, in line with a suggestion made by Allan Arvastson (1971), that the psalm originated, or was at least popularized, by the thousands of pilgrims who journeyed to Vadstena cloister. We have then an interesting set of poetical texts in this quire of UUB C 4, int. al., a Golliard poem, a Marian poem, Latin hymns, and the Old Swedish poem under discussion. Perhaps the phrase that concludes *Trollmöte*, "Mary, Jesus, Blessed Trinity" (*maria jhesus o beata trinitas*), should be interpreted as signaling not only the end of that specific text, but perhaps also of that section of poems as a whole, that is, five texts, two in Latin and three in Swedish, understood to be related to the pilgrimage experience.

---

[22] See Geete 1903:84 and *Tungulus*, 27–34.

Conclusion

What then should we make of the little-known 48-line Old Swedish poem that begins *Mik mötte en gamul kerling* ("I met an old crone")? And, in particular, what sort of window on poetry and popular tradition in medieval Sweden does it offer the modern reader? First of all, as we have seen, it is a very tightly composed work as regards meter, indeed, one of a small handful of particularly complex and skillfully wrought Old Swedish works that appear to have their roots in the Birgittine motherhouse in Vadstena (and thus ultimately further afield to the Continent). This exotic metrical quality is employed in the service of themes that are on one level built on the widespread Christian theme of pilgrimage, of life as a journey, yet at the same time, the work possesses a particular Nordic twist, the age-old theme of the encounter with a troll-like creature. And the manuscript context in which we find the text of *Mik mötte en gamul kerling* suggests that poem may itself, in turn, have been intended to form part of the pilgrimage experience—and here it is important to recall that Vadstena was late medieval Sweden's most popular pilgrimage destination.

Thus, in this Old Swedish text we find not only the deft hand of a poet conversant with sophisticated versification schemes and projects, but also one who possessed an intimate knowledge of vernacular and ecclesiastical narrative traditions concerned with otherworldly beings, i.e., trolls and demons, and otherworldly journeys as allegories, a fitting image for an audience that should perhaps be understood to consist largely of current or past pilgrims. As regards the question of titles, Linderholm's *Trollmöte* may be something of a leap, although by no means completely inappropriate; yet at the same time, Geete's anodyne descriptive tag, *En allegorisk dikt (dröm eller saga)*, may ultimately be closer to the mark.

"En allegorisk dikt (dröm eller saga)," ed. Robert Geete

Bilaga till Svenska Fornskrift-sällskapets årsmöte 1902:43–44.

   Mik mötte en gamul kerling
   henna färdh war swa undirlik
   hon stegh swa hoght oc stunde
   medh annan fot stegh hon nidh
5 som thän a styltom gaar
   ¶ hon var som än rumffelling
   jak helsadhe hänne hon suaradhe mik
   swa stuntlik j thesse lunde
   ey thorff thu swa vndra a mik
10 hwi jak swa | löslik staar
   Vil thu vita hwat jak kan
   tha gak thän vegh jak gangir
   mik haffwir fölght swa mangin man
   badhe j gledhi lost oc angir
15 jak hafwir farit j skoghin vil
   mära än thusan[d] aar

2.

   Min vägh fiol tha medh hänne
   äpte thän veg[h] hon sidhan stegh
   hon haffdhe swa thunkt at bära
   mik thikke thik vara än vndirlik gek
5 jak sigher thik son min hwj
   ¶ Radh vil jak thik känna
   än tho at se gamul oc ey fegh
   vil thu thik hiälpa. oc nära
   thu tak medh oc bär [nu] min sek[23]
10 oc haff thet är ij.
   Then är j siälff vel thusand mark
   gul oc ädhla stena
   gud gaffwe at jak vare än man swa stark
   jak vrkadhe bära han ena.
15 liffte hon sekin vppa min bak
   oc hedhan gingin vj

---

[23] Linderholm: *oc bær nu min sek.*

3.

        Thän kerling fik än lathir
        hon lo at mik, at jak var flather
        thet jak bar swa at jak stunde
        swa haffwir jak darath mangin man
5   medh thesse ssamu list
        ¶ The äru än flere athir
        ther bära skulu oc getas väl aat
        til the dö ther vnde
        swa haffwir jak än mikt gul oc silff
10   oc the haffua allo mist
        Nu vil jak e[y] fordarva thik[24]
        jak giffwer thik aff eet stykke
        thu gak vm kring thu skodha mik
        tha se thu huru thik thikke
15   jak teer mik mangom lundum väl
        thet a . . . . . ful vist
        maria jhesus o beata trinitas

        I met an old crone,
        her gait was so remarkable:
        she stepped so high and groaned,
        with the other foot, she stepped down,
5   like one who goes on crutches.
        She was like a stumbler.
        I hailed her, she answered me
        so lovingly in this fashion:
        "You need not wonder about me,
10   I stand so 'wobbly'.
        Would you know what I know (alt., can do),
        then accompany me on the road I travel!
        So many men have followed me
        in joy, lust and sorrow,
15   I have journeyed in the forest well
        more than a thousand years."

2.

        My path fell [in] with hers.
        going the way she then tread,

---

[24] Linderholm: "Geete har, felaktigt, läst *en*," > *Nu vil jak ey fordarva thik*.

          she had so heavy [a burden] to bear:
          "It seems to me you are a remarkable fool,
    5   I tell you, my son, why.
          I would give you some advice,
          it may be old yet not fey.
          Would you help and nurture yourself,
          now take and bear my sack
    10   and have that which is in it!
          In it is silver [worth] more than a thousand marks,
          gold and gemstones.
          God grant, that I should be a man so strong,
          [that] I should be able to bear it alone."
    15   She lifted the sack up on my back,
          and hence we went.

3.

          The crone smiled,
          she laughed at me, that I was simple,
          as I bore, such that I groaned:
          "Thus have I fooled many a man
    5   with the same 'trick'."
          There are yet others,
          who should bear [it] and be well pleased
          until they die there under.
          have I yet much gold and silver,
    10   and all have missed them.
          Now I would not corrupt you,
          I give to you from a piece:
          you went about, you beheld me,
          then you see, how to it seems to you:
    15   I declare in many ways
          it is . . . . . fully shown.
          Maria, Jesus, Blessed Trinity.

(Efter Upsala Uni.-bibl:s handskrift C 4; detta stycke från förra hälften af 1400-talet; skrifvet som prosa)

Anm. Uti v. 3, r. 16 *är det andra ordet oläsligt.*

[Following Uppsala University Library manuscript C 4; this piece from the first half of the 1400s; written as prose.]

Works Cited

- Articles in English (a, the) are not observed in alphabetization but those in other languages (e.g., en, den, Der) are.
- Family names beginning with de, von, van are filed under the second element.
- Icelandic authors are listed by given names, not patronymics.
- For Danish authors, Danish filing rules apply.
- Vowel length (á, é, í, ó, ú, ý) does not impact alphabetical order.
- Characters not used in English adhere to the following scheme: å = aa; æ/ä = ae; ǫ/ø/ö = oe; ü = ue; ð = dh; þ follows z.

Abbreviations

ARV = *ARV. Tidskrift för nordisk folkminnesforskning, ARV. The Yearbook of Scandinavian Folklore, ARV. The Nordic Yearbook of Folklore.*

Íslenzk fornrit editions are cited by volume number rather than title.

KLNM = *Kulturhistorisk leksikon for nordisk middelalder fra vikingetid til reformasjonstid*, ed. Johannes Brøndsted et al. Copenhagen, 1982 (1956–1978).

SFSS = Svenska Fornskrift-Sällskapets Samlingar, Samlingar utg. af Svenska Fornskrift-Sällskapet, etc.

Primary sources

Unpublished

Cambridge, Massachusetts. Milman Parry Collection of Oral Literature. Harvard University:
> Međedović, Avdo. *Ženidba Smailagić Meha*. PN 6840, July 5-12, 1935; LN 35, May 23, 1950.
> Parry, Milman. 1935. "The Singer of Tales." Typewritten ms.

Uppsala. Uppsala universitetsbibliotek. UUB C 4.

Published

Abbo of Fleury. *Corolla Sancti Eadmundi. The Garland of Saint Edmund, King and Martyr*, ed. and trans. Lord Francis Hervey, 10-59. London, 1907.

Adam of Bremen. See *Gesta Hammaburgensis*.

Äldre Västgötalagen. In *SGL*. 1:1-74.

Ælfric. *Life of Saint Edmund* = "XXXII. Passio Sancti Eadmvndi Regis et Martyris." In *Ælfric's Lives of Saints, being A Set of Sermons on Saints' Days Formerly Observed by the English Church*, ed. and trans. Walter W. Skeat, 2:314-335. Early English Text Society. London, 1900.

Alfræði íslenzk. Islandsk encyklopædisk litteratur, ed. Natanael Beckman and Kristian Kålund. SUGNL, 37, 41, 45. Copenhagen, 1908-1918.

Alvíssmál = *Edda. Die Lieder des Codex Regius*, 124-129. Translation: *All-wises's Sayings* in *The Poetic Edda*, 105-109.

Árna saga byskups. In *Íslenzk fornrit*, 17, ed. Sigurgeir Steingrímsson, Ólafur Halldórsson, and Peter Foote. Reykjavík, 1998

Ásmundar saga kappabana = *FAS* 1954, 1:383-408. Translation: *The Saga of Asmund Champion-Killer*. In *Six Old Icelandic Sagas*, trans. W. Bryant Bachman and Guðmundur Erlingsson, 85-102. Lanham, MD, 1993.

Baldrs draumar = *Edda. Die Lieder des Codex Regius*, 277-279. Translation: *Baldr's Dreams* in *The Poetic Edda*, 235-237.

Beowulf = *Beowulf and The Fight at Finnsburg*, ed. Francis Klaeber. 3rd ed. Boston, 1941.

Beowulf 1977 = *Beowulf: A Dual-Language Edition*, ed. and trans. Howell D. Chickering, Jr. Garden City NY, 1977.

Bósa saga ok Herrauðs = *FAS*, 3:191-234.

Bósa saga ok Herrauðs 1954 = *FAS* 1954, 3:281–322. Translation: *Bosi and Herraud*. In *Seven Viking Romances*, trans. Hermann Pálsson and Paul Edwards, 199–227. Harmondsworth, 1985.

Brennu-Njáls saga. In *Íslenzk fornrit*, 12, ed. Einar Ól. Sveinsson. Reykjavík, 1971 (1954). Translation: *Njal's saga*, trans. Magnus Magnusson and Hermann Pálsson. The Penguin Classics. Baltimore, 1960.

Brevis Historia Regvm Dacie = Sven Aggesen, *Historia Regum Dacie Compendiosa* = *En Ny Text af Sven Aggesøns Værker Genvunden paa Grundlag af Codex Arnæmagnæanus 33, 4to*, ed. M. Cl. Gertz, 94–143. Copenhagen, 1916. Translation: *The Works of Sven Aggesen, Twelfth-Century Danish Historian*, trans. Eric Christiansen. Viking Society for Northern Research. Text Series, 9. London, 1992.

Brynolf Algotssons samlade diktverk, ed. and trans. Tryggve Lundén. *Credo*, 27.2 (1946):73–121.

CCF = *Føroya kvæði. Corpus Carminum Færoensium*, ed. Christian Matras, Sven Grundtvig, and Jørgen Bloch. Universitets-Jubilæets Danske Samfunds Skriftserie. Copenhagen, 1944–2003.

Celebremus karissimi = *S:t Sigfrid besjungen: Celebremus karissimi, ett helgonofficium från 1200-talet*, ed. Ann-Marie Nilsson. Runica et mediævalia. Scripta maiora, 6. Stockholm, 2010.

Cimbrorum et Gothorum origines = Nicolaus Petreius (alt., Niels Pedersen), *Cimbrorum et Gothorum origines*. Leipzig: ex officina Johann Melchior Lieben, 1695 (written ca. 1573–1579).

Codex diplomaticus Lubecensis, Lübeckisches Urkundenbuch 1. Abt. Urkundenbuch der Stadt Lübeck. vol. 3. Hrsg. von dem Vereine für Lübeckische Geschichte und Altertumskunde. Lübeck, 1871.

The Complete Sagas of Icelanders, including 49 Tales, ed. and trans. Viðar Hreinsson et al. 5 vols. Reykjavík, 1997.

Corpus iuris canonici, ed. Emil Friedberg and Aemilius Ludwig Richter. 2nd ed. Leipzig, 1879.

Danmarks runeindskrifter, ed. Lis Jacobsen and Erik Moltke. Copenhagen, 1941–1942.

De Lapidibus = Marbod of Rennes, *"De lapidibus," considered as a Medical Treatise with Text, Commentary, and C. W. King's Translation, together with Text and Translation of Marbode's Minor Works on Stones*, ed. John M. Riddle. Sudhoffs Archiv. Beihefte, 20. Wiesbaden, 1977.

Den norske-islandske Skjaldedigtning. See *Skj*.

Den vises sten = "Den vises sten. En hittils okänd rimdikt från 1300-talet. Efter en Upsalahandskrift från år 1379 (Bilaga till Sv. Fornskr.-Sällsk:s årsmöte 1900)," ed. Robert Geete, 1–16. In *Småstycken på fornsvenska*. Andra serien. SFSS. Stockholm, 1900.

Deutsche Sagen. Herausgegeben von den Brüdern Grimm, ed. Jacob Grimm and Wilhelm Grimm. Berlin, 1816–1818. Translation: *German Legends of the Brothers Grimm*, trans. Donald Ward. Philadelphia, 1981.

DgF = *Danmarks gamle Folkeviser*, ed. Svend Grundtvig, Axel Olrik, Hakon Grüner-Nielsen, and Erik Dal. Copenhagen, 1966–1976 (1853–1965).

Diplomatarium Danicum = Diplomatarium Danicum, Danish National Archives and the Carlsberg Foundation. https://diplomatarium.dk/search?from_ z date=&to_date=&search=Sams%C3%B8 (accessed March 11, 2020).

Diplomatarium suecanum. See *SD* (*Svenskt diplomatarium*).

DN = *Diplomatarium Norvegicum*, ed. C. R. Unger, C. A. Lange, H. J. Huitfeldt, Alexander Bugge et al. Christiania, 1847–.

Dudo Sancti Quintini. *De moribus et actis primorum Normannorum ducum*, ed. Jules Lair. Mémoires de la Société des antiquaires de Normandie, 23. Paris, 1865. Translation: Dudo, Dean of St Quentin. *History of the Normans*, trans. Eric Christiansen. Woodbridge, 1998.

Duggals leiðsla, ed. Peter Cahill. Rit / Stofnun Árna Magnússonar á Íslandi, 25. Reykjavík, 1983.

Edda = *Edda. Die Lieder des Codex Regius nebst verwandten Denkmälern. I. Text*, ed. Gustav Neckel and Hans Kuhn. 5th rev. Heidelberg, 1983. Translation: *The Poetic Edda*, trans. Carolyne Larrington. Oxford World's Classics. 2nd ed. Oxford, 2014.

Edda Sn 1 = *Snorri Sturluson. Edda. Prologue and Gylfaginning*, ed. Anthony Faulkes. 2nd ed. London, 2005 (1982). Translation: *Snorri Sturluson. Edda*, trans. Anthony Faulkes. Everyman Classics. London, 1987.

Edda Sn 2 = *Snorri Sturluson. Edda. Skáldskaparmál. I. Introduction, Text and Notes*, ed. Anthony Faulkes. London, 1998. Translation: *Snorri Sturluson. Edda*, trans. Anthony Faulkes. Everyman Classics. London, 1987.

Edda Sn 1848–1887 = *Edda Snorra Sturlusonar. Edda Snorronis Sturlæi*, ed. Jón Sigurðsson et al. 3 vols. Copenhagen, 1848–1852.

Edda Sn 1931 = *Edda Snorra Sturlusonar*, ed. Finnur Jónsson. Kommissionen for Det Arnamagnaeanske Legat. Copenhagen, 1931.

Egils saga Skalla-Grímssonar. In *Íslenzk fornrit*, 2, ed. Sigurður Nordal. Reykjavík, 1979 (1933). Translation: *Egil's Saga*, trans. Hermann Pálsson and Paul Edwards. Harmondsworth, 1980 (1976).
Eiríks saga rauða. In *Íslenzk fornrit*, 4, ed. Einar Ól. Sveinsson and Matthías Þórðarson, 193–237. Reykjavík, 1957 (1935). Translation: *Vinland Sagas: The Norse Discovery of America*, trans. Magnus Magnusson and Hermann Pálsson, 73–105. Harmondsworth, 1983.
Eiríks saga víðfǫrla, ed. Helle Jensen. Editiones Arnamagnæanæ. Series B, 29. Copenhagen, 1983.
En allegorisk dikt (dröm eller saga). See *Tröllmöte*.
En giftmordares bekännelser. In *Röster från svensk medeltid: latinska texter i original och översattning*, ed. and trans. Hans Aili, Olle Ferm, and Helmer Gustavson, 14–21. Stockholm, 1990.
Erikskrönikan, enligt Cod. Holm. D2 jämte avvikande läsarter ur andra handskrifter, ed. Rolf Pipping. SFSS, 47. Uppsala, 1963. Translation: *The Chronicle of Duke Erik: A Verse Epic from Medieval Sweden*, trans. Erik Carlquist and Peter C. Hogg. Lund, 2012.
Eyrbyggja saga. In *Íslenzk fornrit*, 4, ed. Einar Ól. Sveinsson and Matthías Þórðarson, 1–184. Reykjavík, 1957 (1935). Translation: *Eyrbyggja saga*, trans. Hermann Pálsson and Paul Geoffrey Edwards. The New Saga Library. Edinburgh, 1973.
Færeyinga saga, ed. Ólafur Halldórsson. Rit / Stofnun Árna Magnússonar á Islandi, 30. Reykjavík, 1987. Translation: *The Faroe Islanders' Saga*, trans. George Johnston. Ottawa, 1975.
FAS = *Fornaldar Sögur Nordrlanda, eptir gömlum handritum*, ed. C. C. Rafn. 3 Vols. Copenhagen, 1829–1830.
FAS 1954 = *Fornaldar sögur Norðurlanda*, ed. Guðni Jónsson. 4 vols. n.p., 1981 (1954).
Faulkes = *Snorri Sturluson. Edda*, trans. Anthony Faulkes. Everyman Classics. London, 1987.
Flateyjarbok, ed. Guðbrandur Vigfússon and C. R. Unger. Norske historiske Kildeskriftfonds Skrifter. Christiania, 1860-1868.
Flores och Blanzeflor. Kritisk upplaga, ed. Emil Olson. SFSS, 46. Lund, 1956.
Florus = *Lucius Annaeus Florus, Epitome of Roman History*, ed. and trans. E. S. Forster. The Loeb Classical Library. Cambridge, MA, 1929.
For Scírnis = *Edda. Die Lieder des Codex Regius*, 69–77. Translation: *Skirnir's Journey* in *The Poetic Edda*, 57–64.
Fornmanna sögur eptir gömlum handritum. Copenhagen, 1825–1837.

Gamal Norsk Homiliebok: Cod. Am 619 4, ed. Gustav Indrebø. Skrifter utgjevne for Kjeldeskriftfondet, 54. Oslo, 1931.

Gammeldansk Bibel = Den ældste danske Bibel-Oversættelse eller det gamle Testamentes otte første Bøger: Fordanskede efter Vulgata, ed. Christian Molbech. Copenhagen, 1828.

Gautreks saga. In *Fornaldar Sögur Nordrlanda, eptir gömlum handritum*, ed. Carl C. Rafn, 3:3–53. Copenhagen, 1829–1830. Translation: *King Gautrek*. In *Seven Viking Romances*, trans. Hermann Pálsson and Paul Edwards, 138–170. Harmondsworth, 1985.

Gautreks saga 1954 = *FAS* 1954, 4:1–50. Translation: *King Gautrek*. In *Seven Viking Romances*, trans. Hermann Pálsson and Paul Edwards, 138–170. Harmondsworth, 1985.

Gesta Danorum = Saxo Grammaticus. *Gesta Danorum. Danmarkshistorien*, ed. Karsten Friis-Jensen. Copenhagen, 2005. Translation: *Saxo Grammaticus: The History of the Danes. (Books 1–9)*, ed. H.R. Ellis Davidson; trans. Peter Fisher. Cambridge, 1979.

Gesta Hammaburgensis = Adam of Bremen. *Adami Gesta Hammaburgensis ecclesiae pontificum*. Monumenta Germaniae historica. Scriptores rerum germanicarum, 2. Hannover, 1876. Translation: Adam of Bremen. *History of the Archbishops of Hamburg-Bremen by Adam of Bremen*, trans. F. J. Tschan. New York, 1959.

Getica = *Iordanis Romana et Getica*, ed. Theodor Mommsen. Monumenta Germaniae historica. Auctores antiquissimi, 5:1. Berlin, 1961. Translation: *The Gothic History of Jordanes in English version*, trans. Charles C. Mierow. 2nd ed. Cambridge: 1966.

Gísla saga Súrssonar. In *Íslenzk fornrit*, 6, ed. Björn K. Þórólfsson and Guðni Jónsson, 1–118. Reykjavík, 1972 (1943). Translation: *The Saga of Gisli the Outlaw*, trans. George Johnston. Toronto. 1973 (1963).

Göngu-Hrólfs saga = *FAS* 3:253-364.

Grænlendinga saga. In *Íslenzk fornrit*, 4, ed. Einar Ól. Sveinsson and Matthías Þórðarson, 239–269. Reykjavík, 1957 (1935). Translation: *Vinland Sagas: The Norse Discovery of America*, trans. Magnus Magnusson and Hermann Pálsson, 47–72. Harmondsworth, 1983.

Grágás. Konungsbók, ed. Vilhjálmur Finsen. Odense: Universitetsforlag, 1974 (1852). Facsimile ed. Translation: *Laws of Early Iceland: Grágás, the Codex Regius of Grágás, with Material from other Manuscripts*. 2 vols, ed. and trans. Andrew Dennis, Peter Foote, and Richard Perkins. University of Manitoba Icelandic Studies 3, 5. Winnipeg, 1980–2000.

Grettis saga Ásmundarsonar. In *Íslenzk fornrit,* 7, ed. Guðni Jónsson, 3–290. Reykjavík, 1964 (1936). Translation: *Grettir's saga,* trans. Denton Fox and Hermann Pálsson. Toronto, 1974.

Grímnismál = *Edda. Die Lieder des Codex regius,* 56–68. Translation: *Grimnir's Sayings* in *The Poetic Edda,* 47–56.

Grógaldr. In *De gamle Eddadigte,* ed. Finnur Jónsson, 171–174. Copenhagen, 1932. Translation: *Gróa's Chant* in *The Poetic Edda,* 256–258.

Guðrúnarqviða ǫnnor = *Edda. Die Lieder des Codex Regius,* 224–231. Translation: *The Second Poem of Gudrun* in *The Poetic Edda,* 191–196.

Guta saga 1959 = *En fornsvensk och några äldre danska översättningar av Gutasagan,* ed. Karl Gustav Ljunggren. SFSS, 64. Lund, 1959.

Guta saga 1999 = *Guta saga: The History of the Gotlanders,* ed. and trans. Christine Peel. Viking Society for Northern Research. Text Series, 12. London, 1999.

Gylfaginning. See *Edda Sn* 1.

Hälsingelagen. In *SGL,* 6:1–93.

Hálfs saga 1829–1830 = *FAS* 2:23–60.

Hálfs saga 1954 = *FAS* 1954, 2:91–134. Translation: *The Sagas of King Half and King Hrolf,* trans. W. Bryant Bachman and Guðmundur Erlingsson, 1–36. Lanham MD, 1991.

Hálfs saga 1981 = *Hálfs saga ok Hálfsrekka,* ed. Hubert Seelow. Stofnun Árna Magnússonar Rit 20. Reykjavík, 1981.

Hamðismál = *Edda. Die Lieder des Codex regius,* 269–274. Translation: *The Lay of Hamdir* in *The Poetic Edda,* 230–234.

Haralds saga Sigurðarsonar. In *Heimskringla* 3:68–202. Translation: *Snorri Sturluson. Heimskringla I-III,* trans. Alison Finlay and Anthony Faulkes, 3:41–122. 2nd ed. London, 2014–2016.

Hárbarðzlióð = *Edda. Die Lieder des Codex regius,* 78–87. Translation: *Harbard's Song* in *The Poetic Edda,* 65–73.

Hávamál = *Edda. Die Lieder des Codex Regius,* 17–44. Translation: *The Sayings of the High One* in *The Poetic Edda,* 13–35.

Hávarðr halti ísfirðingr. In *Den norske-islandske Skjaldedigtning. B. Rettet Tekst,* ed. Finnur Jónsson, 182. Copenhagen, 1973 (1912–1915).

Heiðarvíga saga. In *Íslenzk fornrit,* 3, ed. Sigurður Nordal and Guðni Jónsson, 213–328. Reykjavík, 1938. Translation: *Heidarvíga saga,* trans. W. Bryant Bachman and Guðmundur Erlingsson. Lanham, MD, 1995.

Heimskringla = *Íslenzk fornrit,* 26–28, ed. Bjarni Aðalbjarnarson. 3 vols. Reykjavík, 1979 (1945– 1961). Translation: *Snorri Sturluson.*

Heimskringla I–III, trans. Alison Finlay and Anthony Faulkes. 2nd ed. London, 2014–2016.

Hemings þáttr Áslákssonar, ed. Gillian Fellows Jensen. Editiones Arnamagnaeanae.Ser. B, 3. Copenhagen, 1962. Translation: *Hemings Þáttr*, trans. Anthony Faulkes. Thorisda, 2016.

Herr Ivan. Kristisk upplaga, ed. Erik Noreen. SFSS, 50. Stockholm, 1931.

Hertig Fredrik av Normandie: kritisk upplaga på grundval av Codex Verelianus, ed. Erik Noreen. SFSS, 49. Uppsala, 1927.

Hervarar saga ok Heiðreks konungs 1 = *FAS* 1:409–512; 513–533

Hervarar saga ok Heiðreks konungs 2 = *Saga Heiðreks konungs ins vitra. The Saga of King Heidrek the Wise*, ed. and trans. Christopher Tolkien. London, 1960.

Historia de antiquitate regum Norwagiensium. See Theodoricus Monachus. *Historia de antiquitate regum Norwagiensium*.

Historia de gentibus septentrionalibus. See Olaus Magnus, *Historia de gentibus septentrionalibus*.

Historia Norwegie. In *Monumenta Historica Norvegiae*, 70–124. Translation: *History of Norway and the Passion and Miracles of the Blessed Óláfr*, ed. Carl Phelpstead; trans. D. Kunin, 1–25. Viking Society for Northern Research Text Series, 13. London, 2001.

Hrafnkels saga Freysgoða. In *Íslenzk fornrit*, 11, ed. Jón Jóhannesson, 98–133. Reykjavík, 1950. Translation: *The Saga of Hrafnkel Frey's Godi*, trans. Terry Gunnell, 5:261–281. In *The Complete Sagas of Icelanders*.

Hrólfs saga kraka ok kappa hans = *FAS* 1954, 1:1–105. Translation: *The Saga of King Hrolf Kraki*, trans. Jesse L. Byock. New York, 1998.

Hyndloljóð. In *Edda. Die Lieder des Codex Regius*, 288–296. Translation: *The Song of Hindla* in *The Poetic Edda*, 245–252.

Illuga saga Gríðarfóstra = *FAS* 1954, 3:411–424. Translation: *The Saga of Illugi, Grid's Foster-Son*. In *Six Old Icelandic Sagas*, trans. W. Bryant Bachman and Guðmundur Erlingsson, 63–72. Lanham, MD, 1993.

Islandske Annaler indtil 1578, ed. Gustav Storm. Christiania, 1888.

Íslenzk fornkvæði (JH) = *Íslenzk fornkvæði / Islandske folkeviser*, ed. Jón Helgason. Editiones Arnamagnaeanae, B: 10–17. Copenhagen, 1962.

Íslenzk fornkvæði (SG) = *Íslenzk fornkvæði*, ed. Sven Grundtvig, Jón Sigurðsson and Pálmi Pálsson. Nordiske Oldskrifter. Copenhagen, 1854–1885.

Íslenzkar gátur, skemtanir, vikivakar og þulur, ed. Jón Árnason and Ólafur Davíðsson. Copenhagen, 1887.

Íslenzkar þjóðsögur og ævintýri, ed. Jón Árnason; 2nd ed. Árni Böðvarsson and Bjarni Vilhjálmsson. Reykjavík, 1954–1961.

Jóns saga Baptista I. In *Postola sögur*, 842–849.

Jóns saga Baptista II. In *Postola sögur*, 849–931.

Knýtlinga saga. In *Íslenzk fornrit*, 35, ed. Bjarni Guðnason, 91–321. Reykjavík, 1982. Translation: *Knytlinga saga. The History of the Kings of Denmark*, trans. Hermann Pálsson and Paul Geoffrey Edwards. Odense, 1986.

Kristi pina. = *Christi pina (also called Kristi lidande)*. In *Svenska medeltids dikter och rim*, ed. Gustaf E. Klemming, 3–6. SFSS, 78–80. Stockholm, 1881–1882.

Kumlbúa þáttr. In *Íslenzk fornrit*, 13, ed. Þórhallur Vilmundarson and Bjarni Vilhjálmsson, 451–455. Reykjavík, 1991. Translation: *The Tale of the Cairn-Dweller*, trans. Marvin Taylor, 2:443–444. In *The Complete Sagas of Icelanders*.

Landnámabók. In *Íslenzk fornrit*, 1, ed. Jakob Benediktsson, 29–397. Reykjavík, 1968. Translation: *The Book of Settlements: Landnámabók*, trans. Hermann Pálsson and Paul Edwards. University of Manitoba Icelandic Studies, 1. Winnipeg, 1997 (1972).

Legenda aurea = *Jacobi a Voragine. Legenda aurea vulgo Historia lombardica dicta*, ed. Johann Georg Theodor Grässe. 2nd ed. Leipzig: Impensis Librariae Arnoldianae, 1850. Translation: *The Golden Legend: Readings on the Saints*, trans. William Granger Ryan. Princeton, 1993.

Life of Saint Edmund. See Ælfric.

Locasenna = *Edda. Die Lieder des Codex Regius*, 96–110. Translation: *Loki's Quarrel* in *The Poetic Edda*, 80–92.

Lucius Annaeus Florus. See *Florus*.

Macarius and the Magicians, Saul and the Witch of Endor = Ælfric. "Macarius and the Magicians, Saul and the Witch of Endor." In *Homilies of Ælfric: A Supplementary Collection*, ed. John Collins Pope, 2:786–798. Early English Text Society, 259. London, 1967.

Magister Mathias Lincopenis. "Testa nucis" and "Poetria," ed. Birger Bergh. SFSS. Ser. 2, Latinska skrifter. IX:2. Arlöv, 1996.

Magnúss saga berfætts. In *Heimskringla* 3:210–237. Translation: *Snorri Sturluson. Heimskringla 1–3*, trans. Alison Finlay and Anthony Faulkes, 3:127–144. 2nd ed. London, 2014–2016.

Mágus saga jarls. In *Fornsögur Suðrlanda. Isländska bearbetningar af främmande romaner från medeltiden*, ed. Gustaf Cederschiöld, 1–42. 2 vols. Lund, 1884.

Malleus maleficarum = Heinrich Institoris and Jakob Sprenger. *Malleus maleficarum*. Nüremberg, 1494. Translation: Heinrich Institoris and Jakob Sprenger. *Malleus maleficarum*, trans. Christopher S. Mackay. Cambridge, 2006.

Materials toward a History of Witchcraft. Collected by Henry Charles Lea; arranged and edited by Arthur C. Howland. Philadelphia, 1939.

Međedović, Avdo. *Ženidba Smailagić Meha*. PN 6840, July 5–12, 1935; LN 35, May 23, 1950. Milman Parry Collection of Oral Literature. Harvard University. Translated as: Međedović, Avdo. *The Wedding of Smailagic Meho*, trans. Albert Bates Lord. Serbo-Croatian Heroic Songs 3. Cambridge, MA, 1974.

Montgomerie, Alexander. *Ane Invectione against Fortun*. In *The Poems of Alexander Montgomerie*, ed. James Cranstoun, 129–131. Edinburgh, 1887.

Monumenta Historica Norvegiae. Latinske Kildeskrifter til Norges Historie i Middelalderen, ed. Gustav Storm. Christiania, 1880.

Morkinskinna. In *Íslenzk fornrit*, 23–24, ed. Ármann Jakobsson and Þórður Ingi Guðjónsson. Reykjavík, 2011. *Morkinskinna. The Earliest Icelandic Chronicle of the Norwegian Kings (1030– 1157)*, trans. Theodore M. Andersson and Kari Ellen Gade. Islandica, 51. Ithaca, NY, 2000.

Namnlös och Valentin. En medeltids-roman., ed. Gustaf E. Klemming. SFSS, Serie 1. Svenska skrifter, 6. Stockholm, 1846.

NGL = *Norges gamle Love indtil 1387*, ed. Rudolf Keyser and Peter Andreas Munch. Christiania, 1846–1895. Translation: *The Earliest Norwegian Laws: Being the Gulathing Law and the Frostathing Law*, trans. Laurence M. Larson. New York, 1935.

Nóregs konunga tal. In *Íslenzk fornrit*, 29, ed. Bjarni Einarsson. Reykjavík, 1984.

Nye and tilforladelig accurat geographisk Charte over Öen Samsoe af aar 1755. Jonas Haas and Laurids Lauridsen de Thurah. Det Kgl. Bibliotek, Digitale samlinger. http://www5.kb.dk/images/billed/2010/okt/billeder/object396722/da/

Örvar-Odds saga (AM 344a, 4to, etc.) = *FAS* 2:159-322.

Óláfs saga helga = *Heimskringla* 2. Translation: *Óláfr Haraldsson (The Saint)*. In *Snorri Sturluson. Heimskringla II*, trans. Alison Finlay and Anthony Faulkes. 2nd ed. London, 2014–2016.

Óláfs saga kyrra. In *Heimskringla* 2:203–209. Translation: *Snorri Sturluson. Heimskringla I-III*, trans. Alison Finlay and Anthony Faulkes, 3:123–126. 2nd ed. London, 2014–2016.

Óláfs saga Tryggvasonar. In *Heimskringla* 1:225–372. Translation: *Snorri Sturluson. Heimskringla I-III*, trans. Alison Finlay and Anthony Faulkes, 1:137–233. 2nd ed. London, 2014–2016.
Olaus Magnus. *Historia de gentibus septentrionalibus* (...). Rome, 1555. Translation: *Description of the Northern Peoples*, ed. and trans. Peter Fisher and Humphrey Higgens. With Annotations derived from the Commentary by John Granlund. The Hakluyt Society. 2nd ser., 182, 187–188 London, 1996–1998.
Om S. Bartholomei moder, eller folk-sagan om Qvinnan utan Händer. In *Ett Forn-Svenskt Legendarium*, ed. George Stephens and F. A. Dahlgren, 1:217–222. SFSS, 7. Stockholm, 1847–1874.
Origines Islandicae. A Collection of the More Important Sagas and Other Native Writings Relating to the Settlement and Early History of Iceland, ed. and trans. Gudbrandur Vigfússon and Frederick York Powell. 2 vols. Oxford, 1905.
Passio Sancti Eadmundi = Abbo of Fleury. *Corolla Sancti Eadmundi. The Garland of Saint Edmund, King and Martyr*, ed. and trans. Lord Francis Hervey, 10–59. London, 1907.
Poetic edda. See *Edda. Die Lieder des Codex Regius.*
Postola sögur. Legendariske fortællinger om apostlernes liv, deres kamp for kristendommens udbredelse, samt deres martyrdod. Efter gamle haandskrifter, ed. C. R. Unger. Christiania, 1874.
Prose edda. See entries under *Edda Sn.*
Regino of Prüm. *Canon episcopi.* See *Corpus Iuris Canonici.*
The Ruin = *The Exeter Book*, ed. George Philip Krapp and Elliott Van Kirk Dobbie, 227-229. The Anglo-Saxon Poetic Records, 3. New York, 1936.
Saga Heiðreks konungs ins vitra. The Saga of King Heidrek the Wise. See *Hervarar saga ok Heiðreks konungs.*
Saga Sverris konúngs. In *Fornmanna sögur, eptir gömlum handritum*, 8:7–448.
Sagan om Sankt Dionysius. In *Ett Forn-Svenskt Legendarium*, ed. George Stephens and F. A. Dahlgren, 1:339–345. SFSS, 7. Stockholm, 1847–1874.
Samnordisk Runtextdatabas (website), ed. Lennart Elmevik, Lena Peterson and Henrik Williams. Institutionen för nordiska språk, Uppsala universitet, 1993–. http://www.runforum.nordiska.uu.se/samnord/Uppsala.
Saxo Grammaticus. *Gesta Danorum.* See *Gesta Danorum.*

SD = *Svenskt Diplomatarium: Diplomatarium Suecanum*, ed. Johan Gustaf Liljegren, Bror Emil Hildebrand, Sven Tunberg, et al. Stockholm, 1829–.

Sermo Lupi ad Anglos = "The Electronic Sermo Lupi ad Anglos" of Wulfstan (website), ed. Melissa Bernstein Ser. http://english3.fsu.edu/~wulfstan/ (accessed October 14, 2011).

SGL = *Samling af Sweriges Gamla Lagar. Corpus iuris Sueco-Gotorum antiqui*, ed. D. C. J. Schlyter (vols. 1–2 ed. with D. H. S. Colin), vols. 1–3, Stockholm; vols. 4–13, Lund, 1822–1877. Translations: Individual titles have and will appear in the series Routledge Medieval Translations: Medieval Nordic Laws, ed. Stefan Brink. London, 2019–.

Signelser ock besvärjelser från medeltid ock nytid, ed. Emanuel Linderholm. Svenska landsmål och svenskt folkliv. B, 41. Stockholm, 1917–1940.

Sigrdrífomál = Edda. *Die Lieder des Codex Regius*, 189–197. Translation: The Lay of Sigrdrífa in *The Poetic Edda*, 162–168.

Skaldic Poetry of the Scandinavian Middle Ages. Series Ed. Margaret Clunies Ross et al. Turnhout, 2007–.

Skáldskaparmál. See *Edda Sn* 2.

Skírnismál. See *For Scírnis*.

Skj. = *Den norske-islandske Skjaldedigtning. B. Rettet Tekst*, ed. Finnur Jónsson. Copenhagen, 1973 (1912–1915).

Sneglu-Halla þáttr F. In *Flateyjarbók*, ed. Guðbrandur Vigfússon and C. R. Unger, 3:415–428. Norske historiske Kildeskriftfonds Skrifter, 4. Christiania, 1860–1868. Translation: *The Tale of Sarcastic Halli*, trans. George Clark, 1:342–357. In *The Complete Sagas of Icelanders*.

Sneglu-Halla þáttr M. In *Morkinskinna*, 1:270–284 (chap. 47) Translation: *Morkinskinna. The Earliest Icelandic Chronicle of the Norwegian Kings (1030–1157)*, trans. Theodore M. Andersson and Kari Ellen Gade, 243–252 (chap. 43). Islandica, 51. Ithaca, NY, 2000.

Snorra edda. See *Edda Sn*.

Snorri Sturluson. *Edda*. See *Edda Sn*.

Snorri Sturluson. *Heimskringla*. See *Heimskringla*.

Södermanlands runinskrifter. 1. Text, ed. Erik Brate and Elias Wessén. Sveriges runinskrifter, 3. Stockholm, 1924–1936.

Speculum lapidum = Camillus Leonardi. *Les pierres talismaniques: Speculum lapidum, livre III*, ed. and trans. Claude Lecouteux and Anne Monfort. Paris, 2003.

SRD = *Scriptores Rerum Danicarum Medii Ævi*, ed. Jacobus Langebek. Copenhagen, 1774.

Stenbog = Henrik Harpestræng (Ny kgl. Saml. 66, 8vo). In *Gamle danske Urtebøger, Stenbøger og Kogebøger*, ed. Marius Kristensen, 174–193. Copenhagen, 1908.
Stenbok = *Peder Månssons skrifter på svenska*, ed. Robert Geete, 457–530. SFSS, 43. Stockholm, 1913–1915.
Stimulus amoris. In *Skrifter till uppbyggelse från medeltiden. En samling af moralteologiska traktater på svenska*, ed. Robert Geete, 3–110. SFSS. Serie 1. Svenska skrifter, 36 Stockholm, 1904–1905.
Stjorn. Gammelnorsk bibelhistorie fra verdens skabelse til det babyloniske fangenskab, ed. C. R. Unger. Christiania, 1862.
Strelow, *Cronica Guthilandorum* = Strelow, Hans Nielssøn. *Cronica Guthilandorum: Den guthilandiske cronica...* (Visby, 1978) Facsimile ed. of 1633 original.
Sturlunga saga = *Sturlunga saga efter membranen Króksfjarðarbók udfyldt efter Reykjarfjarðarbók*, ed. Kristian Kålund. 2 vols. Copenhagen, 1906–1911. Translation: *Sturlunga saga I-II*, trans. Julia H. McGrew and R. George Thomas. The Library of Scandinavian Literature, 9–10. New York, 1970–1974.
Svarfdæla saga. In *Íslenzk fornrit*, 9, ed. Jónas Kristjánsson, 127–211. Reykjavík, 1956. Translation: *The Saga of the People of Svarfadardal*, trans. Fredrik J. Heinemann, 4:149–192. In *The Complete Sagas of Icelanders*.
Svenska medeltids dikter och rim, ed. Gustaf E. Klemming. SFSS, 78–80. Stockholm, 1881–1882.
Svenska medeltids-postillor, ed. Gustaf E. Klemming, Robert Geete and Bertil Ejder. SFSS, 23. Stockholm, 1879–.
Tacitus. *Histories, Books IV–V; Annals Books I–III*. Tacitus Vol. 3, ed. and trans. Clifford H. Moore and John Jackson. Loeb Classical Library, 249. Cambridge, MA, 1931.
Theodoricus Monachus. *Historia de antiquitate regum Norwagiensium*. In *Monumenta Historica Norvegiae*, 1–68. Translation: *Historia de antiquitate regum Norwagiensium: An Account of the Ancient History of the Norwegian Kings*, trans. David McDougall and Ian McDougall. Viking Society for Northern Research Text Series, 11. London, 1998.
Tóka þáttr Tókasonar = *FAS* 1954, 2:135–141.
Trójumanna saga, ed. Jonna Louis-Jensen. Editiones Arnamagnaeanae. Series A., 8. Copenhagen, 1963.
Trollmöte 1902 = *En allegorisk dikt (dröm eller saga)*. In "Två svenska rimdikter från medeltiden efter gamla handskrifter. 1. En allegorisk dikt (dröm

eller saga). 2. Jungfru Marias sju fröjder," ed. Robert Geete, 43–44. In *Bilaga till Svenska Fornskrift-sällskapets årsmöte*. Stockholm, 1902.

Trollmöte 1917. In *Signelser ock besvärjelser från medeltid ock nytid*, ed. Emanuel Linderholm, 86– 88. Svenska landsmål och svenskt folkliv. B, 41. Stockholm, 1917–1940.

Tungulus. In *S. Patriks-sagan, innehållande S. Patrik och hans järtecken, Nicolaus i.S. Patriks skärsild, och Tungulus*, ed. George Stephens and Johan August Ahlstrand, 27–48. SFSS, 2. Stockholm, 1844.

Upphaf allra frásagna. In *Íslenzk fornrit*, 35, ed. Bjarni Guðnason, 39–40. Reykjavík, 1982.

Vafðrúðnsimál = *Edda. Die Lieder des Codex Regius*, 45–55. Translation: *Vafthrudnir's Sayings* in *The Poetic Edda*, 36–45.

Víga-Glúms saga. In *Íslenzk fornrit*, 9, ed. Jónas Kristjánsson, 1–98. Reykjavík, 1956. Translation: *Killer-Glum's Saga*, trans. John McKinnell, 2:267–327. In *The Complete Sagas of Icelanders*.

Visbyfranciskanernas bok: Handskriften B 99 i Kungliga biblioteket, ed. Eva Odelman and Evert Melefors. Arkiv på Gotland, 5. Visby, 2008.

Vǫlospá = *Edda. Die Lieder des Codex Regius*, 1–16. Translation: *The Seeress's Prophecy* in *The Poetic Edda*, 3–12.

Völsa þáttr. In *Stories from the Sagas of the Kings*, ed. and trans. Anthony Faulkes, 51–61. London, 1980.

Ynglinga saga. In *Heimskringla* 1:9–83. Translation: *Snorri Sturluson. Heimskringla*, trans. Alison Finlay and Anthony Faulkes, 1:6–47. 2nd ed. London, 2016.

Yngvars saga víðförla = *FAS* 1954, 2:423–459. Translation: *Yngvar's Saga*. In *The Vikings in Russia: Yngvar's Saga and Eymund's Saga*, trans. Hermann Pálsson and Paul Edwards, 44–68. Edinburgh, 1989.

Þorgils saga ok Hafliða. In *Sturlunga saga*, 1:7–46. Translation: *Sturlunga saga*, 2:25–70.

Þorleifs þáttr jarlsskálds. In *Íslenzk fornrit*, 9, ed. Jónas Kristjánsson, 215–229. Reykjavík, 1956. Translation: *The Tale of Thorleif, the Earl's Poet*, trans. Judith Jesch, 1:362–369. In *The Complete Sagas of Icelanders*.

Þorsteins þáttr uxafóts. In *Íslenzk fornrit*, 13, ed. Þórhallur Vilmundarson and Bjarni Vilhjálmsson, 341–370. Reykjavík, 1991. Translation: *The Tale of Thorstein Bull's-Leg*, trans. George Clark, 4:340–354. In *The Complete Sagas of Icelanders*.

Secondary sources

Aarne, Antti, and Stith Thompson, eds. 1961. *The Types of the Folktale: A Classification and Bibliography*. 2nd ed. Helsinki.
Abrahams, Roger D. 1962. "Playing the Dozens." *Journal of American Folklore* 75:209–220.
———. 1968. "Introductory Remarks to a Rhetorical Theory of Folklore." *Journal of American Folklore* 81:143–156.
———. 1972. "The Literary Study of the Riddle." *Texas Studies in Literature and Language* 14 (1):177–197.
Abrahams, Roger D., and Alan Dundes. 1972. "Riddles." In *Folklore and Folklife*, ed. Richard M. Dorson, 129–143. Chicago.
Abram, Christopher. 2003. "Representations of the Pagan Afterlife in Medieval Scandinavian Literature." PhD diss., University of Cambridge.
Acker, Paul. 1998. *Revising Oral Theory: Formulaic Composition in Old English and Old Icelandic Verse*. New York.
Adamsen, Christian 1995. "Stavns Fjord: Et natur- and kulturhistorisk forskningsområde på Samsø." In *Stavns Fjord i jernalder and vikingetid*, ed. Hanne Hansen and Bent Aaby, 68–96. Copenhagen.
Adriansen, Inge. 2003. *Nationale symboler i det danske rige 1830–2000*. Etnologiske studier, 8. Copenhagen.
———. 2011. *Erindringssteder i Danmark*. Etnologiske studier, 14. Copenhagen
Ahola, Joonas. 2014. *Outlawry in the Icelandic Family Sagas*. PhD diss., University of Helsinki.
Almgren, Oscar. 1903. "Ett guldmynt från en Gotländsk graf." In *Studier tillägnade Oscar Montelius, 1903 af lärjungar*, 89–98. Stockholm.
Alver, Brynjulf. 1954. "Norrøne gåter fra mellomalderen." *Syn og Segn* 60:29–36.
———. (1956–1978) 1982. "Gåter." In *KLNM* 5: cols. 648–651.
———. 1962. "Historiske segner og historisk sanning." *Norveg* 9:89–116.
Andersen, John Roth. 1981. *Der ligger en ø--Samsø*. Tranebjerg.
Anderson, Walter. 1923. *Kaiser und Abt. Die Geschichte eines Schwanks*. Helsinki.
Andersson, Björn. 1995. *Runor, magi, ideologi: en idéhistorisk studie*. Umeå.
Andersson, Ingvar. 1959. *Erikskrönikans författare*. 2nd ed. Stockholm.
Andersson, Theodore M. 1962. "The Doctrine of Oral Tradition in the *Chanson de Geste* and Saga." *Scandinavian Studies* 34:19–36.

———. 1964. *The Problem of Icelandic Saga Origins: A Historical Survey.* New Haven, CT.

———. 1966. "The Textual Evidence for an Oral Family Saga." *Arkiv för nordisk filologi* 81:1–23.

Andersson-Schmitt, Margarete, and Monica Hedlund, eds. 1988. *manuscripta mediaevalia: Mittelalterliche Handschriften der Universitätsbibliothek Uppsala: Katalog über die C- Sammlung: Bd. 1. C I–IV, 1–50.* Stockholm. http://www.manuscriptamediaevalia.de/hs/katalog-seiten/HSK0506a_b0059_jpg.htm.

———. 1991. *Mittelalterliche Handschriften der Universitätsbibliothek Uppsala: Katalog über die C- Sammlung.* Stockholm.

Andrén, Anders. 1989. "Dörrar till förgångna myter. En tolkning av de gotländska bild- stenarna." In *Medeltidens födelse,* ed. Andrén Anders, 287–319. Krapperup.

———. 1993. "Doors to Other Worlds: Scandinavian Death Rituals in Gotlandic Perspectives." *Journal of European Archaeology* 1:33–56.

———. 1998. "En centralort utan textbelägg?—Uppåkra som ett historiskt-arkeologiskt problem." In *Centrala platser, centrala frågor: Samhällsstrukturen under järnåldern. En vänbok till Berta Stjernquist,* ed. Lars Larsson and Birgitta Hårdh, 137–146. Uppåkrastudier, 1. Stockholm.

———. 2000. "Re-reading Embodied Texts—an Interpretation of Runestones." *Current Swedish Archaeology* 8:7–32.

———. 2012. "Från solnedgång till solnedgång. En tolkning av de tidiga gotländska bildstenarna." In *Gotlands bildstenar. Järnålderns gåtfulla budbärare,* ed. Maria Herlin Karnel, 49–58. Visby.

———. 2013. "Places, Monuments, and Objects: The Past in Ancient Scandinavia." *Scandinavian Studies* 85 (3):267–281.

———. 2014. *Tracing Old Norse Cosmology: The World Tree, Middle Earth, and the Sun from Archaeological Perspectives.* Lund.

———. 2018. "Archaeology." In *The Handbook of Pre-Modern Nordic Memory Studies,* ed. Jürg Glauser, Pernille Hermann, and Stephen A. Mitchell, 136–150. Berlin.

Andrews, A. LeRoy. 1928. "Old Norse Notes: 7. Some Observations on Mímir." *Modern Language Notes* 43:166–171.

Ármann Jakobsson. 2008a. "A Contest of Cosmic Fathers: God and Giant in Vafþrúðnismál." *Neophilologus* 92:263–277.

———. 2008b. "The Trollish Acts of Þorgrímr the Witch: The Meanings of Troll and *Ergi* in Medieval Iceland." *Saga-Book* 32:39–68.

———. 2008c. "Vad är ett troll? Betydelsen av ett isländskt medeltidsbe-grepp." *Saga och sed*, 101–117.
———. 2011. "Vampires and Watchmen: Categorizing the Mediaeval Icelandic Undead." *Journal of English and Germanic Philology* 110:281–300.
Ármann Jakobsson and Sverrir Jakobsson, eds. 2017. *The Routledge Research Companion to the Medieval Icelandic Sagas.* Abingdon, UK.
Arnold, Bettina. 2006. "'Arierdämmerung': Race and Archaeology in Nazi Germany." *World Archaeology* 38 (1):8–31.
Arnold, Martin. 2005. "*Hvat er troll nema þat?* The Cultural History of the Troll." In *The Shadow- Walkers: Jacob Grimm's Mythology of the Monstrous*, ed. T. A. Shippey, 111–155. Tempe, AZ.
Arvastson, Allan. 1971. *Imitation och förnyelse. Psalmhistoriska studier.* Lund.
Ásdísardóttir, Ingunn. See Ingunn Ásdísardóttir.
Assmann, Aleida, Jan Assmann, and Christof Hardmeier, eds. 1983. *Schrift und Gedächtnis: Beiträge zur Archäologie der literarischen Kommunikation.* Munich.
Assmann, Jan. 1992. *Das kulturelle Gedächtnis: Schrift, Erinnerung und politische Identität in frühen Hochkulturen* (trans. as *Cultural Memory and Early Civilization: Writing, Remembrance, and Political Imagination*, 2011). Munich.
———. 1995. "Collective Memory and Cultural Identity." *New German Critique* 65:125–133.
———. 2006. "Introduction: What Is 'Cultural Memory'?" In *Religion and Cultural Memory: Ten Studies*, trans. Rodney Livingstone, 1–30. Stanford, CA.
———. 2008. "Communicative and Cultural Memory." In *Cultural Memory Studies. An International and Interdisciplinary Handbook*, ed. Astrid Erll and Ansgar Nünning, 109–118. Berlin.
AT. See Antti Aarne and Stith Thompson, *The Types of the Folktale*.
Avis, Robert. 2009. "Writing origins: the development of communal identity in some Old Norse foundation-myths and their analogues in Guta saga." In *Á austrvega. Saga and East Scandinavia Preprint papers of the 14th International Saga Conference*, ed. Agneta Ney, Henrik Williams, and Fredrik Charpentier Ljungqvist, 1:52–59. Uppsala.
Bäckvall, Maja. 2013. *Skriva fel och läsa rätt?: Eddiska dikter i Uppsalaeddan ur ett avsändar- och mottagarperspektiv.* Nordiska texter och under-sökningar, 31. Uppsala.
Baert, Barbara, Anita Traninger, and Catrien Santing, eds. 2013. *Disembodied Heads in Medieval and Early Modern Culture.* Leiden.

Bandle, Oskar. 1988. "Die Fornaldarsaga zwischen Mündlichkeit und Schriftlichkeit: Zur Entstehung und Entwicklung der *Örvar-Odds saga.*" In *Zwischen Festtag und Alltag. Zehn Beiträge zum Thema 'Mündlichkeit und Schriftlichkeit'*, ed. Wolfgan Raible, 199–213. Tübingen.

Bartsch, K. 1872. "Altschwedische Schreiberverse." *Germania* 17:444.

Bauman, Richard. 1975. "Verbal Art as Performance." *American Anthropologist* 77:290–311.

———. 1977. "Verbal Art as Performance." In *Verbal Art as Performance*, 3–58. Rowley, MA.

———. 1986a. "Performance and Honor in 13th-Century Iceland." *Journal of American Folklore* 99:131–150.

———. 1986b. *Story, Performance, and Event: Contextual Studies of Oral Narrative.* Cambridge.

———. 1992. "Contextualization, Tradition, and the Dialogue of Genres: Icelandic Legends of the Kraftaskald." In *Rethinking Context: Language as an Interactive Phenomenon*, ed. Charles Goodwin, 125–145. Cambridge.

———. 1996. "Folklore as a Transdisciplinary Dialogue." *Journal of Folklore Research* 33:15–20.

Bauman, Richard, and Charles L. Briggs. 1990. "Poetics and Performance as Critical Perspectives on Language and Social Life." *Annual Review of Anthropology* 19:59–88.

Bauman, Richard, and Joel Sherzer. 1975. "The Ethnography of Speaking." *Annual Review of Anthropology* 4:95–119.

Bauschatz, Paul. 1978. "The Germanic Ritual Feast." In *Proceedings of the Third International Conference of Nordic and General Linguistics*, ed. John Weinstock, 289–295. Austin, TX.

Bax, Marcel, and Tineke Padmos. 1983. "Two Types of Verbal Dueling in Old Icelandic: The Interactional Structure of the *senna* and the *mannajafnaðr* in Hárbarðsljóð." *Scandinavian Studies* 55:149–174.

———. 1993. "*Senna - Mannajafnaðr.*" In *Medieval Scandinavia: An Encyclopedia*, ed. Phillip Pulsiano et al., 571–573. New York.

Beck, Heinrich. 1968. "Die Stanzen von Torslunda und die literarische Überlieferung." *Frühmittelalterliche Studien* 2:237–250.

Beckman, Bjarne. 1947. "Om tiden och sätt för Hertig Fredriks försvenskning." *Arkiv för nordisk filologi* 62:263–267.

Behringer, Wolfgang. 1998. "Das „Ahnenerbe" der Buchgesellschaft. Zum Neudruck einer Germanen-Edition des NS-Ideologen Otto Höfler." SoWi (= *Sozialwissenschaftliche Informationen. Das Journal für Geschichte, Politik, Wirtschaft und Kultur*) 27:283–289.

Ben-Amos, Dan. 1976. "Solutions to Riddles." *Journal of American Folklore* 89:249–254.

———. 1984. "The Seven Strands of Tradition: Varieties in Its Meaning in American Folklore Studies." *Journal of Folklore Research* 21 (2–3):97–131.

———. 2020. "A Definition of Folklore: A Personal Narrative." In *Folklore Concepts: Histories and Critiques*, ed. Henry Glassie and Elliott Oring, 203–223. Bloomington, IN.

Ben-Amos, Dan, and Liliane Weissberg, eds. 1999. *Cultural Memory and the Construction of Identity*. Detroit.

Bendix, Regina. 1997. *In Search of Authenticity: The Formation of Folklore Studies*. Madison, WI.

Bennett, Lisa. 2018. "Saga Burial Mounds." In *The Handbook of Pre-Modern Nordic Memory Studies*, ed. Jürg Glauser, Pernille Hermann, and Stephen A. Mitchell, 613–619. Berlin.

Berg Petersen, Irene. 2012. "An Entire Army Sacrificed in a Bog." *Science Nordic*. https://sciencenordic.com/anthropology-archaeology-denmark/an-entire-army-sacrificed-in-a-bog/1375773 (accessed August 1, 2014).

Berlin, Brent, Dennis E Breedlove, and Peter H Raven. 1973. "General Principles of Classification and Nomenclature in Folk Biology." *American Anthropologist* 75 (1):214–242.

Bessinger, Jess B. 1974. "Kenning." In *Princeton Encyclopedia of Poetry and Poetics*, ed. Alex Preminger, Frank J. Warnke, and O. B. Hardison, 434. Princeton, NJ.

Bidney, David. 1947. "Human Nature and the Cultural Process." *American Anthropologist* 49 (3):375–399.

Blaney, Benjamin. 1993. "Berserkr." In *Medieval Scandinavia: An Encyclopedia*, ed. Phillip Pulsiano et al., 37–38. New York.

Blomkvist, Nils, Stefan Brink, and Thomas Lindkvist. 2007. "The Kingdom of Sweden." In *Christianization and the Rise of Christian Monarchy: Scandinavia, Central Europe and Rus' c. 900–1200*, ed. Nora Berend, 167–213. Cambridge.

Boberg, Inger M. 1932. "Sagn and Overlevering om Samsøs Høje and Bakker." *Årbog for Historisk Samfund for Holbæk Amt*, 26:5–41.
———. 1953. *Folkemindeforskningens historie i Mellem- og Nordeuropa*. Danmarks Folkeminder, 60. Copenhagen.
———, ed. 1966. *Motif-Index of Early Icelandic Literature*. Copenhagen.
Bødker, Laurits, Brynjulf Alver, Bengt Holbek, and Leea Virtanen, eds. 1964. *The Nordic Riddle: Terminology and Bibliography*. Nordisk Institut for Folkedigtning. Skrifter, 3. Copenhagen.
Borgene på Samsø: En arkæologisk jakt på historien bag øens fem middelalderborge. 2018, ed. Vivian Etting, University of Southern Denmark Studies in History and Social Sciences, 558. Odense.
Bridges, Margaret. 1999. "The King, the Foreigner, and the Lady with a Mead Cup: Variations on a Theme of Cross-Cultural Contact." *Multilingua* 18 (2–3):185–207.
Brink, Stefan. 2003. "Legal Assemblies and Judicial Structure in Early Scandinavia." In *Political Assemblies in the earlier Middle Ages*, ed. Paul S. Barnwell and Marco Mostert, 61–72. Studies in the Early Middle Ages, 7. Turnhout.
———. 2007. "How Uniform was the Old Norse Religion?" In *Learning and Understanding in the Old Norse World: Essays in Honour of Margaret Clunies Ross*, ed. Judy Quinn, Kate Heslop, and Tarrin Wills, 105–136. Turnhout.
———. 2014. "*Minnunga mæn*: The Usage of Old Knowledgeable Men in Legal Cases." In *Minni and Muninn. Memory in Medieval Nordic Culture*, ed. Pernille Herrman, Stephen A. Mitchell and Agnes S. Arnórsdóttir, 197–210. Turnhout.
———. 2017. "Law, Society and Landscape in Early Scandinavia." In *Comparative Law and Anthropology*, ed. James A.R. Nafziger, 319–337, Research Handbooks in Comparative Law Series. Cheltenham.
———. 2018. "Onomastics." In *The Handbook of Pre-Modern Nordic Memory Studies*, ed. Jürg Glauser, Pernille Hermann, and Stephen A. Mitchell, 565–574. Berlin.
———. 2020. "Laws and Assemblies." In *Pre-Christian Religions of the North. Histories and Structures, Volume 2: Social, Geographical, and Historical Contexts, and Communication between Worlds*, ed. Anders Andrén, John Lindow, and Jens Peter Schjødt, 45–77. Turnhout.
Brink, Stefan, and Neil Price, eds. 2008. *The Viking World*. New York.

Brix, Hans. 1943. "Oldtidens og Middelalderens Litteratur i Danmark." In *Litteraturhistoria. A. Danmark, Finland och Sverige*, ed. Sigurður Nordal, 3–63. Stockholm.
Brøndum-Nielsen, Johannes. 1929. "Skriververset i Kölner Dombibliotheks Codex CXXX." *Acta Philologica Scandinavica* 4:65–71.
Bronner, Simon J. 1998. *Following Tradition: Folklore in the Discourse of American Culture*. Logan, UT.
———. 2000. "The Meaning of Tradition: An Introduction." *Western Folklore* 59 (2):87–104.
Bruce, Alexander M. 2002. *Scyld and Scef: Expanding the Analogues*. New York.
Buck, Carl Darling. 1988. *A Dictionary of Selected Synonyms in the Principal Indo-European Languages: A Contribution to the History of Ideas*. Chicago.
Bugge, Sophus. 1881–1889. *Studier over de nordiske Gude- og Heltesagns Oprindelse*. Christiania.
Bulfinch, Thomas. 1855. *The Age of Fable; or, Stories of Gods and Heroes*. Boston.
Burke, Peter. 1997. *Varieties of Cultural History*. Oxford.
Burns, Thomas A. 1976. "Riddling: Occasion to Act." *Journal of American Folklore* 89:139–165.
Byock, Jesse L. 1982. *Feud in the Icelandic Saga*. Berkeley, CA.
———. 1984. "Saga Form, Oral Prehistory, and the Icelandic Social Context." *New Literary History* 16:153–173.
Carruthers, Mary J. 1990. *The Book of Memory: A Study of Memory in Medieval Culture*. Cambridge Studies in Medieval Literature, 10. Cambridge.
———. 1998. *The Craft of Thought: Meditation, Rhetoric, and the Making of Images, 400–1200*. Cambridge.
Carruthers, Mary, and Jan M. Ziolkowski, eds. 2002. *Medieval Craft of Memory: An Anthology of Texts and Pictures*. Philadelphia.
Catholic Encyclopedia: An International Work of Reference, ed. Charles George Herbermann. (1917) 2003. New York. http://www.newadvent.org/cathen/ (accessed October 23, 2015).
Celander, Hilding. 1920. "Julkärve och Odinskult." *Rig*: 168–176.
———. 1943. "Oskoreien och besläktade föreställningar i äldre och nyare nordisk tradition." *Saga och sed*: 71–175.
Chadwick, Nora K. 1946. "Norse Ghosts (A Study in the *Draugr* and the *Haugbúi*)." *Folklore* 57:50–65, 106–127.

Christensen, Kjeld. 1995. "Kanhave-kanalen." In *Stavns Fjord i jernalder and vikingetid*, ed. Hanne Hansen and Bent Aaby, 98–117. Copenhagen.
Christensen, Peter Birkedahl. 1983. "Søby—A Viking Age Settlement on Samsø." *Journal of Danish Archaeology* 2 (1):149–155.
Christensen, Tom. 2010a. "Lejre beyond the legend—the archaeological evidence." In *Gedächtnis-Kolloquium / Memorial Colloquium Werner Haarnagel (1907–1984)*, 237– 255, Siedlungs- und Küstenforschung im südlichen Nordseegebiet, 33. Rahden, Westf.
———. 2010b. "Lejreskatten." *Danefæ - Skatte fra den danske muld*: 183–186.
———. 2010c. "En sølvfigurin fra Lejre i Danmark." *Viking. Norsk arkeologisk årbok* 73:143–156.
———. ed. 2016. *Lejre bag myten. De arkæologiske udgravninger*. Jysk Arkæologisk Selskabs Skrifter 87. Århus.
Christiansen, Torben Trier, et al. 2014. "Beretning for arkæologisk udgravning ved FHM 5216 Tønnesminde, Brundby By, Tranebjerg sogn, Samsø herred, tidl. Århus and Holbæk amt." Arkæologisk Felt Rapport Sb.nr. 138. Sted nr. 03.05.05. Højbjerg.
———. 2015. "Beretning for arkæologisk udgravning ved FHM 5216 Tønnesminde, Brundby By, Tranebjerg sogn, Samsø herred, tidl. Århus and Holbæk amt." Arkæologisk Felt Rapport Sb.nr. 138. Sted nr. 03.05.05. Højbjerg
Ciklamini, Marlene. 1966. "The Combat Between Two Half-Brothers: A Literary Study of the Motif in *Ásmundar saga kappabana* and *Saxonis gesta Danorum*." *Neophilologus* 50:269–279, 370–379.
Clarke, D. E. Martin. 1923. *The Hávamál, with Selections from Other Poems of the Edda, Illustrating the Wisdom of the North in Heathen Times*. Cambridge.
Clarke, M. G. 1911. *Sidelights on Teutonic History during the Migration Period, being Studies from Beowulf and other Old English Poems*. Girton College Studies, 3. Cambridge.
Cleasby, Richard, and Gudbrand Vigfusson, eds. 1874. *An Icelandic-English Dictionary*. Oxford.
———, eds. (1957) 1982. *An Icelandic-English Dictionary*. 2nd ed. Oxford.
Clover, Carol J. 1978. "Skaldic Sensibility." *Arkiv för nordisk filologi* 93:63–81.
———. 1982. *The Medieval Saga*. Ithaca, NY.
———. 1985. "Icelandic Family Saga (Íslendingasögur)." In *Old Norse-Icelandic Literature: A Critical Guide*, ed. Carol J. Clover and John Lindow, 239–315. Ithaca, NY.

———. 1986a. "The Long Prose Form." *Arkiv för nordisk filologi* 101:10–39.
———. 1986b. "Maiden Warriors and Other Sons." *The Journal of English and Germanic Philology*, 85 (1):35-49.
———. 1993. "Regardless of Sex: Men, Women, and Power in Early Northern Europe." *Speculum* 68 (2):363–387.
Clunies Ross, Margaret. 1994–1998. *Prolonged Echoes. I. Old Norse Myths in Northern Society. Prolonged Echoes. II. The Reception of Norse Myths in Medieval Iceland.* Odense.
———. 1997. "The Intellectual Complexion of the Icelandic Middle Ages: Towards a New Profile of Old Icelandic Literature." *Scandinavian Studies* 69 (4):443-453.
———. 2010. *The Cambridge Introduction to the Old Norse-Icelandic Saga.* Cambridge.
———. 2014. "Authentication of Poetic Memory in Old Norse Skaldic Verse." In *Minni and Muninn. Memory in Medieval Nordic Culture*, ed. Pernille Hermann, Stephen A. Mitchell, and Agnes S. Arnórsdóttir, 74–90. Turnhout.
———. 2020. "Archaeology and Textuality in the Study of Pre-Christian Religion." In *Old Norse Myths as Political Ideologies: Critical Studies in the Appropriation of Medieval Narratives*, ed. Nicolas Meylan and Lukas Rösli, 117–128. Turnhout.
Coffin, Tristram P. 1968. *Our Living Traditions: An Introduction to American Folklore.* New York.
Cohen, Esther. 2013. "The Meaning of the Head in High Medieval Culture." In *Disembodied Heads in Medieval and Early Modern Culture*, ed. Barbara Baert, Anita Traninger, and Catrien Santing, 59–76. Leiden.
Colbert, David. 1989. *The Birth of the Ballad: The Scandinavian Medieval Genre.* Stockholm.
Cole, Richard. 2012. "The Jew Who Wasn't There: Anti-Semitism, Absence and Anxiety in Medieval Scandinavia." 15th International Saga Conference, Sagas and the Use of the Past, August 5–11, 2012, Aarhus University, Denmark.
———. 2020. *The Death of Tidericus the Organist: Plague and Conspiracy Theory in Hanseatic Visby.* Viking Society Texts. London.
Crosby, Ruth. 1936. "Oral Delivery in the Middle Ages." *Speculum* 11:88–110.
Cunningham, Graham. 1999. *Religion and Magic: Approaches and Theories.* Edinburgh.

Damico, Helen. 1984. *Beowulf's Wealhtheow and the Valkyrie Tradition*. Madison, WI.

Danmarks Stednavne (website). Institut for Nordiske Studier og Sprogvidenskab: Navneforskning. Copenhagen University. http://danmarksstednavne.navneforskning.ku.dk/ (accessed March 9, 2020).

Davidson, H. R. Ellis. 1943. *The Road to Hel: A Study of the Conception of the Dead in Old Norse Literature*. Cambridge.

———. 1983. "Insults and Riddles in the Edda Poems." In *Edda: A Collection of Essays*, ed. Robert James Glendinning and Haraldur Bessason, 25–46. The University of Manitoba Icelandic Studies, 4. Manitoba.

———. 1988. *Myths and Symbols in Pagan Europe: Early Scandinavian and Celtic Religions*. Manchester.

Davidson, Olga. 1985. "The Crown-Bestower in the Iranian Book of Kings." In *Acta Iranica, Hommages et Opera Minora 10: Papers in Honour of Professor Mary Boyce*, ed. Jacques Duchene-Guillemin and Pierre Lecoq, 61–148. Leiden.

Del Rio, Anthony B. 2020. "Central Transit Places. The Archaeology of Man-Made Navigable Waterways in Iron Age Scandinavia A.D. 400–800." Master's thesis, Harvard University. Cambridge, MA.

Dillmann, François-Xavier. 2006. *Les magiciens dans l'Islande ancienne. Études sur la représentation de la magie islandaise et de ses agents dans les sources littéraires norroises*. Uppsala.

Dinzelbacher, Peter. 1988. "Zur Interpretation erlebnismystischer Texte des Mittelalters." *Zeitschrift für deutsches Altertum und deutsche Literatur* 117 (1):1–23.

———. 2005. "Die mittelalterliche Allegorie der Lebensreise." In *Monsters, Marvels and Miracles. Imaginary Journeys and Landscapes in the Middle Ages*, ed. Leif Søndergaard and Rasmus Thorning-Hansen, 65–112. Odense.

Doht, Renate. 1974. *Der Rauschtrank im germanischen Mythos*. Vienna.

Dollard, John. 1939. "The Dozens: Dialect of Insult." *American Imago* (1):1–21.

Dorson, Richard M. 1961. "Ethnohistory and Ethnic Folklore." *Ethnohistory* 8 (1):12–30.

———. 1972. "Introduction." In *Folklore and Folklife: An Introduction*, ed. Richard Dorson, 1–50. Chicago.

Dow, James R., and Hannjost Lixfeld, eds. 1994. *The Nazification of an Academic Discipline: Folklore in the Third Reich*. Bloomington, IN.

Driscoll, Matthew J. 1996. "The Oral, the Written, and the In-Between: Textual Instability in the Post-Reformation *Lygisaga*." In *(Re) Oralisierung*, ed. H. L. C. Tristram, 127–154. Tübingen.

Dronke, Ursula Brown. 1947–1948. "The Saga of Hrómund Gripsson and Þorgilssaga." *Saga- Book* 13 (2):51–77.

DuBois, Thomas A. 2006. *Lyric, Meaning, and Audience in the Oral Tradition of Northern Europe*. Notre Dame, IN.

———. 2013. "Ethnomemory: Ethnographic and Culture-Centered Approaches to the Study of Memory." *Scandinavian Studies* 85 (3):306–331.

Dumézil, Georges. 1970. *The Destiny of the Warrior*, trans. Alf Hiltebeitel, Chicago (French original, *Heur et malheur du guerrier: aspects mythiques de la fonction guerrière chez les Indo-Européens*, 1969).

———. 1973. *Gods of the Ancient Northmen*, ed. Einar Haugen, Berkeley, CA. (French originals 1952–1959).

Dundes, Alan, Jerry W. Leach, and Bora Özkök. 1970. "The Strategy of Turkish Boys' Verbal Dueling Rhymes." *Journal of American Folklore* 83:325–349.

Egeler, Matthias. 2011. *Walküren, Bodbs, Sirenen. Gedanken zur religionsgeschichtlichen Anbindung Nordwesteuropas an den mediterranen Raum*. Berlin.

———. 2013. *Celtic Influences in Germanic Religion: A Survey*. Munich.

Egilsson, Sveinbjörn. See Sveinbjörn Egilsson

Ehler, Christine, and Ursula Schaefer. 1998. "Aspekte des Medienwechsels in verschiedenen Kulturen und Epochen. Eine Einleitung." In *Verschriftung und Verschriftlichung: Aspekte des Medienwechsels in verschiedenen Kulturen und Epochen*, ed. Christine Ehler and Ursula Schaefer, 1–9. Tübingen.

Einar Ól. Sveinsson. 1953. *Age of the Sturlungs: Icelandic Civilization in the Thirteenth Century*, trans. Jóhann S. Hannesson. Ithaca, NY. (Icelandic original 1940).

Einarsson, Stefán. See Stefán Einarsson.

Elmevik, Lennart, and Lena Peterson. 1993. See *Samnordisk runtextdatabas*.

Enright, Michael J. 1988. "Lady with a Mead-Cup: Ritual, Group Cohesion and Hierarchy in the Germanic Warband." *Frühmittelalterliche Studien* 22:170–203.

Erll, Astrid. 2008. "Cultural Memory Studies: An Introduction." In *Cultural Memory Studies. An International and Interdisciplinary Handbook*, ed. Astrid Erll and Ansgar Nünning, 1–15. Berlin.

Erll, Astrid, and Ansgar Nünning. 2005. "Where Literature and Memory Meet: Towards a Systematic Approach to the Concept of Memory Used in Literary Studies." In *Literature, Literary History, and Cultural Memory*, ed. H. Grabes, 261–294. Tübingen.

Etting, Vivian. 2018a. "Samsøs middelalderhistorie—De skriftlige kilder til øens historie." In *Borgene på Samsø: En arkæologisk jakt på historien bag øens fem middelalderborge*, ed. Vivian Etting. University of Southern Denmark Studies in History and Social Sciences, 558, 23–42. Odense.

———, ed. 2018b. *Borgene på Samsø: En arkæologisk jakt på historien bag øens fem middelalderborge*. University of Southern Denmark Studies in History and Social Sciences, 558. Odense.

Evans-Pritchard, E. E. 1937. *Witchcraft, Oracles and Magic among the Azande*. Oxford.

Fabech, Charlotte. 1999. "Centrality in Sites and Landscapes." In *Settlement and Landscape*, ed. C. Fabeck and J. Ringstved. 455–473. Moesgård, Højbjerg.

Falk, Hjalmar. 1924. *Odensheite*. Christiania.

Falk, Hjalmar, and Alf Torp, eds. 1904–1906. *Etymologisk ordbog over det norske og det danske sprog*. Oslo.

Finnur Jónsson. 1893. "Um þulur og gátur." In *Germanistische Abhandlungen zum 70. Geburtstag Konrad von Maurers*, ed. Oscar Brenner et al., 489–520. Göttingen.

———. 1907. *Den islandske Litteraturs Historie tilligemed den oldnorske*. Copenhagen.

———. 1922. "Mera om folkminnen och filologi." *Folkminnen och folktankar* 8:129–132.

Finnur Jónsson and Sveinbjörn Egilsson, eds. 1931. *Lexicon poeticum antiquae linguae septentrionalis*. See *Lexicon poeticum antiquae linguae septentrionalis*.

Flint, Valerie I. J. 1991. *The Rise of Magic in Early Medieval Europe*. Princeton, NJ.

Foley, John Miles. 1976. "'Riddle I' of the Exeter Book: The Apocalyptical Storm." *Neuphilologische Mitteilungen* 77:347–357.

———. 1977. "Riddles 53, 54, and 55: An Archetypal Symphony in Three Movements." *Studies in Medieval Culture* 11:25–31.

———. 1981. "*Lǽcdom* and *Bajanje*: A Comparative Study of Old English and Serbo-Croatian Charms." *Centerpoint: A Journal of Interdisciplinary Studies* 4 (3):33–40.

———, ed. 1985. *Oral-Formulaic Theory and Research: An Introduction and Annotated Bibliography*. New York.

———. 1988. *The Theory of Oral Composition: History and Methodology*. Bloomington, IN.

———. 1990. *Traditional Oral Epic: The Odyssey, Beowulf, and the Serbo-Croatian Return Song*. Berkeley, CA.

———. 1991. *Immanent Art: From Structure to Meaning in Traditional Oral Epic*. Bloomington, IN.

———. 1992. "Word-Power, Performance, and Tradition." *Journal of American Folklore* 105:275–301.

———. 1995. *The Singer of Tales in Performance*. Bloomington, IN.

———. 1998. "Individual Poet and Epic Tradition: Homer as Legendary Singer." *Arethusa* 31:149–178.

———. 1999. *Homer's Traditional Art*. University Park, PA.

———. 2002. *How to Read an Oral Poem*. Urbana, IL.

———. 2011. "Oral-Derived Text." In *The Homer Encyclopedia*, ed. Margalit Finkelberg 2:603. Chichester, West Sussex and Malden, MA.

———. 2012. *Oral Tradition and the Internet: Pathways of the Mind*. Urbana, IL.

Foote, Peter. 1955–1956. "Sagnaskemtan: Reykjahólar 119." *Saga-Book* 14:226–239.

Frake, Charles O. 1964. "How to ask for a drink in Subanun." In *Ethnography of Communication*, ed. John H. Gumperz and Dell H. Hymes. *American Anthropologist*, 66:127–132.

Frandsen, Ernst. 1935. *Folkevisen. Studier i middelalderens poetiske litteratur*. Copenhagen.

Frank, Roberta. 1978. *Old Norse Court Poetry: The Dróttkvætt Stanza*. Ithaca, NY.

———. 1981. "Snorri and the Mead of Poetry." In *Specvlvm Norrœnvm: Norse Studies in Memory of Gabriel Turville-Petre*, ed. Ursula Dronke et al., 155–170. Odense.

———. 1985. "Skaldic Poetry." In *Old Norse-Icelandic Literature: A Critical Guide*, ed. Carol J. Clover and John Lindow, 157–196. Ithaca, NY.

Fried, Johannes. 2012. *Der Schleier der Erinnerung: Grundzüge einer historischen Memorik*. Munich.

Fritzner, Johan, ed. (1886) 1973. *Ordbok over Det gamle norske Sprog*. 4th ed. Oslo.

Frye, Northrop. 1976. "Charms and Riddles." In *Spiritus mundi: Essays on Literature, Myth, and Society*, 123–147. Bloomington, IN.

Fuglesang, Signe Horn. 1989. "Viking and Medieval Amulets in Scandinavia." *Fornvännen* 84:15–25.

Gachanja, Muigai Wa, and Charles Kebaya. 2013. "Pedagogical Aspects of Riddles: A Critical Examination of Abagusii Riddles." *International Journal of Humanities and Social Science* 3 (3):293–298.

Gailey, Alan. 1989. "The Nature of Tradition." *Folklore* 100 (2):143–161.

Gaiman, Neil. 2017. *Norse Mythology*. New York.

Garberding, Petra 2010. "Den nazistiska raspolitiken—'en förolämpning mot majoriteten av det tyska folket': 1930-talets föreställningar om vetenskap, politik, kultur och ras i det svensk-tyska samarbetet inom folkminnes- och folklivsforskningen." *RIG: Kulturhistorisk tidskrift* 4:193–209.

Gardeła, Leszek, and Kamil Kajkowski, eds. 2013. *Motywy głowy w dawnych kulturach w perspektywie porównawczej/The Head Motif in Past Societies in a Comparative Perspective*. Bytów.

Geertz, Clifford. 1973. "Thick Description: Toward an Interpretive Theory of Culture." In *Interpretations of Culture*, 3–30. New York.

Geete, Robert, ed. 1903. *Fornsvensk bibliografi. Förteckning öfver Sveriges medeltida bokskatt på modersmålet samt därtill hörande literära hjälpmedel*. Stockholm.

Geijer, Herman, and Åke Campbell. 1930. "Gåtor." *Svenska landsmål ock svenskt folkliv* 191:5–68.

Georges, Robert A., and Alan Dundes. 1963. "Toward a Structural Definition of the Riddle." *Journal of American Folklore* 76:111–118.

Gerschenkron, Alexander. 1971. "The Concept of Continuity in German Anthropology" (review article, *Kontinuitaet? Geschichtlichkeit und Dauer als ein volkskundliches Problem*, ed. Hermann Bausinger and Wolfgang Brueckner). *Comparative Studies in Society and History* 13 (3):351–357.

Ginzburg, Carlo. 1991. *Ecstasies: Deciphering the Witches' Sabbath*, trans. Raymond Rosenthal). New York (Italian original 1989).

Gísli Pálsson. 1994. "Enskilment at Sea." *Man* n.s. 29 (4):901–927.

Gísli Sigurðsson. 2002. *Túlkun íslendingasagna í ljósi munnlegrar hefdar: tilgáta um afer*. Reykjavík. (Trans. as *The Medieval Icelandic Saga and Oral Tradition: A Discourse on Method*, trans. Nicholas Jones, Cambridge, MA, 2004.)

———. 2003. "Medieval Icelandic Studies." *Oral Tradition* 18 (2):207–209.

———. 2008. "Orality Harnessed: How to Read Written Sagas from an Oral Culture?" In *Oral Art Forms and their Passage into Writing*, ed. Else Mundal and Jonas Wellendorf, 19–28. Copenhagen.

Glassie, Henry H. 1995. "Tradition." *Journal of American Folklore* 108:395–412.

Glauser, Jürg. 1994. "Spätmittelalterliche Vorleseliteratur und frühneuzeitliche Handschriftentradition. Die Veränderungen der Medialität und Textualität der isländischen Märchensagas zwischen dem 14. und 19. Jahrhundert." In *Text und Zeittiefe*, ed. Hildegard L. C. Tristram, 377–438. Tübingen.

———. 1996. "Tendenzen der Vermündlichung isländischer Sagastoffe." In *(Re)Oralisierung*, ed. Hildegard L. C. Tristram, 111–125. Tübingen.

———. 1998. "Textüberlieferung und Textbegriff im spätmittelaterichen Norden: Das Beispiel der *Riddarasögur*." *Arkiv för nordisk filologi* 113:7–27.

———. 2007. "The Speaking Bodies of Saga Texts." In *Learning and Understanding in the Old Norse World. Essays in Honour of Margaret Clunies Ross*, ed. Judy Quinn, Kate Heslop, and Tarrin Wills, 13–26. Turnhout.

———. 2009. "Sinnestäuschungen. Medialitätskonzepte in der Prosa-Edda." In *Greppaminni. Rit til heiðurs Vésteini Ólasyni sjötugum 14. febrúar 2009*, ed. Margrét Eggertsdóttir et al., 165–174. Reykjavík.

———. 2010. "Staging the Text: On the Development of a Consciousness of Writing in the Norwegian and Icelandic Literature of the Middle Ages." In *Along the Oral-Written Continuum: Types of Texts, Relations, and Their Implications*, ed. Slavica Rankovic, Leidulf Melve, and Else Mundal, 311–334. Turnhout.

Glauser, Jürg, Pernille Hermann, and in collaboration with Stefan Brink and Joseph Harris, eds. 2021. *Myth, Magic, and Memory in Early Scandinavian Narrative Culture: Studies in Honour of Stephen A. Mitchell*. Acta Scandinavinca, 11. Turnhout.

Glauser, Jürg, Pernille Hermann, and Stephen A. Mitchell, eds. 2018. *Handbook of Pre-Modern Nordic Memory Studies*. 2 vols. Berlin.

Goetsch, Paul. 1985. "Fingierte Mündlichkeit in der Erzählkunst entwickelter Schriftkulturen." *Poetica* 17:202–218.

Goffman, Erving. 1959. *The Presentation of Self in Everyday Life*. Garden City, NY.

Goldstein, Kenneth S. 1963. "Riddling Traditions in Northeastern Scotland." *Journal of American Folklore* 76:330-36.

Goody, Jack. 1987. *The Interface between the Written and the Oral*. Cambridge.
Grabka, Gregory. 1953. "Christian Viaticum: A Study of Its Cultural Background." *Traditio* 9:1– 43.
Gräslund, Anne-Sofie. 1965–1966. "Charonsmynt i vikingatida gravar?" *Tor* 11:168–197.
Gräslund, Bo, and Neil Price. 2012. "Twilight of the Gods? The 'Dust Veil Event' of AD 536 in Critical Perspective." *Antiquity* 86 (332):428–443.
Green, Thomas A., and W. J. Pepicello. 1984. "The Riddle Process." *Journal of American Folklore* 97:189–203.
Grimm, Jacob. 1835. *Deutsche Mythologie*. Göttingen.
———. 1875. *Deutsche Mythologie*. Berlin. 4th ed. (Trans. as *Teutonic Mythology*, trans. James Steven Stallybrass, New York, (1882) 1966.)
Grinsell, Levi V. 1957. "The Ferryman and His Fee: A Study in Ethnology, Archaeology, and Tradition." *Folklore* 68 (1):257–269.
Grønvik, Ottar. 1981. *Runene på Tunesteinen: Alfabet, språkform, budskap*. Oslo.
———. 1982. *The Words for "heir," "inheritance" and "funeral feast" in early Germanic. An Etymological Study of ON arfr m, arfi m, erfi n, erfa vb and the Corresponding Words in the Other Old Germanic Dialects*. Oslo.
Grundtvig, Nikolai Frederik Severin. 1832. *Nordens Mythologi eller Sindbilled-Sprog historisk-poetisk udviklet og oplyst*. 2nd ed. Copenhagen.
Gumperz, John H., and Dell H. Hymes, eds. 1964. *The Ethnography of Communication*, Special issue of *American Anthropologist*, 66.
Gunnell, Terry. 1993. "Skírnisleikur og Freysmál. Endurmat eldri hugmynda um 'forna norræna helgileiki'." *Skírnir* 167:421–459.
———. 1995. *The Origins of Drama in Scandinavia*. Cambridge.
———. 2001a. "Hof, Halls, Goðar and Dwarves: An Examination of the Ritual Space in the Pagan Icelandic Hall." *Cosmos* 17 (1):3–36.
———. 2001b. "Mists, Magicians and Murderous Children: International Migratory Legends Concerning the 'Black Death' in Iceland." In *Northern Lights: Following Folklore in North Western Europe: Essays in Honour of Bo Almqvist*, ed. Séamas Ó Catháin, 47–59. Dublin.
———. 2006a. "Narratives, Space and Drama: Essential Spatial Aspects Involved in the Performance and Reception of Oral Narrative." *Folklore: An Electronic Journal* 33:7–26.
———. 2006b. "'Til holts ek gekk': Spacial and Temporal Aspects of the Dramatic Poems of the *Elder Edda*." In *Old Norse Religion in Long Term Perspectives: Origins, Changes and Interactions*, ed. Anders Andrén, Kristina Jennbert, and Catharina Raudvere, 238–242. Lund.

———. 2008. "The Performance of the Poetic Edda." In *The Viking World*, ed. Stefan Brink in collaboration with Neil Price, 199–203. New York.
———. 2011. "The Drama of the *Poetic Edda*: Performance as a Means of Transformation." In *Pogranicza teatralności: Poezja, poetyka, praktyka*, ed. Andrzeja Dąbrówki, 13–40. Warsaw.
———. 2012. "Waking the Dead: Folk Legends Concerning Magicians and Walking Corpses in Iceland." In *News from Other Worlds: Studies in Nordic Folklore, Mythology and Culture in Honor of John F. Lindow*, ed. Merrill Kaplan and Timothy R. Tangherlini, 235–266. Berkeley, CA.
———. 2013. "*Vǫluspá* in Performance." In *The Nordic Apocalypse: Approaches to Vǫluspá and Nordic Days of Judgement*, ed. Terry Gunnell and Annette Lassen, 63–77. Turnhout.
———. 2016. "Eddic Performance and Eddic Audiences." In *A Handbook to Eddic Poetry: Myths and Legends of Early Scandinavia*, ed. Carolyne Larrington, Judy Quinn and Britanny Schorn, 92–113. Cambridge.
———. 2018. "Performance Studies." In *Handbook of Pre-Modern Nordic Memory Studies*, ed. Jürg Glauser, Pernille Hermann, and Stephen A. Mitchell, 1:107–119. Berlin.
———. 2019. "Folke Ström and *kultdrama*." In *Religionshistorikern Folke Ström*, ed. Andreas Nordberg and Olof Sundqvist, 137–146. Uppsala.
———. 2020. "Performance Archaeology, *Eiríksmál*, *Hákonarmál* and the Study of Old Nordic Religions." In *John Miles Foley's World of Oralities: Text, Tradition, and Contemporary Oral Theory*, ed. Mark C. Amodio, 137–153. Leeds.
———. 2022. "Introduction." In *Old Norse Poetry in Performance*, ed. Brian McMahon and Annemari Ferreira, 1–15. London.
Gunnell, Terry, and Owe Ronström. 2013. "Folklore och Performance Studies: En introduktion." In *Folkloristikens akutella utmaningar: Vänbok till Ulf Palmenfelt*, ed. Owe Rönström, Georg Drakos, and Jonas Engman, 21–55. Visby.
Gurević, Elena A. 1992. "Zur genealogie der þula." *Alvíssmál* 1:65–98.
Gurevitch, A. Ya. 1968. "Wealth and Gift-Bestowal among the ancient Scandinavians." *Scandinavica* 7:126–138.
Gutenbrunner, Siegfried. 1936. "Zur Gutasaga." *Zeitschrift für deutsches Altertum und deutsche Literatur* 73 (3):159–163.
———. 1976. *Von Hildebrand und Hadubrand. Lied-Sage-Mythos*. Heidelberg.
Hållans Stenholm, Ann-Mari. 2018, "Landscape and Mounds." In *The Handbook of Pre-Modern Nordic Memory Studies*, ed. Jürg Glauser, Pernille Hermann, and Stephen A. Mitchell, 607–612. Berlin.

Hafstein, Valdimar Tr. See Valdimar Tr. Hafstein.
Halbwachs, Maurice. 1925. *Les cadres sociaux de la mémoire*. Travaux de l'Année sociologique. Paris. (Trans. as *On Collective Memory*, trans. Lewis A. Coser, Chicago, 1992.)
———. 1950. *La mémoire collective*. Bibliothèque de sociologie contemporaine. Paris. (Trans. as *The Collective Memory*, trans. Francis J. Ditter, Jr., and Vida Yazdi Ditter, New York, 1980.)
Hald, Kristian. 1971. *Personnavne i Danmark. I. Oldtiden*. Copenhagen.
Hall, Alaric. 2007. *Elves in Anglo-Saxon England: Matters of Belief, Health, Gender and Identity*. Woodbridge.
Hallberg, Peter. 1962. *Snorri Sturluson och Egils saga Skallagrímssonar: Ett forsok till språklig författarbestämning*. Reykjavík.
Halvorsen, Eyvind Fjeld. (1956–1978) 1982. "Mimir el. Mímr." In *KLNM* 11: cols. 629–630.
Harb, F. 1990. "Wine Poetry (khamriyyāt)." In *'Abbasid Belles-Lettres*, ed. Julia Ashtiany et al., 219–234. Cambridge.
Haring, Lee. 1974. "On Knowing the Answer." *Journal of American Folklore* 87:197–207.
Harris, Joseph. 1972. "Genre and Narrative Structure in some *Íslendinga þættir*." *Scandinavian Studies* 44:1–27.
———. 1976a. "The Masterbuilder Tale in Snorri's *Edda* and Two Sagas." *Arkiv för nordisk filologi* 91:66–101.
———. 1976b. "Theme and Genre in some *Íslendinga þættir*." *Scandinavian Studies* 48:1–28.
———. 1979. "The *senna*: From Description to Literary Theory." *Michigan Germanic Studies* 5:65–74.
———. 1983. "Eddic Poetry as Oral Poetry: The Evidence of Parallel Passages in the Helgi Poems for Questions of Composition and Performance." In *Edda: A Collection of Essays*, ed. Robert J. Glendinning and Haraldur Bessason, 210–242. Winnepeg.
———. 1985. "Eddic Poetry." In *Old Norse-Icelandic Literature: A Critical Guide*, ed. C. Clover and J. Lindow, 68–156. Ithaca, NY.
———. 1988. "Hadubrant's Lament." In *Heldensage und Heldendichtung in Germanischen*, ed. Heinrich Beck, 81–114. Berlin.
———. 1997. "The Prosimetrum of Icelandic Sagas and some Relatives." In *Prosimetrum: Crosscultural Perspectives on Narrative in Prose and Verse*, ed. Joseph Harris and Karl Reichl, 131–163. Cambridge.
———. 1998. "The Icelandic Sagas." In *Teaching Oral Traditions*, ed. John Miles Foley, 382–390. New York.

———. 2000a. "The Performance of Old Norse Eddic Poetry: A Retrospective." In *The Oral Epic: Performance and Music*, ed. Karl Reichl, 225–232. Berlin.

———. 2000b. "Performance, Textualization, and Textuality of 'Elegy' in Old Norse." In *Textualization of Oral Epics*, ed. Lauri Honko, 89–99. Berlin.

———. 2006. "Myth and Meaning in the Rök Inscription." *Viking and Medieval Scandinavia* 2:45–109.

———. 2008. "Romancing the Rune: Aspects of Literacy in Early Scandinavian Orality." In *"Speak Useful Words or Say Nothing": Old Norse Studies by Joseph Harris*, ed. Susan E. Deskis and Thomas D. Hill, 319–347. Ithaca, NY. First published in 1996.

———. 2010a. "Old Norse Memorial Discourse between Orality and Literacy." In *Along the Oral-Written Continuum: Types of Texts, Relations, and Their Implications*, ed. Slavica Rankovic, Leidulf Melve, and Else Mundal, 120–133. Turnhout.

———. 2010b. "Varin's Philosophy and the Rök Stone's Mythology of Death." In *New Perspectives on Myth: Proceedings of the Second Annual Conference of the International Association for Comparative Mythology, Ravenstein (the Netherlands), 19–21 August, 2008*, ed. Wim M. J. van Binsbergen and Eric Venbrux, 91–105. Haarlem.

———. 2016. "Traditions of Eddic Scholarship." In *A Handbook to Eddic Poetry: Myths and Legends of Early Scandinavia*, ed. Carolyne Larrington, Judy Quinn, and Brittany Schorn, 33–57. Cambridge.

Harris, Joseph, and Karl Reichl. 2011. "Performance and Performers." In *Medieval Oral Literature*, ed. Karl Reichl, 141–202. Berlin.

Harrison, Dick. 2000. *Stora döden: Den värsta katastrof som drabbat Europa*. Stockholm.

Hartmann, Elisabeth. 1936. *Die Trollvorstellungen in den Sagen und Märchen der skandinavischen Völker*. Stuttgart and Berlin.

Hatto, A. T. 1973. "On the Excellence of the *Hildebrandslied*: A Comparative Study in Dynamics." *The Modern Language Review* 68 (4):820–838.

Hedeager, Lotte. 2011. *Iron Age Myth and Materiality: An Archaeology of Scandinavia, AD 400–1000*. London.

Heide, Eldar. 2011. "Holy Islands and the Otherworld: Places beyond Water." In *Isolated Islands in Medieval Nature, Culture and Mind*, ed. Gerhard Jaritz and Torstein Jørgensen, 57–80. CEU Medievalia, 14. Budapest/Bergen.

———. 2012. "The early Viking ship types." *Sjøfartshistorisk Årbok*: 81–153.

Helgason, Jón. See Jón Helgason.
Helgesson, Bertil. 1998. "Vad är centralt?—fenomen och funktion; lokalisering och person." In *Centrala platser, centrala frågor: Samhällsstrukturen under järnåldern. En vänbok till Berta Stjernquist*, ed. Lars Larsson and Birgitta Hårdh, 39–45. Uppåkrastudier, 1. Stockholm
Hellqvist, Elof, ed. 1957. *Svensk etymologisk ordbok*. 3rd ed. Lund.
Helmbrecht, Michaela. 2012. "A Winged Figure from Uppåkra." *Fornvännen* 107 (3):171–178.
Hermann Pálsson. 1962. *Sagnaskemmtun Íslendinga*. Reykjavík.
Hermann, Pernille. 2009. "Concepts of Memory and Approaches to the Past in Medieval Icelandic Literature." *Scandinavian Studies* 81 (3):287–308.
——. 2010. "Founding Narratives and the Representation of Memory in Saga Literature." *ARV* 66:69–87.
——. 2014. "Key Aspects of Memory and Remembering in Old Norse-Icelandic Literature." In *Minni and Muninn. Memory in Medieval Nordic Culture*, ed. Pernille Hermann, Stephen A. Mitchell, and Agnes S. Arnórsdóttir, 13–49. Turnhout.
——. 2017. "Methodological Challenges to the Study of Old Norse Myths: The Orality and Literacy Debate Reframed." In *Old Norse Mythology – Comparative Perspectives*, ed. Pernille Hermann, Stephen A. Mitchell, and Jens Peter Schjødt, with Amber J. Rose, 29–51. Publications of the Milman Parry Collection of Oral Literature, 3. Cambridge, MA.
——. 2018a. "Danish Perspectives." In *The Handbook of Pre-Modern Nordic Memory Studies*, ed. Jürg Glauser, Pernille Hermann, and Stephen A. Mitchell, 771–781. Berlin.
——. 2018b. "Memorial Landscapes." In *The Handbook of Pre-Modern Nordic Memory Studies*, ed. Jürg Glauser, Pernille Hermann, and Stephen A. Mitchell, 627–637. Berlin.
——. 2020. "Memory, Oral Tradition, and Sources." In *Pre-Christian Religions of the North. Histories and Structures. Volume I. Basic Premises and Consideration of Sources*, ed. Anders Andrén, John Lindow, and Jens Peter Schjødt, 41–62. Turnhout.
Hermann, Pernille, and Stephen A. Mitchell, eds. 2013. *Memory and Remembering: Past Awareness in the Medieval North*. Special issue of *Scandinavian Studies*.
Hermann, Pernille, Stephen A. Mitchell, and Agnes S. Arnórsdóttir, eds. 2014. *Minni and Muninn. Memory in Medieval Nordic Culture*. Turnhout.

Heslop, Kate. 2014. "Minni and the Rhetoric of Memory in Eddic, Skaldic and Runic Texts." In Minni *and* Muninn. *Memory in Medieval Nordic Culture,* ed. Pernille Hermann, Stephen A. Mitchell, and Agnes S. Arnórsdóttir, 75–107. Turnhout.

Heusler, Andreas. 1901. "Die altnordischen Rätsel." *Zeitschrift des Vereins für Volkskunde* 11:117–149.

———. 1914. *Die Anfänge der isländischen Saga.* Berlin.

———. 1923. *Die altgermanische Dichtung.* Handbuch der literaturwissenschaft. Berlin- Neubabelsberg.

Höfler, Otto. 1934. *Kultische Geheimbünde der Germanen.* Frankfurt am Main.

———. 1937. *Das germanische Kontinuitätsproblem.* Hamburg.

———. 1938. "Das germanische Kontinuitätsproblem." *Historische Zeitschrift* 157 (1):1–26.

Hofmann, Dietrich. 1971. "Vers und Prosa in der mündlich gepflegten mittelalterlichen Erzählkunst der germanischen Länder." *Frühmittelalterliche Studien* 5:135–175.

———. 1981. "Die *Yngvars saga víðfǫrla* und Oddr munkr inn fróði." In *Speculum norroenum: Norse Studies in Memory of Gabriel Turville-Petre*, ed. Ursula Dronke, 182–222. Odense.

Hollander, Lee M. 1945. *The Skalds: A Selection of their Poems.* Princeton, NJ.

Hollowell, Ida Masters. 1978. "*Scop* and *woðbora* in OE Poetry." *Journal of English and Germanic Philology* 77:317–329.

Holmbäck, Åke, and Elias Wessén, ed. and trans. (1933–1946) 1979. *Svenska Landskapslagar, tolkade och förklarade för nutidens svenskar.* 2nd ed. 5 vols. Stockholm.

Holst, Mads Kähler, Jan Heinemeier et al. 2018. "Direct evidence of a large North European Roman period martial event and postbattle corpse manipulation." *Proceedings of the National Academy of Sciences* 115 (23):5920–5925.

Holthausen, Ferdinand, ed. 1948. *Vergleichendes und etymologisches Wörterbuch des Altwestnordischen, Altnorwegisch-isländischen, einschliesslich der Lehn- und Fremdwörter sowie der Eigennamen.* Göttingen.

Holtsmark, Anne. 1945. "Bil og Hjuke." *Maal og Minne*: 139–154.

———. (1956–1978) 1982a. "Lovkvad." In *KLNM* 10: cols. 700–704.

———. (1956–1978) 1982b. "Skaldediktning." In *KLNM* 15: cols. 386–390.

———. 1964. *Studier i Snorres mytologi.* Oslo.

Honko, Lauri. 1998. *Textualising the Siri Epic*. Folklore Fellows Communications, 264. Helsinki.
Hornemann, Johanne Duus. "Folkemøderne i Herthadalen genoplives," *Kristeligt Dagblad*. June 4, 2007. https://www.kristeligt-dagblad.dk/danmark/folkemøderne-i-herthadalen-genoplives
Hughes, Shaun F. D. 1978. "'Völsunga rímur' and 'Sjúrðar kvæði': Romance and Ballad, Ballad and Dance." In *Ballads and Ballad Research*, ed. Patricia Conroy, 37–45. Seattle.
———. 1982. "Rímur." In *Dictionary of the Middle Ages*, ed. Joseph Strayer, 401–407. New York.
Hultkrantz, Åke. 1999. *Vem är vem i nordisk mytologi. Gestalter och äventyr i Eddans gudavärld*. 2. uppl. Stockholm.
Hutton, Patrick. 1981. "The History of Mentalities: The New Map of Cultural History." *History and Theory* 20:237–259.
Huxley, Julian S. 1955. "Guest Editorial: Evolution, Cultural and Biological." *Yearbook of Anthropology*: 2–25.
Hyltén-Cavallius, Gunnar Olof. 1863–1868. *Wärend och Wirdarne. Ett försök i Svensk Ethnologi*. 2 vols. Stockholm.
Hymes, Dell H. 1962. "The Ethnography of Speaking." In *Anthropology and Human Behavior*, 13–53. Washington, DC.
———. 1964. "Introduction: Toward Ethnographies of Communication." In *Ethnography of Communication*, ed. John H. Gumperz and Dell H. Hymes. *American Anthropologist*, 66:1–34.
———. 1971. "The Contribution of Folklore to Sociolinguistic Research." *The Journal of American Folklore* 84:42–50.
Ingunn Ásdísardóttir. 2007. *Frigg og Freyja. Kvenleg goðmögn í heiðnum sið*. Reykjavík.
Inomata, Takeshi, and Lawrence S. Coben. 2006. *Archaeology of Performance: Theaters of Power, Community, and Politics*. Lanham, MD.
Iversen, Frode. 2009. "Royal Villas in Northern Europe." In *The Archaeology of Early Medieval Villages in Europe*, ed. Juan Antonio Quirós Castillo, 99–112. Documentos de Arqueología e Historia. Bilbao.
Jacobsen, Lis. 1911. "Gamle danske Oversættelser af Gutasaga." *Arkiv för nordisk filologi* 27:50–75.
Jacobsson, Bengt. 2002. *Pestbacken: En begravningsplats för pestoffer från åren 1710 och 1711, Blekinge, Olofströms kommun, Jämshögs socken, Holje 5:68 och 5:69*. Lund.
Jakobsson, Ármann. See Ármann Jakobsson.
Jansson, Valter. 1945. *Eufemiavisorna. En filologisk undersökning*. Uppsala.

———. (1956–1978) 1982. "Fornsvenska Legendariet." In *KLNM* 5: cols. 518–522.
Janzén, Assar, ed. 1948. *Personnamn*. Stockholm.
Jesch, Judith. 2001. *Ships and Men in the late Viking Age. The Vocabulary of Runic Inscriptions and Skaldic Verse*. Woodbridge.
———. 2005. "Memorials in Speech and Writing." In *Runesten, magt og mindesmærker: Tværfagligt symposium på Askov Højskole 3. –5. oktober 2002*, ed. Gunhild Øeby Nielsen, 95–104. Højbjerg.
———. 2008. "Myth and Cultural Memory in the Viking Diaspora." *Viking and Medieval Scandinavia* 4:221–226.
Jespersen, Poul Helveg. 1938. "Sneglen i digtning, tale og folketro." *Danske Studier* 1938:147–164.
Jokipii, Mauno, and Ilkka Nummela, eds. 1981. *Ur nordisk kulturhistoria: Universitetsbesöken i utlandet före 1660, I. XVIII Nordiska historikermötet*. Jyväskylä.
Jón Helgason. 1953. "Norges og Islands Digtning." In *Litteraturhistorie. B: Norge og Island*, ed. Sigurður Nordal, 3–179. Nordisk kultur 8B. Stockholm.
Jones, Steven. 1979. "Slouching towards Ethnography: The Text/Context Controversy Reconsidered." *Western Folklore* 38:42–47.
Jonsson, Bengt R. 1978. "The Ballad in Scandinavia: Its Age, Prehistory and Early History. Some Preliminary Reflections." In *The European Medieval Ballad: A Symposium*, ed. Otto Holzapfel, 9–15. Odense.
———. 1991. "Oral Literature, Written Literature, and the Ballad: Relations between Old Norse Genres." In *The Ballad and Oral Literature*, ed. Joseph Harris, 139–170. Cambridge, MA.
Jonsson, Bengt R., Svale Solheim et al., eds. 1978. *Types of the Medieval Scandinavian Ballad*. See *TSB*.
Jónsson, Finnur. See Finnur Jónsson.
Kanerva, Kirsi. 2011. "The Role of the Dead in Medieval Iceland: A Case Study of *Eyrbyggja Saga*." *Collegium Medievale* 24:23–49.
———. 2013. "Rituals for the Restless Dead: The Authority of the Deceased in Medieval Iceland." In *Authorities in the Middle Ages: Influence, Legitimacy, and Power in Medieval Society*, ed. Sini Kangas, Mia Korpiola, and Tuija Ainonen, 201–223. Berlin.
Kaplan, Merrill. 2000. "Prefiguration and the Writing of History in *Þáttr Þiðranda ok Þórhalls*." *Journal of English and Germanic Philology* 99 (3):379–394.

———. 2004. "The Past as Guest: Mortal Men, King's Men, and Four *gestir* in *Flateyjarbók*." *Gripla* 15:91–120.

———. 2011. *Thou Fearful Guest: Addressing the Past in Four Tales in Flateyjarbók*. Helsinki.

Kaul, Flemming. 1998. *Ships on Bronzes: A Study in Bronze Age Religion and Iconography*, trans. Gillian Fellows Jensen and Lone Gebauer Thomsen. Copenhagen.

———. 2004. *Bronzealderens religion. Studier af den nordiske bronzealders ikonografi*. Copenhagen.

Keary, Annie, and Eliza Keary. 1857. *The Heroes of Asgard and the Giants of Jötunheim; or, the Week and its Story*. London.

Kershaw, Kris. 2000. *The One-Eyed God: Odin and the Indo-Germanic Männerbünde*. Washington, DC.

Kieckhefer, Richard. 1990. *Magic in the Middle Ages*. Cambridge.

———. 1997. *Forbidden Rites: A Necromancer's Manual of the Fifteenth Century*. University Park, PA.

Kiening, Christian. 2003. *Zwischen Körper und Schrift: Texte vor dem Zeitalter der Literatur*. Frankfurt am Main.

Klare, Hans-Joachim. 1933–1934. "Die Toten in der altnordischen Literatur." *Acta Philologica Scandinavica* 8:1–56.

Klockars, Birgit. 1967. "Medeltidens religiösa litteratur." In *Ny illustrerad svensk litteraturhistoria*, ed. E. N. Tigerstedt, I, 125–225. Stockholm.

Knight, K., ed. (1907) 2003. *The Catholic Encyclopedia*. See *The Catholic Encyclopedia*.

Knirk, James E. 1981. *Oratory in the Kings' Sagas*. Oslo.

Knudsen, Gunnar, Viggo Brøndal, and Svend Aakjær, eds. *Samsøs Stednavne*. 1922. Stednavneudvalget, Københavns Universitet, Institut for Navneforskning, Danmarks Stednavne, 1. Copenhagen.

Knuuttila, Seppo. 1993. "Some Questions Concerning Mentalities, Ethnomethodology and Rhetorics in the Folkloristic Study of Community." In *Nordic Frontiers: Recent Issues in the Study of Modern Traditional Culture in the Nordic Countries*, ed. Pertti J. Anttonen and Reimund Kvideland, 121–130. Turku.

———. 1995. "Mentalities and Modalities." *Suomen Antropologi* 20 (1):18–25.

Kock, Axel. 1899. "Etymologisch-mythologische Untersuchungen." *Indogermanische Forschungen* 10:90–111.

Köngäs-Maranda, Elli-Kaija. 1963. "The Concept of Folklore." *Midwest Folklore* 13 (2):69–88.

Körner, Sten. 2008. *Slottsprästen Petreius berättar: Gotlands äldsta historiekrönika i gotländskt och europeiskt perspektiv*. Visby.
Kragerud, Alv. 1981. "De mytologiske spørsmål i Fåvnesmål." *Arkiv för nordisk filologi* 96:9–48.
Krappe, Alexander Haggerty. 1930. *The Science of Folk-Lore*. London.
Krause, Wolfgang. 1971. *Die Sprache der urnordischen Runeninschriften*. Heidelberg.
Kroeber, Alfred L. 1917. "The Superorganic." *American Anthropologist* 19 (2):163–213.
———. 1918. "The Possibility of a Social Psychology." *The American Journal of Sociology* 23 (5):633–650.
Kroeber, Alfred L., and Lila M. O'Neale. 1926. *Archaeological Explorations in Peru*. Anthropology Memoirs 2:1–4. Chicago.
Krohn, Kaarle. 1911. "Tyrs högra hand, Freys svärd." In *Festskrift til H.F. Feilberg fra nordiske sprog- og folkemindesforskere på 80 års dagen den 6. august 1911*. Pub. as *Svenska landmål* 1911; *Maal og minne* 1911; and *Danske Studier* 1911:541–547.
———. 1926. *Die folkloristische Arbeitsmethode, begründet von Julius Krohn und weitergeführt von nordischen Forschern, erläutert von Kaarle Krohn*. Oslo and Cambridge, MA. (Trans. as *Folklore Methodology, formulated by Julius Krohn and expanded by Nordic Researchers*, Austin, TX.)
La Cour, Vilhelm. 1921. "Lejrestudier." *Danske Studier*: 147–166.
Labov, William. 1973. *Language in the Inner City*. Philadelphia.
Läffler, L. F. 1908. "Till 700-årsminnet af slaget vid Lena 31 januari 1208. 3. Ett stadgande i *Gutasaga*, som ytterst föranledts af slaget vid Lena. En laghistorisk undersökning." *Fornvännen*: 137–177.
Lang, Andrew. (1884) 1893. "The Method of Folklore." Rev. ed. In *Custom and Myth*, 10–28. London.
Larrington, Carolyne. 1993. *A Store of Common Sense: Gnomic Theme and Style in Old Icelandic and Old English Wisdom Poetry*. Oxford.
———. 2017. "A Textscape: On Sámsey." In *Skandinavische Schriftlandschaften: Vänbok till Jürg Glauser*, ed. Klaus Müller-Wille et al., 84–89. Beiträge zur Nordischen Philologie, 59. Tübingen.
Larsson, Lars. 2007. "The Iron Age ritual building at Uppåkra, southern Sweden." *Antiquity* 81:11–25.
Larsson, Lars-Olof. 1975. *Den helige Sigfrid: I kult, legend och verklighet*. Växjö.
Larsson, Lars, and Birgitta Hårdh, eds. 1998. *Centrala platser, centrala frågor: Samhällsstrukturen under järnåldern. En vänbok till Berta Stjernquist*. Uppåkrastudier, 1. Stockholm.

Laugerud, Henning. 2010. "Memory Stored and Reactivated – Some Introductory Reflections." *ARV* 66:7–20.
Layher, William. 2008. "The Big Splash: End-rhyme and Innovation in Medieval Scandinavian Poetics." *Scandinavian Studies* 80:407–436.
———. 2010. *Queenship and Voice in Medieval Northern Europe*. New York.
Le Goff, Jacques. 1988. *Histoire et mémoire*. Collection Folio/histoire 20. Paris. (Trans. as *History and Memory*, New York, 1992, Italian original 1986.)
Lexicon poeticum antiquae linguae septentrionalis: Ordbog over det norsk-islandske skjaldesprog. 1931. Ed. Sveinbjörn Egilsson. 2nd ed. Finnur Jónsson. Copenhagen.
Leyen, Friedrich von der. 1899. *Das Märchen in den Göttersagen der Edda*. Berlin.
Lie, Hallvard. (1956–1978) 1982. "Lausavísur." In *KLNM* 10: cols. 355–356.
Lieber, Michael D. 1976. "Riddles, Cultural Categories, and World View." *Journal of American Folklore* 89:255–265.
Liestøl, Knut. 1945. "Til spørsmålet om dei eldste islendske danskvæde." *ARV* 1:70–75.
Lind, Erik Henrik. 1905–1931. *Norsk-isländska dopnamn ock fingerade namn från medeltiden*. Uppsala.
Lindahl, Carl. 2000. "Folklore." In *Medieval Folklore: An Encyclopedia of Myths, Legends, Tales, Beliefs, and Customs*, ed. Carl Lindahl, John McNamara, and John Lindow, 333–342. Santa Barbara, CA.
Lindahl, Carl, John McNamara, and John Lindow, eds. 2000. *Medieval Folklore: An Encyclopedia of Myths, Legends, Tales, Beliefs, and Customs*. Santa Barbara, CA.
Lindow, John. 1975. "Riddles, Kennings, and the Complexity of Skaldic Poetry." *Scandinavian Studies* 47 (3):311–327.
———. 1976. *Comitatus, Individual and Honor: Studies in North Germanic Institutional Vocabulary*. University of California Publications in Linguistics, 83. Berkeley, CA.
———, ed. 1983. *Scandinavian Mythology: A Bibliography*. New York.
———, ed. 2001. *Handbook of Norse Mythology*. Santa Barbara, CA.
———, ed. 2002. *Norse Mythology: A Guide to the Gods, Heroes, Rituals, and Beliefs*. Oxford.
———. 2014. *Trolls. An Unnatural History*. London.
———. 2016. "Groups, Lists, Features: Snorri's Ásynjur." In *Theorizing Old Norse Myth*, ed. Stefan Brink and Lisa Collinson, 131–149. Turnhout.
———. 2021. *Old Norse Mythology*. New York.

Lindqvist, Sune. 1914. "Ramsundsbron vid Sigurdsristningen och en storbondesläkt från missionstiden." *Fornvännen*: 203–230.
Lindroth, Sten. (1975) 1989. *Svensk lärdomshistoria*. 4 vols. Stockholm.
Lixfeld, Hannjost. 1994. *Folklore and Fascism: The Reich Institute for German Volkskunde*, trans. James R. Dow. Bloomington, IN.
Lobell, Jarrett A. 2012. "The Bog Army." *Archaeology* 65 (6):14.
Löfqvist, Karl-Erik. 1935. *Om riddarväsen och frälse i nordisk medeltid: Studier rörande adelsståndets uppkomst och tidigare utformning*. Lund.
Lönnroth, Lars. 1971. "Hjálmar's Death-Song and the Delivery of Eddic Poetry." *Speculum* 46:1–20.
———. 1976. *Njáls saga: A Critical Introduction*. Berkeley, CA.
———. 1977. "*Skírnismál* och den fornisländska äktenskapsnormen." In *Opuscula Septentrionalia. Festskrift til Ole Widding. 10.10.1977*, ed. Bent Chr. Jakobsen et al., 154–178. Copenhagen.
———. 1978. *Den dubbla scenen: Muntlig diktning fran Eddan till ABBA*. Stockholm.
———. 1980. "New Dimensions and Old Directions in Saga Research." *Scandinavica* 19:57–61.
———. 2009. "Old Norse Text as Performance." *Scripta Islandica* 60:49–60.
Lord, Albert B. 1953. "Remarks." In *Four Symposia on Folklore. Midcentury International Folklore Conference 1950*, ed. Stith Thompson, 316. Bloomington, IN.
———. 1956. "Avdo Međedović, Guslar." *Journal of American Folklore* 69:320–330.
———. (1960) 2000. *The Singer of Tales*. 2nd ed., ed. Stephen Mitchell and Gregory Nagy. Cambridge, MA.
———. 1986. "The Merging of Two Worlds: Oral and Written Poetry as Carriers of Ancient Values." In *Oral Tradition in Literature: Interpretation in Context*, ed. John Miles Foley, 19–64. Columbia, MO.
———. 1991. "Homer as Oral-Traditional Poet." In *Epic Singers and Oral Tradition*, 72–103. Ithaca, NY.
Loumand, Ulla. 2006. "The Horse and its Role in Icelandic Burial Practices, Mythology, and Society." In *Old Norse Religion in Long Term Perspectives: Origins, Changes and Interactions, an International Conference in Lund, Sweden, June 3–7, 2004*, ed. Anders Andrén, Kristina Jennbert, and Catharina Raudvere, 130–134. Lund.
Love, Jeffrey Scott. 2013. *The Reception of* Hervarar Saga ok Heiðreks *from the Middle Ages to the Seventeenth Century*. Münchner nordistische Studien, 14. Munich.

Lucas, Gavin, and Thomas McGovern. 2007. "Bloody Slaughter: Ritual Decapitation and Display at the Viking Settlement of Hofstaðir, Iceland." *European Journal of Archaeology* 10 (1):7–30.

Lütjens, August. 1912. *Herzog Friedrich von der Normandie. Eine Beitrag zur Geschichte der deutschen und schwedischen Literatur des Mittelalters*. Munich.

Lukman, Niels. (1956–1978) 1982. "Heltesagn." In *KLNM* 6: cols. 420–425.

Lundén, Tryggve. 1967. "Medeltidens religiösa litteratur." In *Ny illustrerad svensk litteraturhistoria*. 2nd ed., ed. E. N. Tigerstedt and Erik Hjalma Linder, 122–222. Stockholm.

Mansa, Frederick Vilhelm. 1873. *Bidrag til Folkesygdommenes og Sundhedspleiens Historie i Danmark, fra de aeldste Tider til Begyndelsen af det attende Aarhundrede*. Copenhagen.

Marchand, James W. 1976. "The Old Icelandic *Joca Monachorum*." *Mediæval Scandinavia* 9:99–126.

Martin, John Stanley. 2000. "From Godan to Wotan: An Examination of Two Langobardic Mythological Texts." In *Old Norse Myths, Literature and Society. The 11th International Saga Conference*, ed. Geraldine Barnes and Margaret Clunies Ross, 303–315. University of Sydney, Australia. http://www.sagaconference.org/SC11/SC11_Martin.pdf.

Martin, Richard P. 1989. *The Language of Heroes: Speech and Performance in the Iliad*. Ithaca, NY.

McDowell, John Holmes. 1979. *Children's Riddling*. Bloomington, IN.

McKinnell, John. 2005. *Meeting the Other in Norse Myth and Legend*. Cambridge.

———. 2007. "Wisdom from the Dead: The *Ljóðatal* section of *Hávamál*." *Medium Aevum* 76 (1):85–115.

McTurk, Rory, ed. 2005. *A Companion to Old Norse-Icelandic Literature and Culture*. Blackwell Companions to Literature and Culture, 31. Oxford.

Medieval Craft of Memory: An Anthology of Texts and Pictures. 2002., ed. and trans. Mary Carruthers and Jan M. Ziolkowski. Philadelphia.

Meier, M. 2001. "Männerbund." In *Reallexikon der germanischen Altertumskunde*, ed. Herbert Jankuhn, Johannes Hoops, and Heinrich Beck, 105–110. Berlin.

Meletinskij, Eleazar M. 1973. "Scandinavian Mythology as a System." *Journal of Symbolic Anthropology* 1:43–57 and 2:57–78.

———. 1977. "Scandinavian Mythology as a System of Oppositions." In *Patterns in Oral Literature*, 251–260. The Hague.

Mellor, Scott A. 2008. *Analyzing Ten Poems from The Poetic Edda: Oral Formula and Mythic Patterns*. Lewiston, NY.
Meulengracht Sørensen, Preben. 1993. *Saga and Society: An Introduction to Old Norse Literature*. Studia Borealia. Monograph Series, 1. Odense. (Danish original 1977.)
Mitchell, Stephen A. 1982. "Ambiguity and Germanic Imagery in Old English Riddle 1: 'Army'." *Studia Neophilologica* 54:39–52.
———. 1983. "*Fǫr Scírnis* as Mythological Model: *frið at kaupa*." *Arkiv för nordisk filologi* 98:108–122.
———. 1984. "On the Composition and Function of *Gutasaga*." *Arkiv för nordisk filologi*, 99:151–174.
———. 1985. "Scandinavian Balladry and the Old Norse Legacy: 'Álvur kongur' (CCF 14) 'Stolt Herr Alf' (ST 5), and *Hálfs saga*." *ARV* 41:1–11.
———. 1987. "The Sagaman and Oral Literature: The Icelandic Traditions of Hjörleifr inn kvensami and Geirmundr heljarskinn." In *Comparative Research on Oral Traditions: A Memorial for Milman Parry*, ed. John Miles Foley, 395–423. Columbus, OH.
———. 1991a. "Heroic Legend, Parricide, and Istaby." In *The Eighth International Saga Conference: The Audience of the Sagas* 2:113–119. Gothenburg.
———. 1991b. *Heroic Sagas and Ballads*. Ithaca, NY.
———. 1993a. "Guta saga." In *Medieval Scandinavia: An Encyclopedia*, ed. Phillip Pulsiano et al., 253. New York.
———. 1993b. "Óðinn." In *Medieval Scandinavia: An Encyclopedia*, ed. Phillip Pulsiano et al., 444–445. New York.
———. 1996. "Literature in Medieval Sweden." In *A History of Swedish Literature*, ed. Lars Warme, 1–57. A History of Scandinavian Literature, 3. Lincoln, NE.
———. 1997a. "*Blåkulla* and its Antecedents: Transvection and Conventicles in Nordic Witchcraft." *Alvíssmál* 7:81–100.
———. 1997b. "Courts, Consorts, and the Transformation of Medieval Scandinavian Literature." In *Germanic Studies in Honor of Anatoly Liberman*, ed. Marvin Taylor, 229–241. Odense.
———. 1998. "Anaphrodisiac Charms in the Nordic Middle Ages: Impotence, Infertility, and Magic." *Norveg* 38:19–42.

———. 2000a. "Folklore and Philology Revisited: Medieval Scandinavian Folklore?" In *Norden og Europa. Fagtradisjoner i nordisk etnologi og folkloristikk*, ed. Bjarne Rogge and Bente Gullveig Alver, 286–294. Olso.

———. 2000b. "Skírnir's Other Journey: The Riddle of Gleipnir." In *Gudar på jorden. Festskrift till Lars Lönnroth*, ed. Matts Malm and Stina Hanson, 67–75. Stockholm.

———. 2001a "Performance and Norse Poetry: The Hydromel of Praise and the Effluvia of Scorn." *Oral Tradition* 16:168–202.

———. 2001b. "Warlocks, Valkyries and Varlets: A Prolegomenon to the Study of North Sea Witchcraft Terminology." *Cosmos* 17 (1):59–81.

———. 2003a. "The *fornaldarsögur* and Nordic Balladry: The Sámsey Episode across Genres." In *Fornaldarsagornas struktur och ideologi*, ed. Ármann Jakobsson, Annette Lassen, and Agneta Ney. Nordiska texter och undersökningar, 28. 245-256. Uppsala.

———. 2003b. "Reconstructing Old Norse Oral Tradition." *Oral Tradition* 18 (2):203–206.

———. 2005. "'An Evil Woman is the Devil's Door Nail': Probing the Proverbial and Pictorial Patriarchate in medieval Scandinavia." In *Neue Wege in der Mittelalterphilologie*, ed. Astrid van Nahl and Susanne Kramarz-Bein, 11–34. Frankfurt am Main/Basel.

———. 2007a. "*DgF* 526 'Lokket med runer', Memory, and Magic." In *Emily Lyle: The Persistent Scholar*, ed. Francis J. Fischer and Sigrid Rieuwerts, 206–211. Trier.

———. 2007b. "*For Scírnis* [*Skírnismál*] and Nordic Charm Magic." In *Reflections on Old Norse Myths*, ed. Pernille Hermann, Jens Peter Schjødt, and Rasmus Tranum Kristensen, 75–94. Turnhout.

———. 2008a. "The n-Rune and Nordic Charms." In *"Vi ska alla vara välkomna!" Nordiska studier tillägnade Kristinn Jóhannesson*, ed. Auður G. Magnúsdóttir et al., 219–229. Gothenburg.

———. 2008b. "*Pactum cum diabolo* og galdur á Norðurlöndum." In *Galdramenn. Galdrar og samfélag á miðöldum*, ed. Torfi H. Tulinius, 121–145. Reykjavík.

———. 2008c. "Spirituality and Alchemy in *Den vises sten* (1379)." in *Lärdomber oc skämptan: Medieval Swedish Literature Reconsidered*, ed. Massimiliano Bampi and Fulvio Ferrari, 97–108. Uppsala.

———. 2009a. "Odin, Magic and a Swedish Trial from 1484." *Scandinavian Studies* 81 (3):263– 286.

———. 2009b. "The Supernatural and the *fornaldarsögur*: The Case of *Ketils saga hængs*." In *Fornaldarsagaerne: Myter og virkelighed: Studier i de oldislandske fornaldarsögur Norðurlanda.*, ed. Agneta Ney, Ármann Jakobsson, and Annette Lassen, 281–298. Copenhagen.

———. 2011. *Witchcraft and Magic in the Nordic Middle Ages*. Philadelphia, PA.

———. 2012a. "Heroic Legend and Onomastics: *Hálfs saga*, the *Hildebrandslied* and the Listerby Stones." In *Donum natalicium digitaliter confectum Gregorio Nagy septuagenario a discipulis collegis familiaribus oblatum / A virtual birthday gift presented to Gregory Nagy on turning seventy by his students, colleagues, and friends*, ed. Leonard Mueller and David Elmer. Washington, DC. http://chs.harvard.edu/wa/pageR?tn=ArticleWrapper&bdc=12&mn=4360

———. 2012b. "*Ketils saga hængs*, *Friðþjófs saga frækna*, and the Reception of the *Canon Episcopi* in Medieval Iceland." In *Skemmtiligastar Lygisögur: Studies in Honour of Galina Glazyrina*, ed. Tatjana N. Jackson and Elena A. Melnikova, 138–147. Moscow.

———. 2012c. "Transvektion und die verleumdete Frau in der skandinavischen Tradition (*TSB D367*): Ein neuerliches Überdenken des Super-Organischen in der Folkloristik." In *Text, Reihe, Transmisson: Unfestigkeit als Phänomen skandinavischer Erzählprosa 1500–1800*, ed. Jürg Glauser and Anna Katharina Dömling, 183–204. Tübingen.

———. 2013. "Memory, Mediality, and the 'Performative Turn': Recontextualizing Remembering in Medieval Scandinavia." *Scandinavian Studies* 85 (3):282–305.

———. 2014a. "Continuity: Folklore's Problem Child?" In *Folklore in Old Norse – Old Norse in Folklore*, ed. Daniel Sävborg and Karen Bek-Pedersen, 34–51. Tartu.

———. 2014b. "Leechbooks, Manuals, and Grimoires. On the early History of Magical Texts in Scandinavia." *Arv. Nordic Yearbook of Folklore* 70:57–74.

———. 2018a. "Folklore Studies." In *Handbook of Pre-Modern Nordic Memory Studies*, ed. Jürg Glauser, Pernille Hermann, and Stephen A. Mitchell, 93–106. Berlin.

———. 2018b. "Orality and Oral Theory." In *The Handbook of Pre-Modern Nordic Memory Studies*, ed. Jürg Glauser, Pernille Hermann, and Stephen A. Mitchell, 120–131. Berlin.

———. 2018c. "U.S. Perspectives." In *The Handbook of Pre-Modern Nordic Memory Studies*, ed. Jürg Glauser, Pernille Hermann, and Stephen A. Mitchell, 866–875. Berlin.

———. 2020a. "Magic and Memory in the Medieval North." *Historisk tidskrift för Finland* 105 (3):336–364.

———. 2020b. "Old Norse Riddles and Other Verbal Contests in Performance." In *John Miles Foley's World of Oralities: Text, Tradition, and Contemporary Oral Theory*, ed. Mark C. Amodio, 123–135. York, UK.

———. 2020c. "Place-names, Periphrasis, and Popular Tradition: Odinic Toponyms on Samsø." In *Making the Profane Sacred in the Viking Age. Essays in Honour of Stefan Brink*, ed. Irene Garcia Losquiño, Olof Sundqvist, and Declan Taggart, 283–295. Turnhout.

———. 2022a. "Framing Old Norse Performance Contexts: The Wedding at Reykjahólar (1119) Revisited." In *Old Norse Poetry in Performance*, ed. Brian McMahon and Annemari Ferreira, 19–44. Abingdon, UK.

———. 2022b. "Margrete of Nordnes in Cult, Chronicle, and Ballad." *Religionsvidenskabeligt Tidsskrift*, 74:262–288.

———. 2022c. "Óðinn's Twin Ravens, Huginn and Muninn." In *Gemini and the Sacred: Twins and Twinship in Religion and Myth*, ed. Kimberley C. Patton, 397–412. London.

Mitchell, Stephen A., and Gregory Nagy. 2000. "Introduction to the Second Edition." In *Albert B. Lord. The Singer of Tales*, ed. Stephen Mitchell and Gregory Nagy, 2nd ed., vii–xxix. Cambridge, MA.

Mogk, Eugen. 1887. "Bragi als Gott und Dichter." *Beiträge zur Geschichte der deutschen Sprache und Literatur* 12:383–392.

———. 1913–1915. "Gnā." In *Reallexikon der Germanischen Altertumskunde*, ed. Johannes Hoops, 2:263. Strassburg.

Müller, Günter. 1970. *Studien zu den theriophoren Personnamen der Germanen*. Cologne and Vienna.

Mundt, Marina. 1997. "A Basic Scheme of Oral Poetry as Found in Ancient Scandinavia." *Tijdschrift voor Skandinavistiek* 18 (2):29–38.

Museum Skanderborg. 2013. "Alken Enge—The Mass Grave at Lake Mossø." http://www.skanderborgmuseum.dk/Alken_Enge-English_version-1070.aspx (accessed July 13, 2014).

Myrdal, Janken. 2003. *Digerdöden, pestvågor och ödeläggelse. Ett perspektiv på senmedeltidens Sverige*. Stockholm.

Näsström, Britt-Mari. 2006. *Bärsärkarna: Vikingatidens elitsoldater*. Stockholm.

Nagy, Gregory. 1990. *Pindar's Homer: The Lyric Possession of an Epic Past.* Baltimore.
———. 1996. *Poetry as Performance: Homer and Beyond.* Cambridge.
———. 2005 (2006). "The Epic Hero." In *A Companion to Ancient Epic*, ed. J. M. Foley), 71–89. Oxford. (2nd ed. online at http://chs.harvard.edu/ publications/)
———. 2011. "A Second Look at the Poetics of Re-enactment in *Ode* 13 of Bacchylides." In *Archaic and Classical Choral Song: Performance, Politics, and Dissemination*, ed. Lucia Athanassaki and Ewen Bowie, 173–206. Berlin.
Nagy, Joseph Falaky. 1985. *The Wisdom of the Outlaw: The Boyhood Deeds of Finn in Gaelic Narrative Tradition.* Berkeley, CA.
Nancke-Krogh, S. 1978. "Søby–en landsby fra vikingetid på Nordsamsø." *Antikvariske studier* 2:81–96.
Naumann, Hans. 1911. *Altnordische Namenstudien.* Berlin.
Naumann, Hans-Peter. 1968–. "Gutasaga." In *Reallexikon der germanischen Altertumskunde*, ed. Herbert Jankuhn, Johannes Hoops and Heinrich Beck, 13:226–228. Berlin.
Nedkvitne, Arnved. 2003. *Møtet med døden i norrøn middelalder: En mentalitetshistorisk studie.* 2nd ed. Oslo.
Neu, Jerome. 2008. *Sticks and Stones: The Philosophy of Insults.* Oxford.
Newell, William Wells. 1888. "On the Field and Work of a Journal of American Folk-Lore." *Journal of American Folk-Lore* 1:3–7.
Nielsen, Niels Åge. 1968. *Runestudier.* Odense.
Niles, John D., Tom Christensen, and Marijane Osborn, eds. 2007. *Beowulf and Lejre.* Medieval and Renaissance Texts and Studies 323. Tempe, AZ.
Nora, Pierre. 1989. "Between Memory and History: Les Lieux de Mémoire." *Representations* 26:7–24.
Nordal, Sigurður. See Sigurður Nordal.
Nordberg, Andreas. (2003) 2004. *Krigarna i Odins sal: Dödsförestallningar och krigarkult i fornnordisk religion.* 2nd ed. PhD diss., Stockholm University. Stockholm.
Noreen, Erik. 1921–1923. *Studier i västnordisk diktning.* Uppsala.
———. 1923–1929. *Studier rörande Eufemiavisorna. I-III.* Uppsala.
———. 1926. *Den norsk-isländska poesien.* Stockholm.
———. 1932. "Ordet bärsärk." *Arkiv för nordisk filologi.* 48:242–254.

Noyes, Dorothy. 1997. "Riddle." In *Folklore: An Encyclopedia of Beliefs, Customs, Tales, Music, and Art*, ed. Thomas A. Green, 728–730. Santa Barbara, CA.

———. 2009. "Three Traditions." *Journal of Folklore Research* 46 (3):233–268.

Nygaard, Simon. 2018. "...*nú knáttu Óðin sjá*: The Function of Hall-Based, Ritualised Performances of Old Norse Poetry in Pre-Christian Nordic Religion." In *The Fortified Viking Age*, ed. Mette Bruus and Jesper Hansen, 26–34. Odense.

Nygaard, Simon, and Jens Peter Schjødt. 2018. "History of Religion." In *Handbook of Pre-Modern Nordic Memory Studies*, ed. Jürg Glauser, Pernille Hermann, and Stephen A. Mitchell, 1:70–78. Berlin.

Nygaard, Simon, and Luke John Murphy. 2017. "Processioner i førkristen nordisk religion." *Religionsvidenskabeligt Tidsskrift* 66:40–77.

Nymark, Lis, and Andreas Nymark. 2018. "Beskrivelse af Samsø – topografi and bebyggelse." In *Borgene på Samsø: En arkæologisk jakt på historien bag øens fem middelalderborge*, ed. Vivian Etting. University of Southern Denmark Studies in History and Social Sciences, 558, 10–22. Odense.

Ohlmarks, Åke. 1936. "Totenerweckungen in Eddaliedern." *Arkiv för nordisk filologi* 52:264–297.

Ólason, Vésteinn. See Vésteinn Ólason.

Olrik, Axel. 1901. "Odinsjægeren i Jylland." *Dania* 8:139–173.

Olsen, Leiv. 2013. "Språkleg tolking av "Danmarkar bót"." *Maal and Minne* 105 (1):1–38.

Olsen, Magnus. 1911. "Hvad betyder oprindelig ordet skald?" In *Festskrift til H.F. Feilberg fra nordiske sprog- og folkemindesforskere på 80 års dagen den 6. august 1911*, 221–225. Pub. as *Svenska landmål 1911; Maal og minne* 1911; & *Danske Studier* 1911.

———. 1916. "Varðlokur. Et Bidrag til Kundskap om gammelnorsk Trolddom." *Maal og Minne*: 1–21.

———. 1936. "Commentarii scaldici, 1:1, Sonatorrek." *Arkiv för nordisk filologi* 52:209–255.

Olsen, Olaf. 1989. "Royal Power in Viking Age Denmark." In *Les mondes normands (VIIIe-XIIe s.) Actes du deuxième congrès international d"archéologie médiévale (Caen, 2–4 octobre 1987)*, 27–32. Actes des congrès de la Société d"archéologie médiévale, 2. Caen.

Ong, Walter J. 1982. *Orality and Literacy: The Technologizing of the Word*. London.

Ordbog over det norrøne prosasprog. A Dictionary of Old Norse Prose, ed. Aldís Sigurðardóttir, Alex Speed Kjeldsen, Bent Chr. Jacobsen et al. Copenhagen. https://onp.ku.dk/onp/onp.php.
Pakis, Valentine A. 2005. "Honor, Verbal Duels, and the New Testament in Medieval Iceland." *TijdSchrift voor Skandinavistiek* 26 (2):163–185.
Pálsson, Gísli. See Gísli Pálsson.
Pálsson, Hermann. See Hermann Pálsson.
Panzer, Friedrich. 1893. *Meister Rûmzlants Leben und Dichten*. Leipzig.
Parks, Ward. 1986. "Flyting, Sounding, Debate: Three Verbal Contest Genres." *Poetics Today* 7 (3):439–458.
———. 1990. *Verbal Dueling in Heroic Narrative: The Homeric and Old English Traditions*. Princeton, NJ.
Patton, Kimberley C. 2009. *Religion of the Gods: Ritual, Paradox, and Reflexivity*. Oxford.
Pearson, Mike, and Michael Shanks. 2001. *Theatre/Archaeology*. New York.
Pernler, Sven-Erik. 1977. *Gotlands medeltida kyrkoliv. Biskop och prosta: En kyrkorättslig studie*. Visby.
———. 1981. "Sankt Olav und Gotland." In *St. Olav, seine Zeit und sein Kult.*, ed. Gunnar Svahnström, 101–114. Visby.
Persson, Charlotte Price. 2014. "Barbarisk fund: Vores forfædre bar ligrester på kæppe." *Videnskab dk*: July 30. http://videnskab.dk/kultur-samfund/barbarisk-fund-vores-forfaedre-bar-ligrester-pa-kaeppe (accessed August 1, 2014).
Peterson, Lena. 2002. *Nordiskt runnamnslexikon med tillägg av frekvenstabeller och finalalfabetisk ordlista*. 4., rev. versionen. Språk- och folkminnesinstitutet (SOFI). http://www.sofi.se/images/runor/pdf/lexikon.pdf (accessed September 20, 2011).
Petsch, Robert. 1899. *Neue Beiträge zur Kenntnis des Volksrätsels*. Palaestra, 4. Berlin.
Phelpstead, Carl. 2009. "Adventure-Time in *Yngvars saga víðförla*." In *Fornaldarsagaerne: Myter of virkelighed*, ed. Agneta Ney, Jakobsson Ármann, and Annette Lassen, 331–346. Copenhagen.
Phillpotts, Bertha S. 1920. *The Elder Edda and Ancient Scandinavian Drama*. Cambridge.
Piltz, Anders. 1987. "Medeltidskyrkans genrer 1150–1520." In *Den svenska litteraturen*, ed. Lars Lönnroth et al., 1:57–92. Stockholm.
———. 2012. *Den signade dag: den nordiska dagvisans ursprungsfunktion. Texter, analyser, hypoteser*. Skellefteå.
Pipping, Rolf. 1928. *Oden i galgen*. Helsinki.

———. 1943. "Den fornsvenska litteraturen." In *Litteraturhistoria. A. Danmark, Finland och Sverige.*, ed. Sigurður Nordal, 64–128. Stockholm, Oslo, and Copenhagen.

Poole, Russell G., ed. 1998. *Old English Wisdom Poetry*. Annotated Bibliographies of Old and Middle English Literature, 5. Cambridge.

———, 2001. *Skaldsagas: Text, Vocation, and Desire in the Icelandic Sagas of Poets*. Berlin.

Potter, Murray Anthony. 1902. *Sohrab and Rustem: The Epic Theme of a Combat between Father and Son, A Study of its Genesis and Use in Literature and Popular Tradition*. London.

Poulsen, Fredrik. 1902. *Historiske and kulturhistoriske efterretninger om Samsø, samlede fra trykte and utrykte kilder*. Copenhagen.

Price, Neil S. 2002. *The Viking Way: Religion and War in Late Iron Age Scandinavia*. Uppsala.

———. 2008. "Bodylore and the Archaeology of Embedded Religion: Dramatic Licence in the Funerals of the Vikings." In *Belief in the Past: Theoretical Approaches to the Archaeology of Religion*, ed. D. M. Whitley and K. Hays-Gilpin, 143–165. Walnut Creek, CA.

———. 2010. "Passing into Poetry: Viking-Age Mortuary Drama and the Origins of Norse Mythology." *Medieval Archaeology* 54:123–156.

———. 2012. "Mythic Acts: Material Narratives of the Dead in Viking Age Scandinavia." In *More than Mythology: Narratives, Ritual Practices and Regional Distribution in Pre-Christian Scandinavian Religions*, ed. Catharina Raudvere and Jens Peter Schjødt, 13–46. Lund.

———. 2014. "Nine Paces from Hel: Time and Motion in Old Norse Ritual Performance." *World Archaeology* 46 (2):178–191.

———. 2019. *The Viking Way: Magic and Mind in late Iron Age Scandinavia*. 2nd ed. Barnsley, UK.

———. 2020. *Children of Ash and Elm: A History of the Vikings*. New York.

Price, Neil S., and Paul Mortimer. 2014. "An Eye for Odin? Divine Role-Playing in the Age of Sutton Hoo." *European Journal of Archaeology* 17:517–538.

Puhvel, Martin. 1987. "The Mighty She-Trolls of Icelandic Saga and Folktale." *Folklore* 98 (2):175–179.

Quinn, Judy. 1992. "Verse Form and Voice in Eddic Poems: The Discourses of *Fáfnismál*." *Arkiv för nordisk filologi* 107:100–130.

———. 1998. "'Ok verðr henni ljóð á munni'—Eddic Prophecy in the *fornaldarsögur*." *Alvíssmál* 8:29–50.

———. 2016. "The Principles of Textual Criticism and the Interpretation of Old Norse Texts Derived from Oral Tradition." In *Studies in the Transmission and Reception of Old Norse Literature: The Hyperborean Muse*, ed. Judy Quinn and Adele Cipolla, 47–78. Turnhout.

Rademann-Veith, Frauke. 2010. *Die skandinavischen Rätselbücher auf der Grundlage der deutschen Rätselbuch-Traditionen (1540–1805)*. Texte und Untersuchungen zur Germanistik und Skandinavistik, 60. Frankfurt am Main.

Ranković, Slavica, Leidulf Melve, and Else Mundal, eds. 2010. *Along the Oral-Written Continuum: Types of Texts, Relations, and Their Implications*. Turnhout.

Raudvere, Catharina, Anders Andrén, and Kristina Jennbert, eds. 2001. *Myter om det nordiska: Mellan romantik och politik*. Lund.

Reichert, Hermann, and Robert Nedoma, eds. 1987. *Lexikon der altgermanischen Namen*. Vienna.

Renoir, Alain. 1988. *A Key to Old Poems: The Oral-Formulaic Approach to the Interpretation of West- Germanic Verse*. University Park, PA.

Rigney, Ann. 2005. "Plenitude, Scarcity and the Circulation of Cultural Memory." *Journal of European Studies* 35 (1):11–28.

Róheim, Géza. 1945. *The Eternal Ones of the Dream. A Psychoanalytic Interpretation of Australian Myth and Ritual*. New York.

Rosén, Helge Ossian. 1918. *Om dödsrike och dödsbruk i fornnordisk religion*. Lund.

Roth, LuAnne. 2010. "Between OT and IT: A visit with John Miles Foley, Professor, Departments of Classical Studies and English." *Syndicate Mizzou*. April 28, 2010. http://syndicate.missouri.edu/articles/show/121 (accessed July 20, 2014).

Russell, Jeffrey Burton. 1972. *Witchcraft in the Middle Ages*. Ithaca, NY.

Rydberg, Viktor. 1886–1889. *Undersökningar i germanisk mythologi*. Stockholm.

Sällström, Åke, Arne Odd Johnsen, Anker Teilgård Laugesen, Jarl Gallén, and Jakob Benediktsson. (1956–1978) 1982. "Studiesresor" (for Sweden, Norway, Denmark, Finland, and Iceland). In *KLNM* 17: cols. 329–442.

Sävborg, Daniel. 2012. "Blockbildningen i Codex Upsalensis." *Maal og Minne* 104 (1):12–53.

Samnordisk runtextdatabas (website), ed. Lennart Elmevik, Lena Peterson and Henrik Williams. http://www.runforum.nordiska.uu.se/samnord/ Uppsala: Institutionen för nordiska språk, Uppsala universitet, 1993–.

Sanmark, Alexandra, Sarah Semple, Natascha Mehler, and Frode Iversen. 2013. "Debating the Thing in the North I. Selected Papers from Workshops Organized by The Assembly Project." *Journal of the North Atlantic* 5:1–4.
SAOB = *Ordbok öfver svenska språket*. 1893–. Svenska akademien. Lund. https://www.saob.se/.
Sawicki, Stanislaw. 1939. *Die Eufemiavisor. Stilstudien zur nordischen Reimliteratur des Mittelalters*. Lund.
Schaefer, Ursula. 1992. *Vokalität: altenglische Dichtung zwischen Mündlichkeit und Schriftlichkeit*. Tübingen.
Schechner, Richard. 1977. *Essays on Performance Theory, 1970–1976*. New York.
Scheindlin, Raymond P. 1984. "A Miniature Anthology of Medieval Hebrew Wine Songs." *Prooftexts: A Journal of Jewish Literary History* 4, no. 2:269–300.
Scheub, Harold. 1998. *Story*. Madison, WI.
Schjødt, Jens Peter. 2008. *Initiation between Two Worlds: Structure and Symbolism in Pre-Christian Scandinavian Religion*. Odense.
Schjødt, Jens Peter, John Lindow, and Anders Andrén, eds. 2020. *Pre-Christian Religions of the North. Histories and Structures*. Turnhout.
Schmid, Hans Ulrich. 2006. "Altnordisch auf Frühneuhochdeutsch. 'Gutalag' und 'Gutasaga' in einer Übersetzung von 1401." *Zeitschrift für deutsches Altertum und deutsche Literatur* 135 (1):62–88.
Schmid, Toni. 1931. *Den helige Sigfrid*. Lund.
Schramm, Gottfried. 1957. *Namenschatz und Dichtersprache. Studien zu den zweigliedrigen Personennamen der Germanen*. Göttingen.
Schröder J. H., and C. A. Weström. 1848. *De visitationibus episcoporum Lincopensium olim per Gotlandiam habitis*, Diss. acad. Uppsala.
Schütte, Gudmund. 1926–1934. *Vor Folkegruppe. Gottjod: De gotiske, tyske, nederlandske, frisiske og nordiske Stammer i etnologisk Fremstilling*. Copenhagen.
Schulte, Michael. 2007. "Memory Culture in the Viking Ages. The Runic Evidence of Formulaic Patterns." *Scripta Islandica* 58:57–74.
Schulz, Katja. 2004. *Riesen: Von Wissenshütern und Wildnisbewohnern in Edda und Saga*. Heidelberg.
See, Klaus von. 1964. "Skop und Skald: Zur Auffassung des Dichters bei den Germanen." *Germanisch-Romanisch Monatsschrift* 45:1–14.

———. 1981. "Das Problem der mündlichen Erzählprosa im Altnordischen. Der Prolog der *Þiðreks saga* und der Bericht von der Hochzeit in Reykjahólar." *Skandinavistik* 11:90–95.
See, Klaus von, Beatrice La Farge, et al., eds. 1993. *Skírnismál: Modell eines Edda-Kommentars*. Heidelberg.
———, eds. 1997–2019. *Kommentar zu den Liedern der Edda*. 7 vols. Heidelberg.
Shetelig, Haakon. 1908. "Færgepengen. Spor av en græsk gravskik i Norge." In *Sproglige og historiske afhandlinger viede Sophus Bugges minde*, ed. Magnus Olsen, 1–7. Christiania.
Shils, Edward. 1981. *Tradition*. Chicago.
Sievers, Eduard. 1894. "Germanisch *ll* aus *ðl*." *Indogermanische Forschungen* 4:335–340.
Sigurðsson, Gísli. See Gísli Sigurðsson.
Sigurður Nordal. 1927. *Völuspá = Vølvens spådom*, trans. Hans Albrectsen. Copenhagen.
———. 1958. *Hrafnkels saga Freysgoða: A Study*, trans. R. George Thomas. Cardiff. (Icelandic original 1940.)
Sijmons, Barend, and Hugo Gering. 1927. *Kommentar zu den Liedern der Edda*. Halle.
Silfverstolpe, Carl. 1898. *Klosterfolket i Vadstena. Personhistoriska anteckningar*. Stockholm.
Simek, Rudolf. 2014. "Memoria Normannica." In *Minni and Muninn. Memory in Medieval Nordic Culture*, ed. Pernille Hermann, Stephen A. Mitchell and Agnes S. Arnórsdóttir, 133–154. Turnhout.
———, ed. 1993. *Dictionary of Northern Mythology*. Cambridge.
———, ed. 1995. *Lexikon der germanischen Mythologie*. Stuttgart.
Simpson, Jacqueline. 1963–1964. "Mímir: Two Myths or One?" *Saga-Book* 16 (1):41–53.
Sjöholm, Elsa. 1976. *Gesetze als Quellen: Mittelalterlicher Geschichte des Nordens*. Stockholm.
Skott, Fredrik. 2008. *Folkets minnen: Traditionsinsamling i idé och praktik 1919–1964*. Gothenburg.
Søndergaard, Leif. 2011. "Dramatic Aspects of Medieval Magic in Scandinavia." *European Medieval Drama* 15:135–151.
Spiegel, Gabrielle M. 1983. "The Cult of St. Denis and Capetian Kingship." In *Saints and Their Cults: Studies in Religious Sociology, Folklore, and History*, ed. Stephen Wilson, 141–168. Cambridge.

Spurkland, Terje. 2004. "Literacy and 'runacy' in medieval Scandinavia." In *Scandinavia and Europe 800–1350. Contact, Conflict, and Coexistence*, ed. Jonathan Adams and Katherine Holman, 333–344. Turnhout.

Ståhle, Carl Ivar. (1952) 1967. "Medeltidens profana litteratur." In *Ny illustrerad svensk litteraturhistoria*. 2nd ed., ed. E. N. Tigerstedt and Erik Hjalmar Linder, 1:37–124. Stockholm.

Stanley, Eric Gerald. 2000. *Imagining the Anglo-Saxon Past*. Cambridge.

Steblin-Kamenskij, M. I. 1969. "On the Etymology of the Word Skald." In *Afmælisrit Jóns Helgasonar 30. juni 1969*, ed. Jakob Benediktsson et al., 421–430. Reykjavík.

Stefán Einarsson. 1957. *A History of Icelandic Literature*. New York.

Stephens, John. 1972. "The Mead of Poetry: Myth and Metaphor." *Neophilologus* 56:259–268.

Stevens, Susan T. 1991. "Charon's Obol and Other Coins in Ancient Funerary Practice." *Phoenix* 45 (3):215–229.

Stjerna, Knut. 1912. *Essays on Questions Connected with the Old English Poem of Beowulf*, trans. John R. Clark Hall. Coventry.

Stobaeus, Per. 2010. "Gutasagan - några tankar om dess uppkomst och ålder." In *Kust och kyrka på Gotland. Historiska uppsatser*, ed. Per Stobaeus, 89–101. Visby.

Ström, Folke. 1947. *Den döendes makt och Odin i trädet*. Gothenburg.

Strömbäck, Dag. 1935. Sejd. *Textstudier i nordisk religionshistoria*. Stockholm.

———. 1975. "The Concept of the Soul in Nordic Tradition." *ARV* 31:5–22.

———. 1976–1977. "Ein Beitrag zu den älteren Vorstellung von der *mara*." *ARV* 32:282–286.

———. 1977. "Marlíðendr." In *Sjötíu ritgerðir helgaðar Jakobi Benediktssyni 20. júli 1977*, ed. Einar G. Petursson and Jonas Kristjansson, 2:705–708. Reykjavík.

———. 1979a. "Folklore and Philology: Some Recollections." *ARV* 35:13–23.

———. 1979b. "To the Readers of ARV." *ARV* 35:9–11.

Stübe, R. 1924. "Kvasir und der magische Gebrauch des Speichels." In *Festschrift Eugen Mogk zum 70. Geburtstag 19. Juli 1924*, 500–509. Halle an der Saale.

Suerbaum, Almut, in collaboration with Manuele Gragnolati. 2010. "Medieval Culture 'betwixt and between': An Introduction." In *Aspects of the Performative in Medieval Culture*, ed. Manuele Gragnolati and Almut Suerbaum, 1–12. Berlin.

Sundqvist, Olof. 2002. *Freyr's Offspring: Rulers and Religion in Ancient Svea Society*. Uppsala.

———. 2009. "The Hanging, the Nine Nights and the 'Precious Knowledge' in *Hávamál* 138–145: The Cultic Context." In *Analecta Septentrionalia: Beiträge zur nordgermanischen Kultur- und Literaturgeschichte*, ed. Wilhelm Heizmann et al., 649–668. Berlin.

———. 2010. "Om hängningen, de nio nätterna och den dyrköpta kunskapen i *Hávamál* 138– 145—den kultiska kontexten." *Scripta Islandica* 61:68–96.

———. 2016. *An Arena for Higher Powers. Ceremonial Buildings and Religious Strategies for Rulership in Late Iron Age Scandinavia*. Numen: Studies in the History of Religions, 150. Leiden.

Sundqvist, Olof, and Anders Hultgård. 2004. "The Lycophoric Names of the 6th to 7th Century. Blekinge Rune Stones and the Problem of their Ideological Background." In *Namenwelten: Orts- und Personennamen in historischer Sicht*, ed. Astrid van Nahl, Lennart Elmevik, and Stefan Brink, 583–602. Berlin.

Sveinbjörn Egilsson and Finnur Jónsson, eds. (1913–1916) 1966. *Lexicon Poeticum antiquæ linguæ Septentrionalis. Ordbog over det norsk-islandske Skjaldesprog*. Rev. ed. Copenhagen.

Sveinsson, Einar Ól. See Einar Ól. Sveinsson.

Svenska akademien. *Ordbok öfver svenska språket*. See *SAOB*.

Sverrir Tómasson. 1988. *Formálar íslenskra sagnaritara á miðöldum*. Reykjavík.

Swenson, Karen. 1991. *Performing Definitions: Two Genres of Insult in Old Norse Literature*. Studies in Scandinavian Literature and Culture, 3. Columbia, SC.

Sydow, Carl von. 1922a. "Folkminnesforskning och filologi." *Folkminnen och folktankar* 8:75– 123.

———. 1922b. "Mera om Folkminnen och filologi." *Folkminnen och folktankar* 8:132–148.

———. 1944. "Folkminnesforskningens uppkomst och utveckling." *Folkkultur* 4:5–35.

Taylor, Archer. 1943. "The Riddle." *California Folklore Quarterly* 2 (2):129–147.

Terdiman, Richard. 1993. *Present Past: Modernity and the Memory Crisis*. Ithaca, NY.

Thompson, Stith, ed. 1966. *Motif-Index of Folk-Literature: A Classification of Narrative Elements in Folktales, Ballads, Myths, Fables, Mediaeval Romances, Exempla, Fabliaux, Jest- Books and Local Legends.* Rev. ed. Bloomington, IN.
Tønnesminde = "Tønnesminde," Wikimedia Foundation. https://en.wikipedia.org/wiki/Tønnesminde, November 11, 2020.
Tolley, Clive. 2009. *Shamanism in Norse Myth and Magic.* Helsinki.
Tómasson, Sverrir. See Sverrir Tómasson.
Toswell, M. Jane. 1993. "Of Dogs, Cawdels, and Contrition: A Penitential Motif in *Piers Plowman*." *The Yearbook of Langland Studies* 7:115–121.
Tracy, Larissa, and Jeff Massey, eds. 2012. *Heads Will Roll: Decapitation in the Medieval and Early Modern Imagination.* Leiden.
TSB = Bengt R. Jonsson, Svale Solheim et al., eds. 1978. *Types of the Medieval Scandinavian Ballad: A Descriptive Catalogue.* Stockholm.
Tubach, Frederic C. 1969. *Index Exemplorum: A Handbook of Medieval Religious Tales.* Helsinki.
Turner, Victor W. 1957. *Schism and Continuity in an African Society. A Study of Ndembu Village Life.* Manchester.
———. 1967. *The Forest of Symbols: Aspects of Ndembu Ritual.* Ithaca, NY.
———. 1971. "An Anthropological Approach to the Icelandic Saga." In *The Translation of Culture*, ed. T. O. Beidelman, 349–374. London.
———. 1980. "Social Dramas and Stories about Them." *Critical Inquiry* 7 (1):141–168.
Turville-Petre, Gabriel. (1964) 1975. *Myth and Religion of the North: The Religion of Ancient Scandinavia.* Westport, CT.
Tylor, Edward B. 1871. *Primitive Culture: Researches into the Development of Mythology, Philosophy, Religion, Art, and Custom.* 2 vols. London.
Valdimar Tr. Hafstein. 2000. "Biological Metaphors in Folklore Scholarship. An Essay in the History of Ideas." *ARV* 57:7–32.
Vésteinn Ólason. 1978. "Ballad and Romance in Medieval Iceland." In *Ballads and Ballad Research*, ed. Patricia Conroy, 26–36. Seattle.
———. 2003. "The Un/Grateful Dead—From Baldr to Bægifótr." In *Old Norse Myths, Literature and Society*, ed. Margaret Clunies-Ross, 153–171. Viborg.
Vikstrand, Per. 2001. *Gudarnas platser: förkristna sakrala ortnamn i Mälarlandskapen.* Acta Academiae Regiae Gustavi Adolphi. Studier till en svensk ortnamnsatlas, 17. Uppsala.
Vilmundarson, Þórhallur. See Þórhallur Vilmundarson.

Vries, Jan de. 1934. "Om Eddaens Visdomsdigtning." *Arkiv för nordisk filologi* 50:1–59.
———. 1935-37. *Altgermanische Religionsgeschichte*. Berlin.
———. 1953. "Das Motiv der Vater-Sohn-Kampfes im *Hildebrandslied*." *Germanisch-Romanisch Monatsschrift*. 34:257–274.
———. 1956–1957. *Altgermanische Religionsgeschichte*. 2nd ed. 2 vols. Berlin.
———, ed. 1961. *Altnordisches etymologisches Wörterbuch*. Leiden.
———. 1962. "Wodan und die Wilde Jagd." *Die Nachbarn* 3:31–59.
Wahlgren, Erik. 1939. "A Swedish-Latin Parallel to the *Joca Monachorum*." *Modern Philology* 36:239–245.
Wald, Elijah. 2012. *The Dozens: A History of Rap's Mama*. Oxford.
Warring, Anette. 2005. *Historie, magt and identitet – Grundlovsfejringer gennem 150 år*. Århus.
Weibull, Curt. 1932. "Folkviseforskning." *Scandia* 5:81–102.
Weiser-Aall, Lilli. 1927. *Altgermanischen Jünglingsweihen und Männerbunde: Ein Beitrag zur deutschen und nordischen Altertums- und Volkskunde*. Bühl in Baden.
Welsh, Andrew. 2000. "Riddle." In *Medieval Folklore: An Encyclopedia of Myths, Legends, Tales, Beliefs, and Custom*, ed. Carl Lindahl, John McNamara, and John Lindow, 824–832. Santa Barbara, CA.
Werlich, Egon. 1964. *Der westgermanische Skop: Der Aufbau seiner Dichtung und sein Vortrag*. Diss. Münster.
———. 1967. "Der westgermanische Skop: Der Ursprung des Sängerstandes in semasiologischer und etymologischer Sicht." *Zeitschrift für deutsche Philologie* 86:352– 375.
Wertsch, James V. 2008. "The Narrative Organization of Collective Memory." *Ethos* 36 (1):120–135.
Wessén, Elias. 1924. "Gestumblindi." In *Festskrift tillägnad Hugo Pipping på hans sextioårsdag den 5 november 1924* (Skrifter utgivna av Svenska Litteratursällskapet i Finland, 175), 537–548. Helsinki.
———. 1928. "Om de nordiska folkvisornas språkform." *Nysvenska studier* 8:43–69.
———. (1956–1978) 1982. "Gutasagan." In *KLNM* 5: col. 603.
Westman, K. G. 1943. "Bidrag till problemet om Nerthus-Frökulten i Sverige." *Saga och Sed*: 199–204.
Wiborg, K. F. 1848. *Fremstillning af Nordens Mythologi*. Copenhagen.
Wilbur, Terrence H. 1958. "Troll, an etymological note." *Scandinavian Studies* 30:137–139.

Wilgus, D. K. 1973. "'The Text Is the Thing.'" *Journal of American Folklore* 86:241–252.
Wolff, Samuel R. 2002. "Mortuary Practices in the Persian Period of the Levant." *Near Eastern Archaeology* (special issue, *The Archaeology of Death*) 65 (2):131–137.
Würth, Stefanie. 2007. "Skaldic Poetry and Performance." In *Learning and Understanding in the Old Norse World: Essays in Honour of Margaret Clunies Ross*, ed. Judy Quinn, Kate Heslop and Tarrin Wills, 263–281. Turnhout
Yates, Frances Amelia. 1974. *The Art of Memory*. Chicago.
Zachrisson, Torun. 2003. "The Queen of Mist and the Lord of the Mountain. Oral Traditions of the Landscape and Monuments in the Omberg area of western Östergötland." *Current Swedish Archaeology*, 11:119–138.
———. 2018. "Sites." In *The Handbook of Pre-Modern Nordic Memory Studies*, ed. Jürg Glauser, Pernille Hermann, and Stephen A. Mitchell, 620–626. Berlin.
Zaleski, Carol G. 1985. "St. Patrick's Purgatory: Pilgrimage Motifs in a Medieval Otherworld Vision." *Journal of the History of Ideas* 46.4:467–485.
Zilmer, Kristel. 2009. "Scenes of Iceland Encounters in Icelandic Sagas: Reflections of Cultural Memory." *Viking and Medieval Scandinavia* 4:227–248.
Zilmer, Kristel, and Judith Jesch, eds. 2012. *Epigraphic Literacy and Christian Identity: Modes of Written Discourse in the Newly Christian European North*. Turnhout.
Zoëga, Geir T. (1910) 1975. *A Concise Dictionary of Old Icelandic*. Oxford.
Zumthor, Paul. 1972. *Essai de poétique médiévale*. Paris. (Trans. as *Toward a Medieval Poetics*, trans. Philip Bennett, Minneapolis, 1992.)
———. 1983. *Introduction à la poésie orale*. Paris. (Trans. as *Oral Poetry: An Introduction*, trans. Kathryn Murphy-Judy, Minneapolis, 1990.)
Zumwalt, Rosemary Lévy. 1988. *American Folklore Scholarship: A Dialogue of Dissent*. Bloomington, IN.
Þórhallur Vilmundarson. 1961. "Fundin Þjóðhildarkirkja. Happaverk Lars Motzfeldts." *Tímarit. Árbók Hins íslenzka fornleifafélags* 58:162–167.

INDEX

Note: Articles in English (*e.g., a, the*) are ignored in alphabetization, but those in other languages (e.g., *Die, den*) are observed. Brief identifying phrases added as an aid: Da = Danish; Nwg = Norwegian; Sw = Swedish

Abbo of Fleury, abbot († 1004), 141
Abrahams, Roger, 18, 85 n18
Adam of Bremen, 5–6, 8, 37, 130, 177, 227
Äldre Västgötalagen, 98
Ælfric of Eynsham, abbot († 1010), 140, 141–42 n33
Æsir gods, 8, 56, 61, 94, 110, 123, 128; war with the Vanir gods, 56
Ahola, Joonas, 132
aft (in memory of), 149–50
Akergarn, Gotland, 196
Alken Enge, Jutland, 131
Alrekr Agnason, legendary Sw king, 211
Alver, Brynjulf, 13, 84
Alvíssmál, 82
Anders Vedel, Da priest and historian († 1616), 181
Andreas Suneson, Da archbishop († 1228), 192, 193
Andrén, Anders, 7 n11, 21, 161 n35, 177, 185 n33
Angantyrs Høj (Angantýr's mound), local onomastic tradition on Samsø, 181
Ansgar, saint. *See* saints

anthroponymy, 215, 222
apprenticeship, 29, 154–55
archaeology, 19, 21, 37–38, 183
Ari Þorgilsson, Icelandic historian († 1148), 158
Ármóðr (Armod), saga figure, 59–60
Árna saga byskups, 177
arnar kjapta órð (seed [or produce] of the eagle's beak), 61
Arngrímr, sons of, 179–80
Arngrímur Jónsson hinn lærði (the learned), Icelandic scholar († 1648), 171
Ásgarðr, mythical location, 56, 120
Ásmundar saga kappabana, 215–17, 224, 227
Ásmundr Ákason, legendary champion, 212, 215, 217
asphyxia, death by, 137
Assmann, Jan, 15, 28, 44, 184 n31, 205 n41
AT 706 "The Maiden without Hands," 252
Augustine of Hippo, saint. *See* saints
authenticity, 38, 157, 241
Baldr, god, 8, 85, 215, 217, 223

Baldrs draumar, 127, 129, 134, 146, 217 n28
ballad(s), 3, 10–11, 23, 49, 177, 179–81, 188, 212, 241–43
Bauman, Richard, 17 n20, 18 n24, 19, 34, 44–45, 52 n3, 54, 76
Bendix, Regina, 38, 137 n22
Beowulf, 215, 217–18
berserkr, pl. *berserkir*, 68, 179–80, 210, 220–21, 226–29, 282; *berserksgangr* (berkerskr fury), 227
Bible passages – Genesis 1:1–2:3, 2:4–2:25, 194; Genesis 6:4, 170; I Samuel 28, 81, 140; Proverbs 4:12, 81, 254; Matthew 14:1–11, 140; Mark 6:14–29, 140; Luke 1:19; 1 Peter 2:8, 254
Bidney, David, 16, 43
Birger Jarl (Magnussson), Sw aristocrat († 1266), 238–39
Birka, 22. 176
Birgitta, saint. *See* saints
biskupasögur (sagas of bishops), 9
Bjarni Kolbeinsson, bishop of the Orkneys († 1222), 103
Björketorp (DR 360). *See* runic inscriptions
Black Death (*digerdöden*), 201
Blåkulla myth, 113
Boberg, Inger, 12, 42, 181 n23
Boccaccio, Giovanni, author († 1375), 249
Bookprose. *See* Freeprose-Bookprose
Botair of Akebäck, figure in *Guta saga*, 187, 199
Bragi, god, 28, 56, 108 n7
Bragi Boddason inn gamli (the old), skald, 55, 250
Brennu-Njáls saga, 5
Brevis Historia Regum Dacie, 171, 175
Brink, Stefan, 8, 13, 23, 185
Brokkr, dwarf, 96

Brynjarr (*haugbúi* in *Þorsteins þáttr uxafóts*), 134, 138
Bulfinch, Thomas, 1
Burchard of Worms, bishop and canonist († 1025), 112
Bureus, Johannes, Sw antiquarian († 1652), 12
Byzantine empire, 5, 6
Camillus Leonardi, 145
Canon episcopi, 112, 121, 122
Celebremus karissimi, 142
central places, 169–70, 171–77, 185–86
cephalophoric saints. *See* saints
charms, xx, 8–9, 99–100, 125–28, 145, 147, 159, 245–47
"Charon's obol," 139–43
Chaucer, Geoffrey, poet († 1400), 249
church murals, 11, 113
collective memory, 14, 28–29, 158, 185, 189, 200 n27, 204
colonialism, inter-Nordic, 30, 53
communicative memory, 15, 17
composition-in-performance, 12, 33, 35, 52, 57, 154
continuity (< hold together), 3, 11, 15, 16, 35–50, 139, 170, 173, 176, 201, 253, 261
Christianity, conversion to, 5, 8, 82, 142, 194, 196–203, 225
Ćor Huso, legendary South Slavic singer, 58
corpse, 105, 119, 125–32, 134–35, 137, 139, 142, 144, 146–47, 178
creative recall or *memoria rerum*, 13, 15, 29
cross-disciplinary, 3–4, 15, 17, 22, 24, 36, 201 n29, 205 n42
cultural memory, 12–16, 23–24, 28–29, 44, 150, 158, 184–87, 201 n29, 205

daemones, demons 111, 112, 115 n21, 253–54, 256
Dante Alighieri, poet († 1321), 248, 255
Davidson, H. R. Ellis, 127 n6, 128 n8
De civitate Dei, 111
De Lapidibus, 144
dead, 112, 116, 121, 127–35, 137, 139, 140, 142–47. 149–50, 180. See also corpse, corpses
deep past, 159, 170, 222–23
Den signade dag, 245 n3, 255
Den vises sten, 248, 249
Denis, saint. *See* saints
Diana, pagan goddess, 112–13
"double bind," 223–24
Draupnir, magic ring, 96
dreams, 115–17; prophecies as dreams and "warning verses," 117
Dudo of Saint-Quentin, Norman chronicler († 1026), 6
Dumézil, Georges, 8, 94
Dundes, Alan, 49, 79 n6
E90 ballad materials (*Angelfyr og Helmer kamp*), 179–81
Edmund of East Anglia, saint. *See* saints
Egill Skallagrímsson, saga figure († 990), 59–62, 63, 154–55, 163, 238
Einar Ól. Sveinsson, 235
Einarr Skúlason, skald († c. 1159) 154, 236
Einarr þambarskelfir (paunch-shaker) Eindriðason, Nwg aristocrat († c. 1050), 178
Erik Magnusson, Sw duke († 1318), 10, 239–40
Erik, saint. *See* saints

Eiríkr I Haraldsson, known as *blóðøx* (blood-axe), Nwg king († c. 954), 153–55, 183,
Eiríkr Emundarson, legendary Sw king, 153
Eiríks saga rauða, 118–19, 123, 155
Eiríks saga víðfǫrla, 111–12
Eiríksmál, 152
Elinsofficiet, 248
Elucidarius, 98, 100
En allegorisk dikt (dröm eller saga), 245,254
encyclopedic literature, 11
"enskilment," 32
erfikvæði (also: *erfidrápa, erfiljóð*), Nordic tradition of elegy, 152
Erikskrönikan (*The Chronicle of Duke Erik*), 16, 241–43
Erll, Astrid, 15, 28
"ethnic memory," 201
ethnobotany, 17 n30
ethnography, 2, 11, 18, 20, 23, 29, 46, 54, 64, 87 n22, 158, 167, 254
"ethnography of communications," 16–20,23, 35; also known as: "ethnography of speaking," 19 n25, 23, 51, 54, 158
ethnohistory, 15, 36, 201
Eufemia of Rügen († 1312). *See* queens and other royal consorts
Eufemiavisor (Eufemia's Songs), 10, 241
Evans-Pritchard, E. E., 167
"evening-riders," "shape-shifters" (*kveldriður eða hamleypur*), 112–13
Exeter Book, 11, 169
Eyrbyggia saga, 129 n8
Eysteinn I Magnússon, Nwg king († 1123), 154
Fabech, Charlotte, 173
Fagrskinna, 178

Fama, Roman goddess (Φήμη among the Greeks), 108–09
Fenrir, "the Binding of Fenrir," 93–95, 96, 99
"Ferryman's Fee" or "Charon's obol, " (Thompson 1966: P613), 126, 139, 142–43, 145
"fictionalized orality" (*Fingierte Mündlichkeit*), 35, 159
Finnish Historical-Geographic School, 18, 42, 44
Finnur Jónsson, 79, 97, 107, 237 n9
Flateyjarbók, 23, 128 n8, 179, 238 n10
flight, flying, 65, 105–06, 108–09, 110–11, 113, 115, 121–23; airborne figures (*marlíðendr, tunríðor, myrkríðor,* and *valkyrjor, englar*), 114–15, 121–22; feathered or falcon cloak (*fjaðrhamr; valshamr*), 111
Flores och Blanzeflor, 240, 243
flyting, 88
Foley, John Miles, 17, 28, 35, 45, 54, 76, 77, 88, 90, 162 n37
"folk memories" (*folkminnen*), 11; "folk memory studies" (*folkminnesforskning, þjóðminjafræði,* etc.), 28
Folk-Lore (neologism for "popular antiquities"), 14, 18, 28, 49
folkloristics, xvii, 1–3, 11, 14, 18–19, 29, 36, 42, 51, 157–58
For Scírnis (also: *Skírnismál*), xix, 93–95, 109, 119–20, 147
fornaldarsaga. pl. *fornaldarsögur* (sagas of antiquity), 9, 83, 170, 178
Fornsvenska legendariet (also: *Ett fornsvenskt legendarium*), 141 n30
frænd-víg "parricide," 216, 223 n42
Frea tricks Godan, 38
Freeprose-Bookprose, 12–13, 31, 34, 52–53, 76, 165

Freiprosa – Buchprosa. See Freeprose-Bookprose
Freyja, 8, 108 n7, 111, 122–23,
Freyr, 8, 93–95, 109, 119–20, 221 n38
Frigg, 103–06, 109–10, 121–22; Frigg as "queen of the Æsir and Asyniur," 110 n12
Fróðafriðr (peace of Fróði), 174
Fuglesang, Signe Horn, 139
Fyrkat, 22
Gabriel, archangel, 120
Gaiman, Neil (*Norse Mythology*, 2017), 2
Galgberget [lit. "Gallows Hill"] in Södermalm, 132
Gallehus horns, 4, 220
gallows-corpse (*virgilnár*), 131, 134
gallows' social functions, 132
Gansum, Terje, 21
Gardrofa, mythical horse, 106
Gautreks saga, 96, 133, 211, 228
Geertz, Clifford, 54, 76, 158 n25
Geete, Robert, 245–47, 256
Geirmundar þáttr heljarskinns, 210
Geirríðr Þórólfsdóttir, 115
genealog/y, -ies, -ical 3, 46, 77, 159, 161, 203, 209–12, 216, 222–24
Georges, Robert, 49
Gerðr, giantess, 93, 95, 119
Gering, Hugo, 107
Gesta Danorum, 3, 5, 7, 83, 134–35, 147, 170, 171, 178–80, 185, 215–18
Gesta hammaburgensis ecclesiae pontificum (*History of the Hamburg-Bremen archbishopric*), 5, 6, 8, 37, 130 n9, 177, 227
"Gesta Saxonum," 164
Gestumblindi, Óðinn in disguise, 83–85, 89

gift, ethnography of giving and receiving, 64, 129, 139, 194, 196, 198, 236, 238
Gísl Illugason, skald († early 12th c.), 152
Gísli Pálsson, 32
Gísli Sigurðsson, 13, 16, 24, 35, 36, 38 n2, 160 n32, 187
Glauser, Jürg, 15, 16, 35, 158 n26, 159 n27, 184, 185 n32, 190 n4
Gleipnir, mythical fetter, 93–98
Gná, goddess, xviii, 103–23
gnomic poetry, wisdom, 33
Goliard verse form, 246, 248
Göngu-Hrólfs saga, 177e
Gormr inn gamli (the old), Da king († c. 960s), 175–76, 186
Gorm stone at Jelling (DR 41). See runic inscriptions
Gotland, 21, 57, 65–66, 111 n15, 134, 139, 189–205
Grabka, Gregory, 143, 144 n37
Grænlendinga saga, 135
Grágás, 131–32
grammatical treatises, 10
Gratianus, monk and canonist († c. 1159), 112
Greenland, Norse colony in, 2, 6, 38, 118, 163, 261
Grettir Ásmundarson, saga figure, 63, 134
Grettis saga Ásmundarsonar, 63, 134
Gríðr, troll, 251
Grimm, Jacob, 12, 51, 109
Grímnismál, 133
Grógaldr, 127, 134, 146 n43
Guðmundr, skald, 235
Guðríðr Þorbjarnardóttir, saga figure, 119, 162–63
Guðrúnarqviða ǫnnor, 210
guest-host relationship, 63–64, 69–71, 74, 156
guldgubbar, 178

Gullinbursti, mythical boar, 96
Gummarp (DR 358 U). See runic inscriptions
Gungnir, mythical spear, 96
Gunnell, Terry, 13, 20–21, 34, 77 n2, 158
Gunnhildr Ǫzuradóttir, Nwg queen, 163
Gunnlaugr Þorbjarnarson, saga figure, 165
Gunnlǫð, giantess, 56
Guta saga, 191–200; manuscript (Cod. Holm. B64), 191–92; Swedish, German, and Danish translations, 192
Gylfaginning, 105, 108, 110, 122, 127, 217 n28
Gyrðr, giantess, 115–16
Haddingus, legendary Da king, 134–35
Hæðcyn, legendary figure, 217–18
Hákonarsaga Hákonarsonar, 234, 235, 243
Halbwachs, Maurice, 14, 28, 44, 157, 184–85, 204
Hálfr Hjǫrleifsson, saga figure, 210–14, 217–18
Hálfr (< haþu-wulfR "battle-wolf" [< haþu- "battle" + wulfR "wolf"]), 213
Hálfs bani (Hálfr's bane), kenning for "fire," 210
Hálfs saga ok Hálfsrekka, 133 n16, 210–15
Hallbjǫrn, known as *hali* (tail), skald, 137–38
Halldór Snorrason, 155
Halli, known as Sneglu-Halli (Sarcastic-Halli), skald, 69–71, 238
Hamskerpir, mythical horse, 105–07
Hans Nielsson Strelow. See Strelow

Harald Hildetand (*hilditǫnn*, "wartooth") legendary king, 171, 174;
  Harald Hildetandshøj (Harald
  Wartooth's mound), 174
Harald stone at Jelling (DR 42). *See*
  runic inscriptions
Haraldr Gormsson, known as *blátǫnn*
  (blue tooth), Da king († c. 985),
  186; Harald's stone at Jelling (DR
  42), 5, 185
Haraldr I Hálfdanarson, known as *inn
  hárfagri* (the fair-haired), Nwg
  king († c. 940), 104
Haraldr III Sigurðarson, known as
  inn harðráði (the hard-rule), Nwg
  king († 1066), 6, 69, 71, 115–16,
  155–56, 178, 238
Haralds saga Sigurðarsonar, 115–16,
  178
Hárbarðzlióð, 221–22, 226
Hariwulfar ("army-wolf" > ON
  Herjólfr), 214, 217, 219
Harris, Joseph, 34–35, 66 n30, 70 n
  36, 77 n2, 88, 126 n3
Harthgrepa, giantess, 127 n6, 134–35,
  147
Hartmann, Elizabeth, 250, 254
Háttstrykr, mythical horse, 107
haugbúi (mound-dweller), pl. *haug-
  búar*, 134, 137–39, 146
Haustlǫng, 8
Hautala, Jouko, 42
Hávamál, 113, 125–27, 130–32,
  134–35, 137, 139, 140, 144–47
Haþuwulfar ("battle-wolf" > ON
  Hálfr), 213–14, 217–18
head of saint, severed, speaks
  (Thompson 1966: V229.25),
  140–42
Heide, Eldar, 178, 184 n28
heilagramanna sögur (sagas of saints),
  9

Helvig of Holstein († c. 1325). *See*
  queens and other royal consorts
Heimskringla, 13, 104, 108 n8, 116,
  178, 210 n4, 226 n52. *See* also
  under the titles of individual
  sagas
Hemings þáttr Áslákssonar, 116, 122
Henrik Institoris Kramer, inquisitor
  († 1505), 253
Herder, Johan Gottfried, 30
Herebeald, legendary figure, 217–18
Herjólfsnes, 163
Herkules vid skiljo-vägen (*Hercules at
  the crossroad*), 255
Hermann, Pernille, 15, 16, 32, 35,
  151 n9, 152, 157, 185, 188
Herodias, 112–13
"heron of forgetfulness" (*óminnis
  hegri*), 152
Herr Ivan Lejonriddare, 240, 243
Herthadalen, 172
Hertig Fredrik af Normandie, 240–43
Heruwulfar ("sword-wolf" > ON
  Hjǫrólfr), 214, 217
Hervarar saga ok Heiðreks konungs, 11,
  20, 64, 98–99, 135, 146, 179,
  181, 216
Hervǫr, legendary figure, daughter of
  Angantýr, 179–80
Heusler, Andreas, 13, 31, 79
Hildebrand, 216, 222
Hildebrandslied, 209, 215–16, 221,
  222, 224–25
Hildólfr (< *hildi-wulfar* "battle-
  wolf"), 221, 222, 226
Hildr, legendary figure, Hjǫrleifr's
  second wife, 211–12
Hirst, Michael, 2
*Historia de antiquitate regum
  Norwagiensium*, 5 n9, 234 n6
Historia Norwegiæ, 115, 157
Historia Sancti Olaí, 242

Hjálmarr, legendary figure, known as *inn hugumstóri* ("the high-hearted"), 179, 180, 262
Hjalti, legendary figure. See Hǫttr
Hjalti Þorðarson, his *erfikvæði*, 152
Hjǫrleifr Hjǫrsson, legendary figure, known as *inn kvensami* ("the womanizer," "the amorous"), 133, 211–12, 226
Hjǫrólfr Hjǫrleifsson, legendary figure, Hálfr's brother, 212, 214
Hǫðr, blind god, 218, 221 n38, 223, 226
Hœnir, god, 127–28
Höfler, Otto, 38–39
Hǫttr (< "hood," "cowl," in *Hrólfs saga kraka*), later called Hjalti (< *hjalt*, the boss of a sword or its guard), 174 n12, 227–29
Hofvarpnir, mythical horse, 106, 109
Holmgeirr, father of Sigrøðr, on the Ramsund inscription (Sö 101), 161
Holocaust, the, 14
Homer and "the Homeric Question," 20, 29, 31, 51–52, 58, 64, 209, 226 n50
hómilíubók, Icelandic, 120
hráki Gleipnis tuggu = "the spittle of Gleipnir's mouthful" = "Fenrir's saliva" = the river Vǫ́n, 99
Hrólfr kraki, 171–72, 211
Hrólfs saga kraka, 171, 172, 227, 228 n58
*Huldar saga, 232, 234–35
Hultgård, Anders, 215, 219, 225, 228–29
Husaby, Västergötland, 142
Huyssen, Andreas, 28
Hyltén-Cavallius, Gunnar Olof, 12–13
Hymes, Dell, 18, 54, 158 n26
Hyndloljóð, 127, 134, 179, 180

Iliad, 21
Illuga saga Gríðarfóstra, 251
Ingibjǫrg of Denmark († 1287). See queens and other royal consorts
Ingibjǫrg († 1318). See queens and other royal consorts
Ingrid Svantepolksdotter, Sw aristocrat and abbess († mid-14th c.), 241
Ingunn Ásdísardóttir, 109, 110 n12, 122
Innsteinn Álfsson, legendary figure, 212
interdisciplinarity, 3–4, 15, 17, 22–24
íslendingasögur (sagas of Icelanders), 9
Istaby (DR 359 U). See runic inscriptions
Jacobus de Voragine, archbishop and chronicler († 1298), 141
Jakob Sprenger, inquisitor († 1495), 253
Jelling, 5, 172, 174–46, 185–86, 188
Joca Monachorum, 82
jǫtunn, jǫtnar (giant, -s), 8, 56, 57, 86, 111, 120, 169–70, 220, 252
John Cassian, saint. See saints
Jómsvíkingadrápa, 103
Jón Guðmundsson lærði, Icelandic scholar and poet († 1658), 12
Jón Helgason, 60, 97
Jóns saga Baptista, 112
journey monomyth, 255
Jungfru Marias sju fröjder, 245
Kalmar, Union of, 7, 30
Kanerva, Kirsi, 126
Kanhave canal, Samsø, 182–84, 186–88
Kaplan, Merrill, 23–24
Karlevi (Öl 1). See runic inscriptions
Karolus Benedicti, general confessor at Vadstena († 1528), 252
Kárr inn gamli (the old), legendary figure in *Grettis saga*), 134

Katla í Holti, saga figure, 115
Keary, Annie and Eliza (*The Heroes of Asgard*, 1857), 1
kenning, -s, 7, 61, 79–80, 86, 89, 99–100, 103–05, 108, 121, 171, 210
Keyser, Rudolf, 51
knights, knighthood, 9–10, 231–32, 241, 243
knittel-verse, 10, 248–49
Knútr, saint. *See* saints
Knútr VI Valdemarsson, Da king († 1202), 178
Knýtlinga saga, 174, 177, 236–37
Köngäs-Maranda, Elli-Kaija, 42–43
Kong Valdemars Jordebog, 184
Konung Alexander, 242
konungasögur (sagas of kings), 9
Konungs skuggsjá (King's Mirror), 10, 98
Krappe, Alexander, 18
Kristi lidande, also known as *Kristi pina* ("Christ's Suffering"), 242, 248
Kroeber, Alfred, 18, 41–42, 143 n36
Krohn, Julius, 42
Krohn, Kaarle, 18, 42
Kulstäde, Gotland, 197
Kumlbúa þáttr, 134
Kunstpoesie (art or elite poetry), 30
Kvasir, mythological figure, 56–57, 60–61
Kvinneby amulet (Öl SAS1989;43). *See* runic inscriptions
L'Anse aux Meadows, Newfoundland, Canada, 6
Lachmann, Karl, 30
Lärbro Stora Hammars stones, Gotland, 57 n13, 64, 133, 137
Landnámabók, 152
Lang, Andrew, 40–42, 205 n41
lapidaries, 10, 144

Last Rites to the dying (*viaticum*), 143–45
Laugerud, Henning, 14
laws, 7–8, 13, 63, 141, 146, 191, 251; canon law, 112; *Grágás*, 131–32; *Laws of Gotland* (*Gutalagen*), 191–92; *Laws of Hälsingland* (*Hälsingelagen*), 190–91; *Laws of Västergötland* (*Västgötalagen*), 80–81; *Older Law of Frǫstaþing* (*Frostatingsloven*), 146
lawman, lawspeaker, 13, 152, 241
Le Goff, Jacques, 28, 44, 200 n27, 201 n29
Lee, Stan, 1–2
Legenda aurea of Jacobus de Voragine, 141
Lejre (ON Hleiðargarðr, now Gammel Lejre), 38, 171–74, 185–86, 188
Lejrekrøniken, 171
Liedertheorie (song theory), 30
Likkair of Stenkyrka, Gotland; later: Likkair Snielli ("the wise"), 197, 199
Lilla rimkrönikan, 82
Linderholm, Emanuel, 245–46, 250, 256
Lindow, John, 80, 86–87, 111, 250, 253
linguistic anthropology, 16, 158,
Listerby-stones (Stentoften, Gummarp, Istaby, Björketorp). *See* runic inscriptions
Locasenna, 122, 178
Loki, 8, 96, 105, 122, 178
Lönnroth, Lars, 34, 151, 159 n27
Lord, Albert B., 17, 20, 27, 29, 31–35, 51, 54
Loumand, Ulla, 110
Love, Jeffrey, 79, 84 n16, 85
lycanthropy, 215
Macarius and the Magicians, 140

magic, 8–9, 118–19, 126–29, 134–35, 144–47, 162–63, 167, 178–79, 191; Bronze Age magico-religious world, 4; magical flight, 111, 119, *seiðr*, 123, 178
Magister Mathias (Matts Övidsson, † 1350), 248
"magnate farms," 173
Magnús I Óláfsson, known as *inn góði* (the good), Nwg king († 1047), 178
Magnús III Óláfsson, known as *berfœttr* (barefoot), Nwg king († 1103), 152
Magnús V Erlingsson, Nwg king († 1184), 237
Magnús VI Hákonarson, known as *lagabœtir* (law-mender), Nwg king († 1280), 71, 74, 166, 235,
Magnús Birgersson, known as Ladulås (barn-lock), Sw king († 1290), 239, 241
Magnúss saga berfœtts, 122
Magus saga jarls, 211
Malinowski, Bronislaw, 29
Malleus maleficarum, 253
Männerbunde, 225, 229
Máni (the Skáld-Máni of *Skáldatal*?) at Nwg court of Magnús Erlingsson († late 12th c.?), 237–38
mannajafnaðr, 221
Marbod of Rennes, bishop and author († 1123), 144
Margrete of Denmark († 1412). See queens and other royal consorts
Margaret of Scotland († 1283). See queens and other royal consorts
marlíðendr (sea-spirits ??), 114–15, 121

Martin, Richard, 75
"Master Builder," 96
Maurer, Konrad von, 51
McKinnell, John, 128,
mead, poetic; myth of the acquisition of the, 56–58, 60–62, 65–67, 76, 111
Međedović, Avdo, 33
mediality, 15, 149.51, 157–60, 164–67, 185, 191
memoria rerum (i.e. creative recall), 15, 29
memoria verborum (i.e. rote memory), 15, 29
memory, xvii, xx, 1–2, 12–17, 22–44, 149–67, 169, 176–80, 183–93, 200–05, 214; as a storehouse," 32, 188
"men of memory." See *minnugha mæn*
mentifact, 16, 18, 43, 201
Meulengracht Sørensen, Preben, 156, 164
Mímir, god, 127–28, 140
"mindscape," 178, 185
minnugha mæn, "men of memory," 190–91
miracle, blind man regains his sight on Sámsey, 178
Mjǫllnir, Þórrs hammer, 8, 96
mnemohistory, 44, 201
Möbius, Theodor, 51, 97
Morkinskinna, 69–71, 116, 154, 155–56, 178, 238 n10
Much, Rudolf, 38–39
Munarvogar (also Mínnívogar), 180
Muninn, news-gathering raven, (< *muna* "to remember"), 152
musical instruments at Nordic courts (e.g., fiddle and pipes), 236–37

myth -s, xvii, 3–4, 7–8, 10, 27, 52, 55, 76, 82, 95, 98–100, 103, 110, 119, 122–23, 125, 146, 152, 198, 201, 221, 222–25, 228; aetiological, 56, 97; creation, 194; Indo-European, 57, 218–19, 225; involving the dead and dying, 126–29, 132; involving flight, 108–09, 111; journey monomyth, 255; of Blåkulla, 113; of the conversion of Gotland, 200; of the making of Gleipnir and the binding of Fenrir, 93–96; of the Mead of Poetry, 58, 62; of Tuisto, the Germanic progenitor, 200; parricidal, 217–18; theoretical approaches to, 93

Nagy, Gregory, 17 n21, 20 n32, 28, 34, 45, 54, 57, 66, 209–10, 222–26, 228

National Socialism, 38–39, 48

náttúrur (spirits), 119, 122–23,

Naturpoesie (natural or "folk" poetry), 30

necromancy, 125–27, 147

New Philology, 35, 158 n26

New World, Vínland, 6, 24, 88, 143, 174, 187

Niels Pedersen (alt., Nicolaus Petreius), author († 1568), 193, 198

Nora, Pierre, 28, 184

Nordic Bronze Age, 4, 169, 171

Nóregs konunga tal, 178

Norse, as term, 3 n4

Norumbega, 274

oblivion, absence of memory, 12, 71, 201 n30, 204, 235

Oddný (in *Þorsteins þáttr uxafóts*), 138–39

Oddr Breiðfirðingr, skald, 152

Oddr (*haugbúi* in *Þorsteins þáttr uxafóts*), 138

"Odin fra Lejre," 173

Óðinn (Odin), 1, 2, 8, 55–65, 83–86, 96, 98, 110–111, 113, 121, 126–31, 133–35, 137, 140, 145–47, 152, 178, 211, 221–22, 226–28, 263; and later folklore traditions, 13, 47–48; and the *berserksgangr* (battlefield fits of frenzy), 227; as "fury," ("Wodan, id est furor"), 227; cognomen "god of the hanged" in various forms, including *hanga-Týr, hangaguð, hangadróttinn, heimþinguðr hanga*, 137; etymology from **Wōþanaz*, 226–27; slandered by Loki, 178; speaks entirely in meter, 55; his priests called songsmiths (*ljóðasmiðir*), 55

Qlvir hnúfa, skald, 104

Qrlygsstaðir, battle of, 117

Örvar-Oddr, legendary figure, xviii, 179–80

Örvar-Odds saga, 179–82

Óláfr Haraldsson, saint. *See* saints

Óláfr III Haraldsson, known as *kyrri* (the quiet), Nwg king († 1093), 231

Ólafs ríma Haraldssonar, 242

Ólafsrímur Tryggvasonar af Indriða þætti ilbreiðs, 242

Óláfs saga helga, 5, 195 n18

Óláfs saga kyrra, 231

Óláfs saga Tryggvasonar, 5

Olaus Magnus, *Historia de gentibus septentrionalibus* (1555) (History of the Northern Peoples), 11, 122, 179, 254

Ole Worm, 12, 174

Olof Skötkonung (ON Óláfr skautkonungr), Sw king († 1022), 142

Om S. Bartholomei moder, eller folksagan om Qvinnan utan Händer, 252

Ong, Walter, 34
oral epic, 17, 20, 29–34
Oral Theory, 15, 17, 27, 31–36, 45
"oral-derived text," 17, 35
oral-written debate, 53. See also Freeprose-Bookprose
orality, oral performance, and oral composition, 12, 28, 33–34, 36, 159, 165–66
Ormika of Hejnum, 194–96, 198–99
Otto, Duke, of Braunschweig († 1252), 240–41
Ottonian empire, 5
Ovid, 109
Owl and the Nightengale, 88
"Palatium Magnum" (Birgittine convent, Rome), 249
parricide, fratricide, and dishonoring of familial ties, 178, 215–17, 222–23, 229
Parry, Milman, 17, 20, 27, 31–34, 51, 54, 58
Passio Sancti Eadmundi, 141
past, mythic, 170; mythologized 189, 203–04; pastness 169–70, 184
Paul the Deacon, monk and historian († c. 899), 38
Peder Månsson, monk and translator († 1534), 145
Pèlerinage de vie humaine (*Life's Pilgrimage*) of Guillaume de Digulleville, 255
performance and mediality, 15, 148, 150–51, 158–60, 164–67
performance archaeology, 21, 23
Peter Algotsson, brother of Brynolf Algotsson, Bishop of Skara († 1299?), 240–41, 243
Petersen, N.M., 51
Petrarch, Francesco († 1374) 249
Petsch, Robert, 28
philology, 2, 13–14, 19, 23–24, 35, 51–52, 76, 158

Philpotts, Bertha, 108, 119
Pilgrim's Progress (1678) by John Bunyan, 255
pilgrimage, 5, 253, 255–56
Piltz, Anders, 248–49, 255
Pipping, Rolf, 126
"places of power," 169, 183
postola sǫgur (sagas of apostles), 9
Pre-Roman Iron Age, 13
Price, Neil, 4 n5, 21–22, 24, 219 n33
proverbs, 3, 11
queens and other royal consorts
– foreign-born, influence on Nordic court culture, 231–43; named: Eufemia of Rügen († 1312), wife of King Hákon V Magnússon, 10, 236, 239–241, 243; Gunnhildr († c. 977?), sometimes referred to as Gormsdóttir, known as *konungamóðir* (mother of kings), wife of Eiríkr *blóðøx*, 163; Helvig of Holstein († c. 1325), wife of King Magnús Ladulås, 239; Ingibjǫrg of Denmark († 1287), wife of King Magnús VI Hákonarson 72–74, 165–66, 232, 234–35, 236, 243; Ingibjǫrg († 1318), daughter of King Hákon V, wife of Duke Erik Magnusson of Södermanland, 240; Margaret of Scotland († 1283), wife of King Eiríkr II Magnússon, 236, 238; Margrete of Denmark († 1412), daughter of Valdemar Atterdag, queen regnant of Denmark, Sweden, and Norway, 7; Þorvé († mid-10th c.?), wife of the Da king Gormr inn gamli 175–76
Rademann-Veith, Frauke, 79
Ragnarǫk (fate of the gods), 8, 95 n4
Ragnars saga loðbrókar, 83 n13, 178

Ragnarsdrápa, 8
Ragnarssona þáttr, 171
Ragnhildr tregagás, 9, 163
Ramsund (Sö 101). *See* Runic inscriptions
"recomposition in performance." *See* "composition in performance,"
Reformation, 10, 11, 192, 194
Regino av Prüm, abbot and chronicler († 915), 112, 121
riddarasögur (sagas of knights), 9
riddle -s, 3, 11, 81–90, 96, 98–100, 181; blocking element in, 78, 80–82; defined and discussed, 77–80; "true riddles," 80, 83, 98–99
Rigney, Ann, 18, 28–29, 188
Rimbert, saint. *See* saints
rímur (rhymes), 10, 242–43, 248
Rímur af Amíkus ok Amilíus, 242
Rök (Ög 136). *See* runic inscriptions
Rolf Kraki. *See* Hrólfr
Romantic nationalism, 30
Rosén, Helge, 126
rote memory. *See memoria verborum*
royal decrees for collecting information on antiquities, 12
Ruin, The, 169–70, 185
Rumelandt von Sachsen, a Minnesinger, 239
Runic inscriptions: DR 41 (Gorm stone at Jelling), 176, 186; DR 42 (Harald stone at Jelling), 5, 186; DR 357 U (Stentoften), 209, 214, 216, 225, 228; DR 358 U (Gummarp), 209, 214, 216, 225, 228; DR 359 U (Istaby), 209, 214, 216, 225, 228; DR 360 (Björketorp), 209, 214, 216, 225, 228; Ög 136 (Rök), 83 n13, 149–51, 167, 220; Öl 1 (Karlevi), 149 n2, 162; Öl SAS1989;43 (Kvinneby amulet), 5; Sö 101 (Ramsund), 161–62; Sö 270 (Tyresta), 214; runacy, 150; runic mediality, 150–51
Saga Sverris konúngs, 237
Sagan om Didrik af Bern, 10
sagas, 3–13, 23–24, 30–31, 34, 37–38, 52–54, 63–64, 69, 75–76, 116, 159–61, 166, 173–74, 177, 181, 187–88, 211–12, 231
sagnaskemmtan "saga entertainment," 67–68, 74, 155, 164, 166, 234–35
saints, 9, 64, 112, 126, 140, 196, 200; cephalophoric saints, 145; St. Ansgar († 865), 5; Augustine of Hippo († 430), 111; St. Birgitta, 8; St. Denis, the first bishop of Paris, 140–41; St. Edmund (*also*: of East Anglia), martyred by the Danish army († 869), 141–42; St. Erik, 8; St. John Cassian, 253; St. Knútr, 8; St. Óláfr/Olaf (Óláfr inn helgi Haraldsson), 5, 8; St. Óláfr on Gotland, 194–97, 200; *Óláfs saga helga*, 5, 195 n1; St. Rimbert, hagiographer of St. Ansgar († 888), 37; St. Sigfrid (*also*: of Sweden), English missionary († mid-11th c.), 142
Samsø (ON Sámsey), 169–88; medieval references to, 177–81; and the mythical-heroic tradition, 178–81
samtíðarsögur (contemporary sagas), 9
Saul and the Witch of Endor, 140
Saxo Grammaticus, 3, 5, 7, 11, 51, 83, 98, 127, 133–35, 137, 139–40, 145, 156, 170–71, 174, 177–80, 185–86, 215, 219–20, 264
Scheub, Harold, 12
Schjødt, Jens Peter, 7 n11, 133 n17, 127, 227, 228 n57

"scripture cake," 81
senna (ritual exchange of insults), 87, 89, 221
Sermo Lupi ad Anglos, 115, 223
sermons, 11, 140, 223 n44, 254
Sigfrid of Sweden, saint. *See* saints
Sigrdrífomál, 127
Sigríðr (Alríkr's mother, Ormr's daughter), 161
Sigtuna, 5, 176
Sigurðr, legendary figure, known as the Dragon-Slayer, 161
Sigurður Nordal, 34, 127 n5, 160
Simek, Rudi, 6 n10, 110
Simon Magus, biblical magician, 111
Singer of Tales, 17, 32, 54. *See* also Albert B. Lord
Sju vise mästare, 10
Skáldskaparmál, 3, 210, 250
Skämtan om Abboten, 10
Skíðblaðnir, mythical ship, 96
Skírnir, god, xix, 93–95, 119, 120, 147, 262
Skjöldunga saga, 171
Slaget på Samsø (the Battle on Samsø), xviii, 179, 180–81, 188
Snæbjǫrn of Sandvík, 117
Sneglu-Halli. *See* Halli
Sneglu-Halla þáttr, 69–71, 238
snekkja, 184, 187
Snorra edda, or the *Prose Edda* of Snorri Sturluson, 3, 7, 93, 96, 100, 103, 105–06, 109, 119–20, 132, 155, 210, 221. *See* also *Gylfaginning* and *Skáldskaparmál*
Snorri Sturluson, Icelandic lawman and author († 1241), 7, 13, 55–56, 60–61, 93, 95–97, 100, 103–105, 107–08, 110–111, 121–22, 156, 190, 210, 226, 250
"social dramas," 17
soundings, alt. dozens, 49–50, 88
Speculum lapidum, 145

speech act theory, 15, 17, 45, 88–89
Spencer, Herbert, 41–42
stave church at Hegge, Norway, 136–37
Stentoften (DR 357 U). *See* runic inscriptions
Stiernhielm, Georg, Sw antiquarian and author († 1672), 255
Stiklastaðir, battle of, 153
Stimulus amoris, 254
Stjórn, 112
Strelow, Hans Nielsson, 193, 198–204
Stríðkeravísur, 99
Strömbäck, Dag, 19, 20 n31, 24, 39 n7, 50, 114–15
Sturla Þórðarson, Icelandic author and skald († 1284), xvii, 62, 71–76, 164–66, 232–35, 238
Sturlu þáttr, 71, 164, 232–33, 235
Sturlunga saga, 9, 233 n4, 236, 238
Sturtevant, Albert Morey, 107–08
Sundqvist, Olof, 126, 214 n16, 215, 219, 225, 228
"superorganic," 16, 18, 41–43, 201
Suttungr, giant, 56, 61
Svabo, Jens Christian, Faroese scholar († 1824), 181
Svarfdælasaga, 116
Sveinn Eiríksson, known as *svíðandi* (singeing), Da king († 1157), 236–37
Sven Aggesen, Da chronicler (*fl.* 12th c.), 171–72, 175–76, 186
Svenska medeltids-postillor, 254
Symphosius, poet (*fl.* 5th c.??), 83, 89
synodal statute, -s, 11, 112, 145, 166
Tacitus, Roman writer († c. 120 CE), 4, 37, 130, 200
Tannr Bjarnason, Icelandic quidnunc and poet, 62
Terdiman, Richard, 28–29

Teutoburg Forest, battle of the (9 CE), 129–30
thanatological rituals, 133, 137
Theodoricus Monachus, Norwegian monk (*fl.* late 12th c.), 5 n9, 11, 157, 234 n6
theriomorphic warriors, 221, 226, 229
"thick description," 38, 75
Thoms, William, 14
Tidericus (burned in Visby), 202, 204
Tissø, 178, 186
Tóka þáttr Tókasonar, 211
Tolkien, J.R.R., 1
Tolley, Clive, 110, 140 n29
tradition, 9–16, 29–35, 42–45, 65, 100, 112–16, 142–47, 149–50, 155–57, 164–67, 185–88; biological metaphor (mycelium, etc.) for, 46, 48; etymology of, 12, 41, 155; expressed in communality, variation, continuity, and function, 15 n18
Trekroner-Gyldehøj, 22
Trier stela (5th-c. CE), 219
Trójumanna saga, 116
troll -s, 12–13, 72–73, 115–16, 146, 165, 233–34, 245–46, 250–54; etymology of, 250–51; Old Swedish terms (*trwll*, *iätun*, *trollkärling*), 250
tunríðor (hedge-riders), 113–14, 121
Turner, Victor, 17, 21, 54 n6, 158 n25
Tylor, Edward, 13
Týr, god, 94, 137
Tyresta (Sö 270). *See* runic inscriptions
Tyrfing, legendary sword, 180
úlfheðnar "wolf-clad warriors," 219
Unaman, Sunaman, and Vinaman, 142
undead dead, 134

Union of Kalmar. *See* Kalmar
Uppåkra, 38, 111 n14, 176–77, 185–86, 188
"Útfarardrápa," 237
Útsteinn, legendary figure, 212
UUB C 4, Vadstena miscellany, 245, 248, 255
Vadstena, Östergötland (Birgittine mother house), 248, 252, 255–56
Vafðrúðnismál, 80, 82, 86, 98, 100, 114, 120
Valdemar IV Kristoffersson, known as Atterdag, Da king († 1375), 203–04
valgaldr (a corpse-reviving spell), 129, 146–47
Valhǫll, 127 n4, 134,
valkyrie, -s, 64, 66, 67, 96, 111, 115
Vanir gods, 8, 56, 105–06, 110, 123, 127–28
Vanlandi, legendary Sw king killed by *seiðkona* 115
Varangian Guard, 6
Varðlokur, 119, 162–63
Varinn, 149–50
Växjö, Småland, 142
Vedic *soma* and *amrita*, 67
Vémóðr, 149
Vésteinn Ólason, 128, 134, 242 n20
Viaticum, 143–45
Vico, Giambattista, scholar and historian († 1744), 20
Viðræða lærisveins ok meistara, 81
Viðræða likams ok sálar, 100
Viðurs þýfi (Óðinn's theft), kenning for Poetic Mead, 61
Víkarr, legendary king, mock sacrifice of, 96, 133
Viking Age, xviii, 2, 4, 6–7, 21, 90, 130, 151, 169, 183–84, 220
Virgil, Roman poet († 19 B.C.E.), 109

Visbyfranciskanernas bok, 202 n35, 203
Visio Tnugdali (The Vision of Tundale), trans. into ON as *Duggals leiðsla*, 255; from Latin into Old Swedish, 155
vocality (the embodied voice), 159
Vǫlospá, 127, 134, 146 n43, 217,
Vǫlsunga saga, 210
Vǫlundr, legendary figure, 111
vǫlva, vǫlur, 129, 134, 147
von Friesen, Otto, 245
Vries, Jan de, 80, 96, 107 n6, 108, 224–25, 228
Wagner, Richard, 1
Wahlgren, Erik, 81–83
Waltharius, 64
warrior bands, bonded through naming conventions, 219, 228
Washington, George, descended from Óðinn, 2
Wealhþeow, legendary figure in *Beowulf*, 64
wedding at Reykhólar (1119), 66, 160
Wilbur, Terrence, 251
Wilgus, D.K., 19
wisdom confrontations, 80, 82, 84, 86–87
witch of Endor (I Sam: 28), 126 n2, 140
witchcraft, 8, 121, 126, 145–46, 162, 167
Witzlaf, Prince, of Rügen, 240
Wolf, Friedrich August, 30
Wulfstan, bishop († 1023), 223
Ynglinga saga, 104, 115, 121, 123, 127–28, 210, 226
Ynglingatal, 210
Yngvars saga víðfǫrla, 164
Younger Futhark, 4
Yves av Chartres, bishop and canonist († 1115), 112
Zacharias, Jewish priest, 120

Zachrisson, Torun, 21, 185 n34, 204 n37
Zaleski, Carol, 255
Ženidba Smailagić Meha (The Wedding of Meho, Son of Smail), 33
Zumthor, Paul, 33–34, 159
Þjazi, giant, 111
Þjóðhildarkirkja, the chapel at Brattahlíð in Greenland, 38
Þjóðhildr Jǫrundardóttir, wife of Eiríkr rauði, 38
Þjóðólfr úr Hvini, skald (*fl.* late 9th– early 10th c.), 210
Þórarinn stuttfeldr (short cloak) (*fl.* early 12th c.), 61
Þorbjǫrg "lítilvǫlva," 118–19, 123, 162–63,
Þorgils saga ok Hafliða, 66, 160
Þorgnýr Þorgnýsson, Sw lawman, 152–53
Þorleifs þáttr jarlsskálds, 137–38
Þórr (Thor), xix, 1, 8, 82, 221–22
Þorsteinn Þórarinsson, saga figure, 134, 138
Þorsteinn Eiríksson, saga figure, 135
Þorsteins þáttr uxafóts, 134, 138, 146
Þorvé († mid-10th c.?). *See* queens and other royal consorts
þula, 103, 108, 177, 197, 238

MYTH AND POETICS
A SERIES EDITED BY
GREGORY NAGY

After Antiquity: Greek Language, Myth, and Metaphor
BY MARGARET ALEXIOU

Helen of Troy and Her Shameless Phantom
BY NORMAN AUSTIN

Poetry in Speech: Orality and Homeric Discourse
BY EGBERT J. BAKKER

The Craft of Poetic Speech in Ancient Greece
BY CLAUDE CALAME, TRANSLATED BY JANICE ORION

Masks of Authority: Fiction and Pragmatics in Ancient Greek Poetics
BY CLAUDE CALAME, TRANSLATED BY PETER M. BURK

Masks of Dionysus
EDITED BY THOMAS H. CARPENTER AND CHRISTOPHER A. FARAONE

The "Odyssey" in Athens: Myths of Cultural Origins
BY ERWIN F. COOK

The Poetics of Supplication: Homer's "Iliad" and "Odyssey"
BY KEVIN CROTTY

Poet and Hero in the Persian Book of Kings
BY OLGA M. DAVIDSON

Gender and Genre in the Folklore of Middle India
BY JOYCE BURKHALTER FLUECKIGER

Ariadne's Thread: A Guide to International Stories in Classical Literature
BY WILLIAM HANSEN

The Ravenous Hyenas and the Wounded Sun: Myth and Ritual in Ancient India
BY STEPHANIE W. JAMISON

Poetry and Prophecy: The Beginnings of a Literary Tradition
EDITED BY JAMES L. KUGEL

The Traffic in Praise: Pindar and the Poetics of Social Economy
BY LESLIE KURKE

Topographies of Hellenism: Mapping the Homeland
BY ARTEMIS LEONTIS

Born of the Earth: Myth and Politics in Athens
BY NICOLE LORAUX, TRANSLATED BY SELINA STEWART

Mothers in Mourning
BY NICOLE LORAUX, TRANSLATED BY CORINNE PACHE

Epic Singers and Oral Tradition
BY ALBERT BATES LORD

The Singer Resumes the Tale
BY ALBERT BATES LORD, EDITED BY MARY LOUISE LORD

The Language of Heroes: Speech and Performance in the "Iliad"
BY RICHARD P. MARTIN

Heroic Sagas and Ballads
BY STEPHEN A. MITCHELL

The Anger of Achilles: Mênis in Greek Epic
BY LEONARD MUELLNER

Greek Mythology and Poetics
BY GREGORY NAGY

Myth and the Polis
EDITED BY DORA C. POZZI AND JOHN M. WICKERSHAM

Knowing Words: Wisdom and Cunning in the Classical Traditions of China and Greece
BY LISA RAPHALS

Singing the Past: Turkic and Medieval Heroic Poetry
BY KARL REICHL

Heroic Poets, Poetic Heroes: The Ethnography of Performance in an Arabic Oral Epic Tradition
BY DWIGHT FLETCHER REYNOLDS

Homer and the Sacred City
BY STEPHEN SCULLY

Singers, Heroes, and Gods in the "Odyssey"
BY CHARLES SEGAL

The Mute Immortals Speak: Pre-Islamic Poetry and the Poetics of Ritual
BY SUZANNE PINCKNEY STETKEVYCH

Phrasikleia: An Anthropology of Reading in Ancient Greece
BY JESPER SVENBRO, TRANSLATED BY JANET E. LLOYD

The Swineherd and the Bow: Representations of Class in the "Odyssey"
BY WILLIAM G. THALMANN

The Jewish Novel in the Ancient World
BY LAWRENCE WILLS

www.ingramcontent.com/pod-product-compliance
Lightning Source LLC
Chambersburg PA
CBHW021335230426
43666CB00006B/298